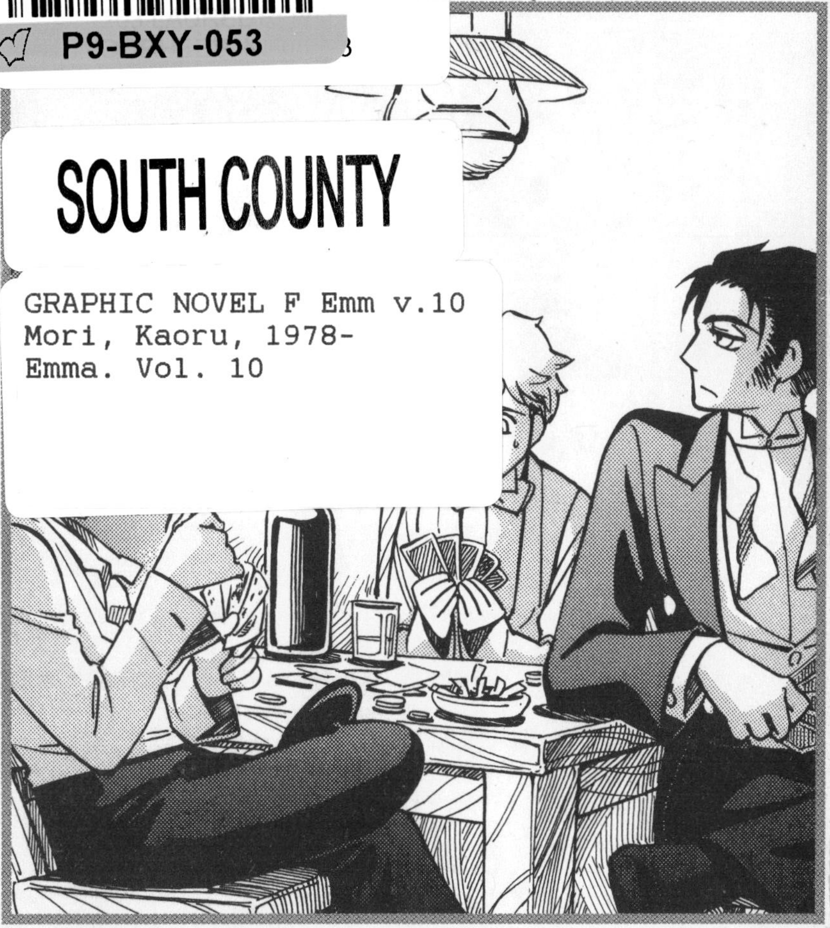

EMMA

Volume 10

By Kaoru Mori

Contents

**CHAPTER 13:
THE
BICYCLE**

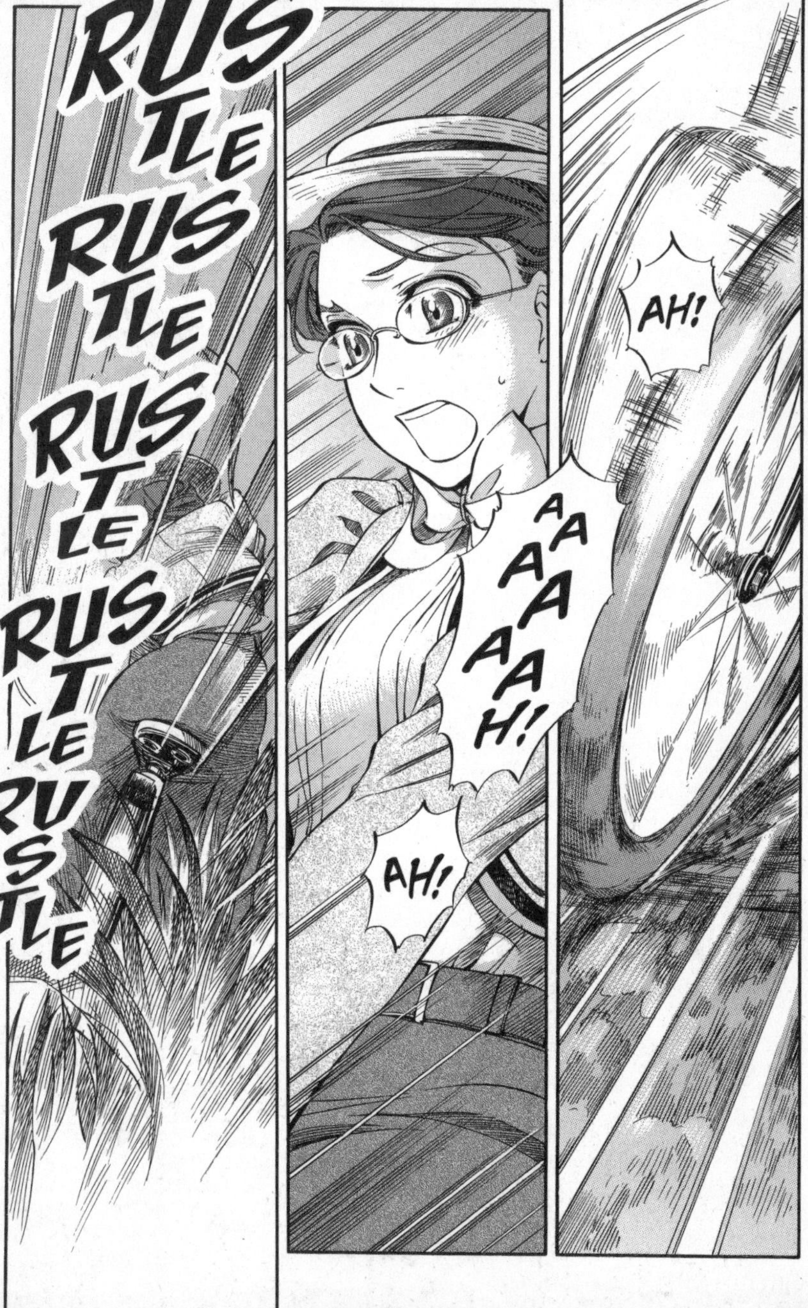
AH!
AAAAAAAH!
AH!
RUSTLE RUSTLE RUSTLE RUSTLE RUSTLE

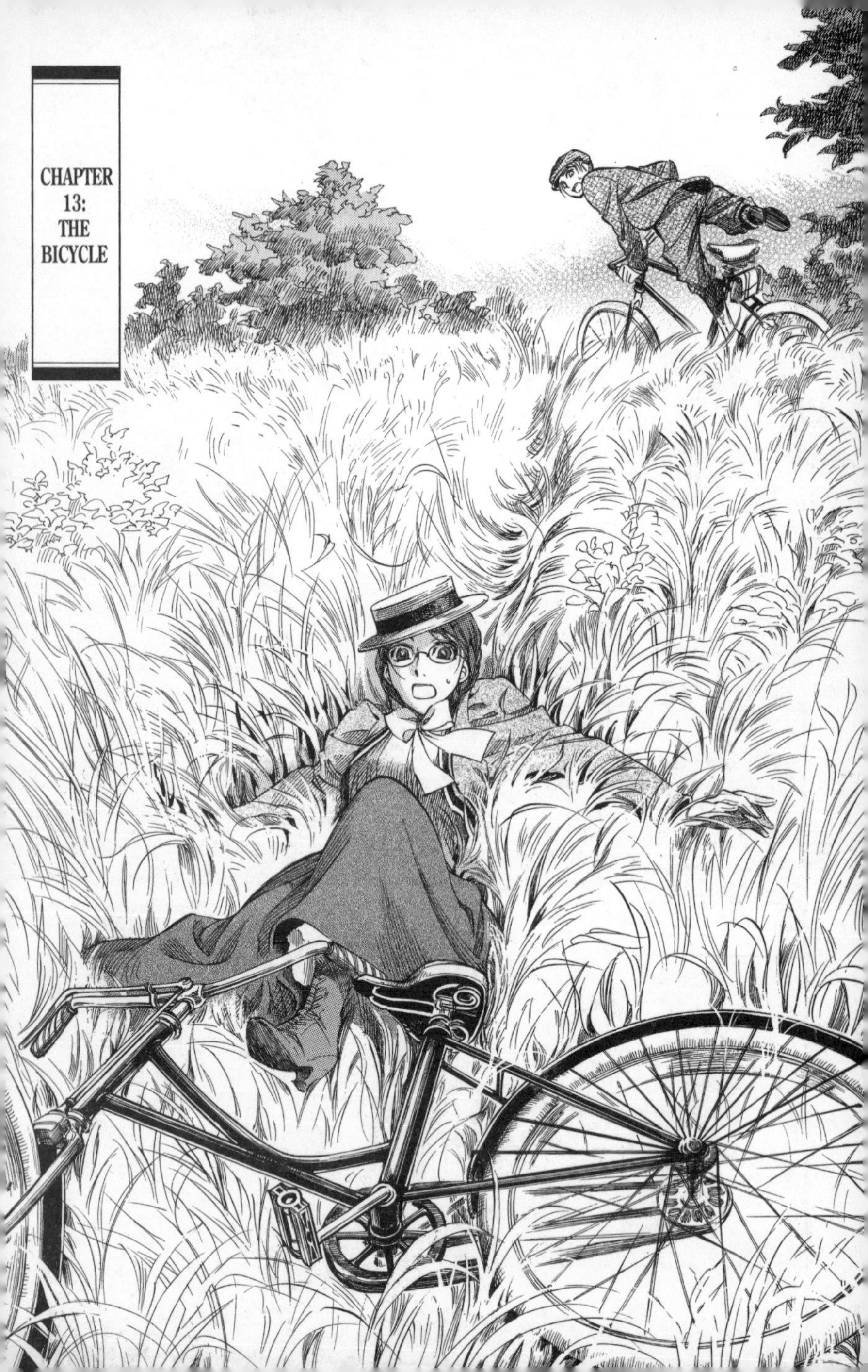
CHAPTER 13: THE BICYCLE

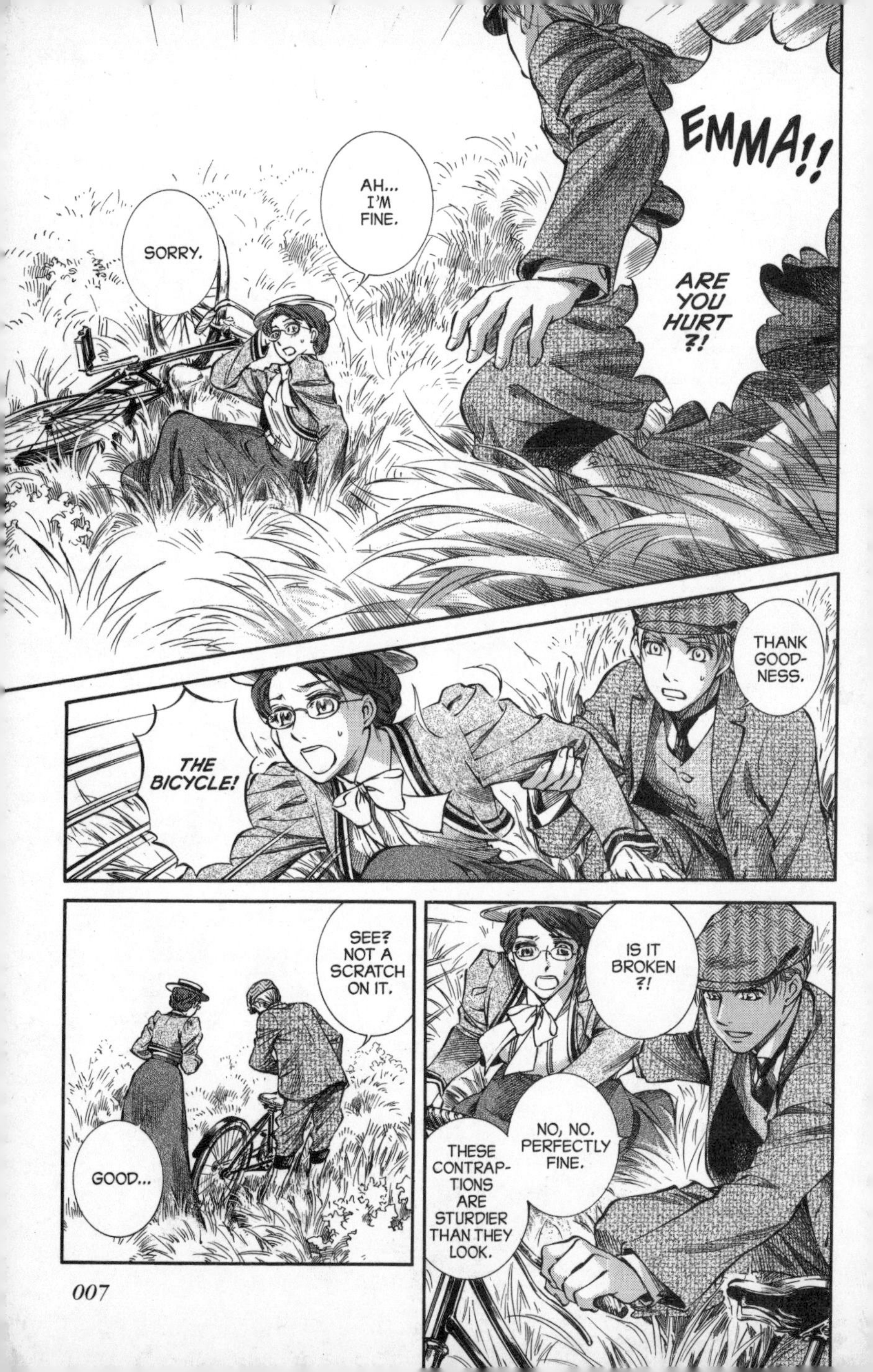

EMMA!!
ARE YOU HURT?!
AH... I'M FINE.
SORRY.
THANK GOODNESS.
THE BICYCLE!
IS IT BROKEN?!
NO, NO. PERFECTLY FINE.
THESE CONTRAPTIONS ARE STURDIER THAN THEY LOOK.
SEE? NOT A SCRATCH ON IT.
GOOD...

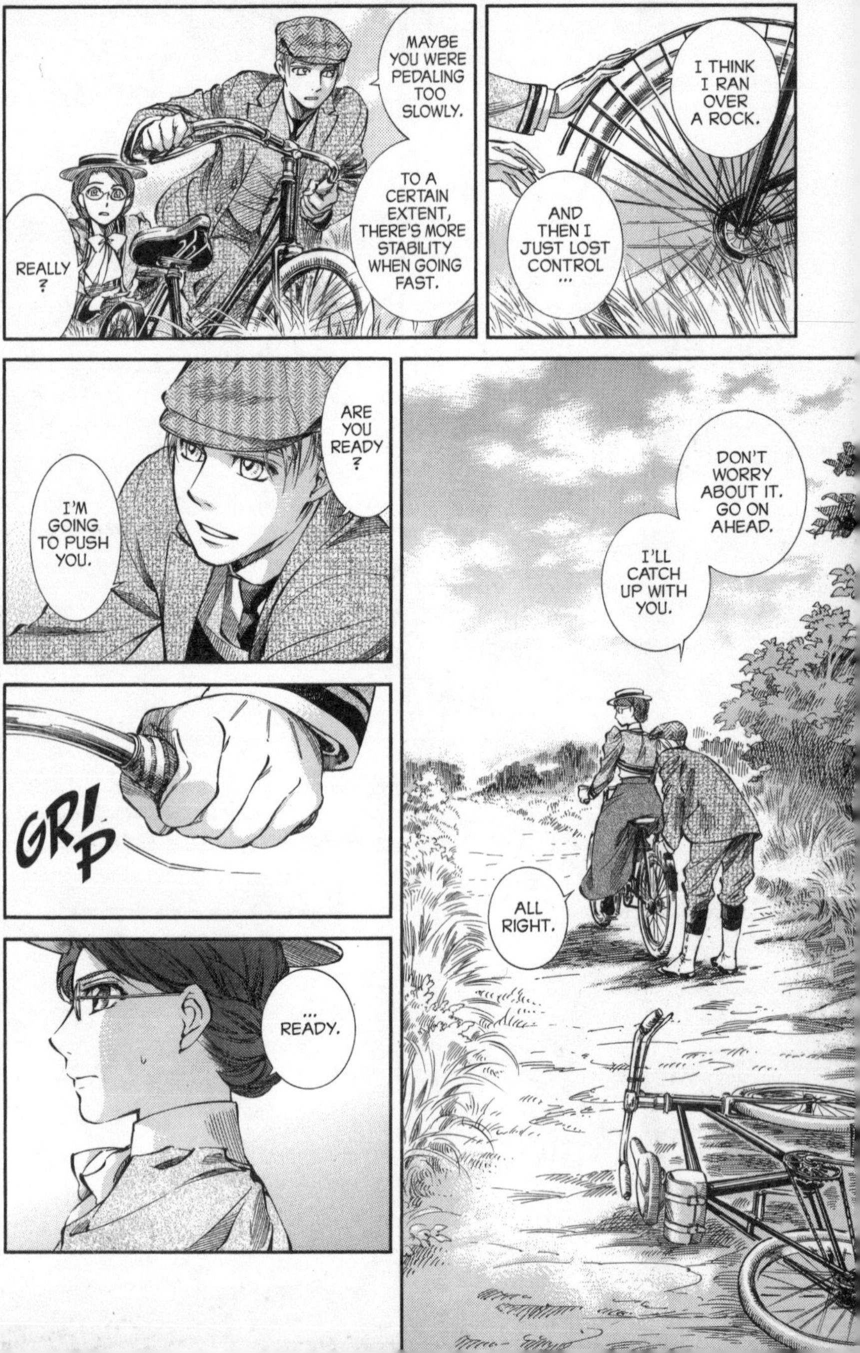
I THINK I RAN OVER A ROCK.
AND THEN I JUST LOST CONTROL ...
MAYBE YOU WERE PEDALING TOO SLOWLY.
TO A CERTAIN EXTENT, THERE'S MORE STABILITY WHEN GOING FAST.
REALLY?
DON'T WORRY ABOUT IT. GO ON AHEAD.
I'LL CATCH UP WITH YOU.
ALL RIGHT.
ARE YOU READY?
I'M GOING TO PUSH YOU.
GRIP
... READY.

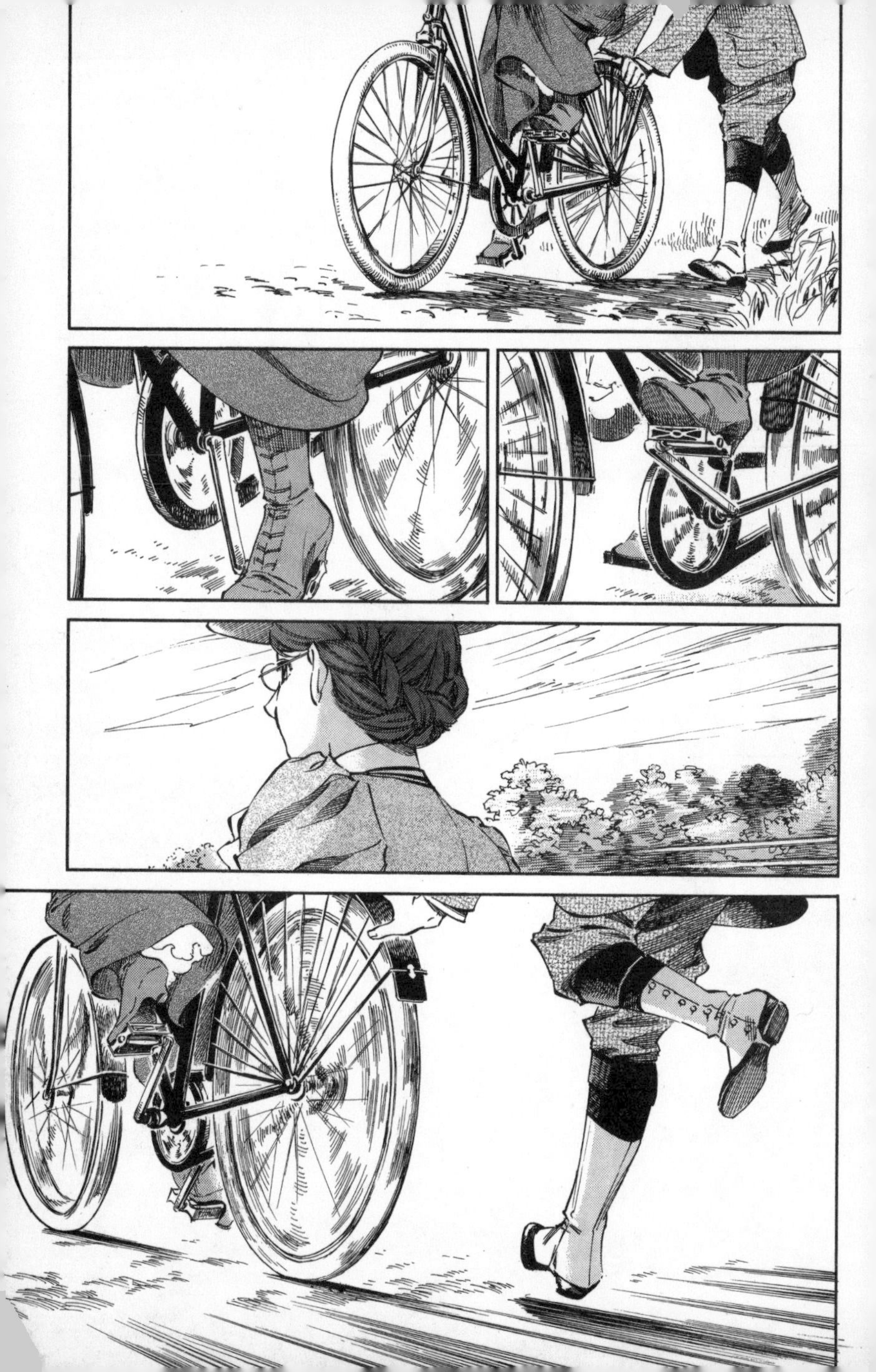

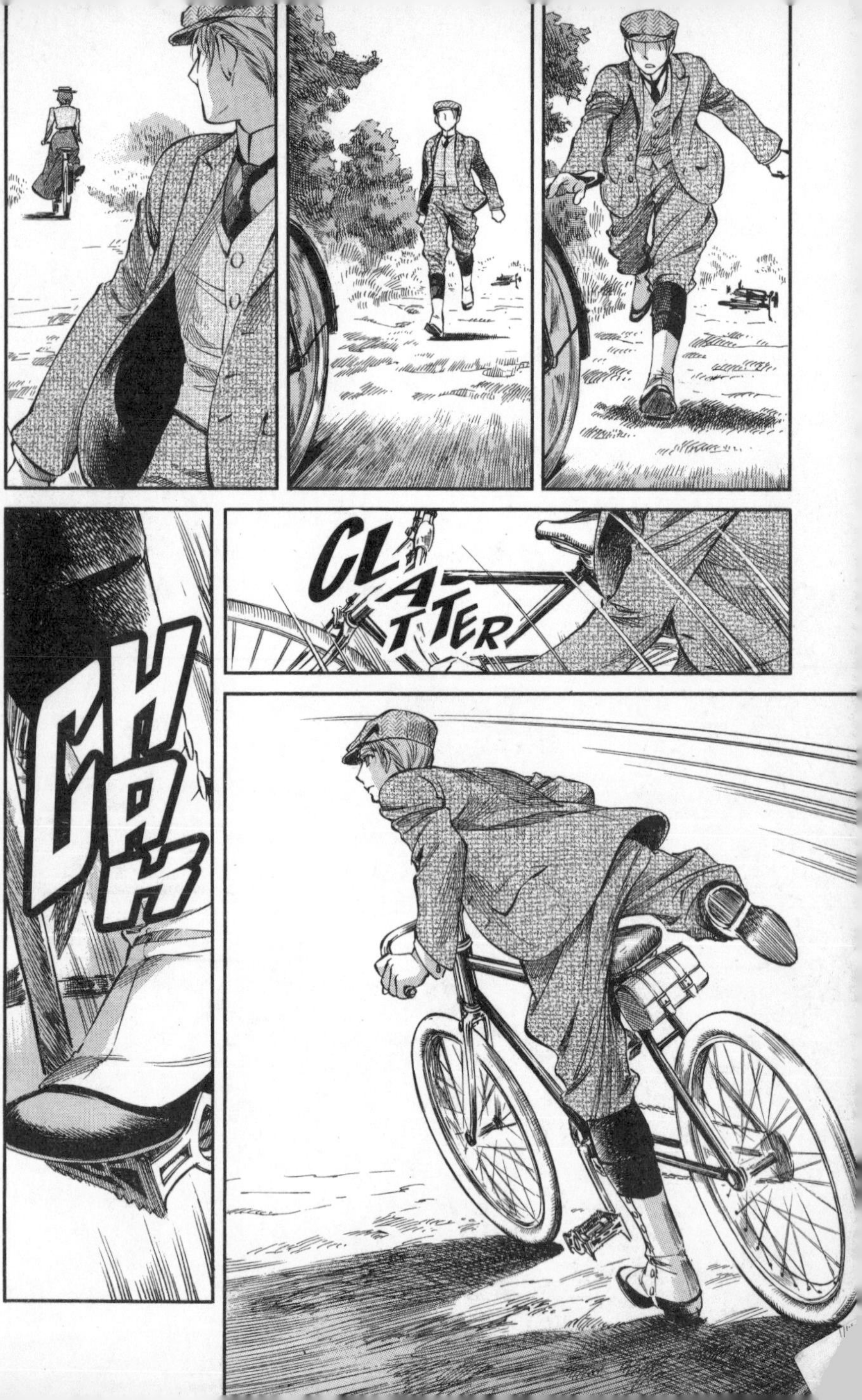
CLATTER
CHAK

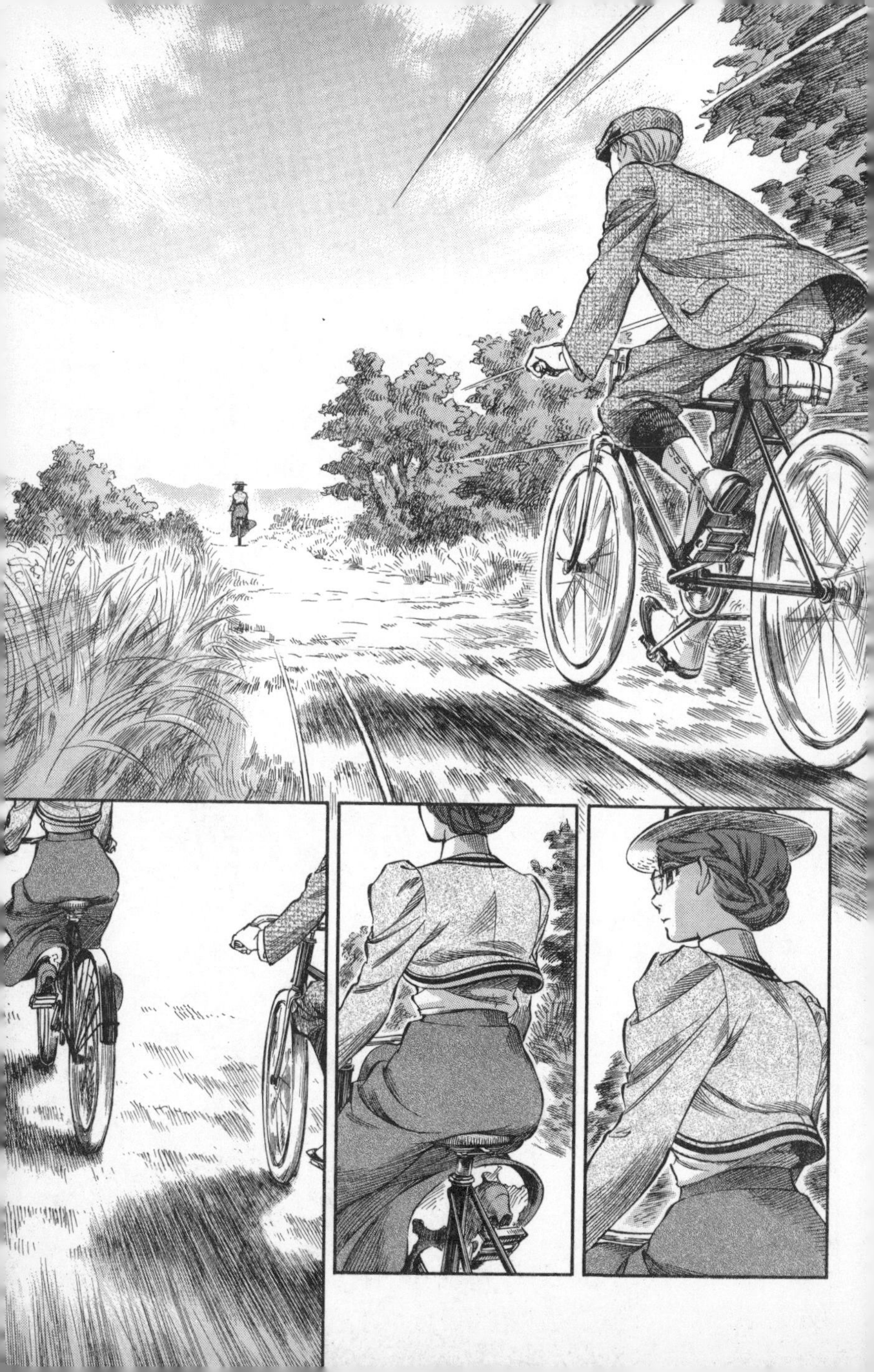

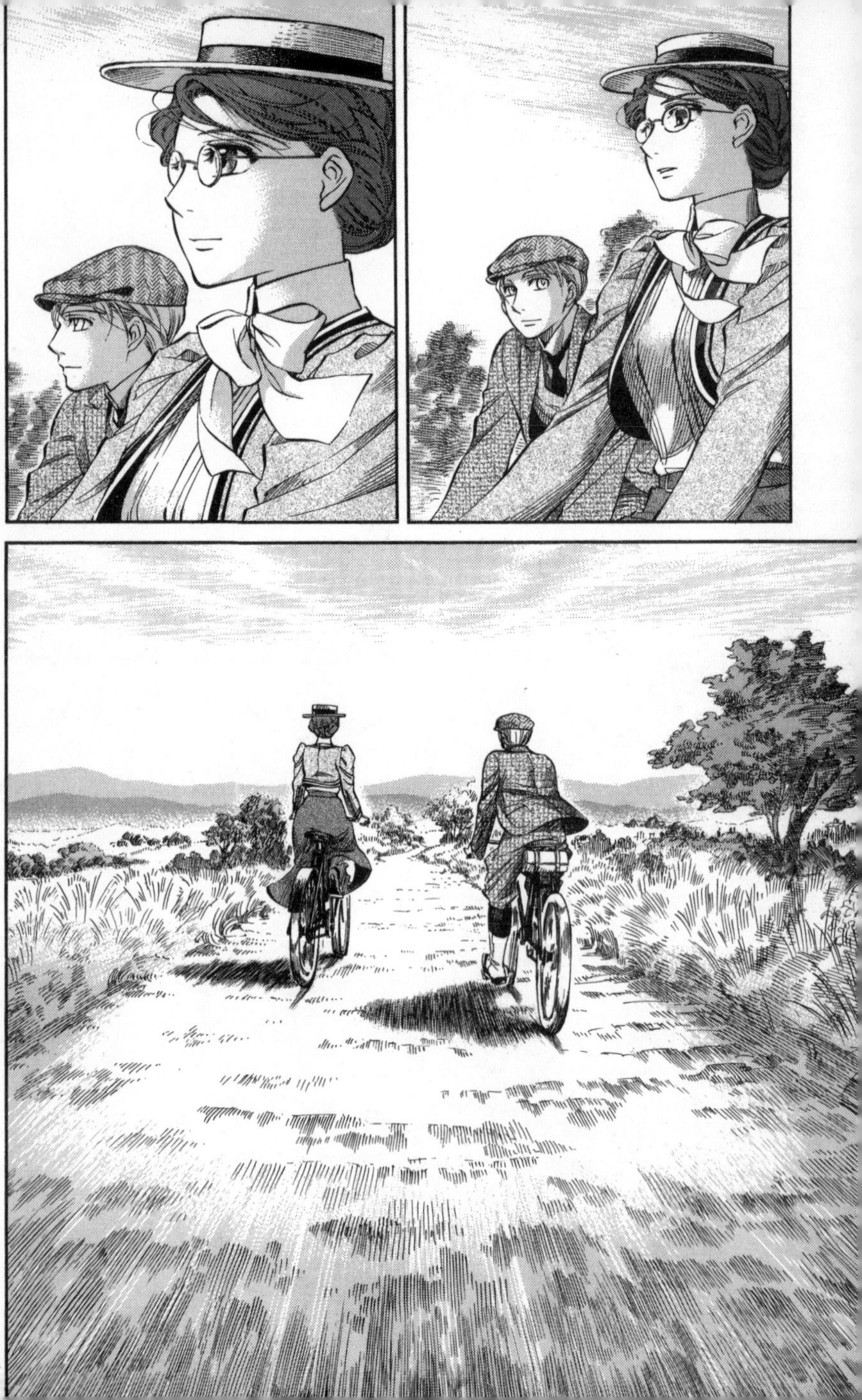

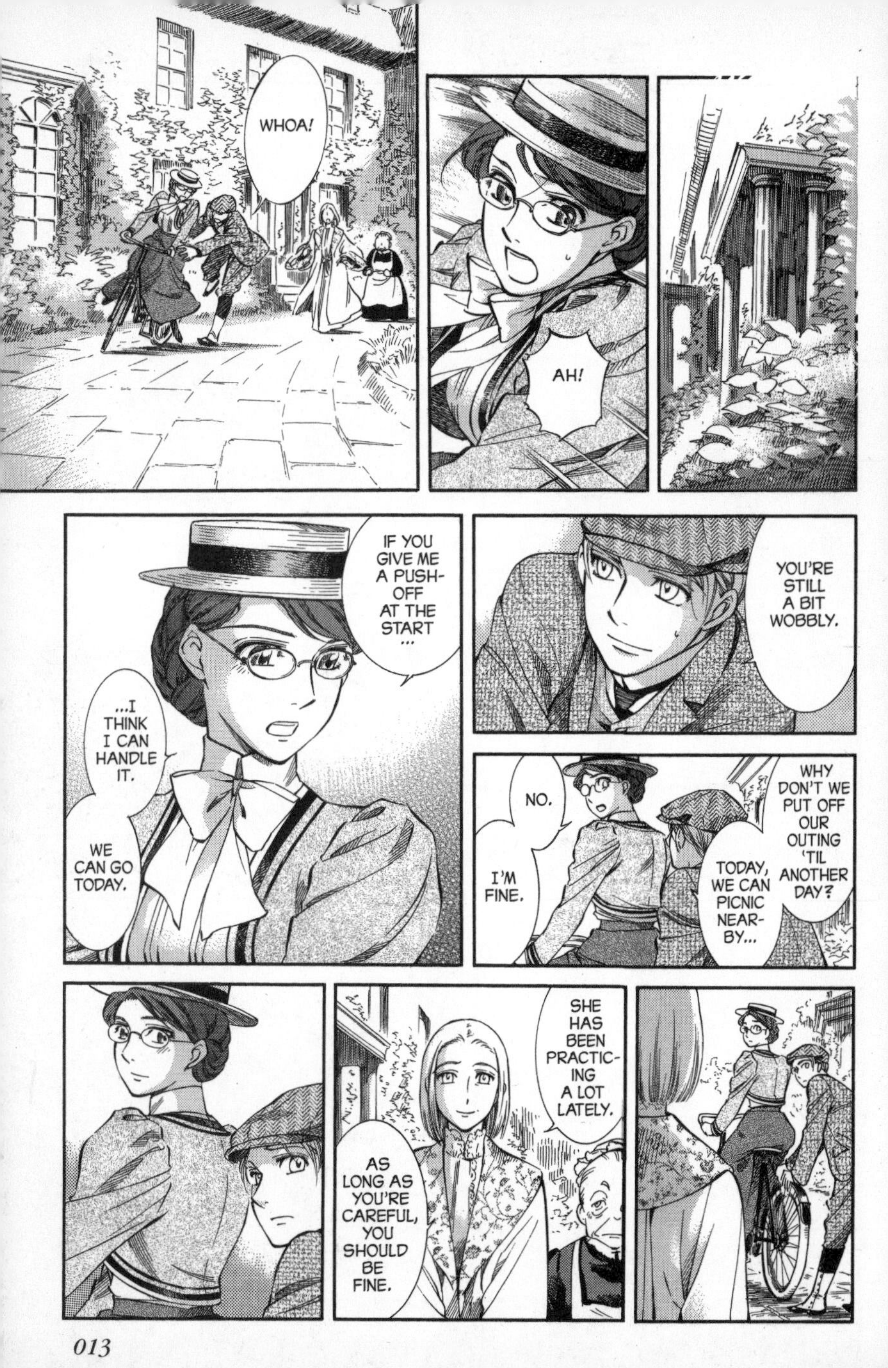
AH!
WHOA!
YOU'RE STILL A BIT WOBBLY.
WHY DON'T WE PUT OFF OUR OUTING 'TIL ANOTHER DAY?
TODAY, WE CAN PICNIC NEARBY...
NO.
I'M FINE.
IF YOU GIVE ME A PUSH-OFF AT THE START ...
...I THINK I CAN HANDLE IT.
WE CAN GO TODAY.
SHE HAS BEEN PRACTICING A LOT LATELY.
AS LONG AS YOU'RE CAREFUL, YOU SHOULD BE FINE.

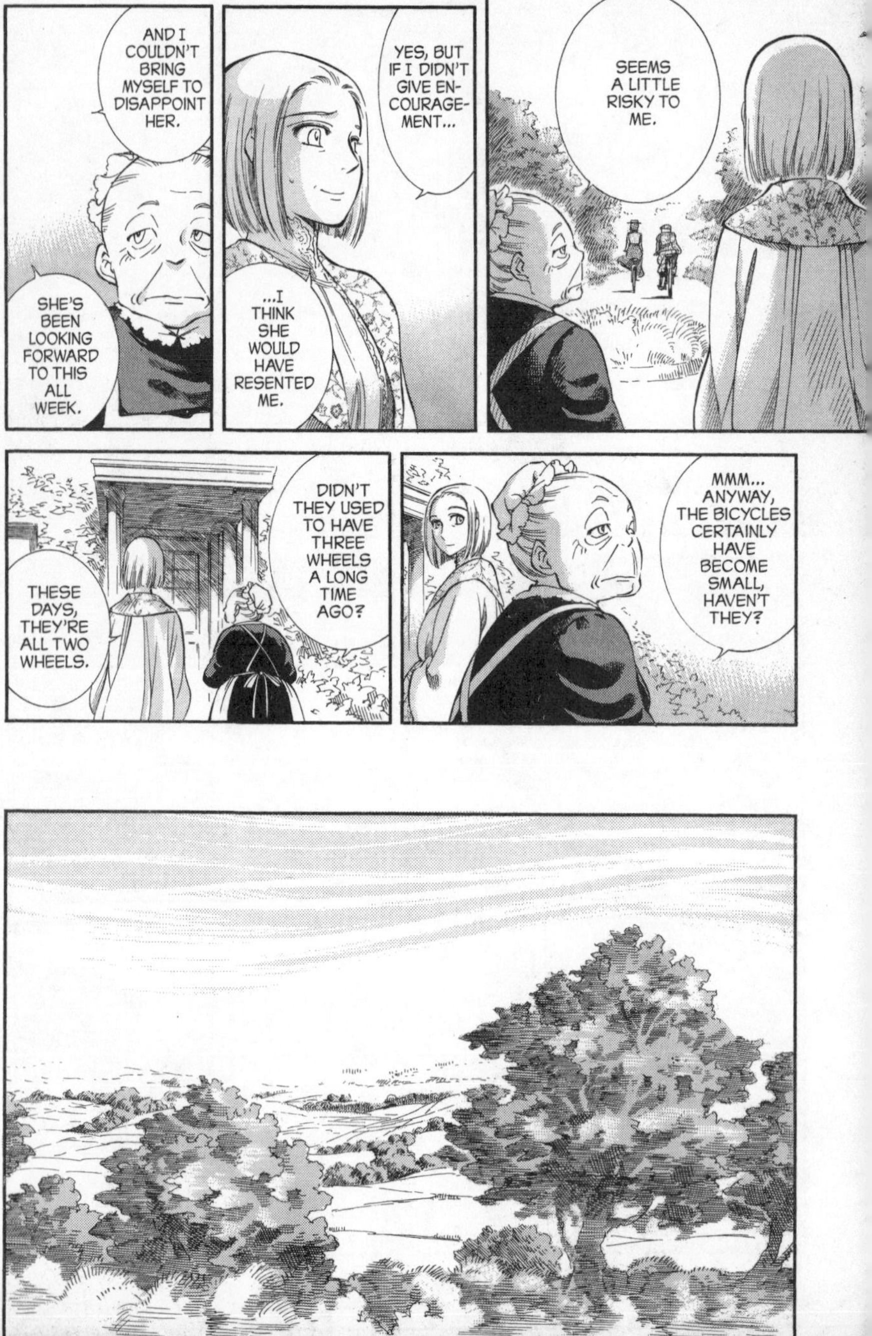
SEEMS A LITTLE RISKY TO ME.
YES, BUT IF I DIDN'T GIVE EN-COURAGE-MENT...
...I THINK SHE WOULD HAVE RESENTED ME.
AND I COULDN'T BRING MYSELF TO DISAPPOINT HER.
SHE'S BEEN LOOKING FORWARD TO THIS ALL WEEK.
MMM... ANYWAY, THE BICYCLES CERTAINLY HAVE BECOME SMALL, HAVEN'T THEY?
DIDN'T THEY USED TO HAVE THREE WHEELS A LONG TIME AGO?
THESE DAYS, THEY'RE ALL TWO WHEELS.

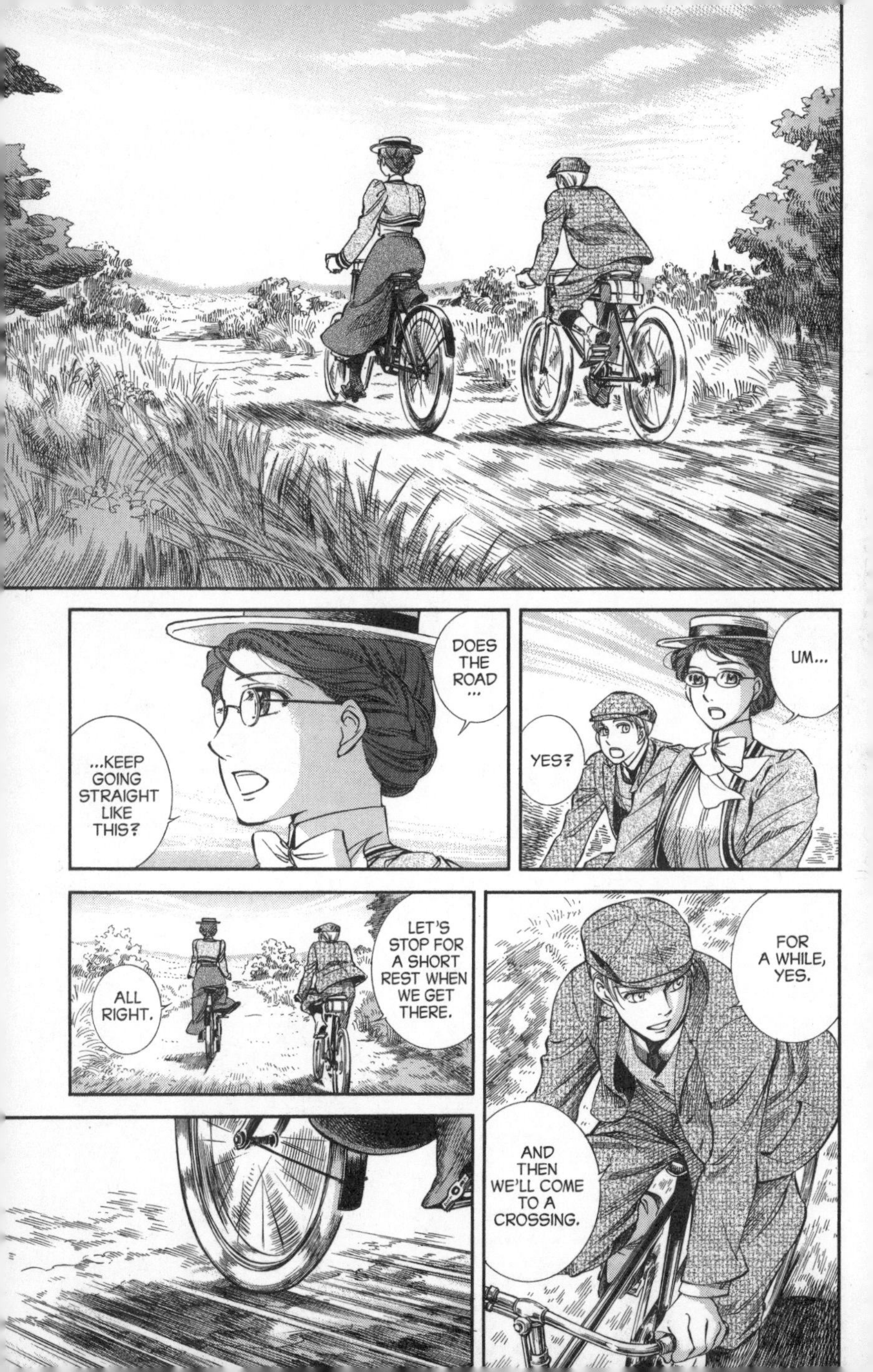
UM...
YES?
DOES THE ROAD ...
...KEEP GOING STRAIGHT LIKE THIS?
FOR A WHILE, YES.
AND THEN WE'LL COME TO A CROSSING.
LET'S STOP FOR A SHORT REST WHEN WE GET THERE.
ALL RIGHT.

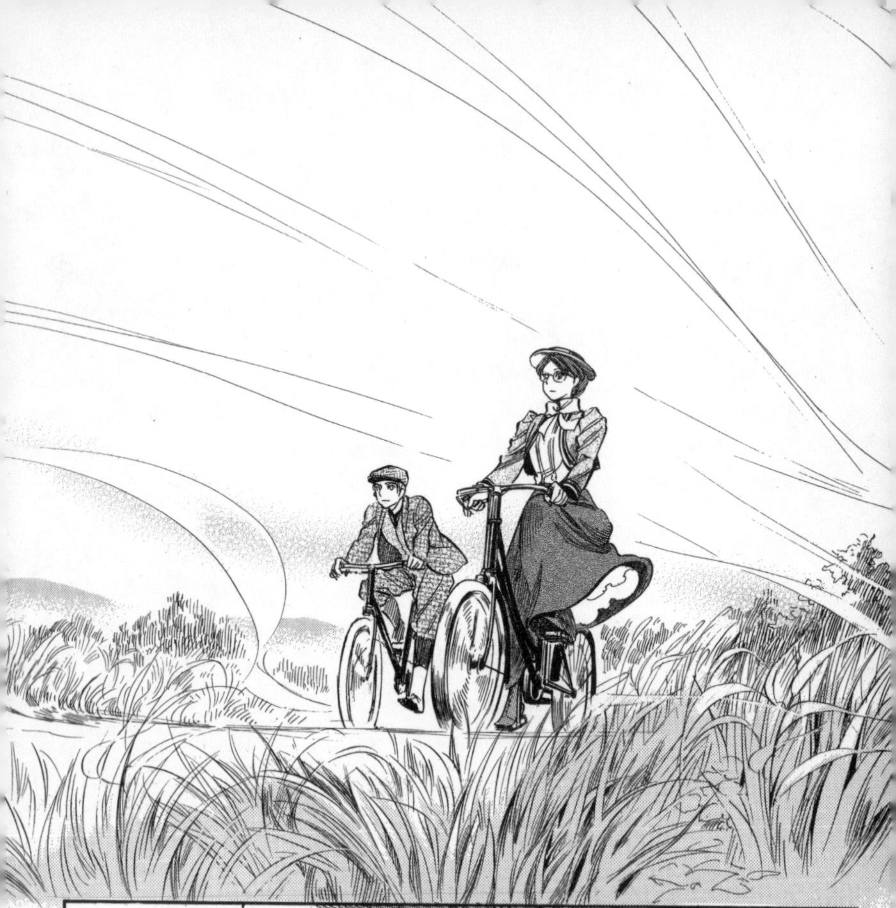

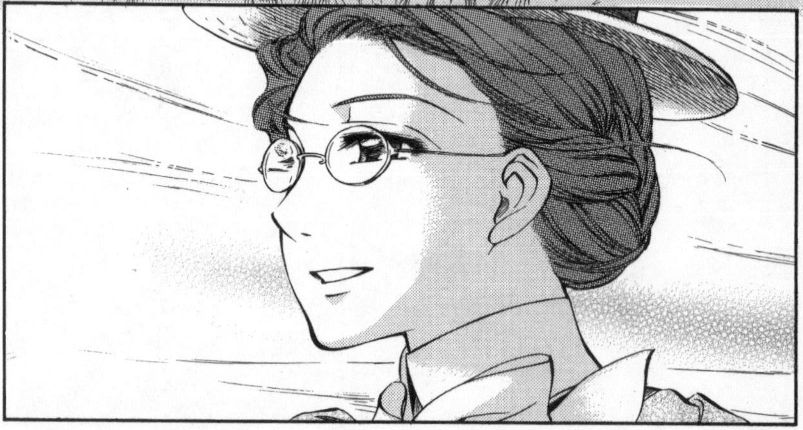

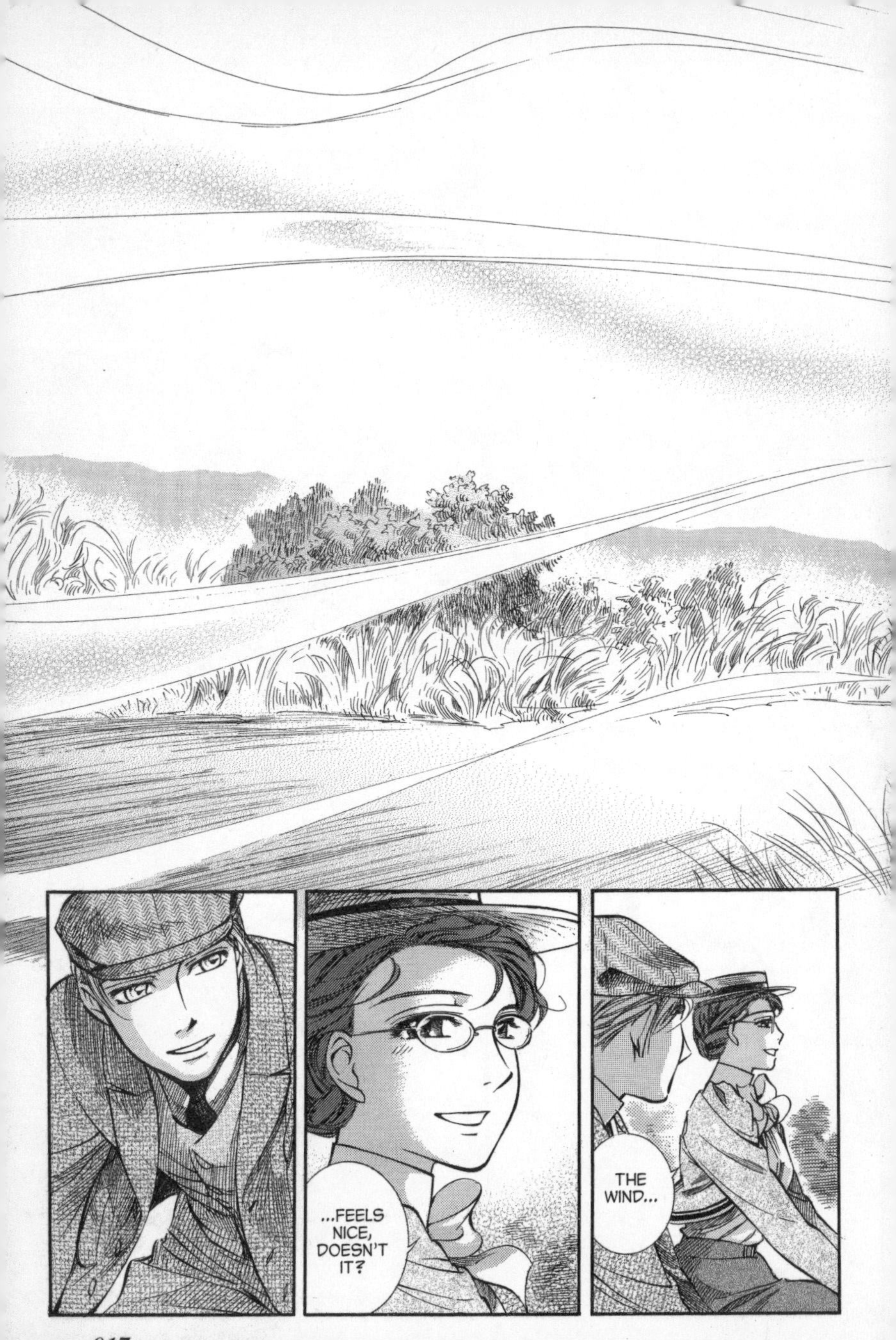
THE WIND...
...FEELS NICE, DOESN'T IT?

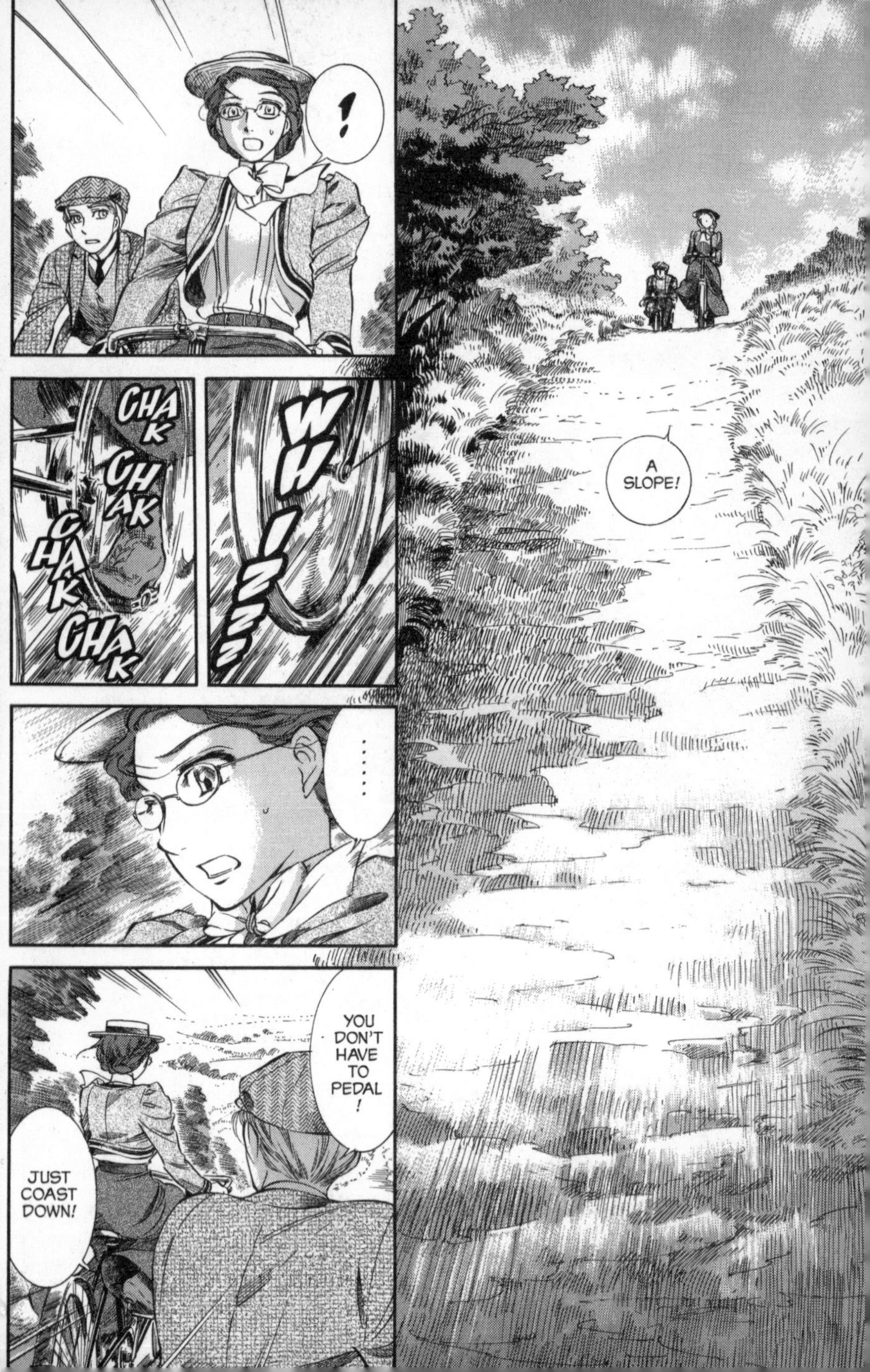
A SLOPE!
!
WHIZZZZ
CHAK CHAK CHAK CHAK
......
YOU DON'T HAVE TO PEDAL!
JUST COAST DOWN!

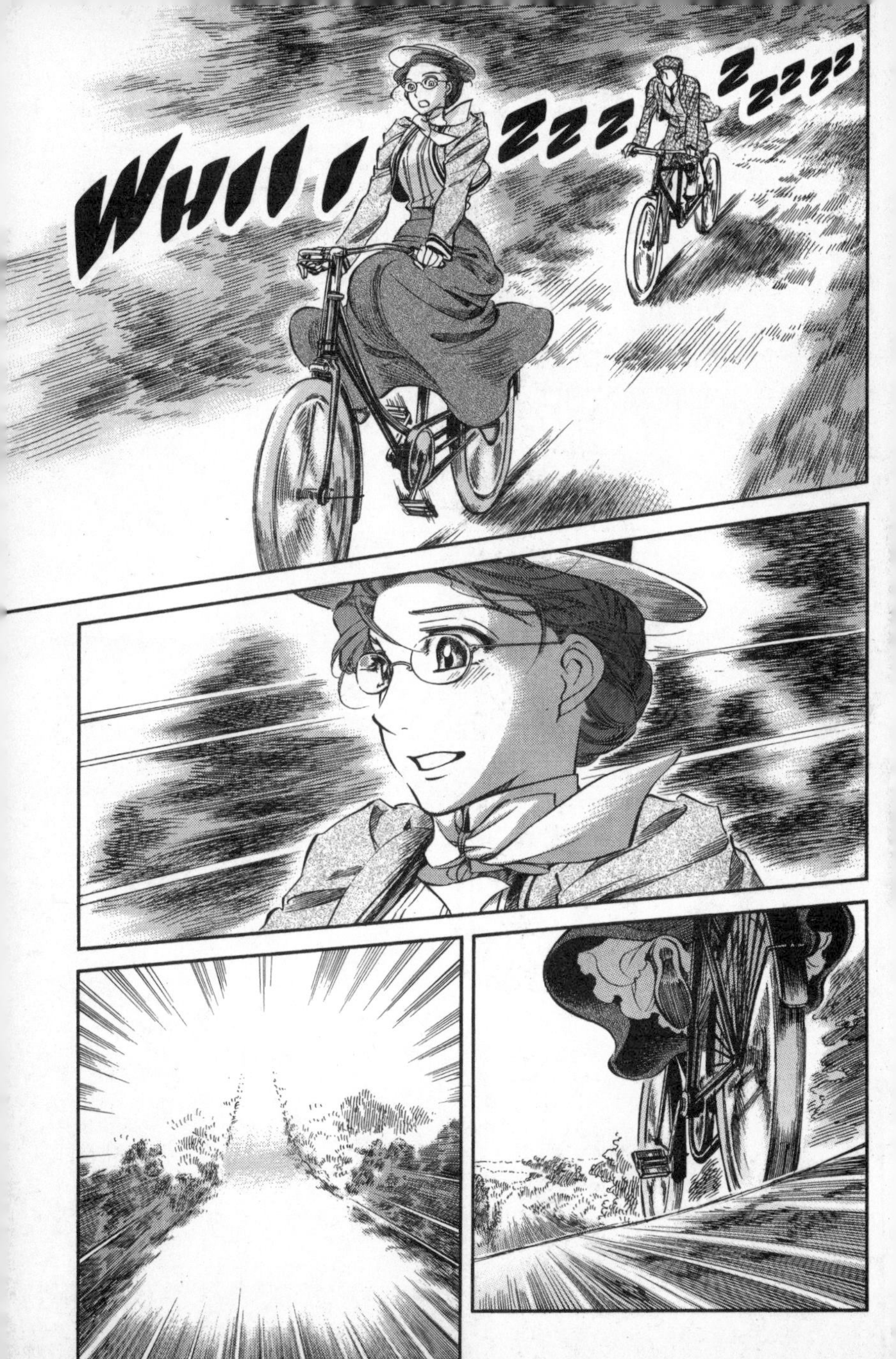
WHIIIZZZZZZZZZ

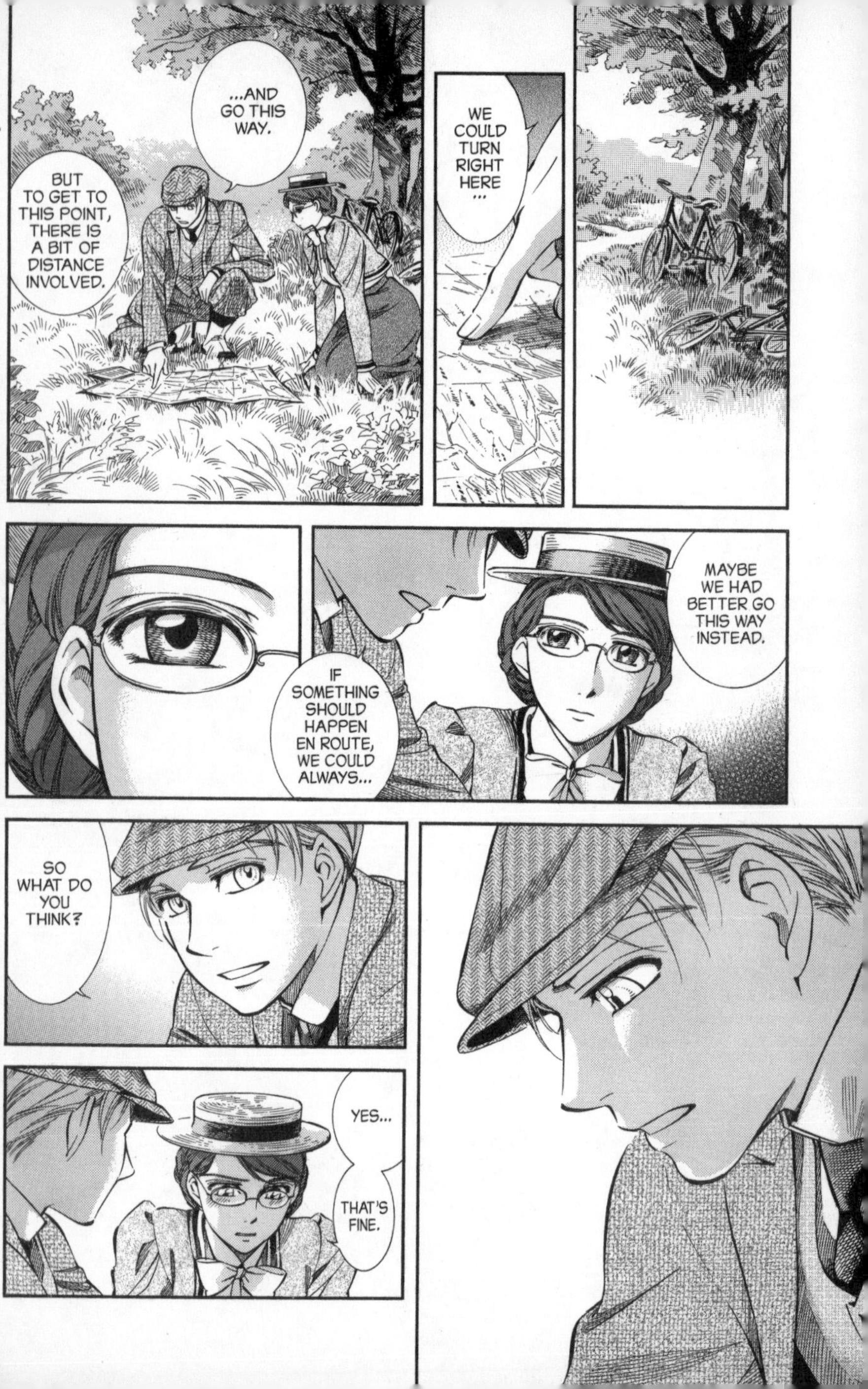
WE COULD TURN RIGHT HERE ...
...AND GO THIS WAY.
BUT TO GET TO THIS POINT, THERE IS A BIT OF DISTANCE INVOLVED.
MAYBE WE HAD BETTER GO THIS WAY INSTEAD.
IF SOMETHING SHOULD HAPPEN EN ROUTE, WE COULD ALWAYS...
SO WHAT DO YOU THINK?
YES...
THAT'S FINE.

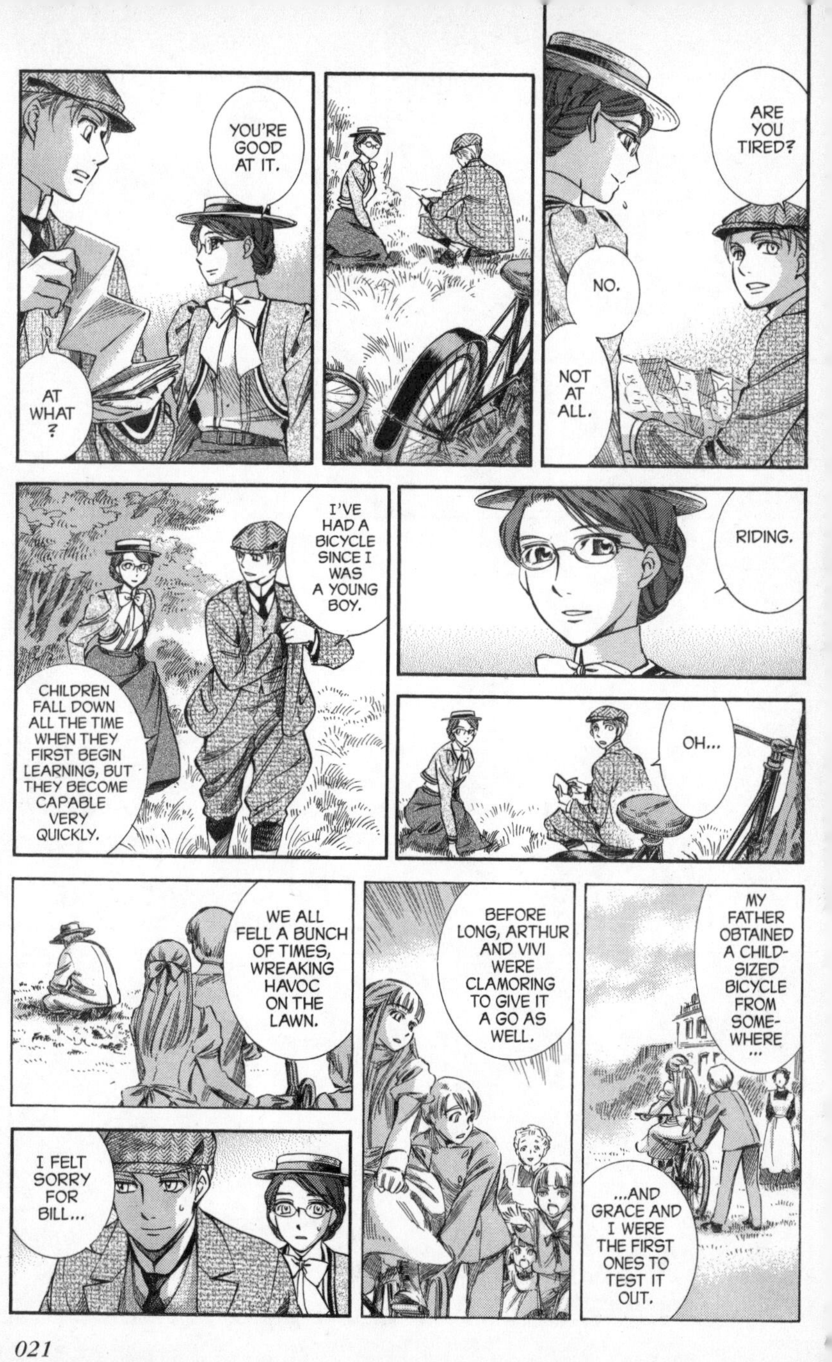
ARE YOU TIRED?
NO.
NOT AT ALL.
YOU'RE GOOD AT IT.
AT WHAT?
RIDING.
OH...
I'VE HAD A BICYCLE SINCE I WAS A YOUNG BOY.
CHILDREN FALL DOWN ALL THE TIME WHEN THEY FIRST BEGIN LEARNING, BUT THEY BECOME CAPABLE VERY QUICKLY.
MY FATHER OBTAINED A CHILD-SIZED BICYCLE FROM SOME-WHERE...
...AND GRACE AND I WERE THE FIRST ONES TO TEST IT OUT.
BEFORE LONG, ARTHUR AND VIVI WERE CLAMORING TO GIVE IT A GO AS WELL.
WE ALL FELL A BUNCH OF TIMES, WREAKING HAVOC ON THE LAWN.
I FELT SORRY FOR BILL...

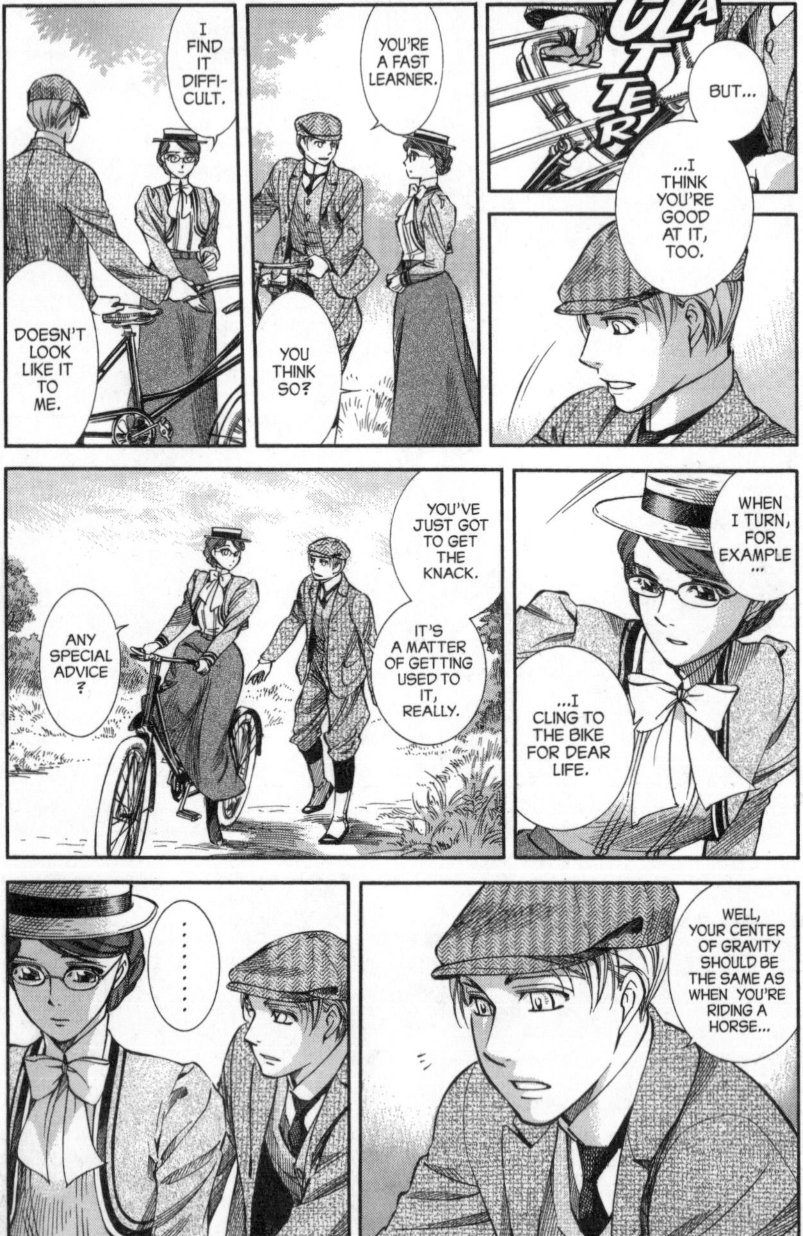
I FIND IT DIFFI-CULT.
DOESN'T LOOK LIKE IT TO ME.
YOU'RE A FAST LEARNER.
YOU THINK SO?
GLATTER!
BUT...
...I THINK YOU'RE GOOD AT IT, TOO.
ANY SPECIAL ADVICE?
YOU'VE JUST GOT TO GET THE KNACK.
IT'S A MATTER OF GETTING USED TO IT, REALLY.
WHEN I TURN, FOR EXAMPLE...
...I CLING TO THE BIKE FOR DEAR LIFE.
....
WELL, YOUR CENTER OF GRAVITY SHOULD BE THE SAME AS WHEN YOU'RE RIDING A HORSE...

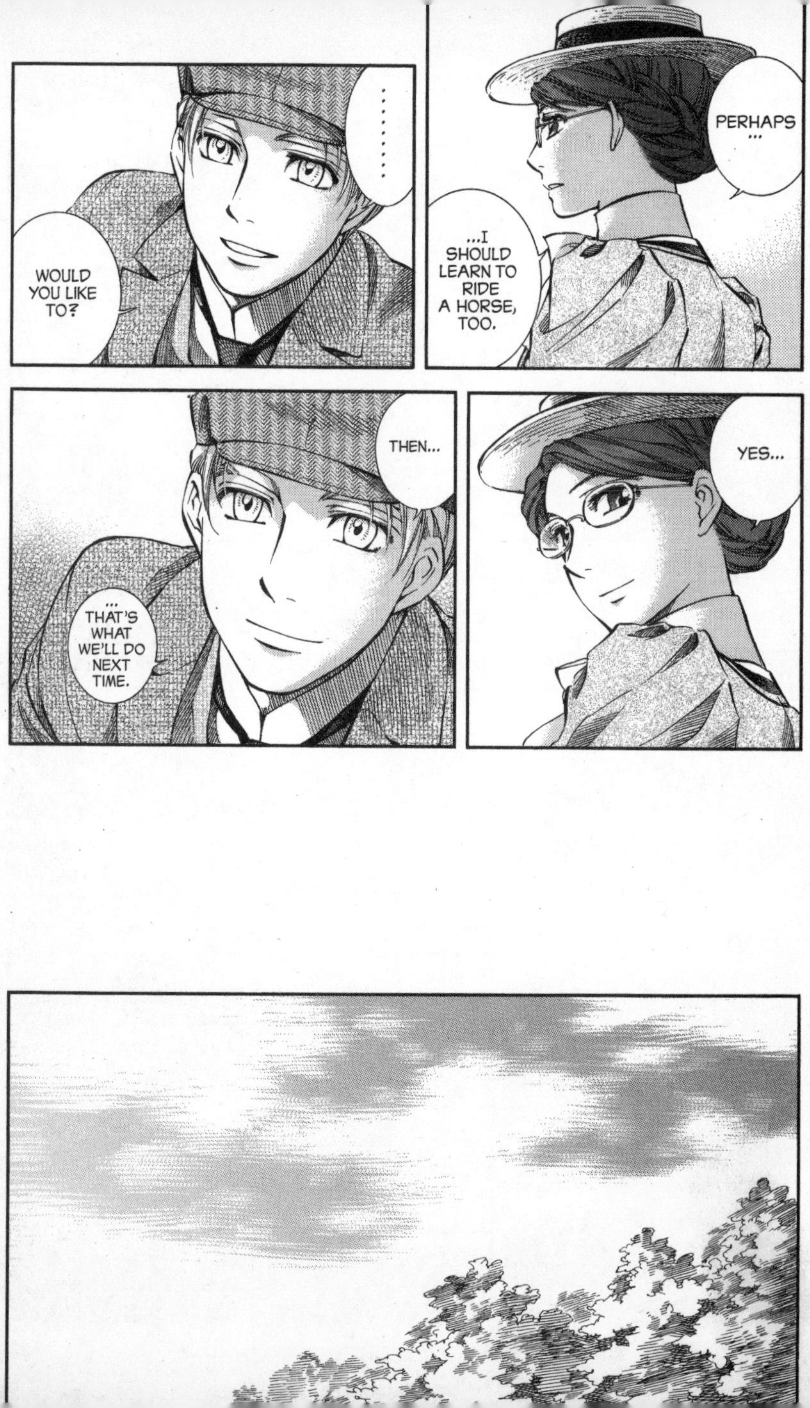
PERHAPS ...
...I SHOULD LEARN TO RIDE A HORSE, TOO.
......
WOULD YOU LIKE TO?
YES...
THEN...
... THAT'S WHAT WE'LL DO NEXT TIME.

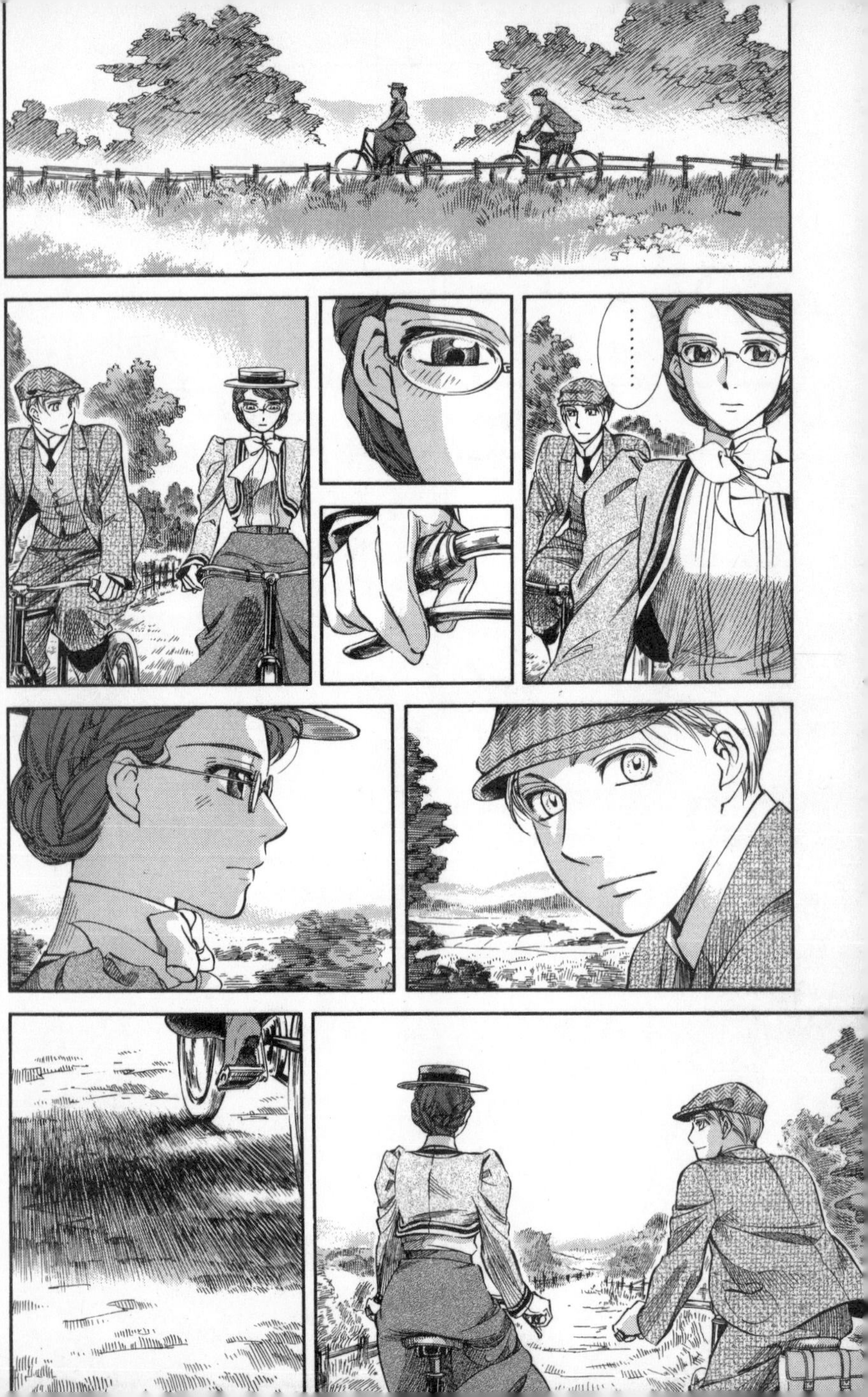
......

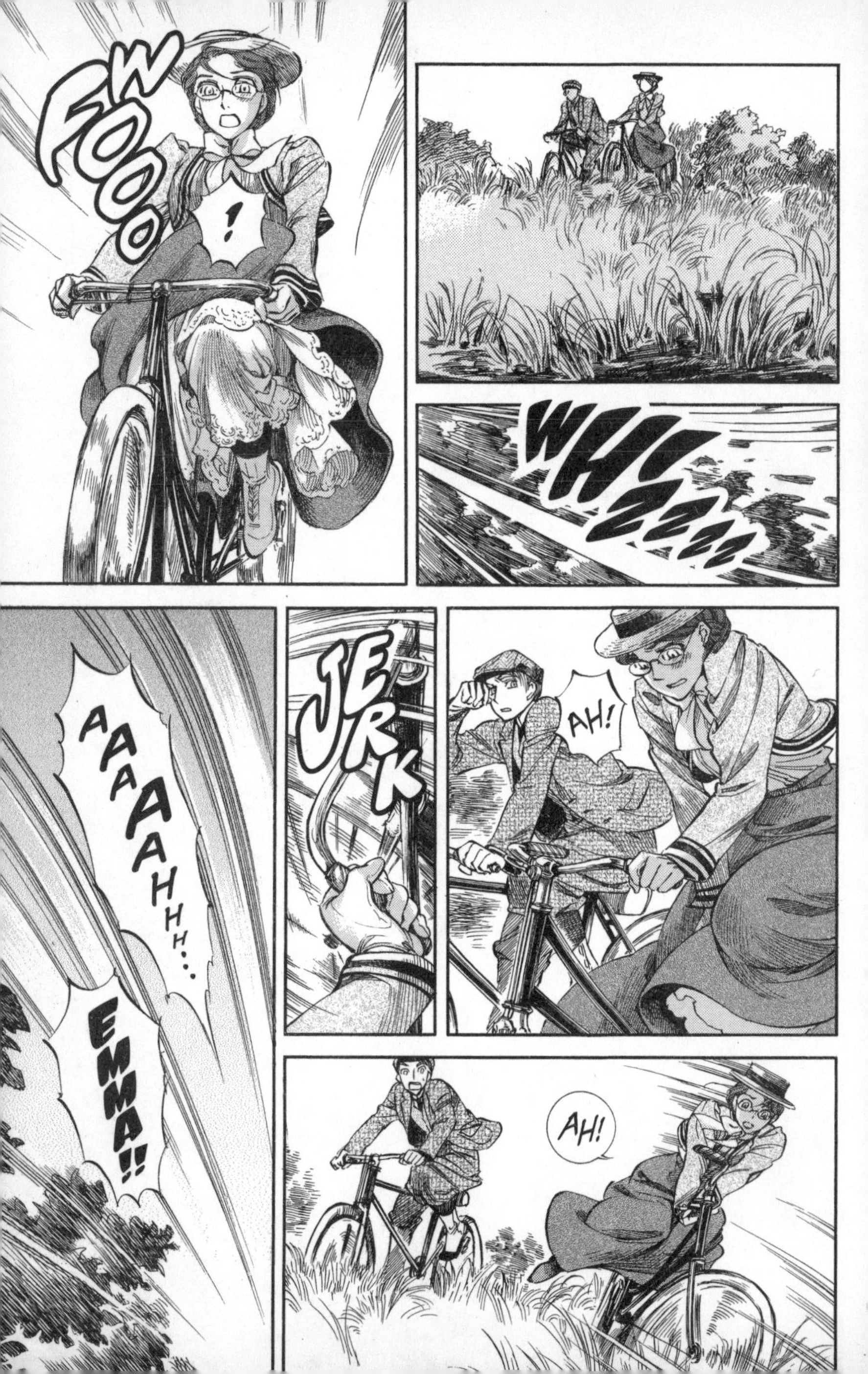
WHIZZZZZ
FWOOOO
!
AH!
JERK
AH!
AAAAHHH...
EMMA!!

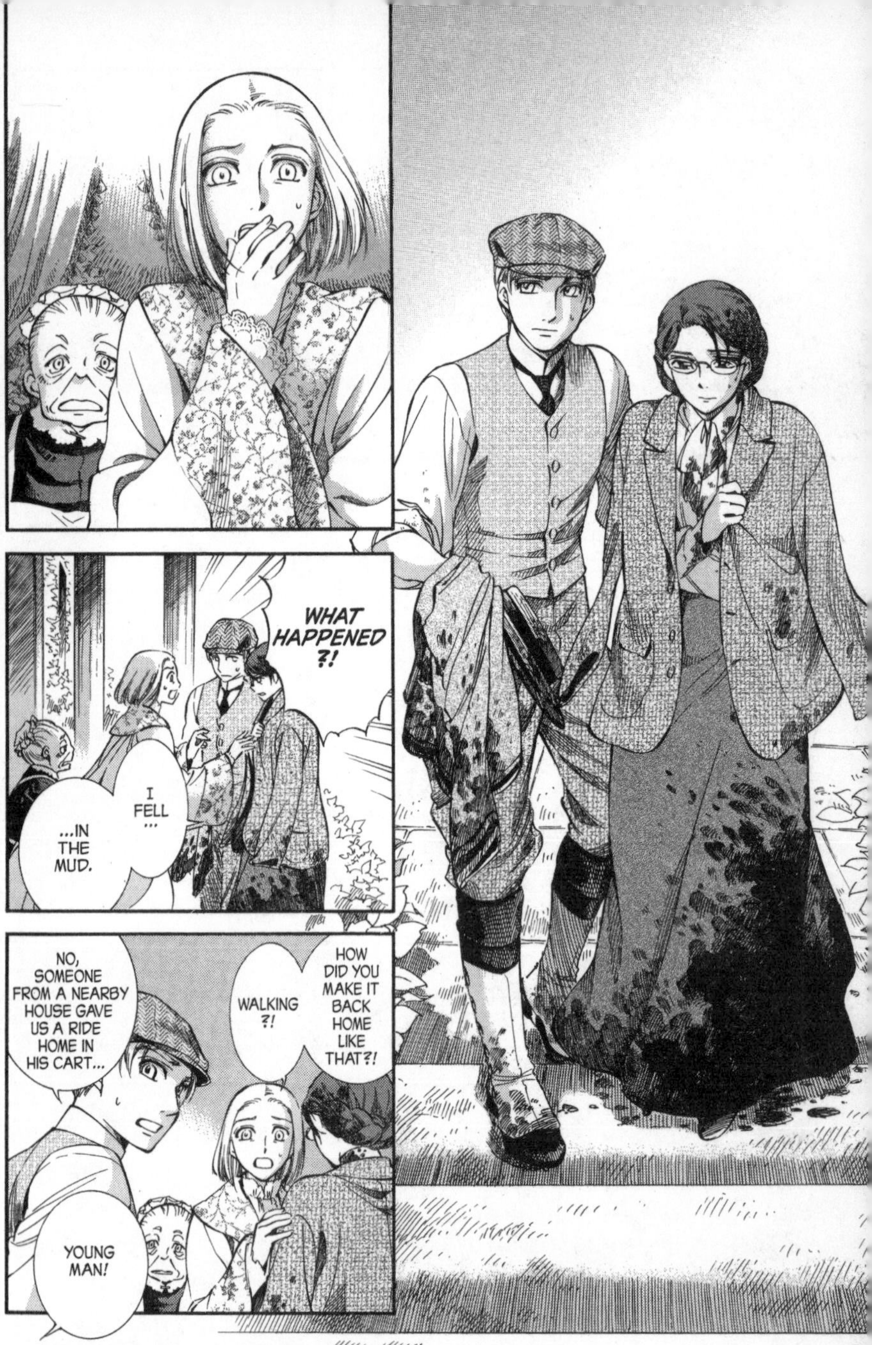
WHAT HAPPENED ?!
I FELL ...
...IN THE MUD.
HOW DID YOU MAKE IT BACK HOME LIKE THAT?!
WALKING ?!
NO, SOMEONE FROM A NEARBY HOUSE GAVE US A RIDE HOME IN HIS CART...
YOUNG MAN!

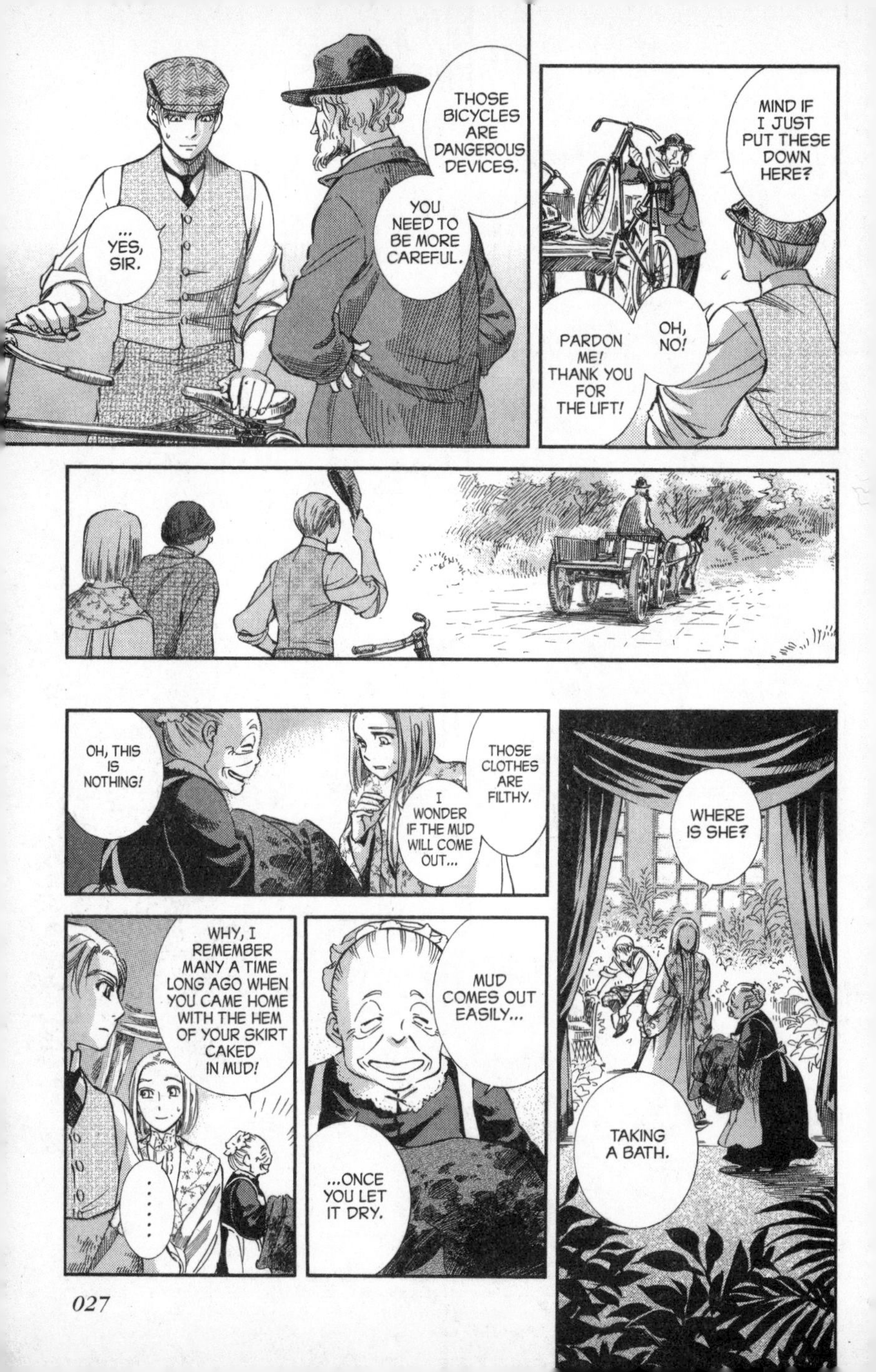
MIND IF I JUST PUT THESE DOWN HERE?
OH, NO!
PARDON ME! THANK YOU FOR THE LIFT!
THOSE BICYCLES ARE DANGEROUS DEVICES.
YOU NEED TO BE MORE CAREFUL.
...YES, SIR.
WHERE IS SHE?
TAKING A BATH.
THOSE CLOTHES ARE FILTHY.
I WONDER IF THE MUD WILL COME OUT...
OH, THIS IS NOTHING!
MUD COMES OUT EASILY...
...ONCE YOU LET IT DRY.
WHY, I REMEMBER MANY A TIME LONG AGO WHEN YOU CAME HOME WITH THE HEM OF YOUR SKIRT CAKED IN MUD!
......

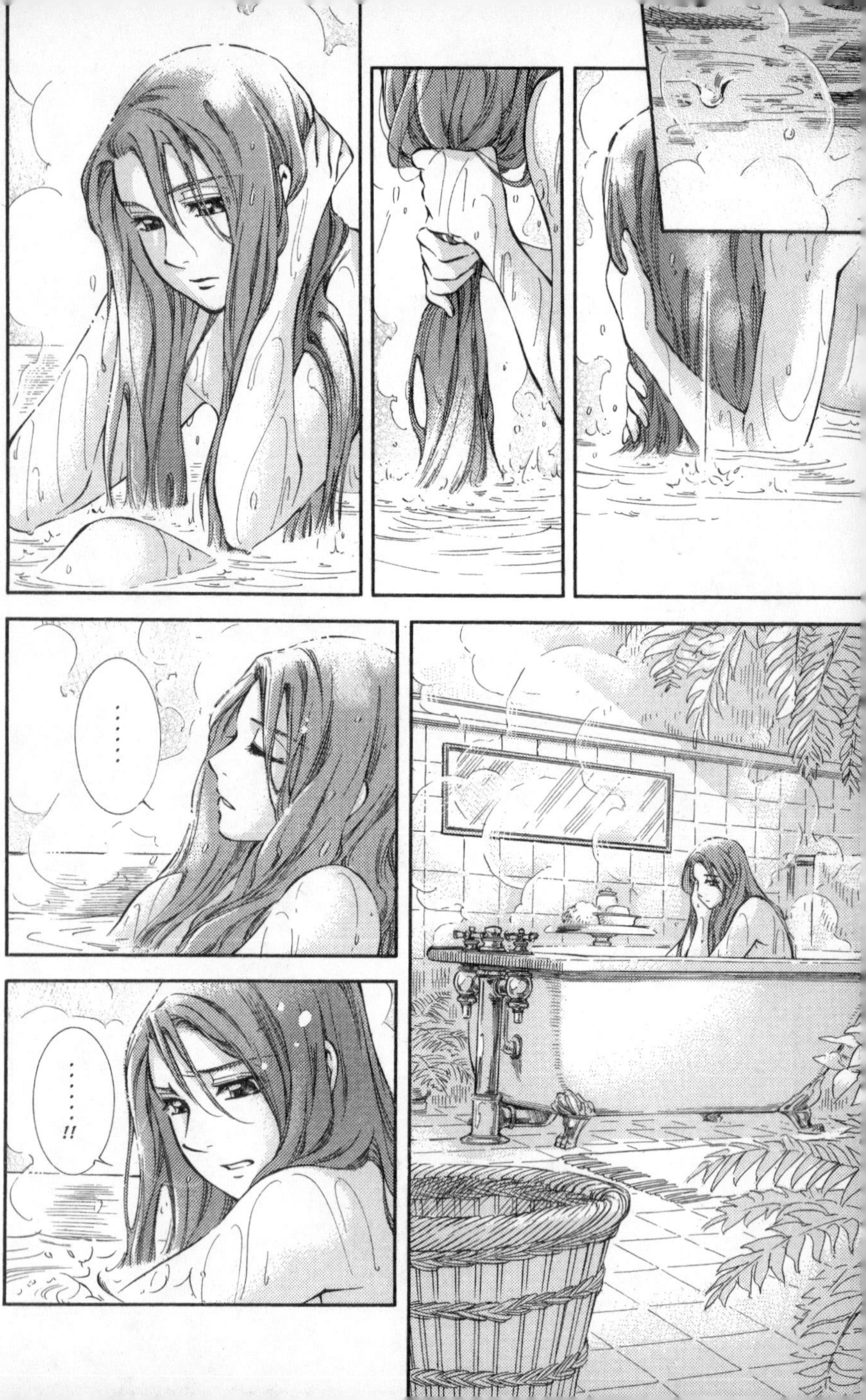
......
......!!

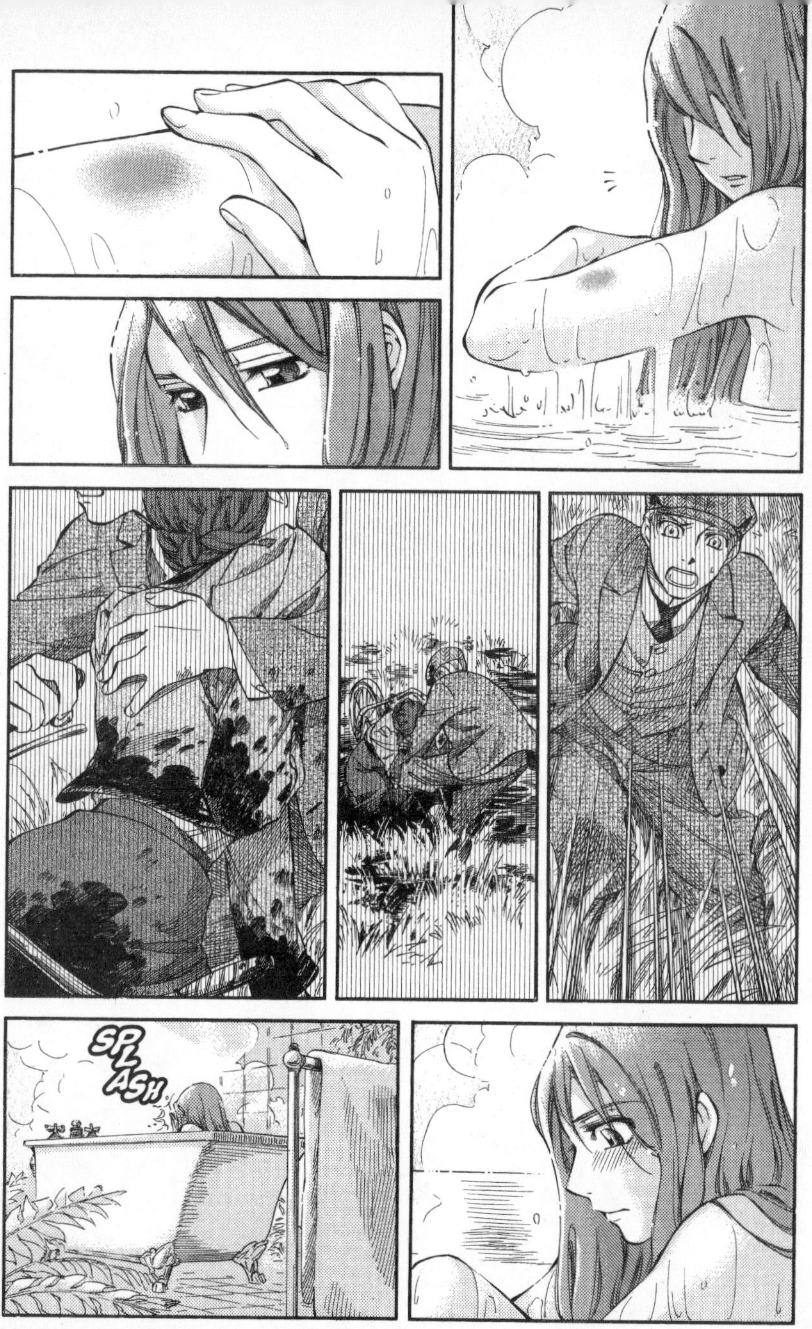
SPLASH

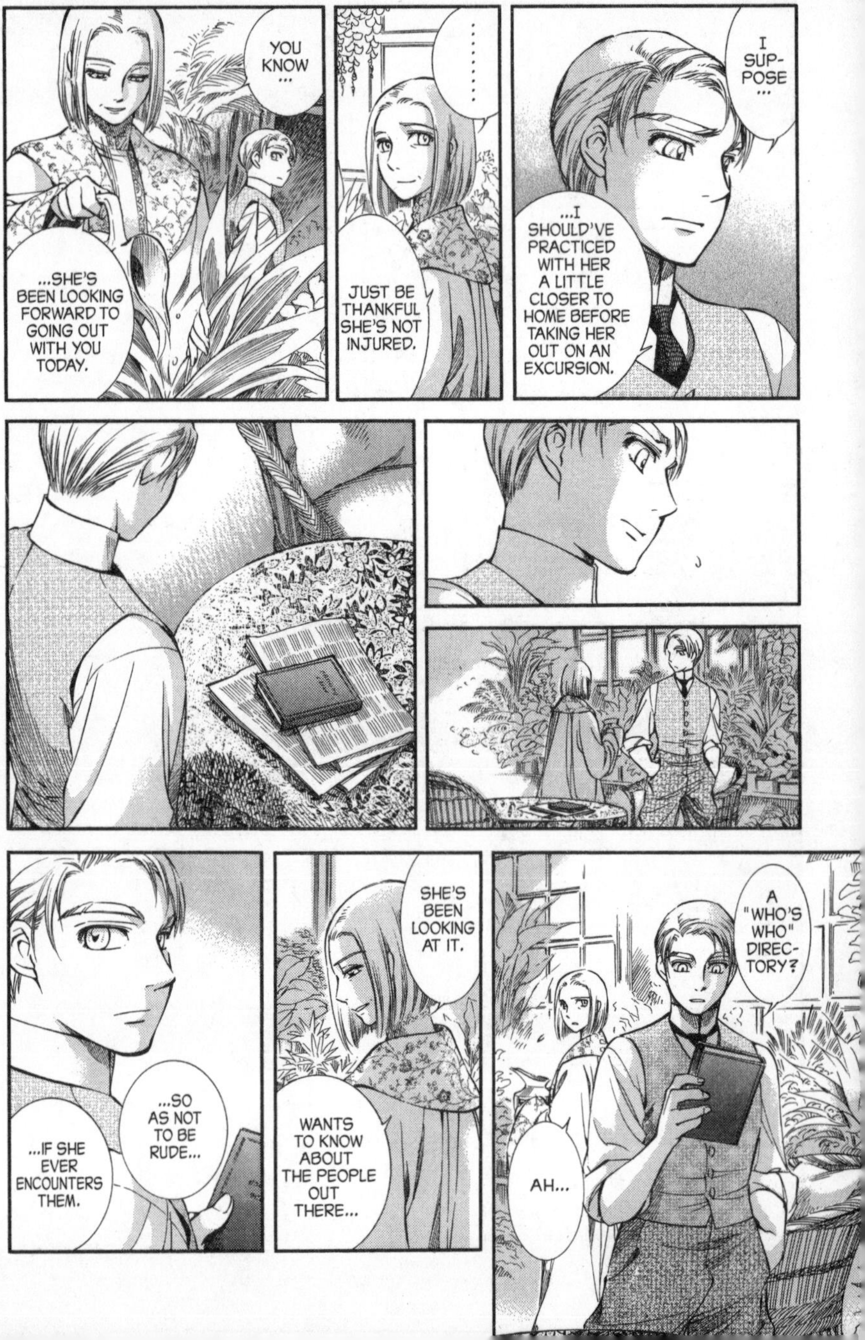
I SUP-POSE...
...I SHOULD'VE PRACTICED WITH HER A LITTLE CLOSER TO HOME BEFORE TAKING HER OUT ON AN EXCURSION.
......
JUST BE THANKFUL SHE'S NOT INJURED.
YOU KNOW...
...SHE'S BEEN LOOKING FORWARD TO GOING OUT WITH YOU TODAY.
A "WHO'S WHO" DIRECTORY?
AH...
SHE'S BEEN LOOKING AT IT.
WANTS TO KNOW ABOUT THE PEOPLE OUT THERE...
...SO AS NOT TO BE RUDE...
...IF SHE EVER ENCOUNTERS THEM.

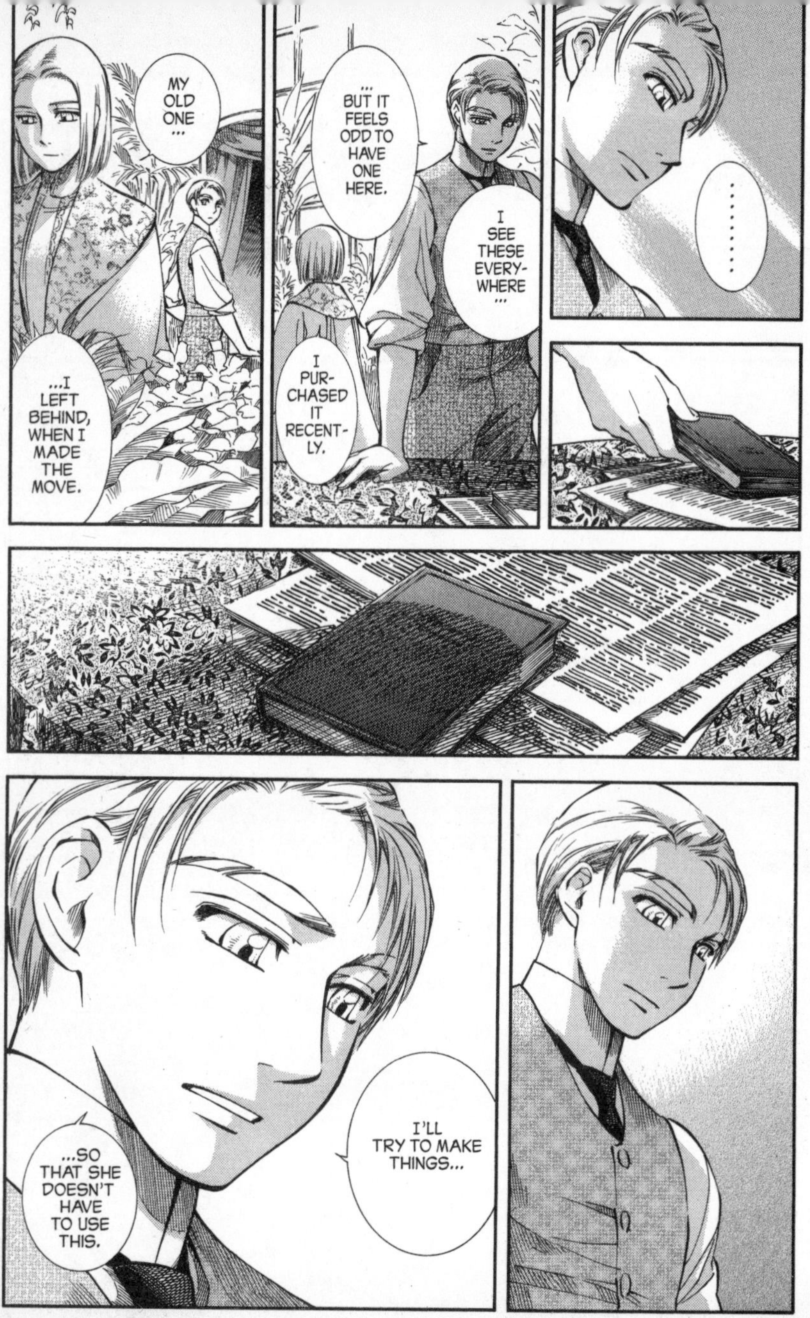

……
I SEE THESE EVERY-WHERE…
… BUT IT FEELS ODD TO HAVE ONE HERE.
I PUR-CHASED IT RECENT-LY.
MY OLD ONE …
…I LEFT BEHIND, WHEN I MADE THE MOVE.
I'LL TRY TO MAKE THINGS…
…SO THAT SHE DOESN'T HAVE TO USE THIS.

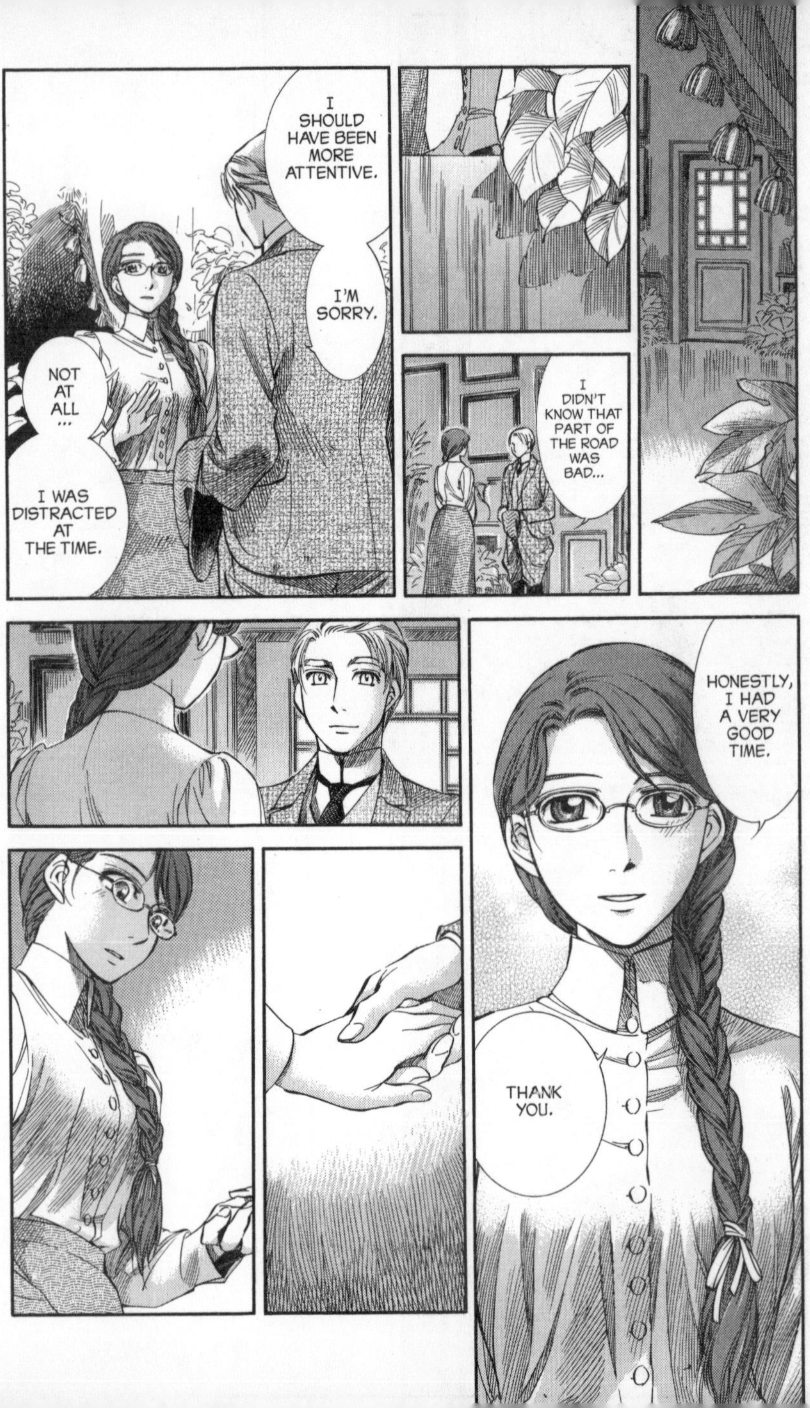
I DIDN'T KNOW THAT PART OF THE ROAD WAS BAD...
I SHOULD HAVE BEEN MORE ATTENTIVE.
I'M SORRY.
NOT AT ALL...
I WAS DISTRACTED AT THE TIME.
HONESTLY, I HAD A VERY GOOD TIME.
THANK YOU.

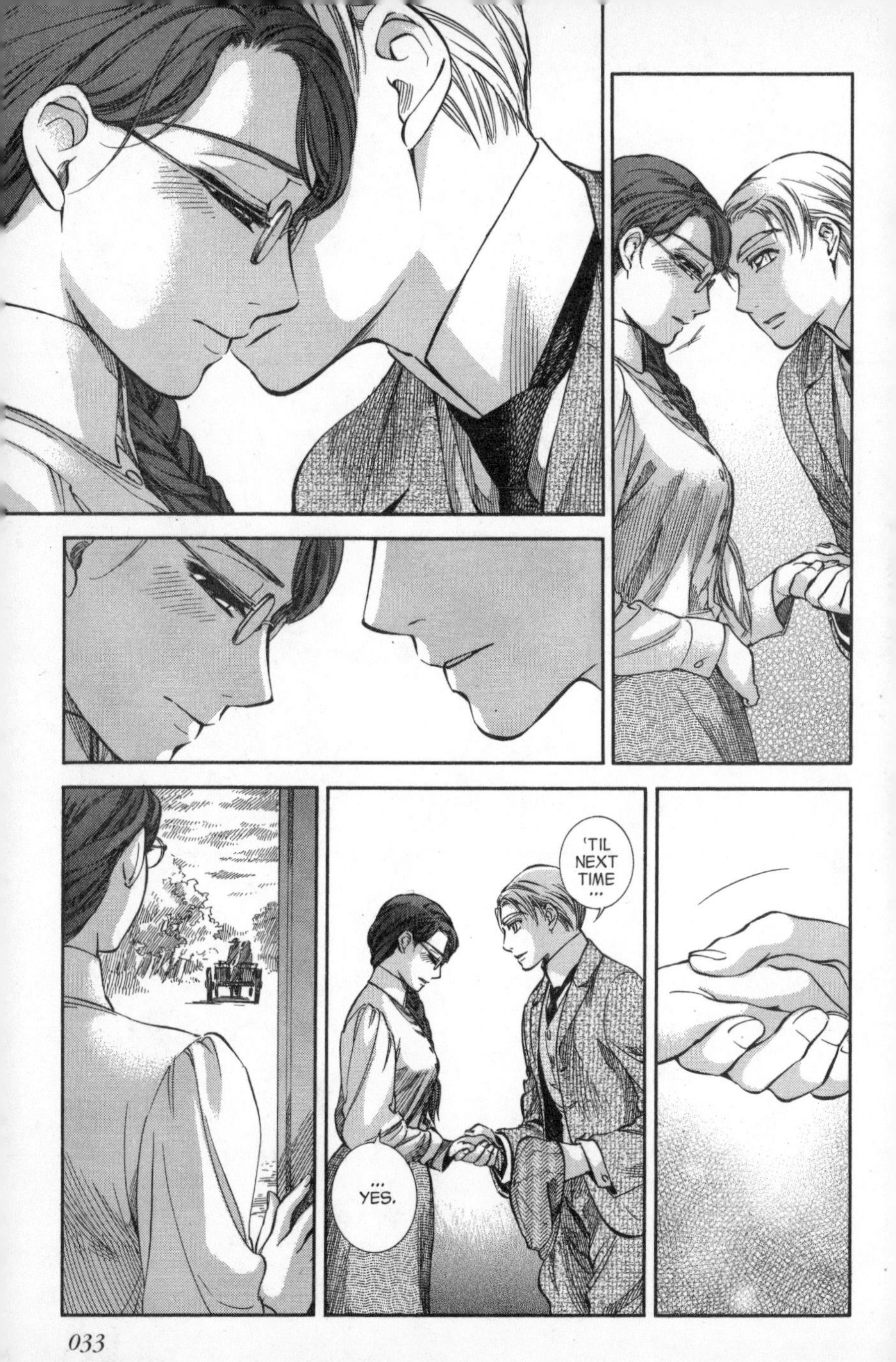
'TIL NEXT TIME ...
... YES.

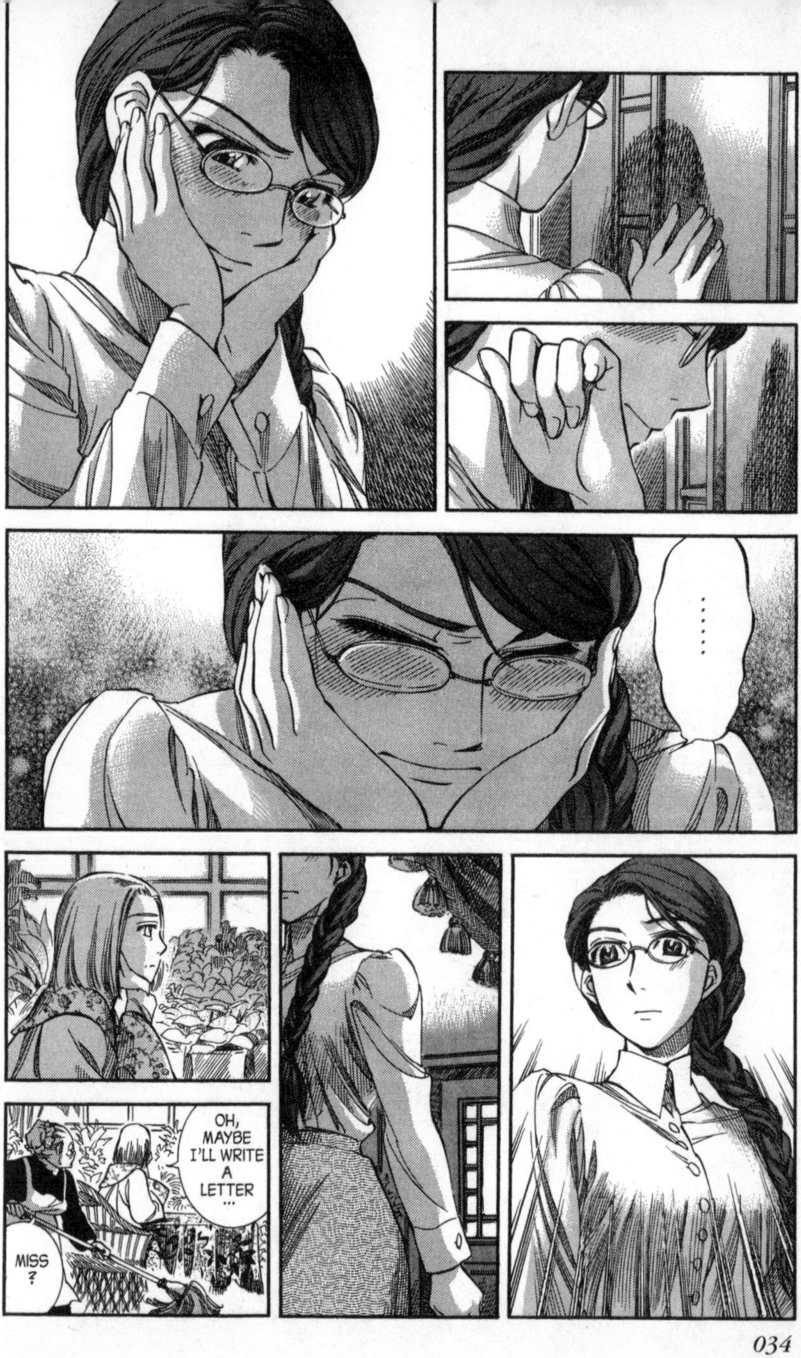
......
OH, MAYBE I'LL WRITE A LETTER ...
MISS ?

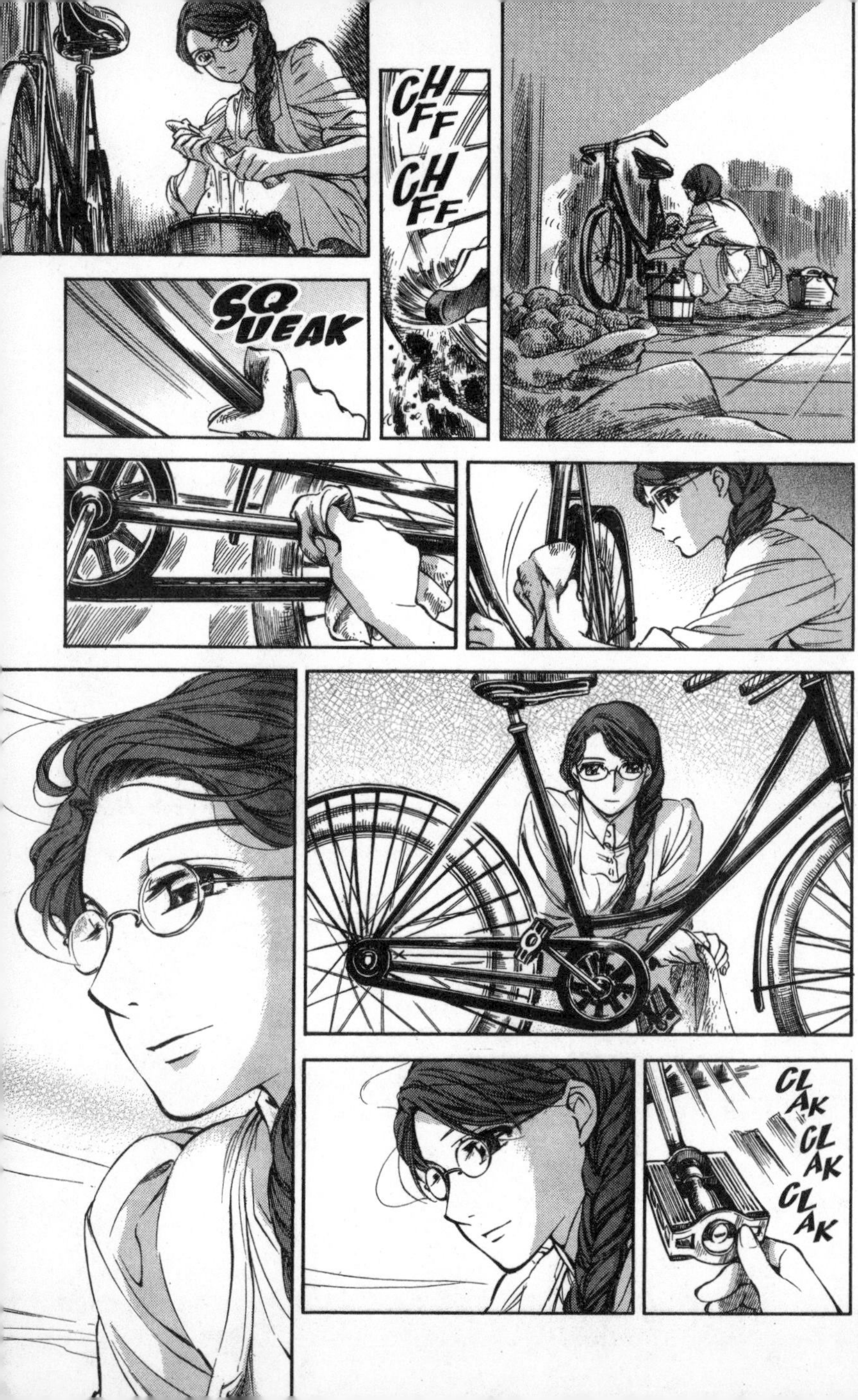
CHFF
CHFF
SQUEAK
CLAK
CLAK
CLAK

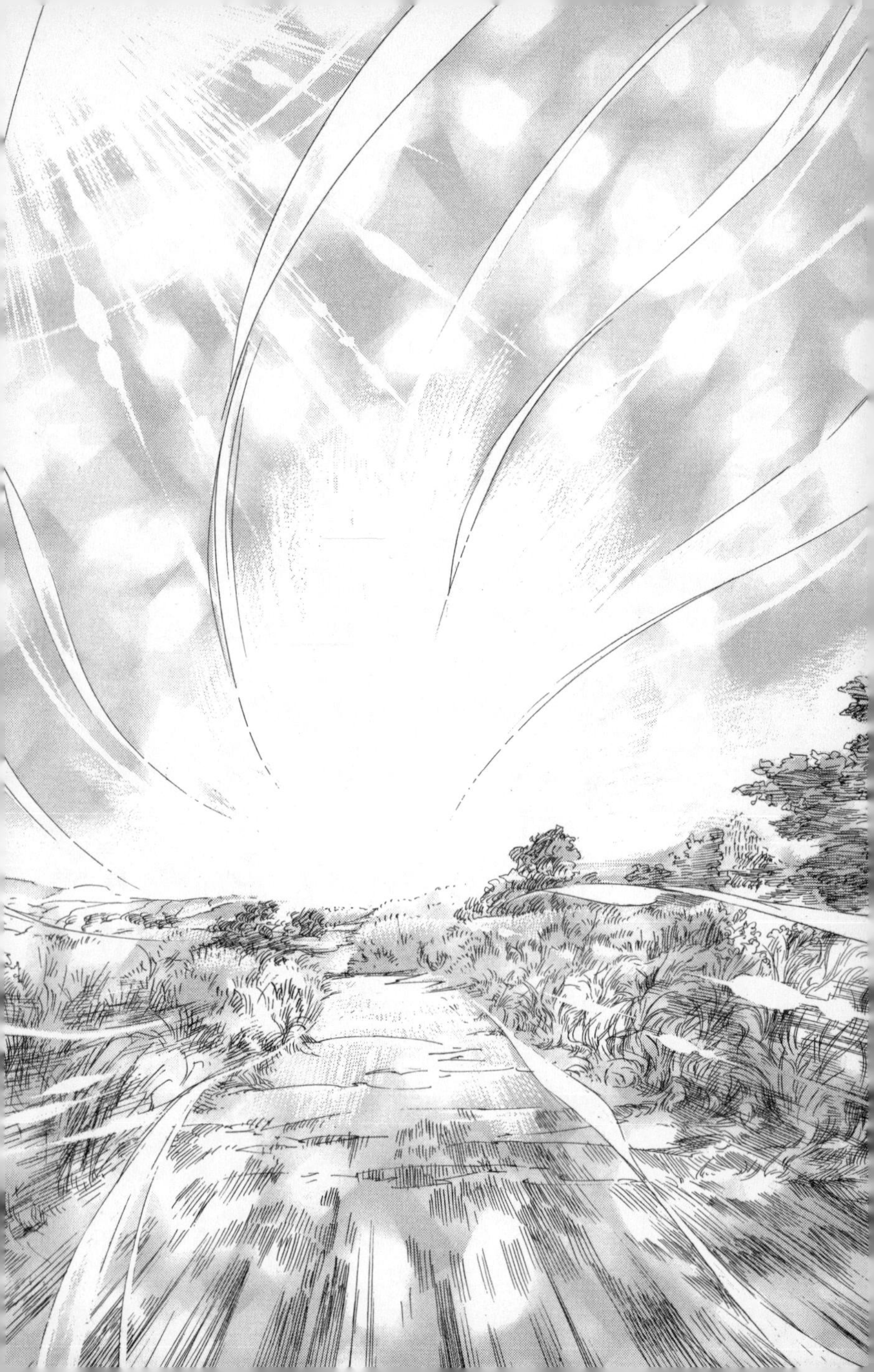

**CHAPTER
14:
ADELE'S
HAPPINESS**

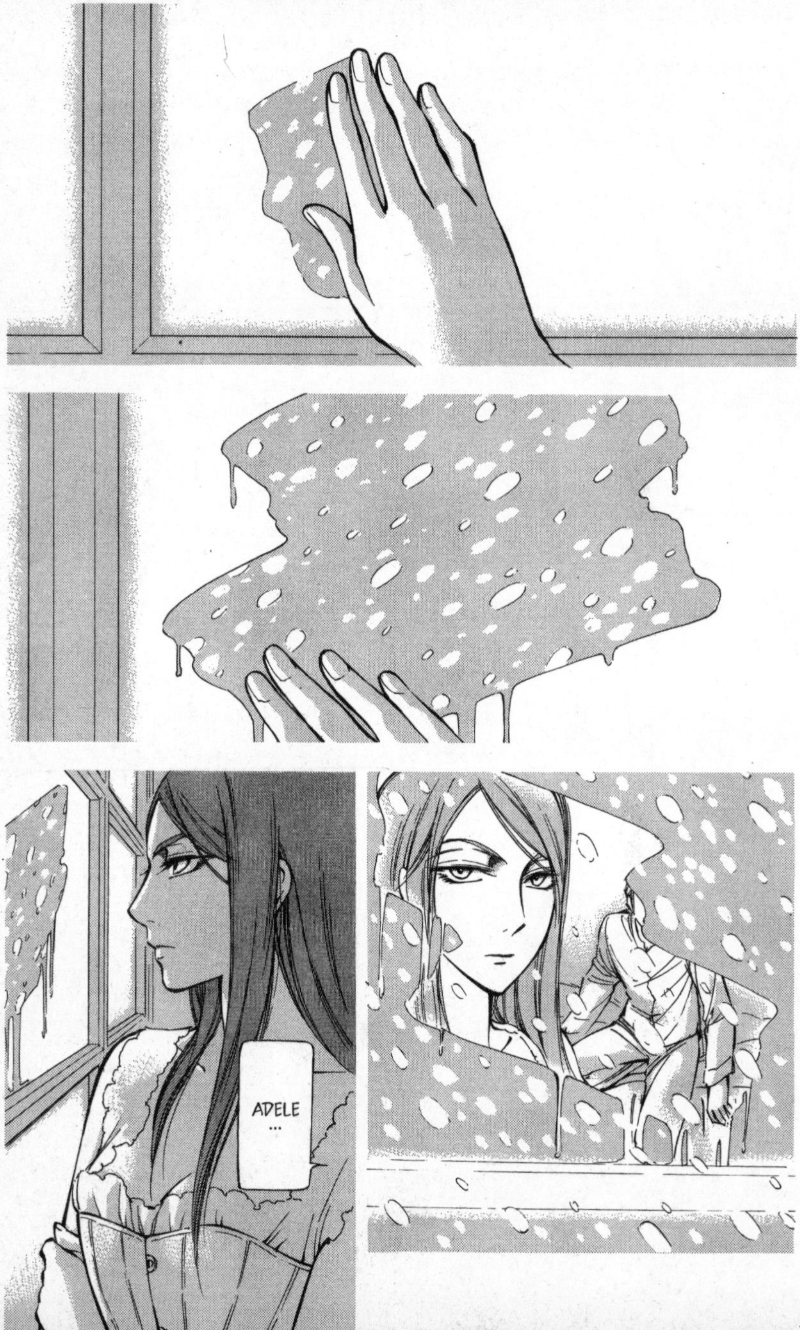
ADELE
...

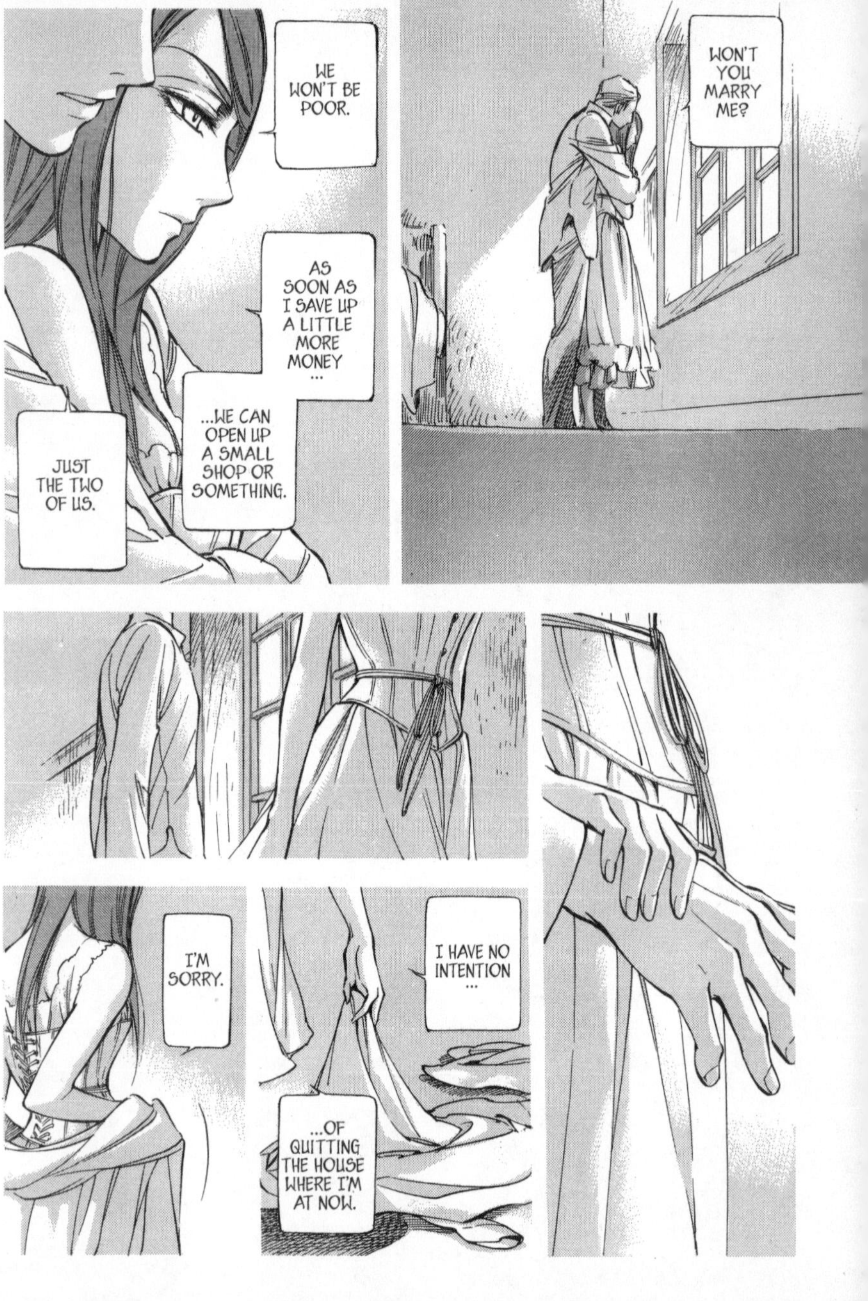
WON'T YOU MARRY ME?
WE WON'T BE POOR.
AS SOON AS I SAVE UP A LITTLE MORE MONEY...
...WE CAN OPEN UP A SMALL SHOP OR SOMETHING.
JUST THE TWO OF US.
I HAVE NO INTENTION...
...OF QUITTING THE HOUSE WHERE I'M AT NOW.
I'M SORRY.

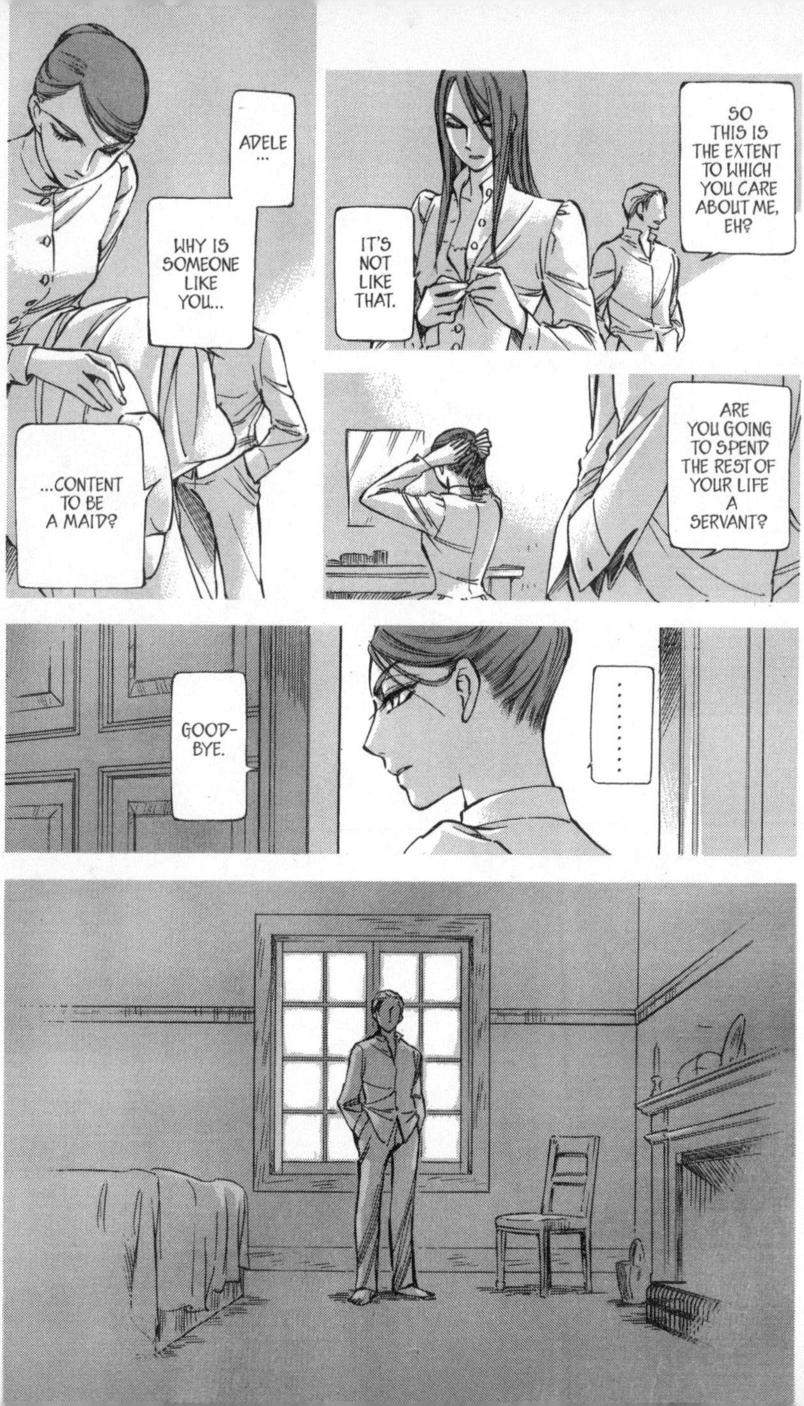
SO THIS IS THE EXTENT TO WHICH YOU CARE ABOUT ME, EH?
IT'S NOT LIKE THAT.
ARE YOU GOING TO SPEND THE REST OF YOUR LIFE A SERVANT?
ADELE ...
WHY IS SOMEONE LIKE YOU...
...CONTENT TO BE A MAID?
....
GOOD-BYE.

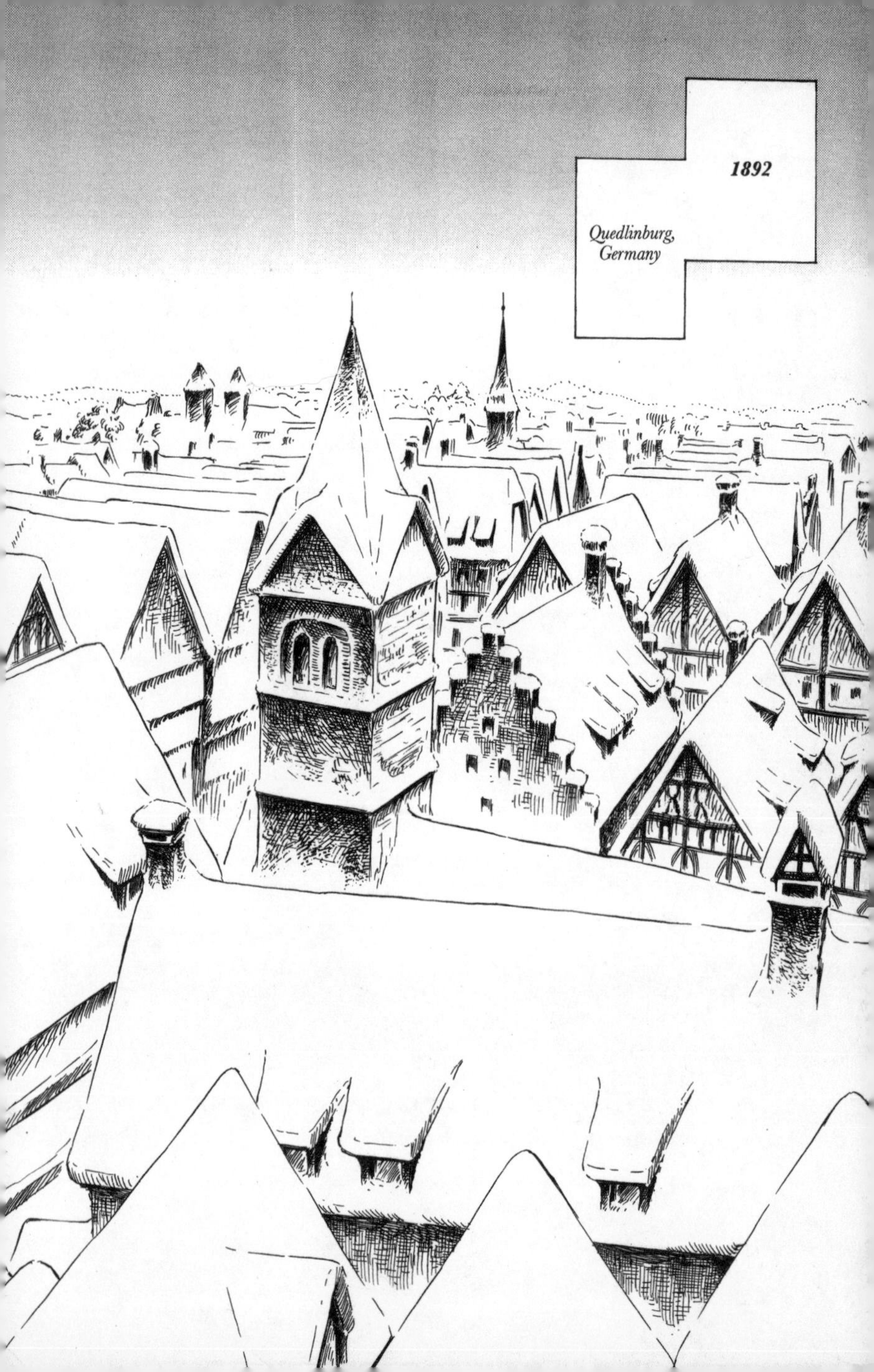
1892
Quedlinburg, Germany

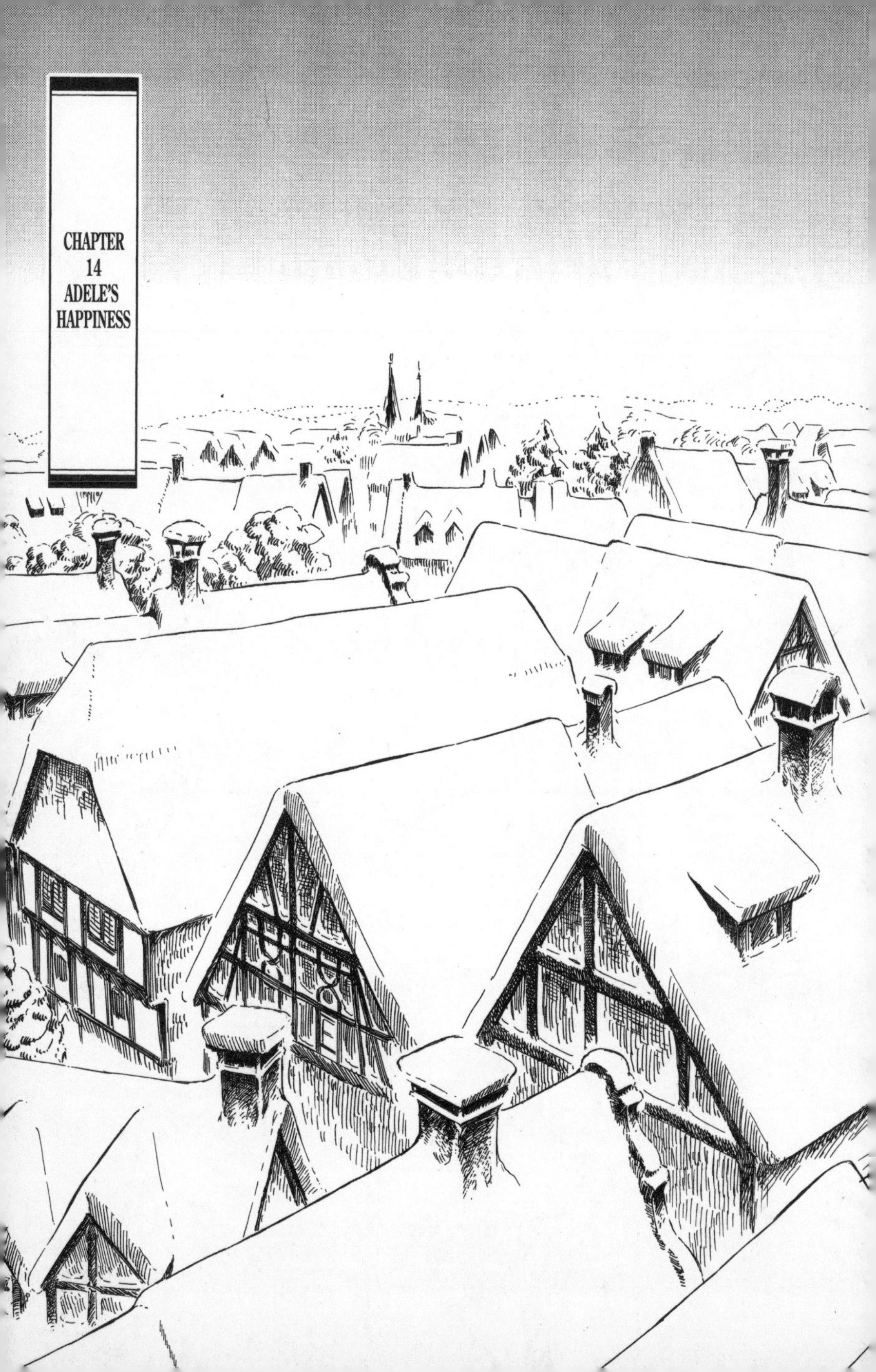
CHAPTER
14
ADELE'S
HAPPINESS

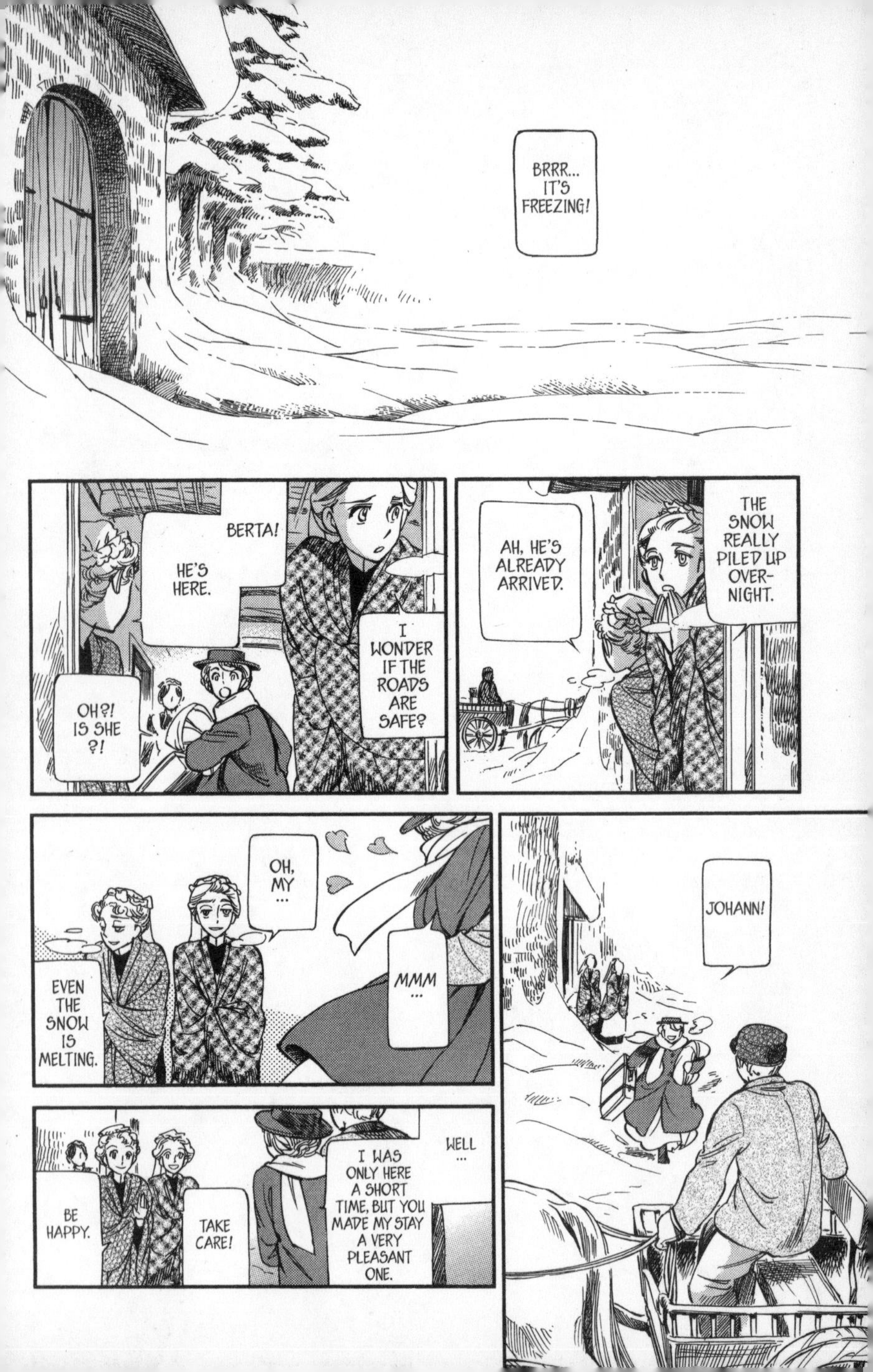
BRRR... IT'S FREEZING!
THE SNOW REALLY PILED UP OVER-NIGHT.
AH, HE'S ALREADY ARRIVED.
I WONDER IF THE ROADS ARE SAFE?
BERTA!
HE'S HERE.
OH?! IS SHE ?!
JOHANN!
OH, MY ...
MMM ...
EVEN THE SNOW IS MELTING.
WELL ...
I WAS ONLY HERE A SHORT TIME, BUT YOU MADE MY STAY A VERY PLEASANT ONE.
TAKE CARE!
BE HAPPY.

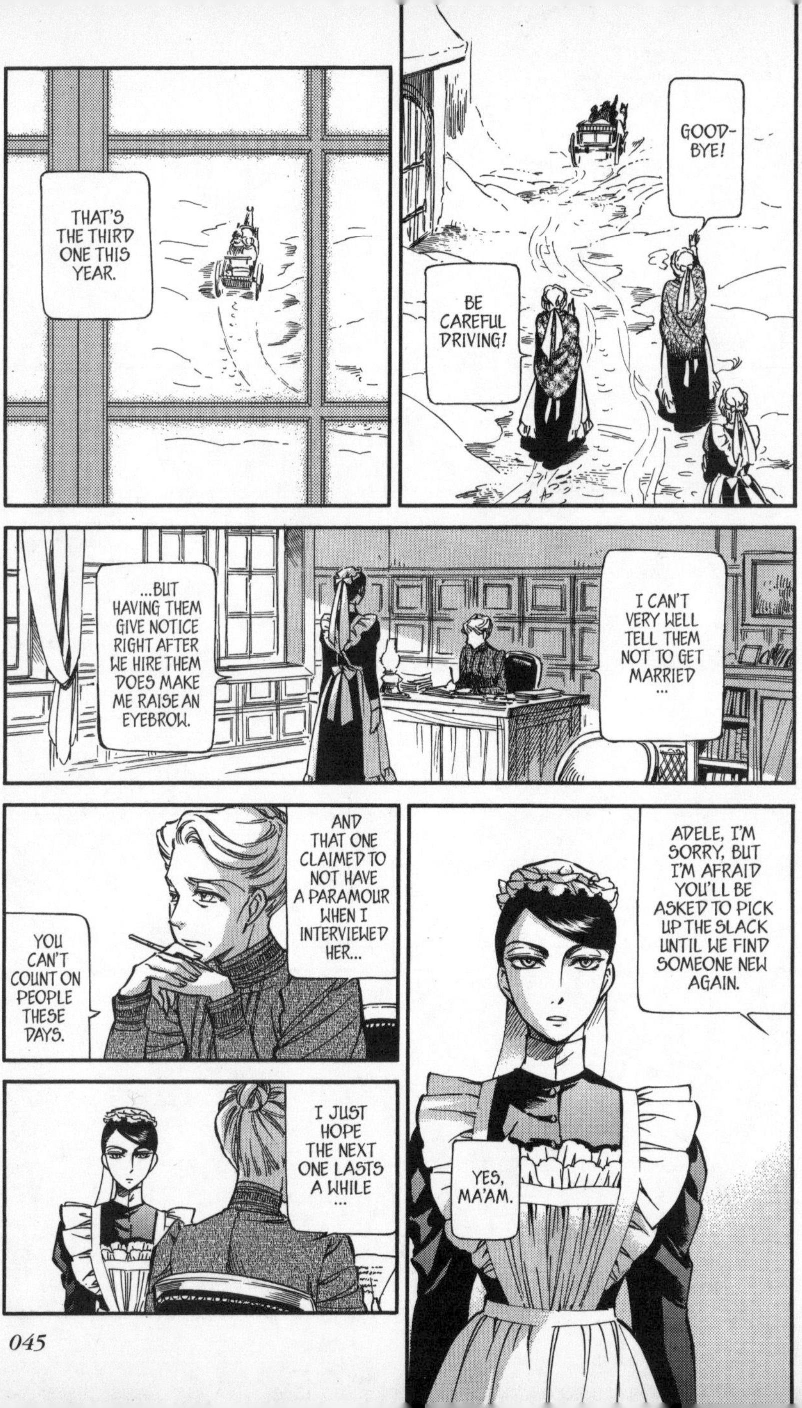
GOOD-BYE!
BE CAREFUL DRIVING!
THAT'S THE THIRD ONE THIS YEAR.
I CAN'T VERY WELL TELL THEM NOT TO GET MARRIED ...
...BUT HAVING THEM GIVE NOTICE RIGHT AFTER WE HIRE THEM DOES MAKE ME RAISE AN EYEBROW.
ADELE, I'M SORRY, BUT I'M AFRAID YOU'LL BE ASKED TO PICK UP THE SLACK UNTIL WE FIND SOMEONE NEW AGAIN.
YES, MA'AM.
AND THAT ONE CLAIMED TO NOT HAVE A PARAMOUR WHEN I INTERVIEWED HER...
YOU CAN'T COUNT ON PEOPLE THESE DAYS.
I JUST HOPE THE NEXT ONE LASTS A WHILE ...

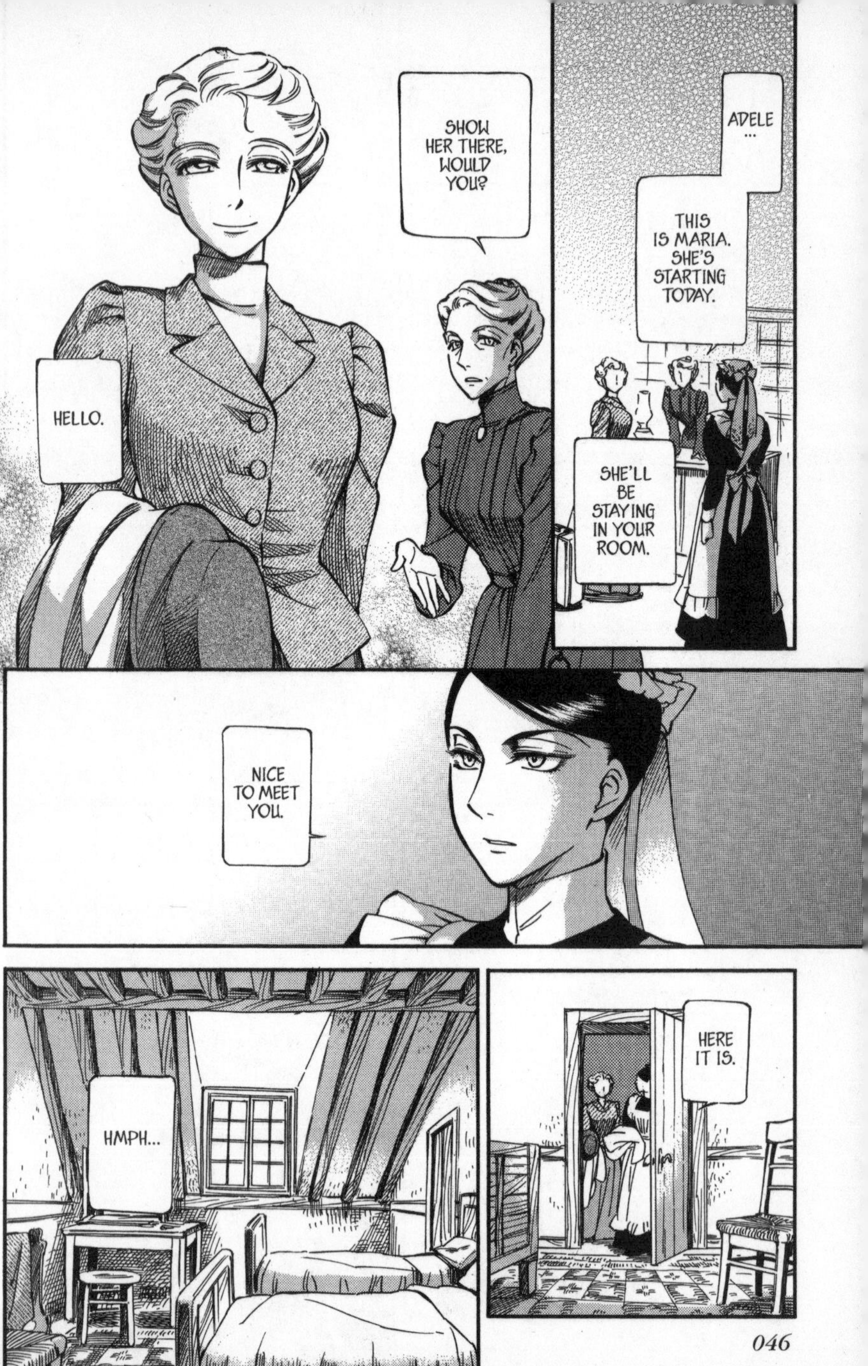
ADELE ...
THIS IS MARIA. SHE'S STARTING TODAY.
SHE'LL BE STAYING IN YOUR ROOM.
SHOW HER THERE, WOULD YOU?
HELLO.
NICE TO MEET YOU.
HERE IT IS.
HMPH...

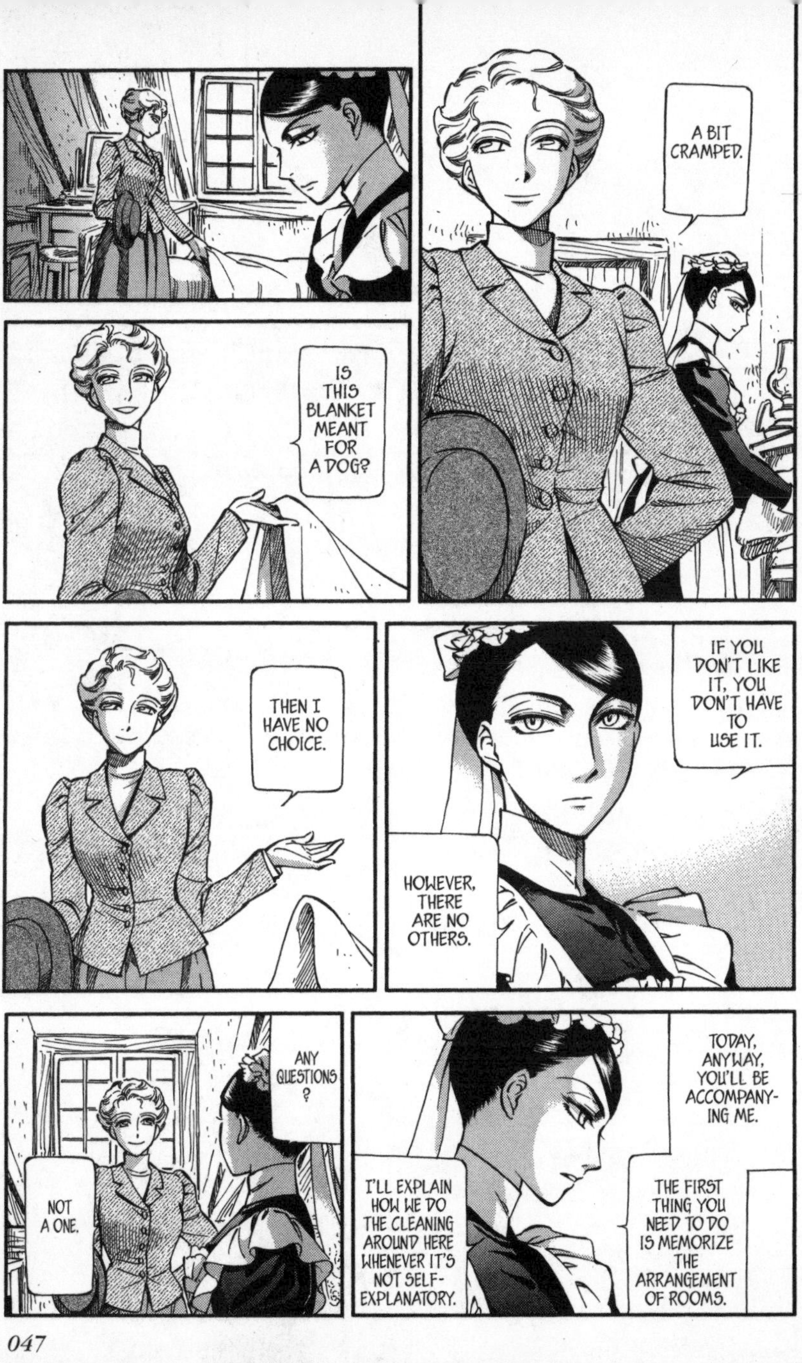
A BIT CRAMPED.
IS THIS BLANKET MEANT FOR A DOG?
IF YOU DON'T LIKE IT, YOU DON'T HAVE TO USE IT.
HOWEVER, THERE ARE NO OTHERS.
THEN I HAVE NO CHOICE.
TODAY, ANYWAY, YOU'LL BE ACCOMPANYING ME.
THE FIRST THING YOU NEED TO DO IS MEMORIZE THE ARRANGEMENT OF ROOMS.
I'LL EXPLAIN HOW WE DO THE CLEANING AROUND HERE WHENEVER IT'S NOT SELF-EXPLANATORY.
ANY QUESTIONS?
NOT A ONE.

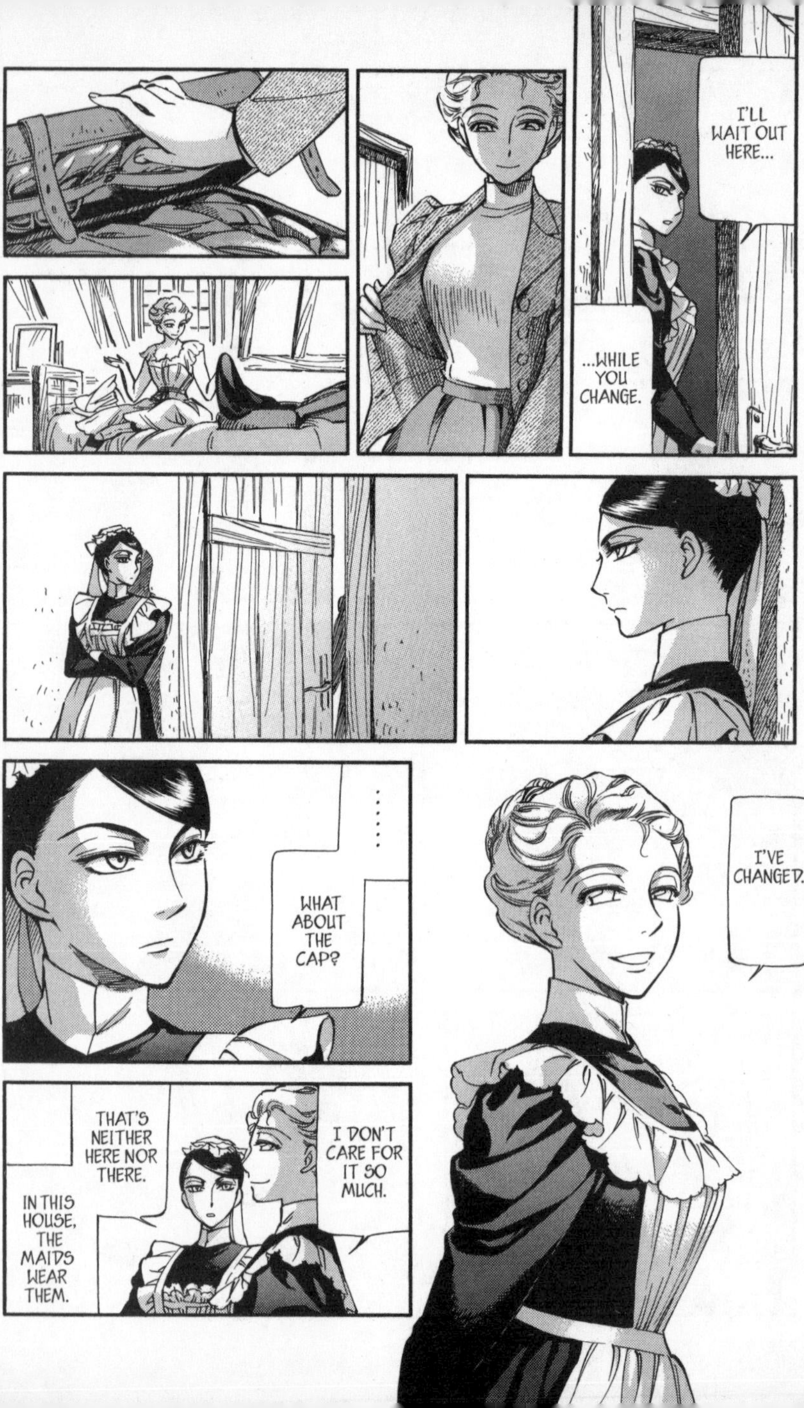
I'LL WAIT OUT HERE...
...WHILE YOU CHANGE.
I'VE CHANGED.
......
WHAT ABOUT THE CAP?
I DON'T CARE FOR IT SO MUCH.
THAT'S NEITHER HERE NOR THERE.
IN THIS HOUSE, THE MAIDS WEAR THEM.

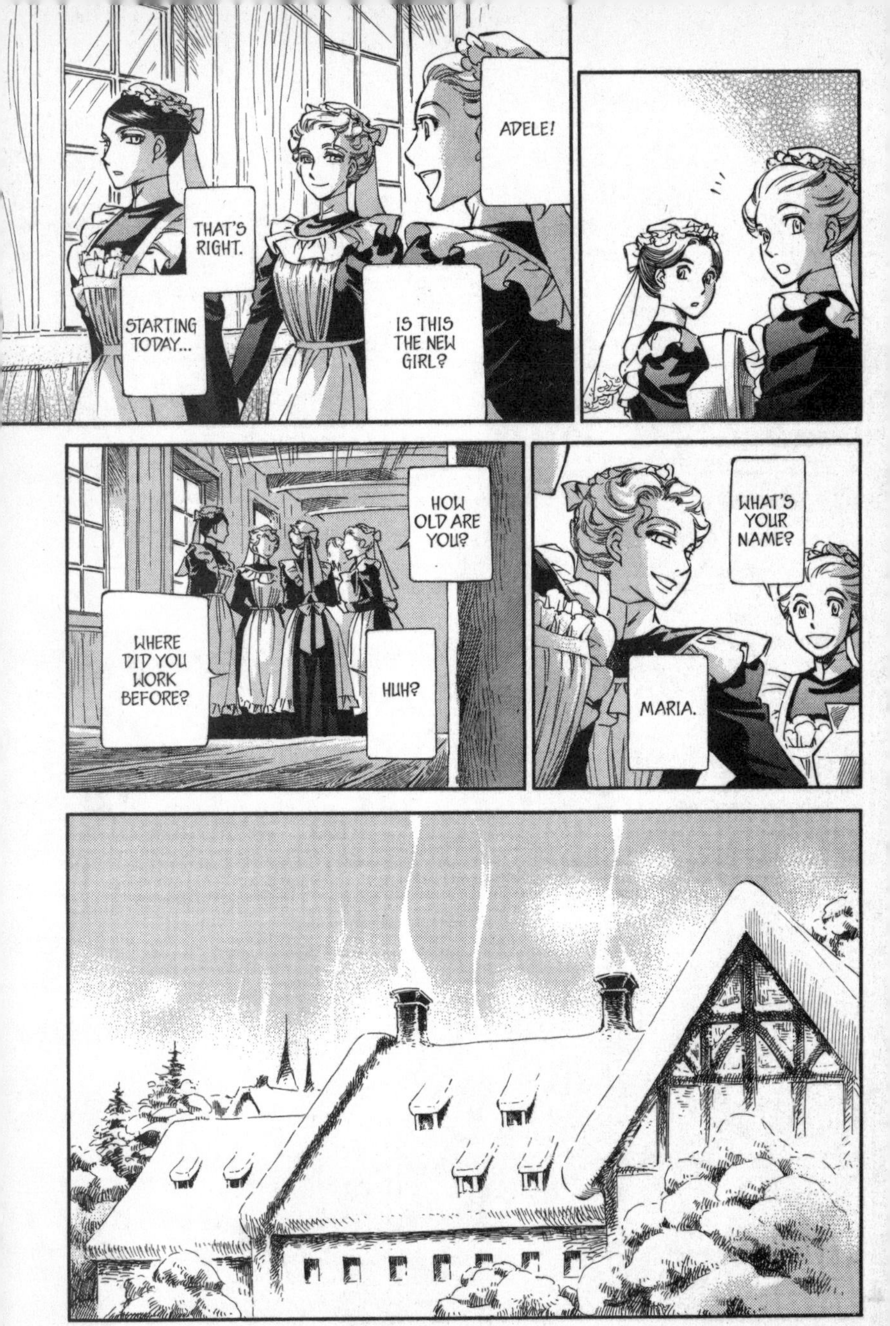
ADELE!
IS THIS THE NEW GIRL?
THAT'S RIGHT.
STARTING TODAY...
WHAT'S YOUR NAME?
MARIA.
HOW OLD ARE YOU?
HUH?
WHERE DID YOU WORK BEFORE?

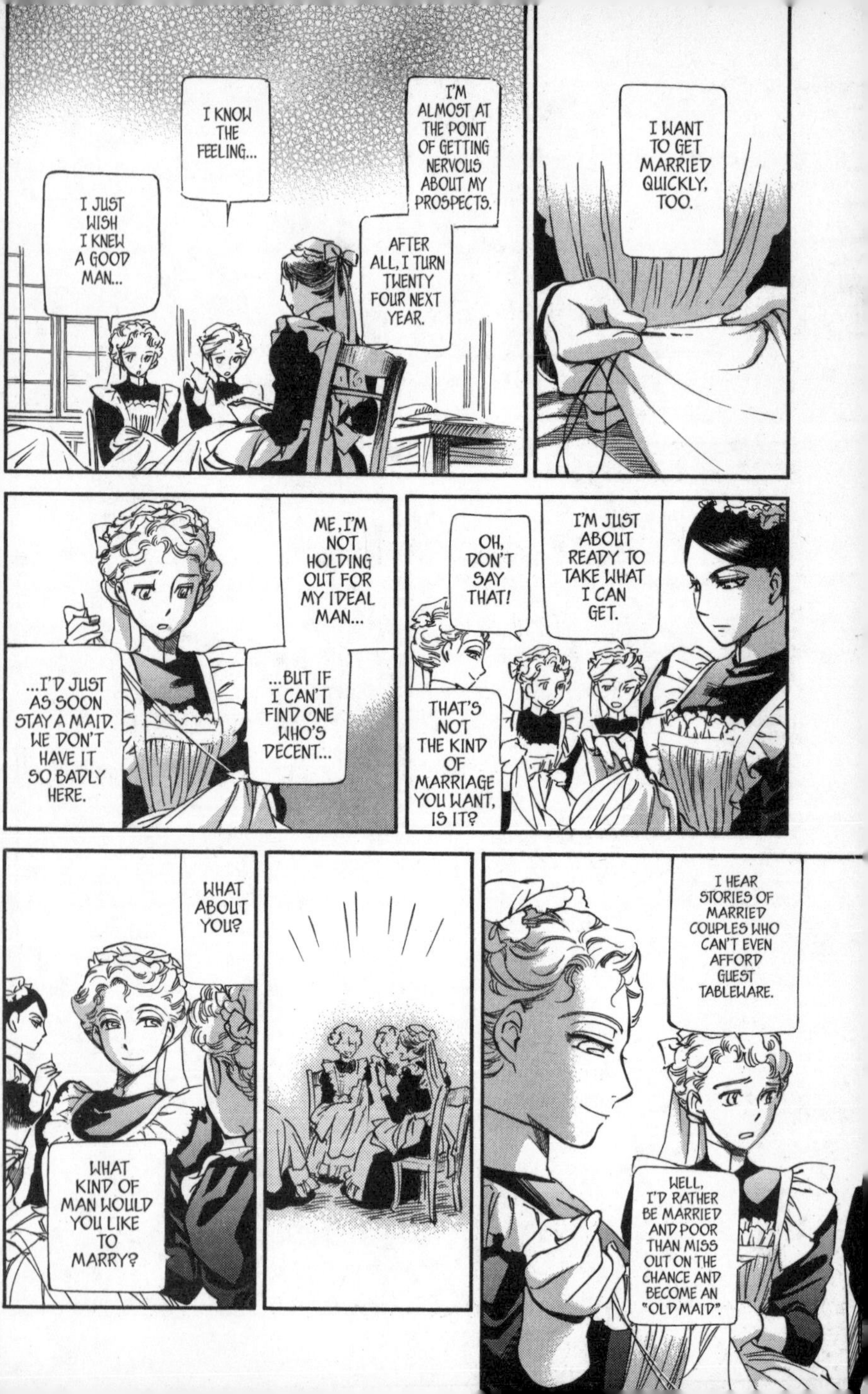
I WANT TO GET MARRIED QUICKLY, TOO.
I'M ALMOST AT THE POINT OF GETTING NERVOUS ABOUT MY PROSPECTS.
AFTER ALL, I TURN TWENTY FOUR NEXT YEAR.
I KNOW THE FEELING...
I JUST WISH I KNEW A GOOD MAN...
I'M JUST ABOUT READY TO TAKE WHAT I CAN GET.
OH, DON'T SAY THAT!
THAT'S NOT THE KIND OF MARRIAGE YOU WANT, IS IT?
ME, I'M NOT HOLDING OUT FOR MY IDEAL MAN...
...BUT IF I CAN'T FIND ONE WHO'S DECENT...
...I'D JUST AS SOON STAY A MAID. WE DON'T HAVE IT SO BADLY HERE.
I HEAR STORIES OF MARRIED COUPLES WHO CAN'T EVEN AFFORD GUEST TABLEWARE.
WELL, I'D RATHER BE MARRIED AND POOR THAN MISS OUT ON THE CHANCE AND BECOME AN "OLD MAID".
WHAT ABOUT YOU?
WHAT KIND OF MAN WOULD YOU LIKE TO MARRY?

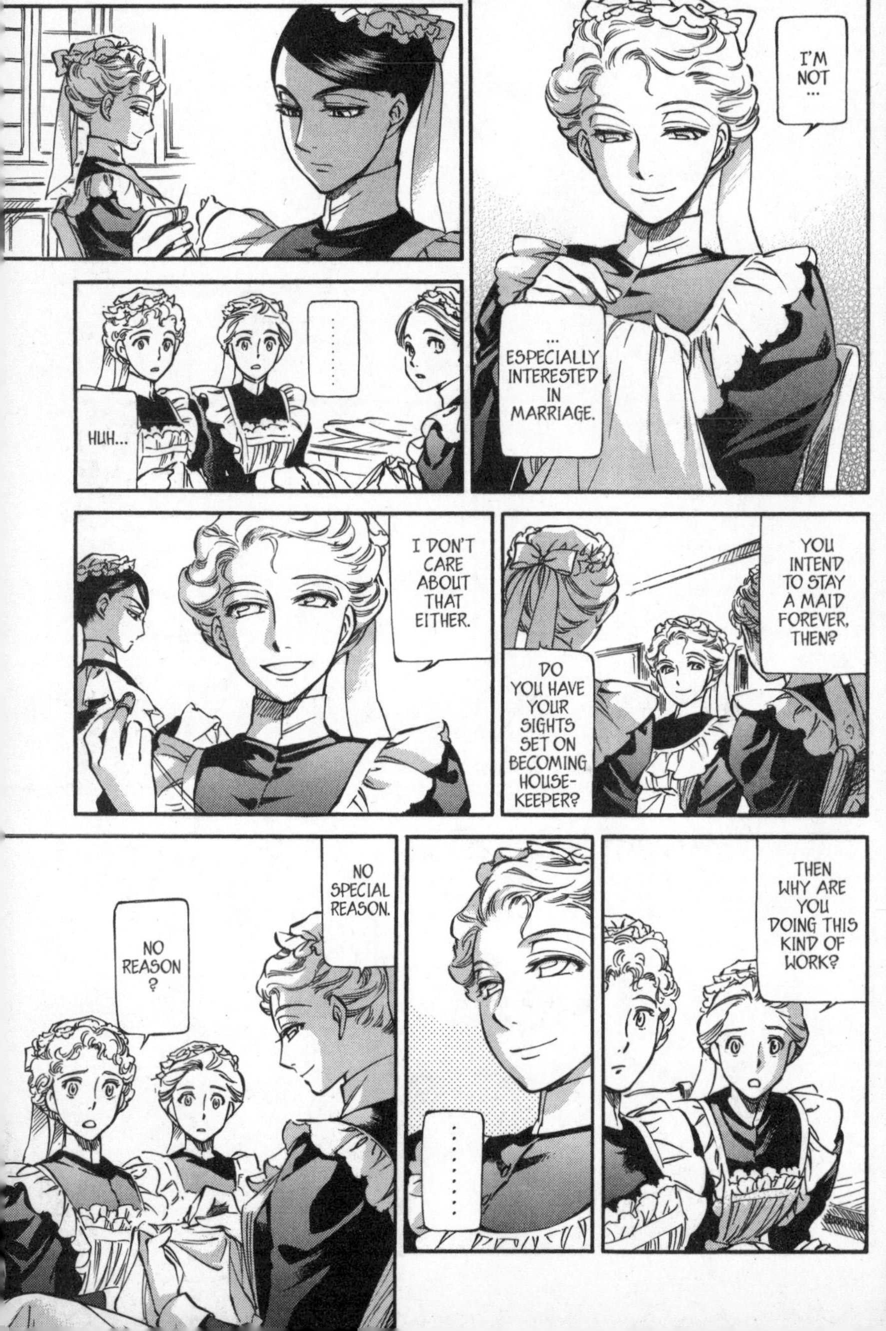
I'M NOT ...
... ESPECIALLY INTERESTED IN MARRIAGE.
......
HUH...
YOU INTEND TO STAY A MAID FOREVER, THEN?
DO YOU HAVE YOUR SIGHTS SET ON BECOMING HOUSE-KEEPER?
I DON'T CARE ABOUT THAT EITHER.
THEN WHY ARE YOU DOING THIS KIND OF WORK?
......
NO SPECIAL REASON.
NO REASON?

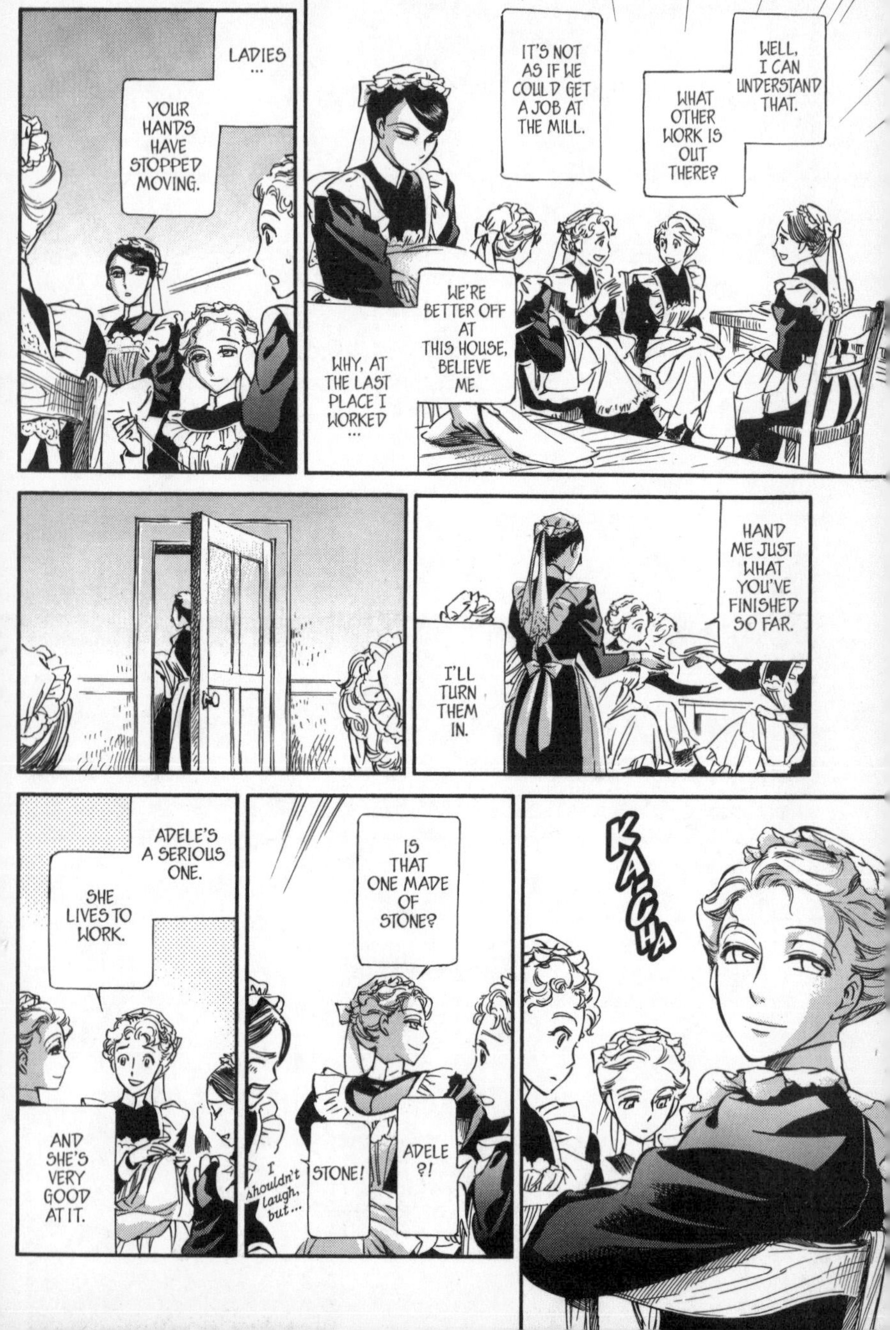
WELL, I CAN UNDERSTAND THAT.
WHAT OTHER WORK IS OUT THERE?
IT'S NOT AS IF WE COULD GET A JOB AT THE MILL.
WE'RE BETTER OFF AT THIS HOUSE, BELIEVE ME.
WHY, AT THE LAST PLACE I WORKED ...
LADIES ...
YOUR HANDS HAVE STOPPED MOVING.
HAND ME JUST WHAT YOU'VE FINISHED SO FAR.
I'LL TURN THEM IN.
KACHA
IS THAT ONE MADE OF STONE?
ADELE ?!
STONE!
I shouldn't laugh, but...
ADELE'S A SERIOUS ONE.
SHE LIVES TO WORK.
AND SHE'S VERY GOOD AT IT.

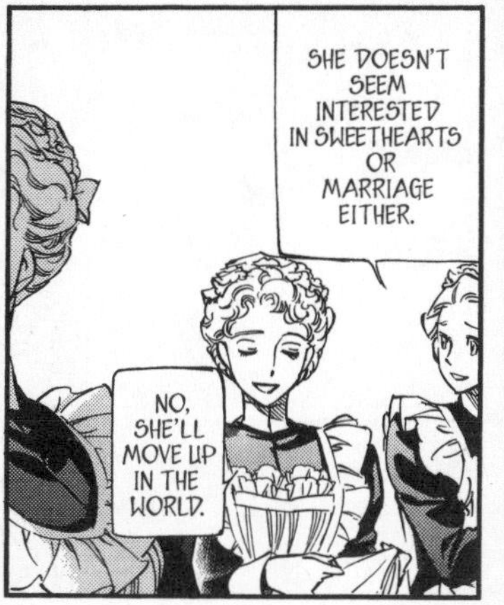
SHE DOESN'T SEEM INTERESTED IN SWEETHEARTS OR MARRIAGE EITHER.
NO, SHE'LL MOVE UP IN THE WORLD.
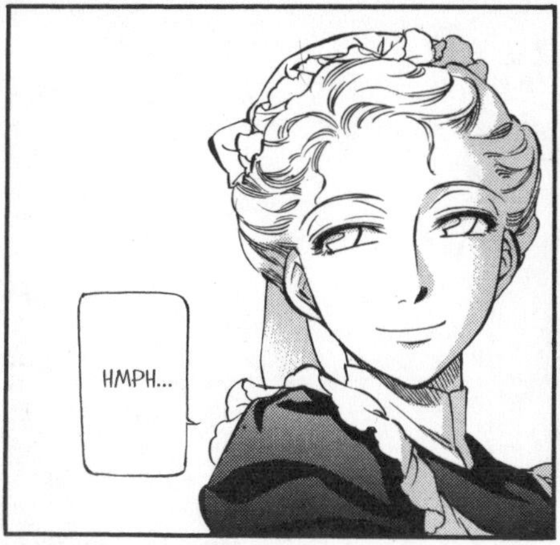
HMPH...
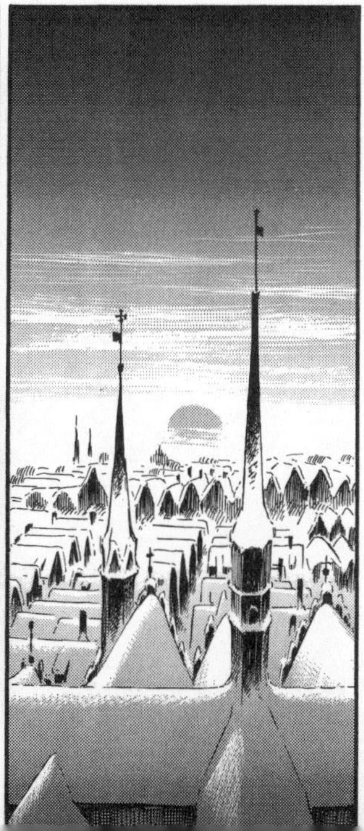
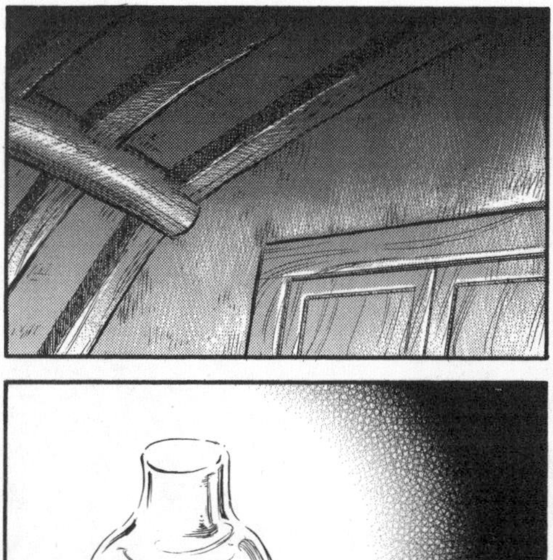
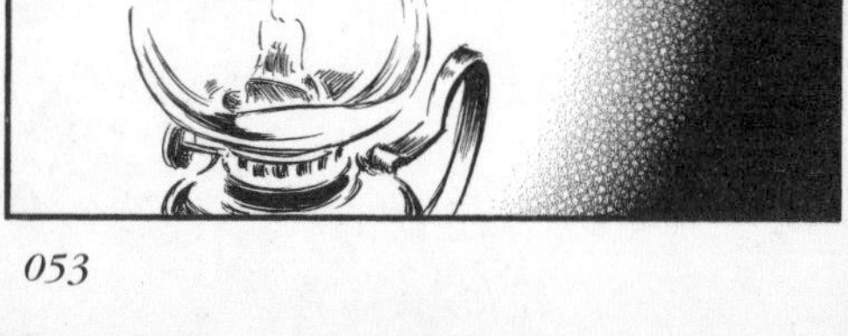

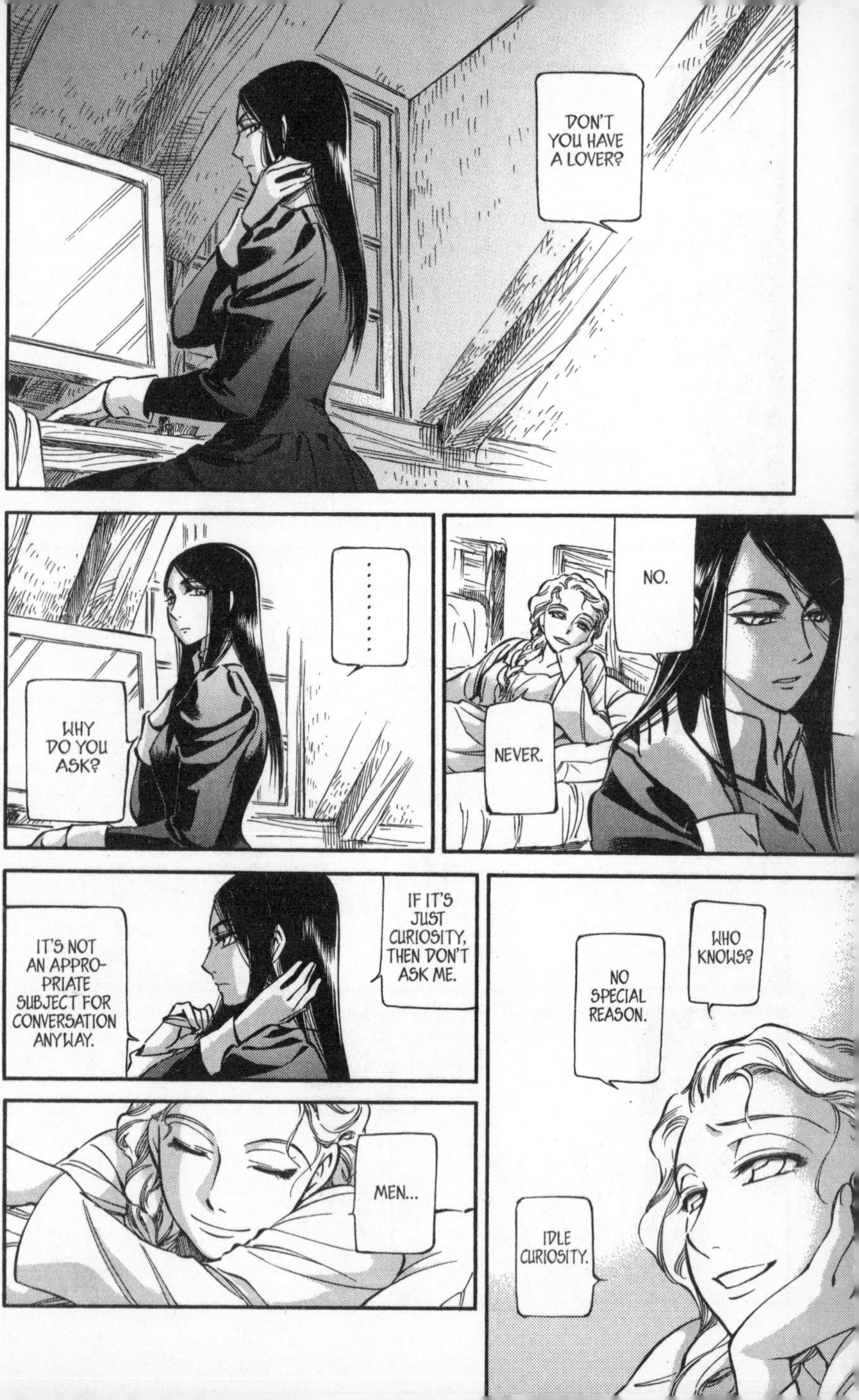
DON'T YOU HAVE A LOVER?
NO.
NEVER.
......
WHY DO YOU ASK?
WHO KNOWS?
NO SPECIAL REASON.
IDLE CURIOSITY.
IF IT'S JUST CURIOSITY, THEN DON'T ASK ME.
IT'S NOT AN APPRO-PRIATE SUBJECT FOR CONVERSATION ANYWAY.
MEN...

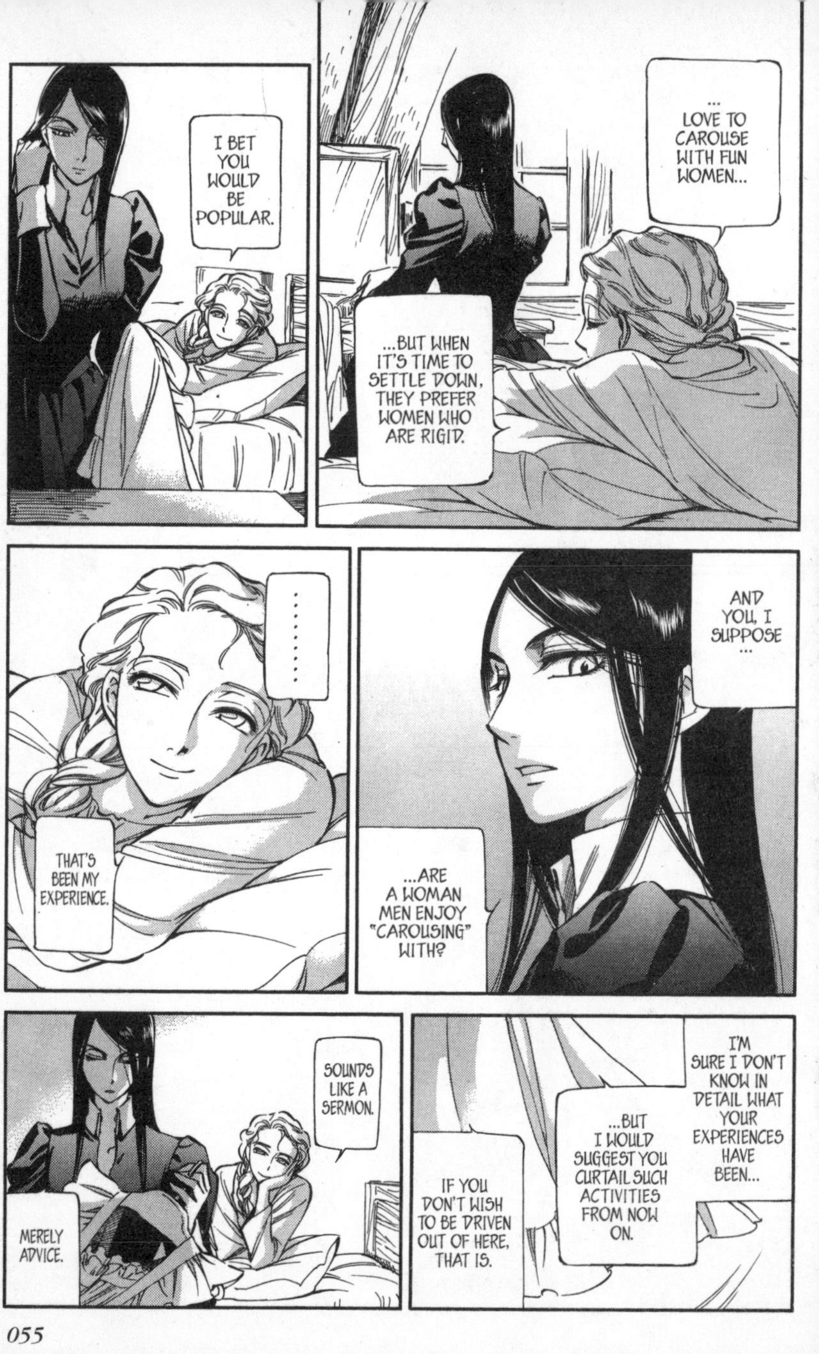
... LOVE TO CAROUSE WITH FUN WOMEN...
...BUT WHEN IT'S TIME TO SETTLE DOWN, THEY PREFER WOMEN WHO ARE RIGID.
I BET YOU WOULD BE POPULAR.
AND YOU, I SUPPOSE ...
...ARE A WOMAN MEN ENJOY "CAROUSING" WITH?
....
THAT'S BEEN MY EXPERIENCE.
I'M SURE I DON'T KNOW IN DETAIL WHAT YOUR EXPERIENCES HAVE BEEN...
...BUT I WOULD SUGGEST YOU CURTAIL SUCH ACTIVITIES FROM NOW ON.
IF YOU DON'T WISH TO BE DRIVEN OUT OF HERE, THAT IS.
SOUNDS LIKE A SERMON.
MERELY ADVICE.

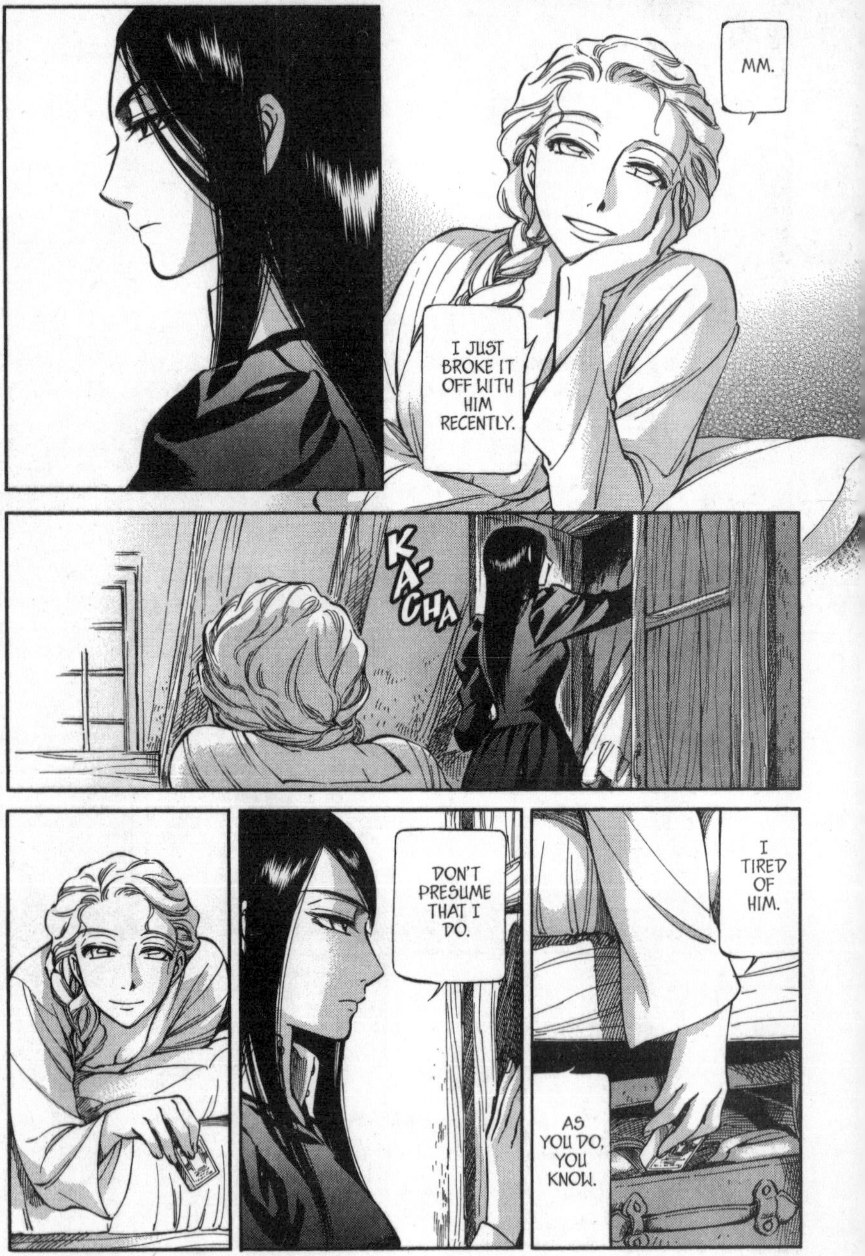
MM.
I JUST BROKE IT OFF WITH HIM RECENTLY.
KA-CHA
I TIRED OF HIM.
AS YOU DO, YOU KNOW.
DON'T PRESUME THAT I DO.

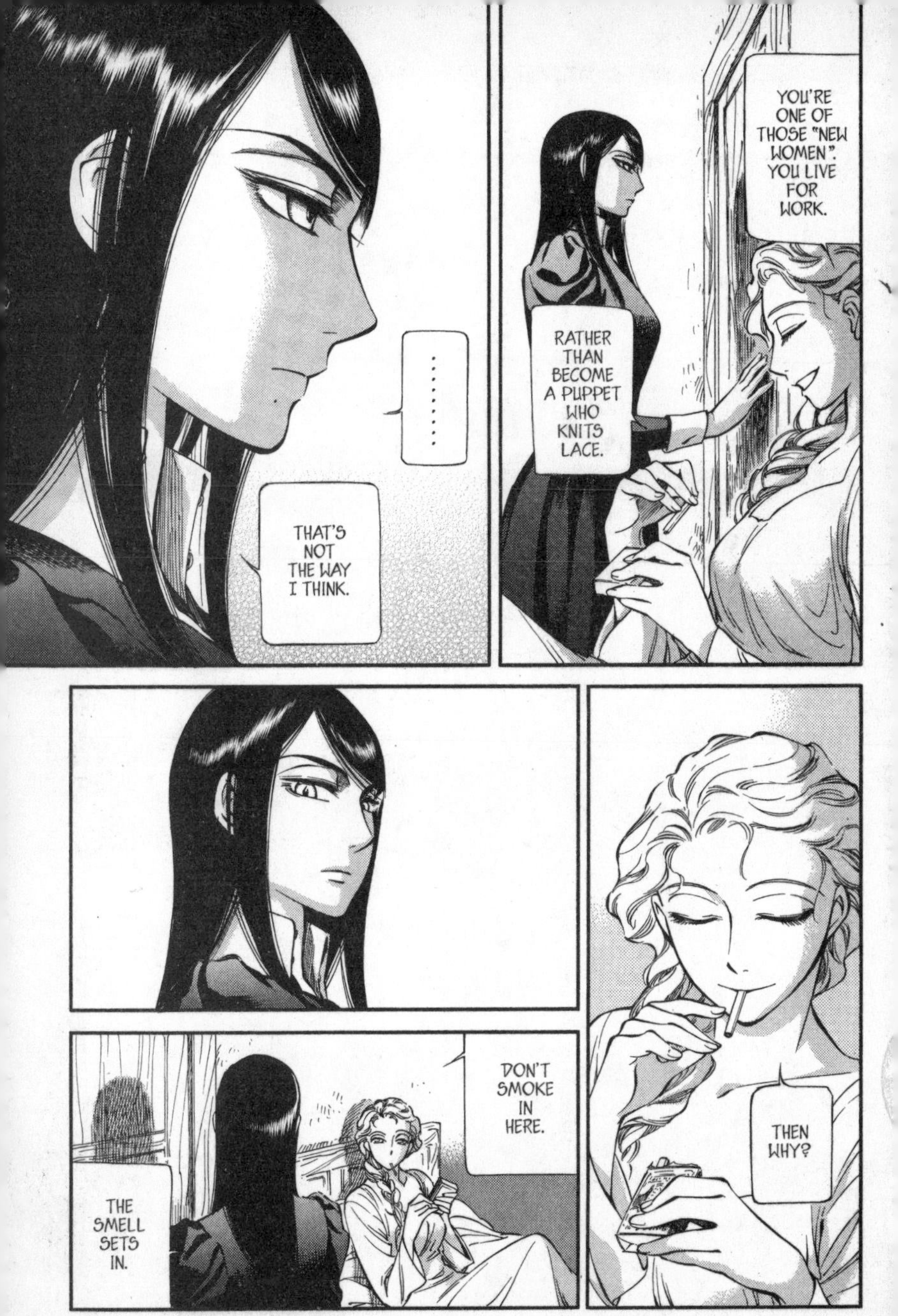
YOU'RE ONE OF THOSE "NEW WOMEN". YOU LIVE FOR WORK.
RATHER THAN BECOME A PUPPET WHO KNITS LACE.
......
THAT'S NOT THE WAY I THINK.
THEN WHY?
DON'T SMOKE IN HERE.
THE SMELL SETS IN.

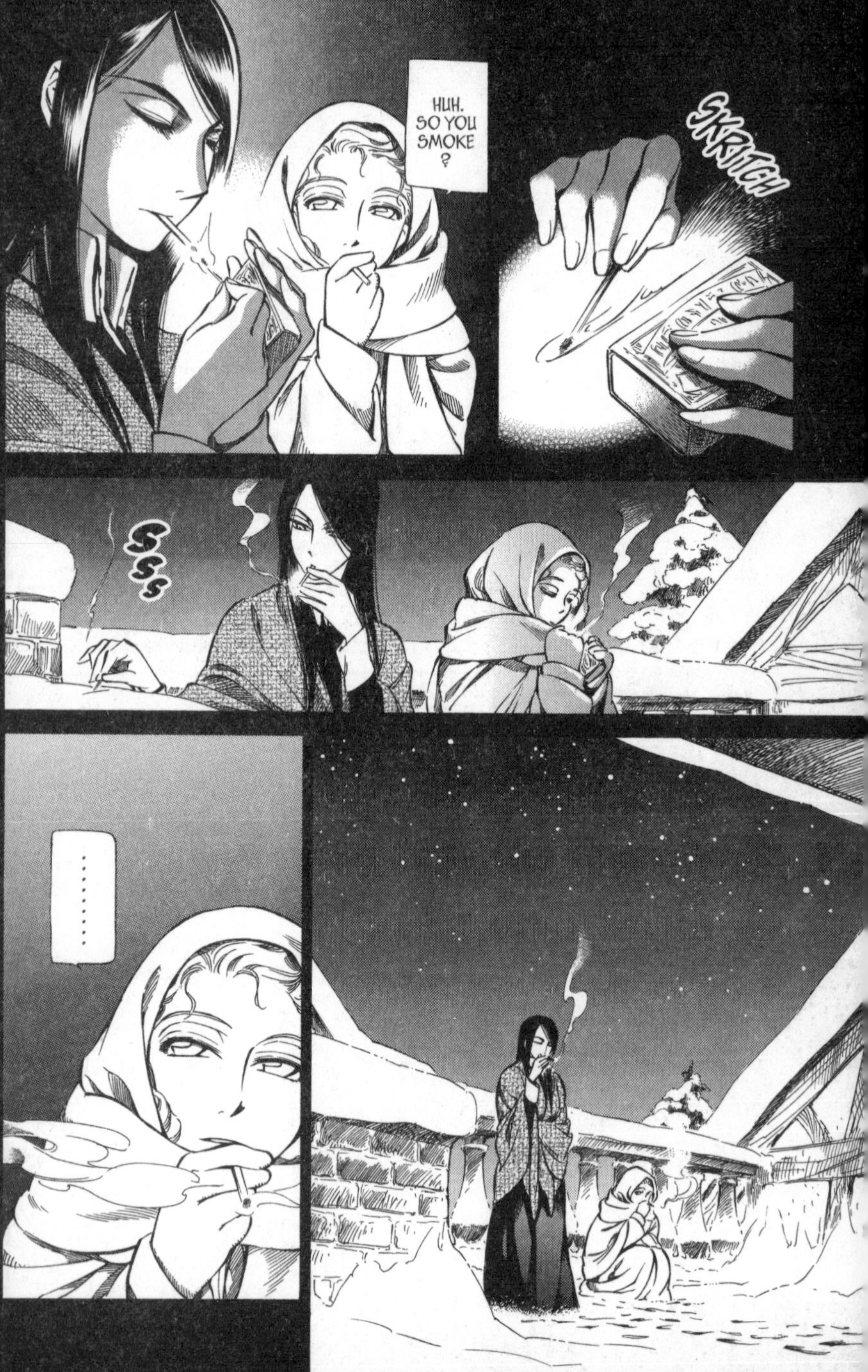
SKRITCH
HUH. SO YOU SMOKE?
SSS
......

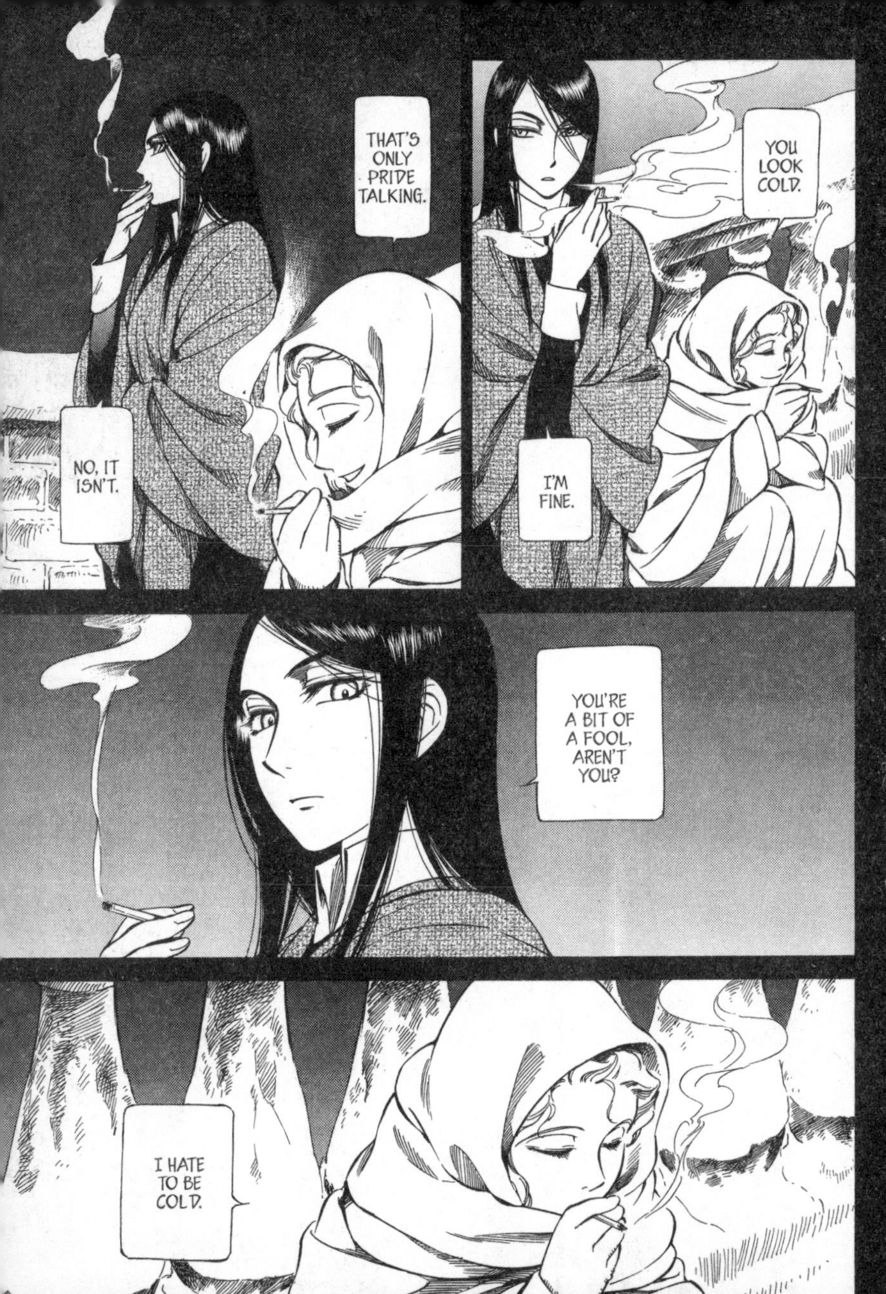
YOU LOOK COLD.
I'M FINE.
THAT'S ONLY PRIDE TALKING.
NO, IT ISN'T.
YOU'RE A BIT OF A FOOL, AREN'T YOU?
I HATE TO BE COLD.

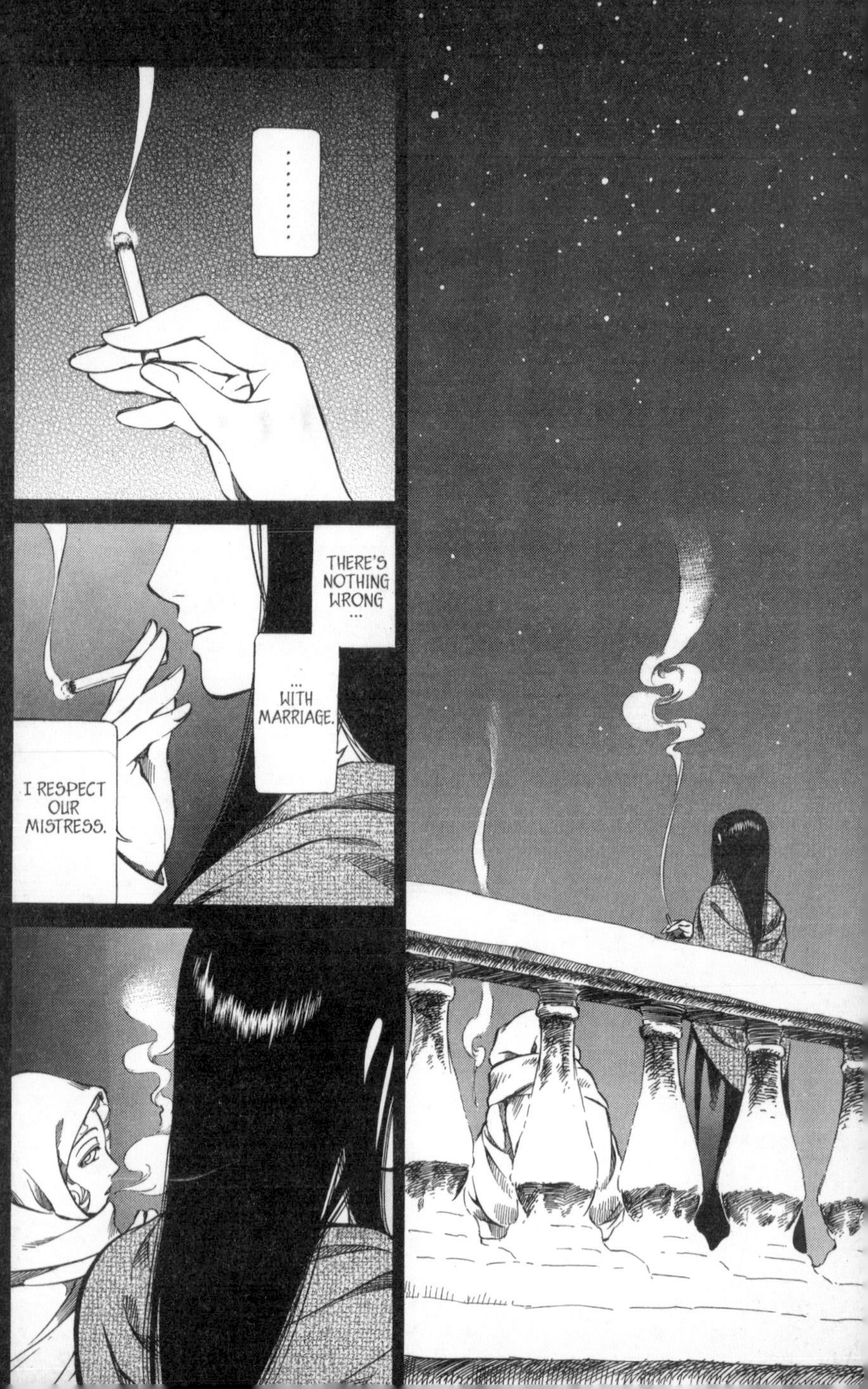
……
THERE'S NOTHING WRONG ...
... WITH MARRIAGE.
I RESPECT OUR MISTRESS.

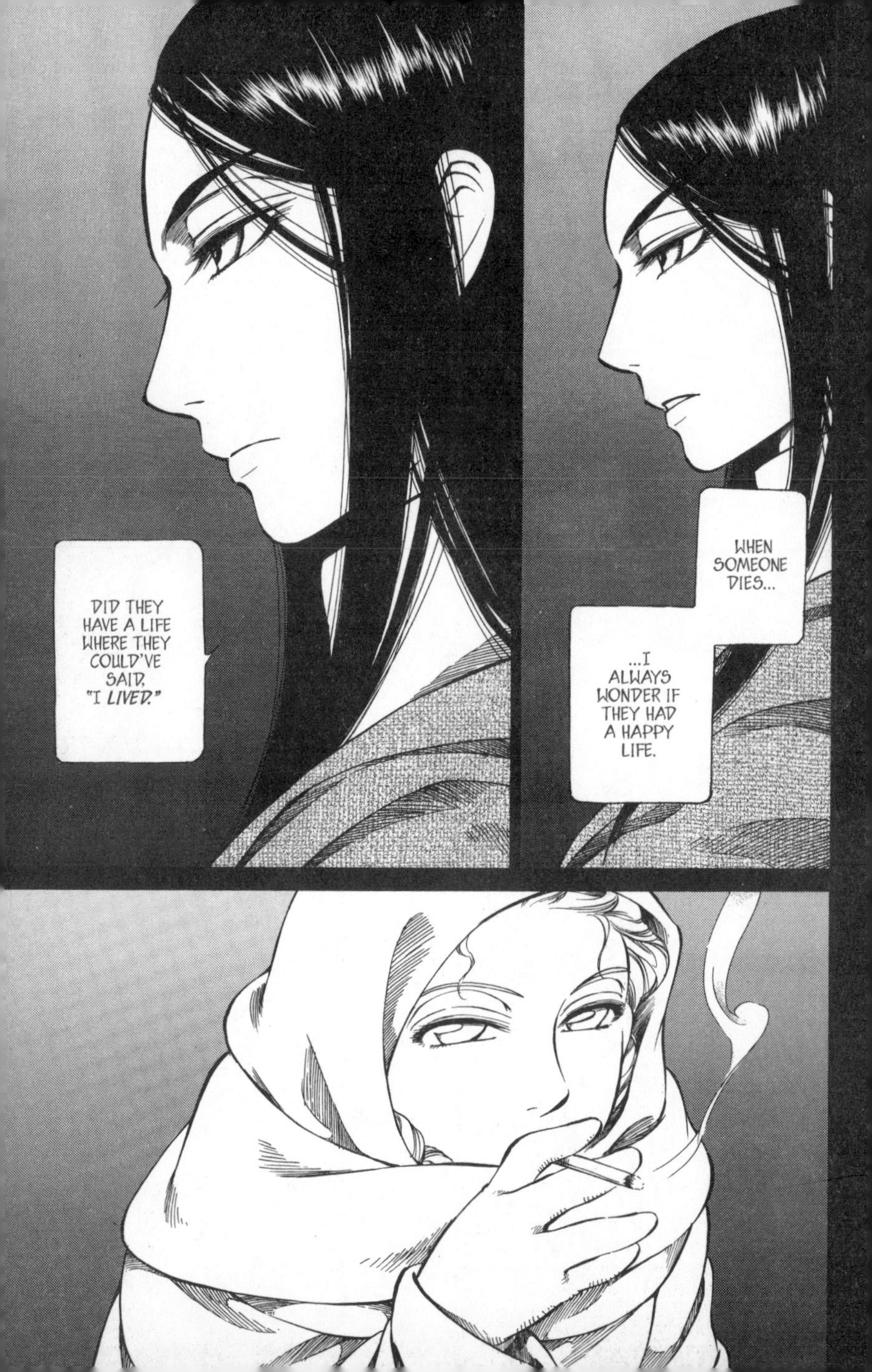
WHEN SOMEONE DIES...
...I ALWAYS WONDER IF THEY HAD A HAPPY LIFE.
DID THEY HAVE A LIFE WHERE THEY COULD'VE SAID, "I *LIVED.*"

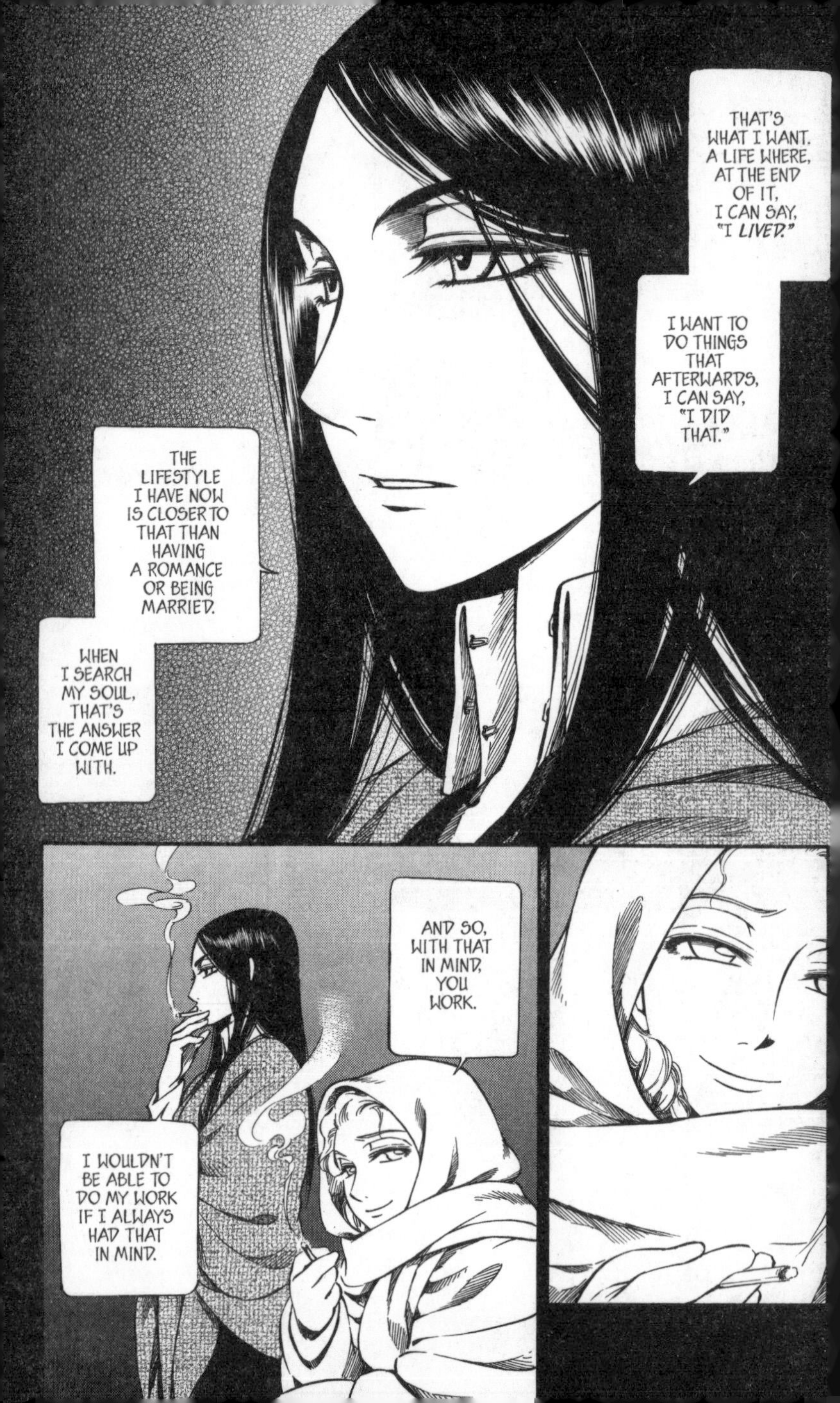
THAT'S WHAT I WANT. A LIFE WHERE, AT THE END OF IT, I CAN SAY, "I *LIVED*."
I WANT TO DO THINGS THAT AFTERWARDS, I CAN SAY, "I DID THAT."
THE LIFESTYLE I HAVE NOW IS CLOSER TO THAT THAN HAVING A ROMANCE OR BEING MARRIED.
WHEN I SEARCH MY SOUL, THAT'S THE ANSWER I COME UP WITH.
AND SO, WITH THAT IN MIND, YOU WORK.
I WOULDN'T BE ABLE TO DO MY WORK IF I ALWAYS HAD THAT IN MIND.

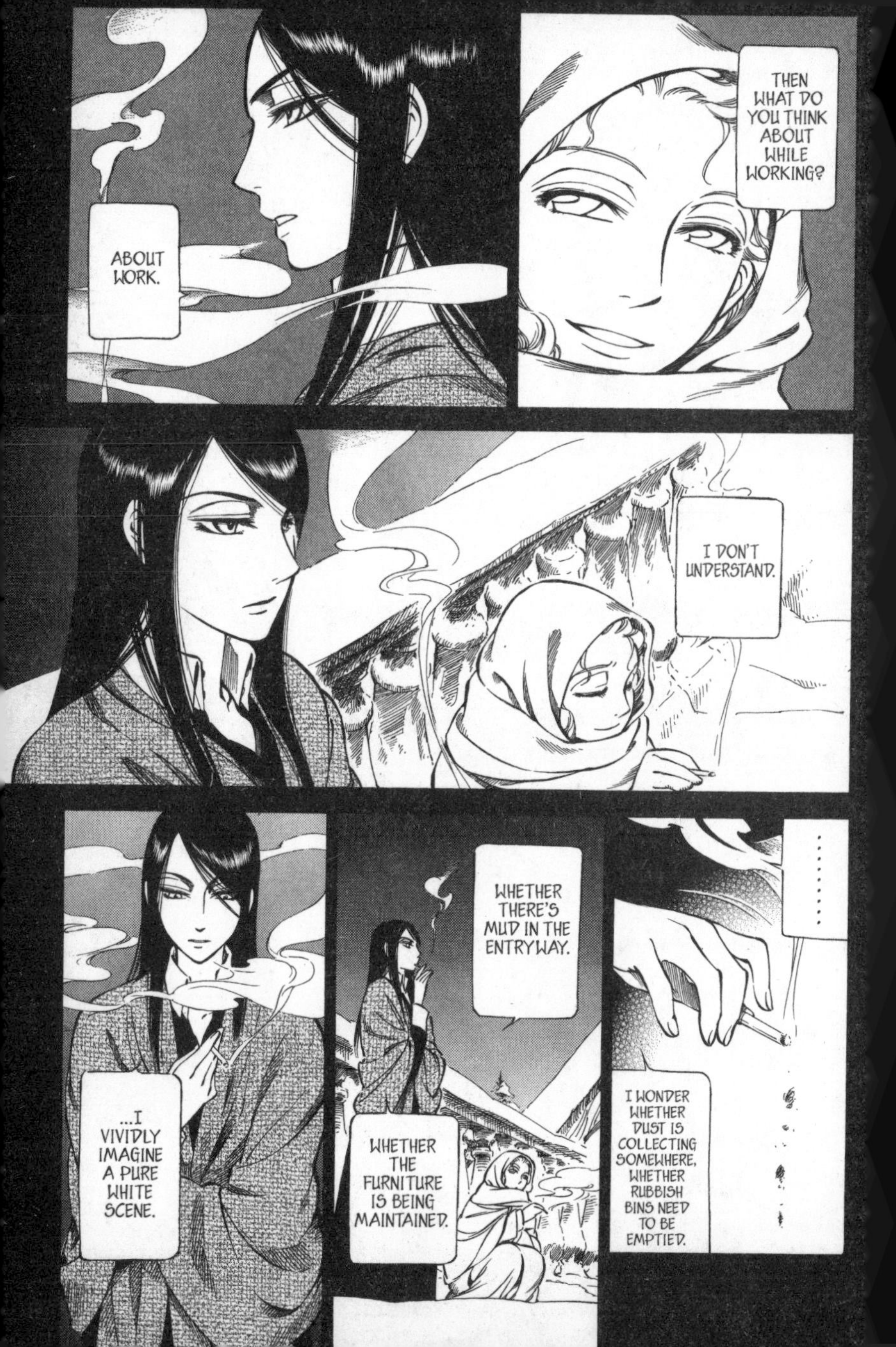
THEN WHAT DO YOU THINK ABOUT WHILE WORKING?
ABOUT WORK.
I DON'T UNDERSTAND.
....
I WONDER WHETHER DUST IS COLLECTING SOMEWHERE, WHETHER RUBBISH BINS NEED TO BE EMPTIED.
WHETHER THERE'S MUD IN THE ENTRYWAY.
WHETHER THE FURNITURE IS BEING MAINTAINED.
...I VIVIDLY IMAGINE A PURE WHITE SCENE.

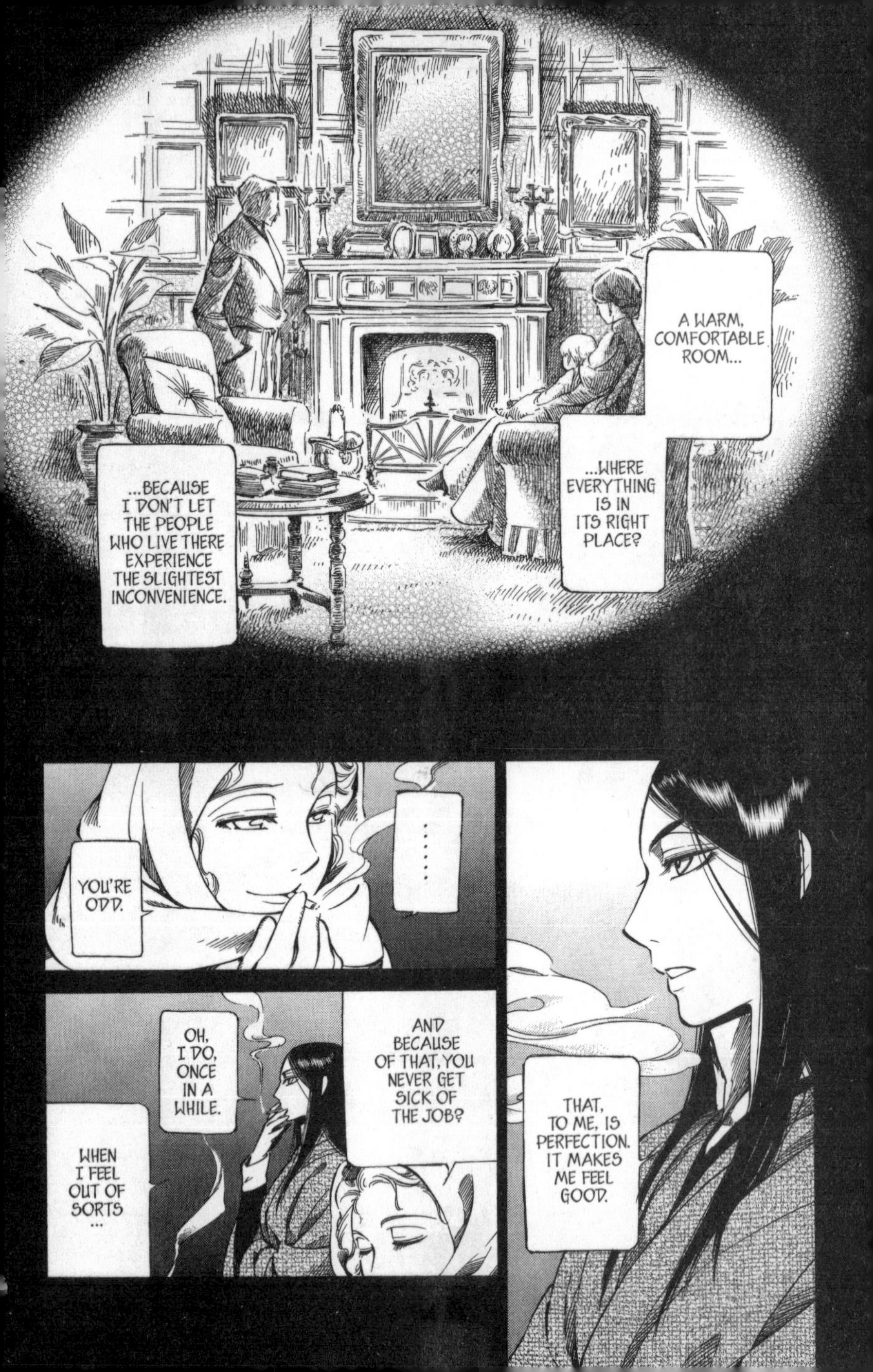
A WARM, COMFORTABLE ROOM...
...WHERE EVERYTHING IS IN ITS RIGHT PLACE?
...BECAUSE I DON'T LET THE PEOPLE WHO LIVE THERE EXPERIENCE THE SLIGHTEST INCONVENIENCE.
THAT, TO ME, IS PERFECTION. IT MAKES ME FEEL GOOD.
......
YOU'RE ODD.
AND BECAUSE OF THAT, YOU NEVER GET SICK OF THE JOB?
OH, I DO, ONCE IN A WHILE.
WHEN I FEEL OUT OF SORTS ...

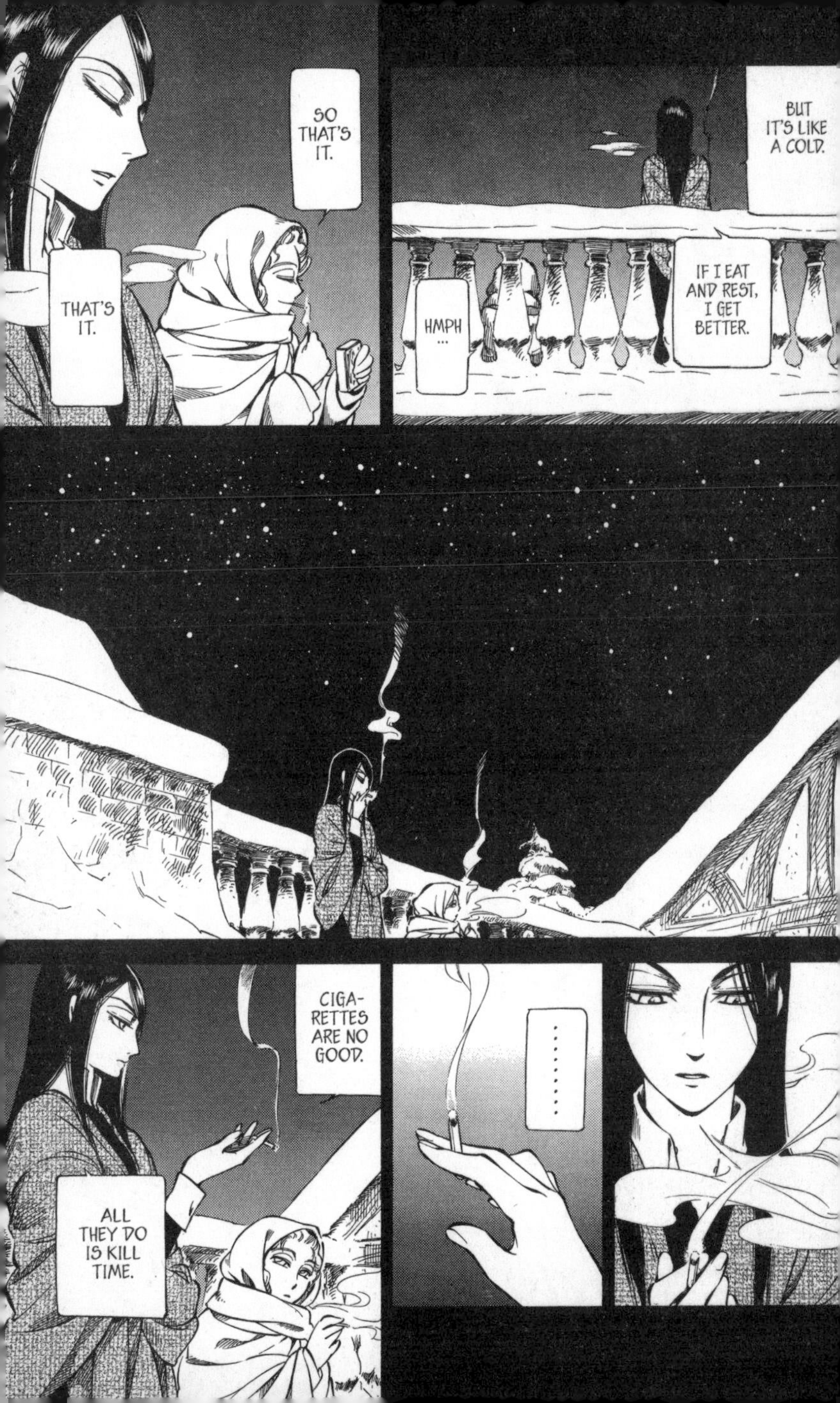
BUT IT'S LIKE A COLD.
IF I EAT AND REST, I GET BETTER.
HMPH...
SO THAT'S IT.
THAT'S IT.
....
CIGA-RETTES ARE NO GOOD.
ALL THEY DO IS KILL TIME.

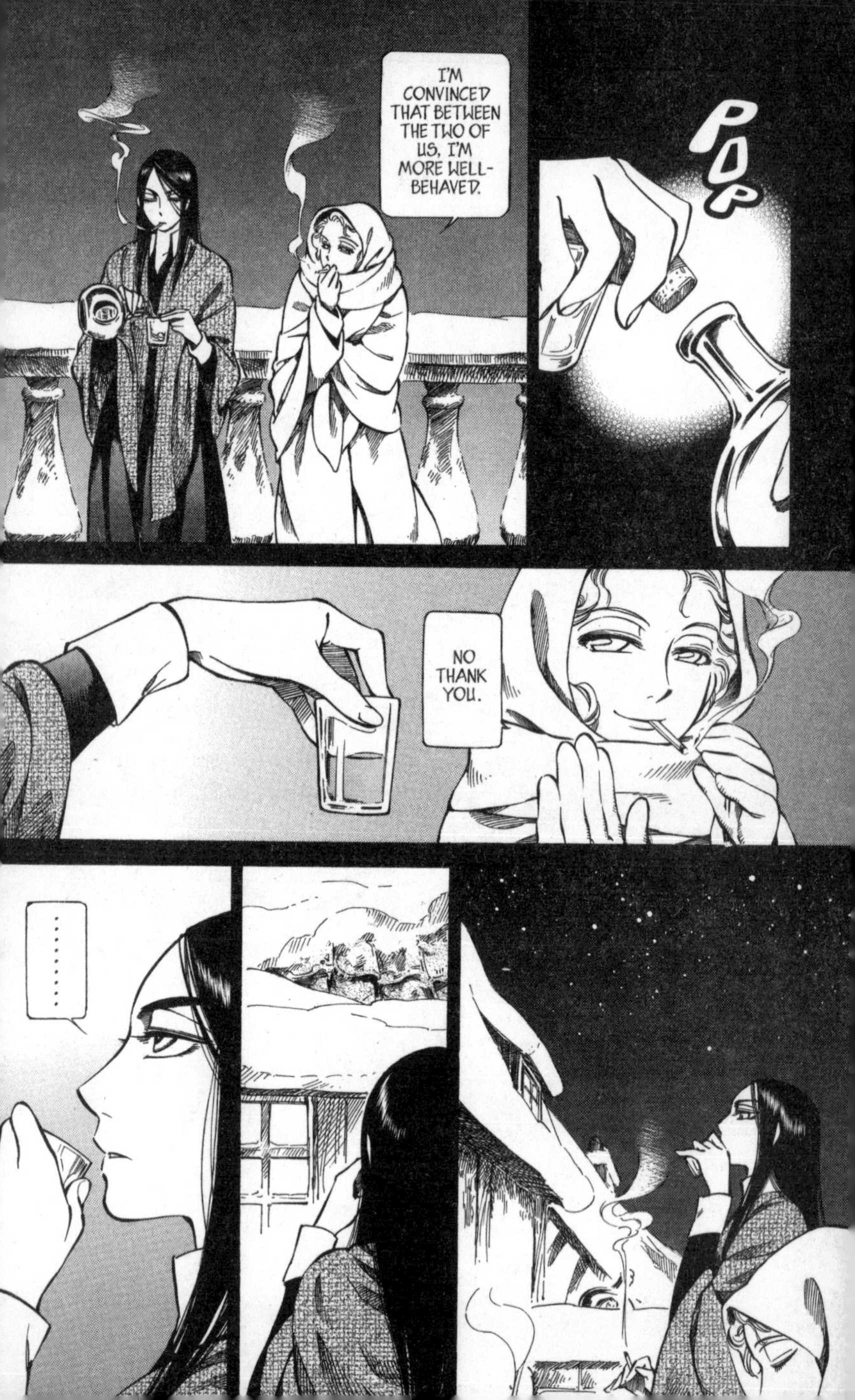
POP
I'M CONVINCED THAT BETWEEN THE TWO OF US, I'M MORE WELL-BEHAVED.
NO THANK YOU.
....

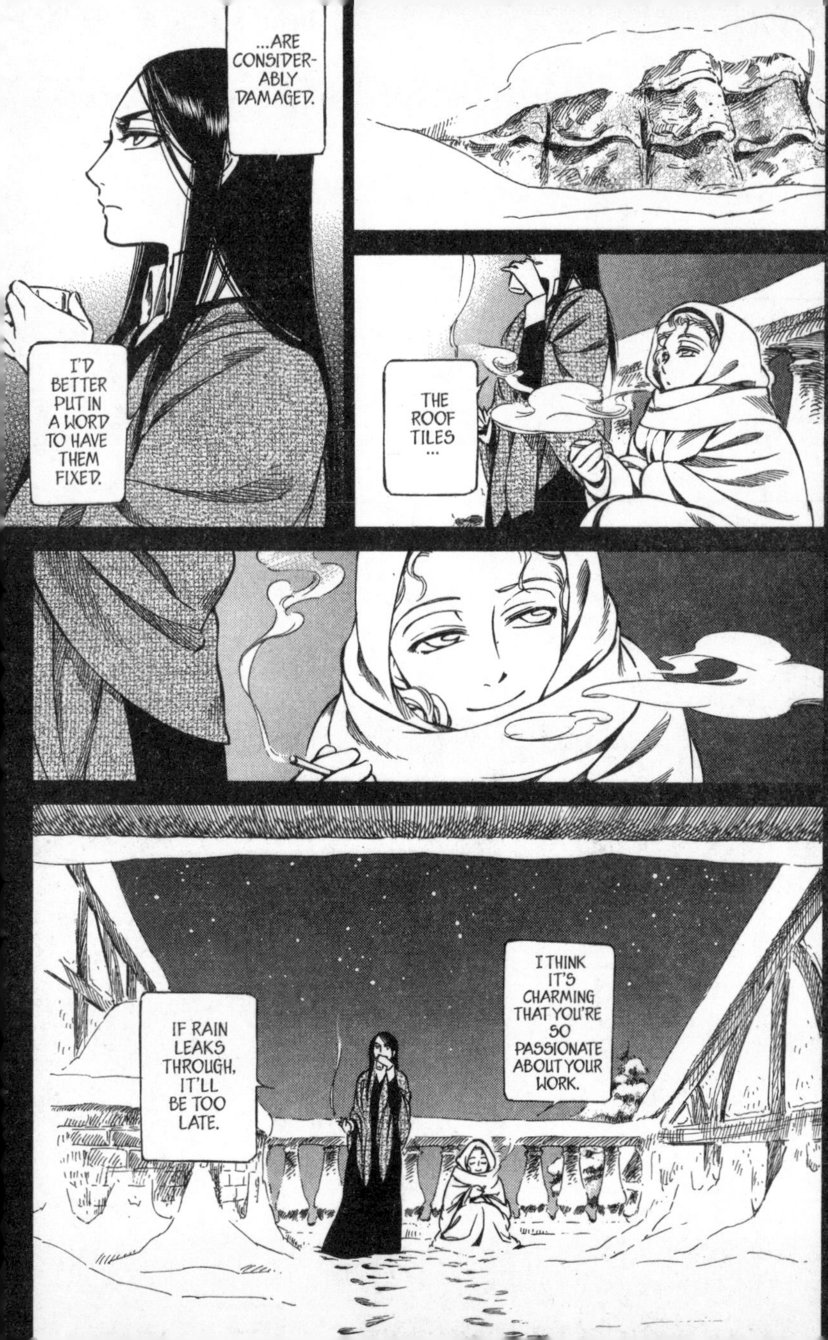
THE ROOF TILES ...
...ARE CONSIDERABLY DAMAGED.
I'D BETTER PUT IN A WORD TO HAVE THEM FIXED.
I THINK IT'S CHARMING THAT YOU'RE SO PASSIONATE ABOUT YOUR WORK.
IF RAIN LEAKS THROUGH, IT'LL BE TOO LATE.

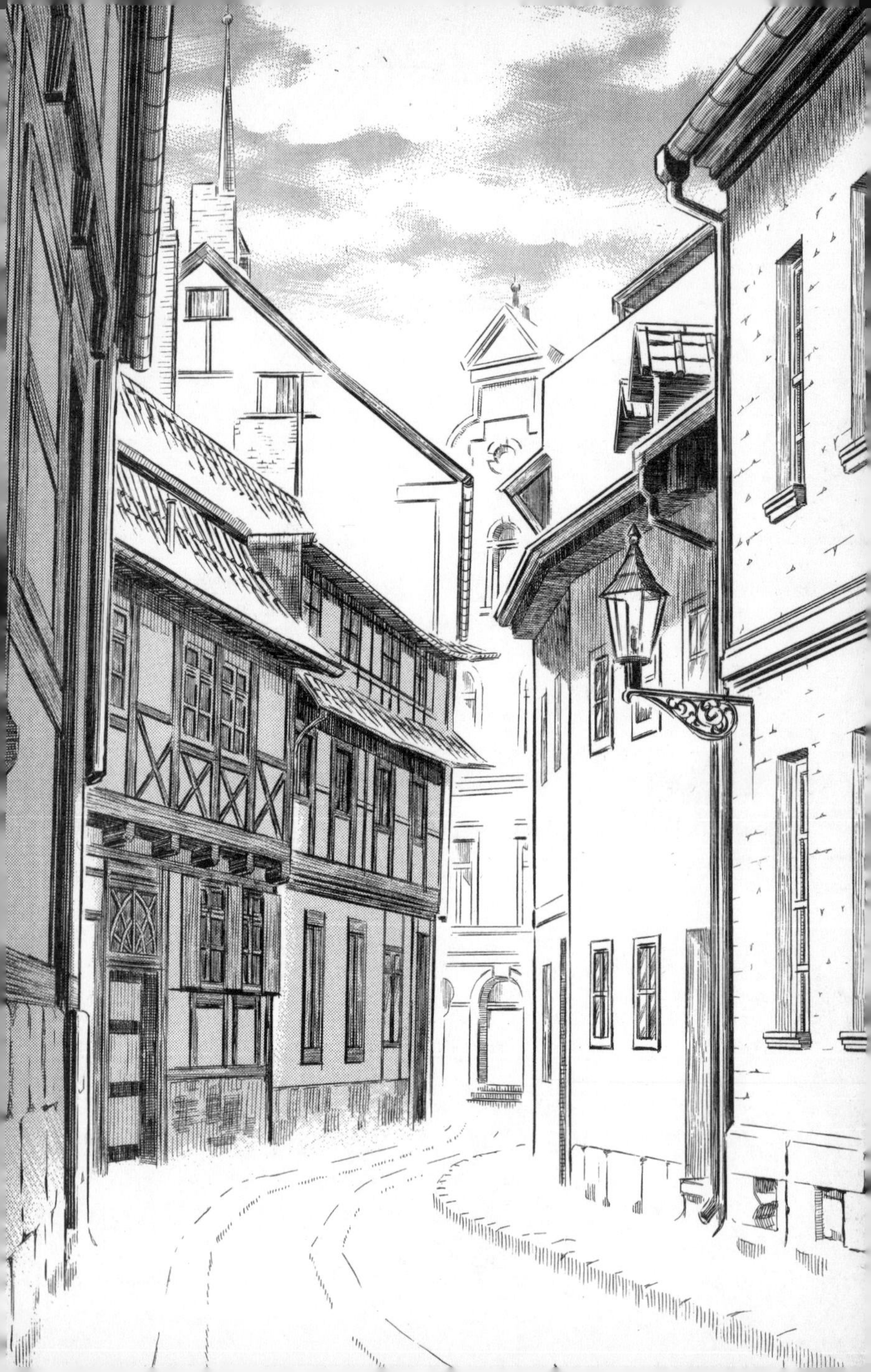

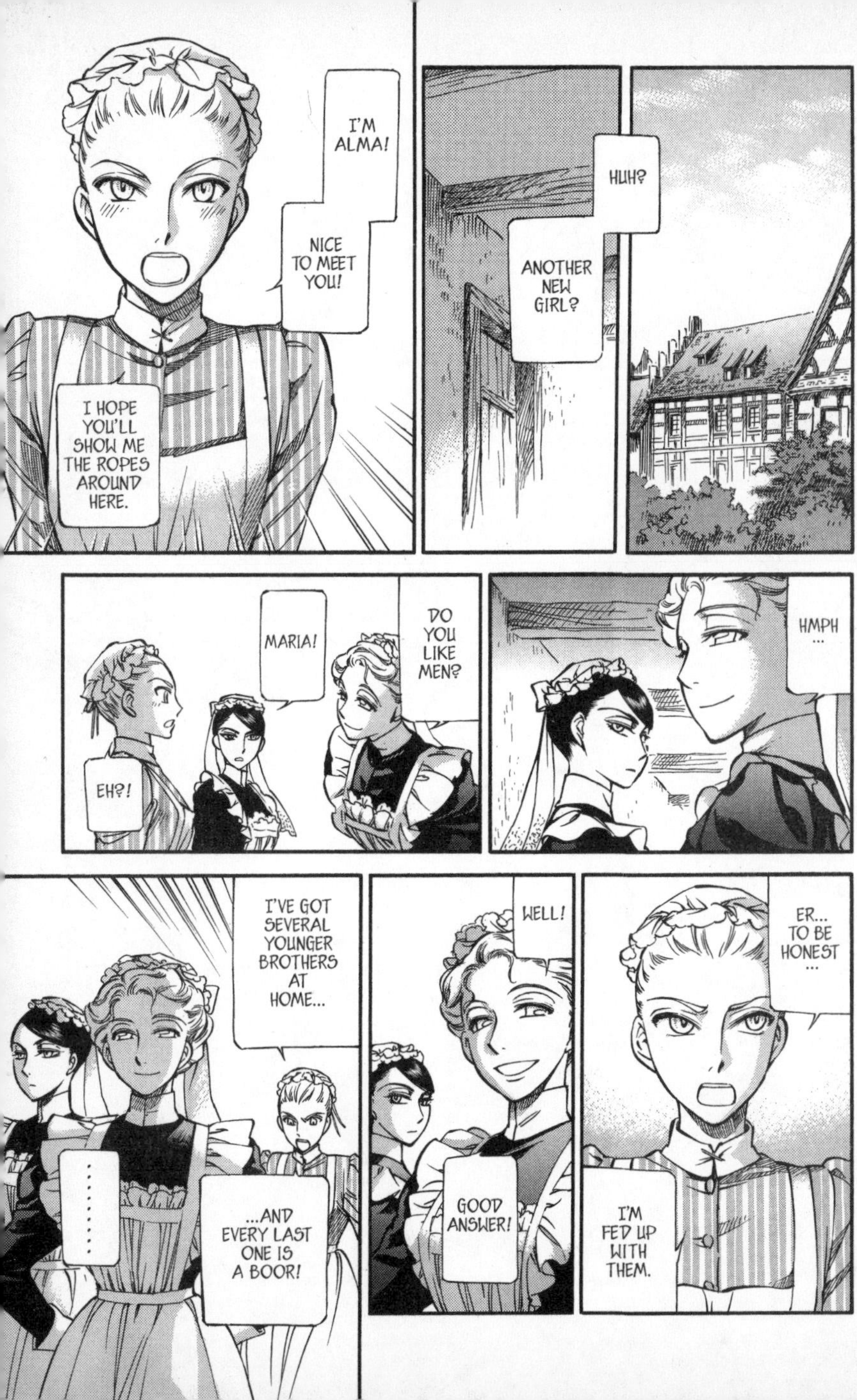
HUH?
ANOTHER NEW GIRL?
I'M ALMA!
NICE TO MEET YOU!
I HOPE YOU'LL SHOW ME THE ROPES AROUND HERE.
HMPH ...
DO YOU LIKE MEN?
MARIA!
EH?!
ER... TO BE HONEST ...
I'M FED UP WITH THEM.
WELL!
GOOD ANSWER!
I'VE GOT SEVERAL YOUNGER BROTHERS AT HOME...
....
...AND EVERY LAST ONE IS A BOOR!

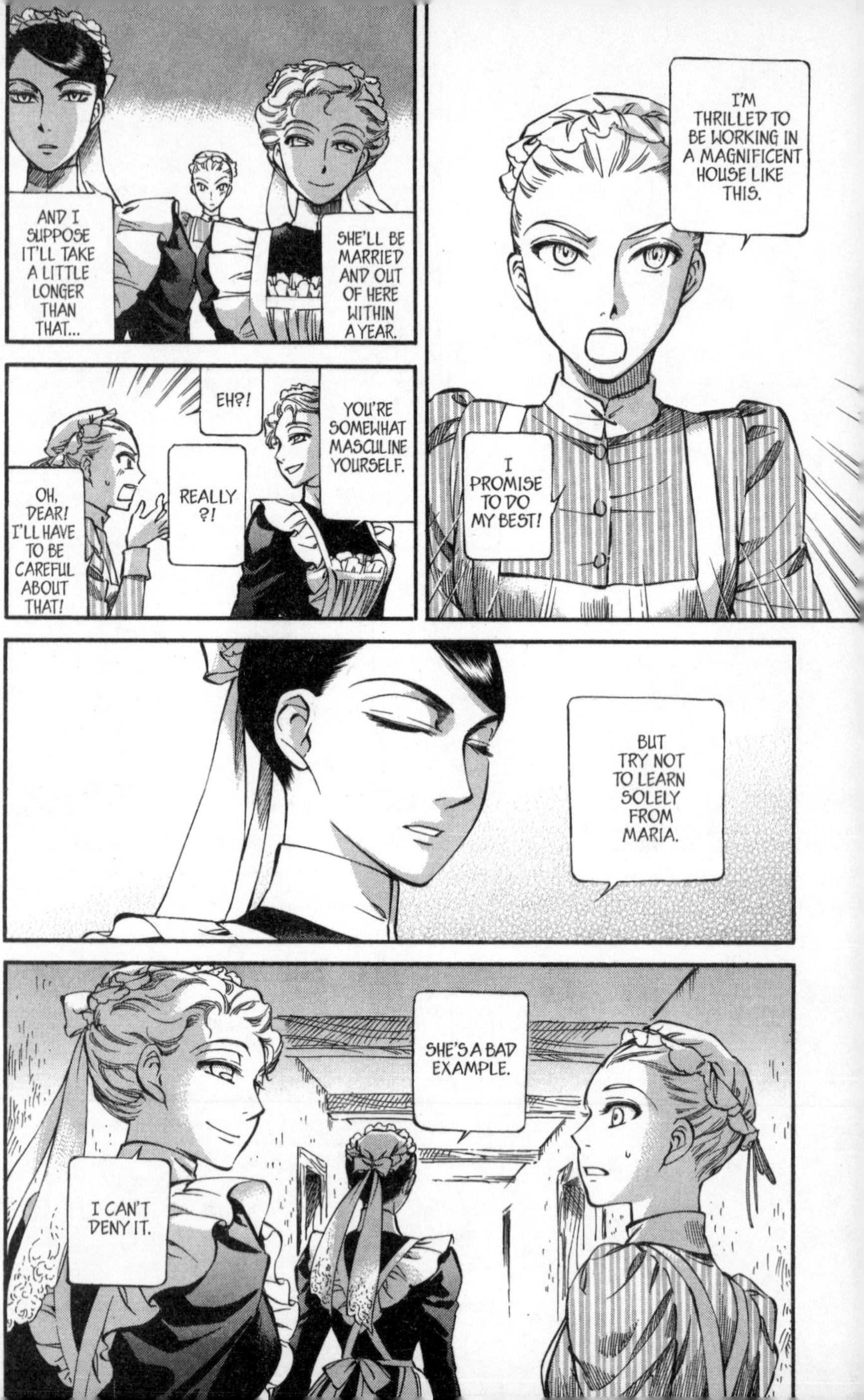
I'M THRILLED TO BE WORKING IN A MAGNIFICENT HOUSE LIKE THIS.
I PROMISE TO DO MY BEST!
SHE'LL BE MARRIED AND OUT OF HERE WITHIN A YEAR.
AND I SUPPOSE IT'LL TAKE A LITTLE LONGER THAN THAT...
YOU'RE SOMEWHAT MASCULINE YOURSELF.
EH?!
REALLY?!
OH, DEAR! I'LL HAVE TO BE CAREFUL ABOUT THAT!
BUT TRY NOT TO LEARN SOLELY FROM MARIA.
SHE'S A BAD EXAMPLE.
I CAN'T DENY IT.

CHAPTER
15:
ORDER

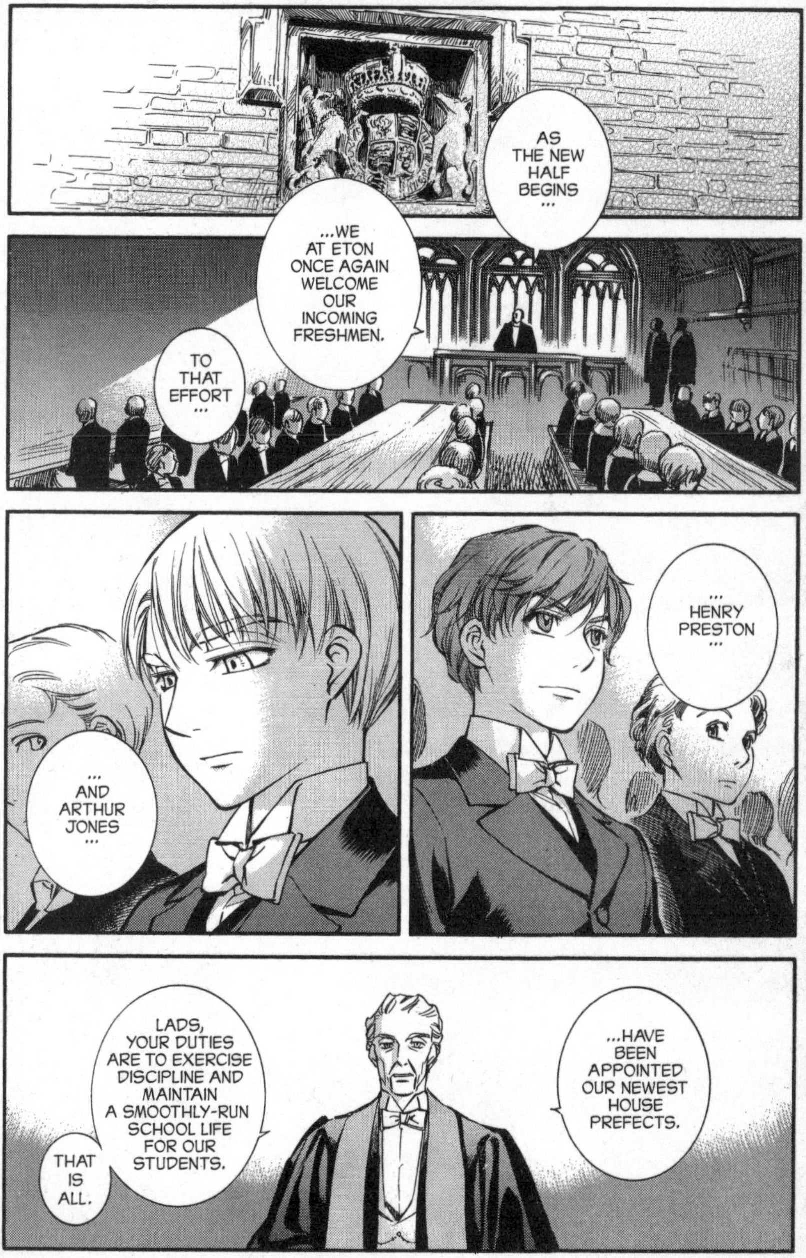
AS THE NEW HALF BEGINS...
...WE AT ETON ONCE AGAIN WELCOME OUR INCOMING FRESHMEN.
TO THAT EFFORT...
...HENRY PRESTON...
...AND ARTHUR JONES...
...HAVE BEEN APPOINTED OUR NEWEST HOUSE PREFECTS.
LADS, YOUR DUTIES ARE TO EXERCISE DISCIPLINE AND MAINTAIN A SMOOTHLY-RUN SCHOOL LIFE FOR OUR STUDENTS.
THAT IS ALL.

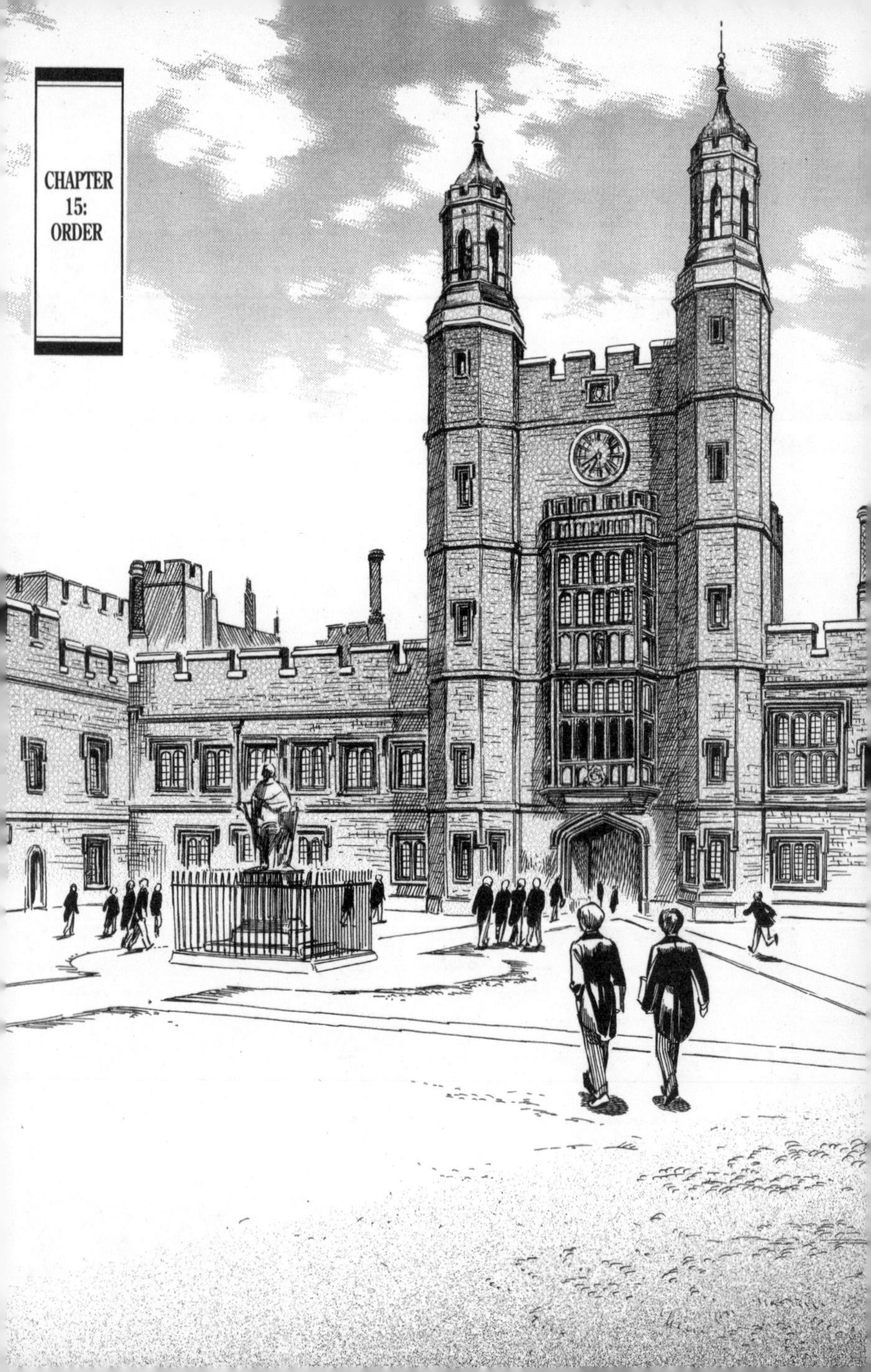
CHAPTER 15: ORDER

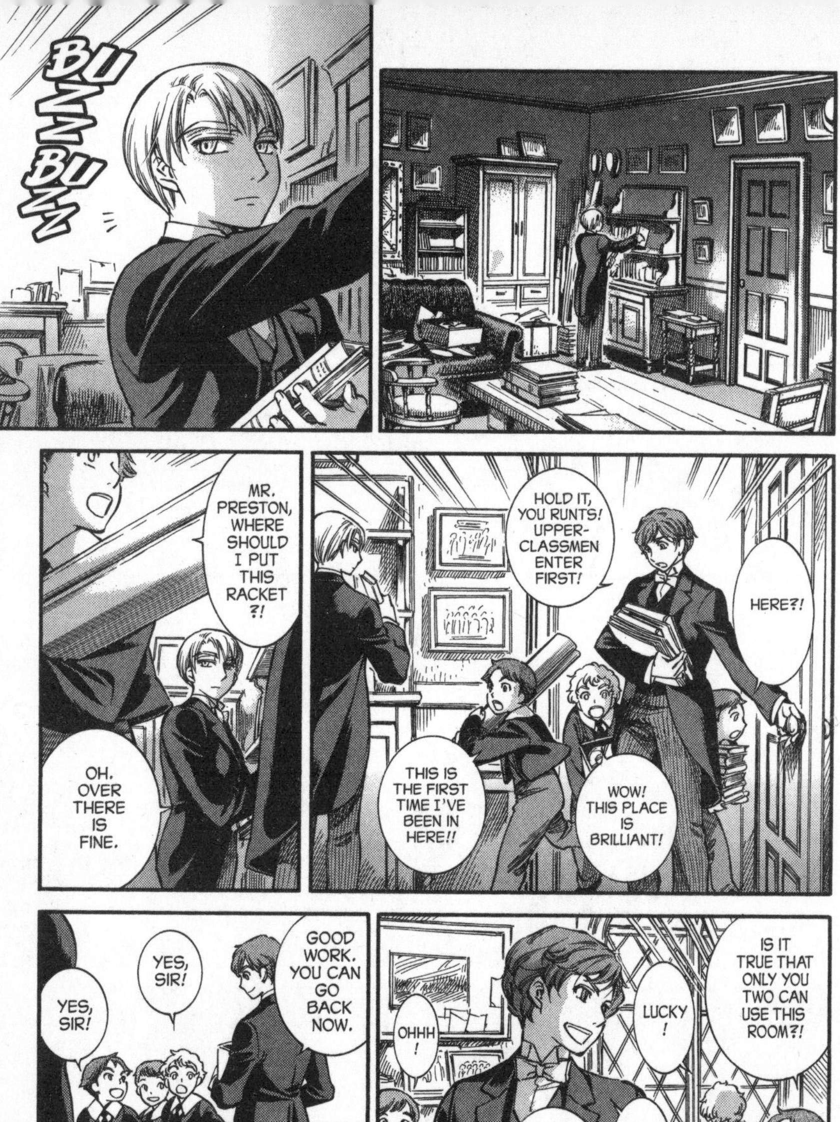
BUZZ BUZZ
HERE?!
HOLD IT, YOU RUNTS! UPPER-CLASSMEN ENTER FIRST!
WOW! THIS PLACE IS BRILLIANT!
THIS IS THE FIRST TIME I'VE BEEN IN HERE!!
MR. PRESTON, WHERE SHOULD I PUT THIS RACKET ?!
OH. OVER THERE IS FINE.
IS IT TRUE THAT ONLY YOU TWO CAN USE THIS ROOM?!
LUCKY !
OHHH !
THAT'S RIGHT.
THIS IS JUST ONE OF THE REWARDS ONE CAN REAP BY BECOMING PREFECT.
YOU BOYS DO YOUR BEST AND ONE DAY, IT COULD BE YOURS, TOO.
GOOD WORK. YOU CAN GO BACK NOW.
YES, SIR!
YES, SIR!
AH, I ALMOST FORGOT.

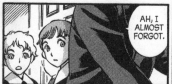

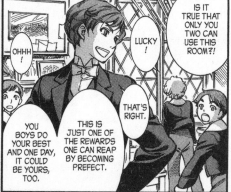

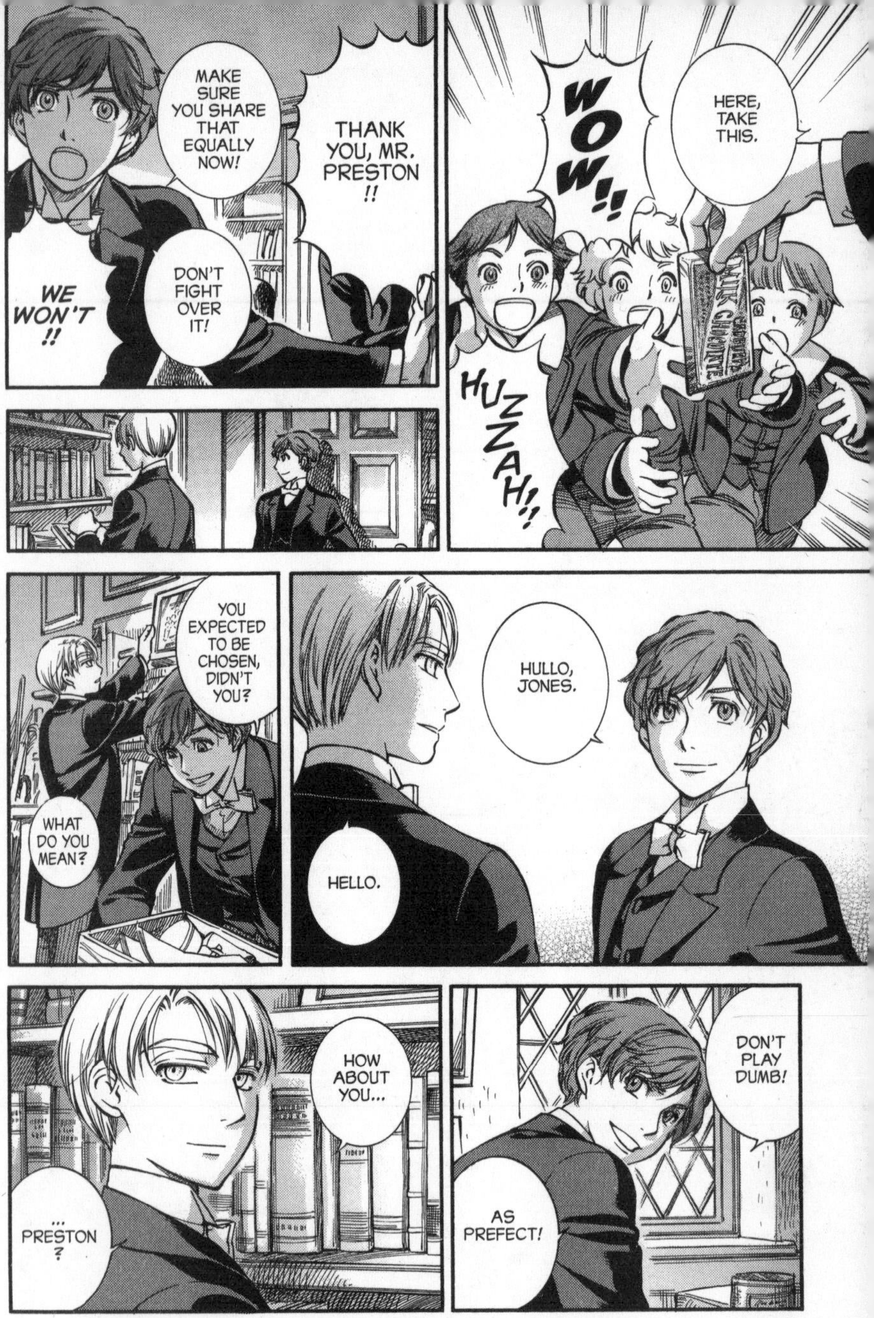
HERE, TAKE THIS.
WOW!!
HUZZAH!!
THANK YOU, MR. PRESTON!!
MAKE SURE YOU SHARE THAT EQUALLY NOW!
DON'T FIGHT OVER IT!
WE WON'T!!
HULLO, JONES.
HELLO.
YOU EXPECTED TO BE CHOSEN, DIDN'T YOU?
WHAT DO YOU MEAN?
DON'T PLAY DUMB!
AS PREFECT!
HOW ABOUT YOU...
...PRESTON?

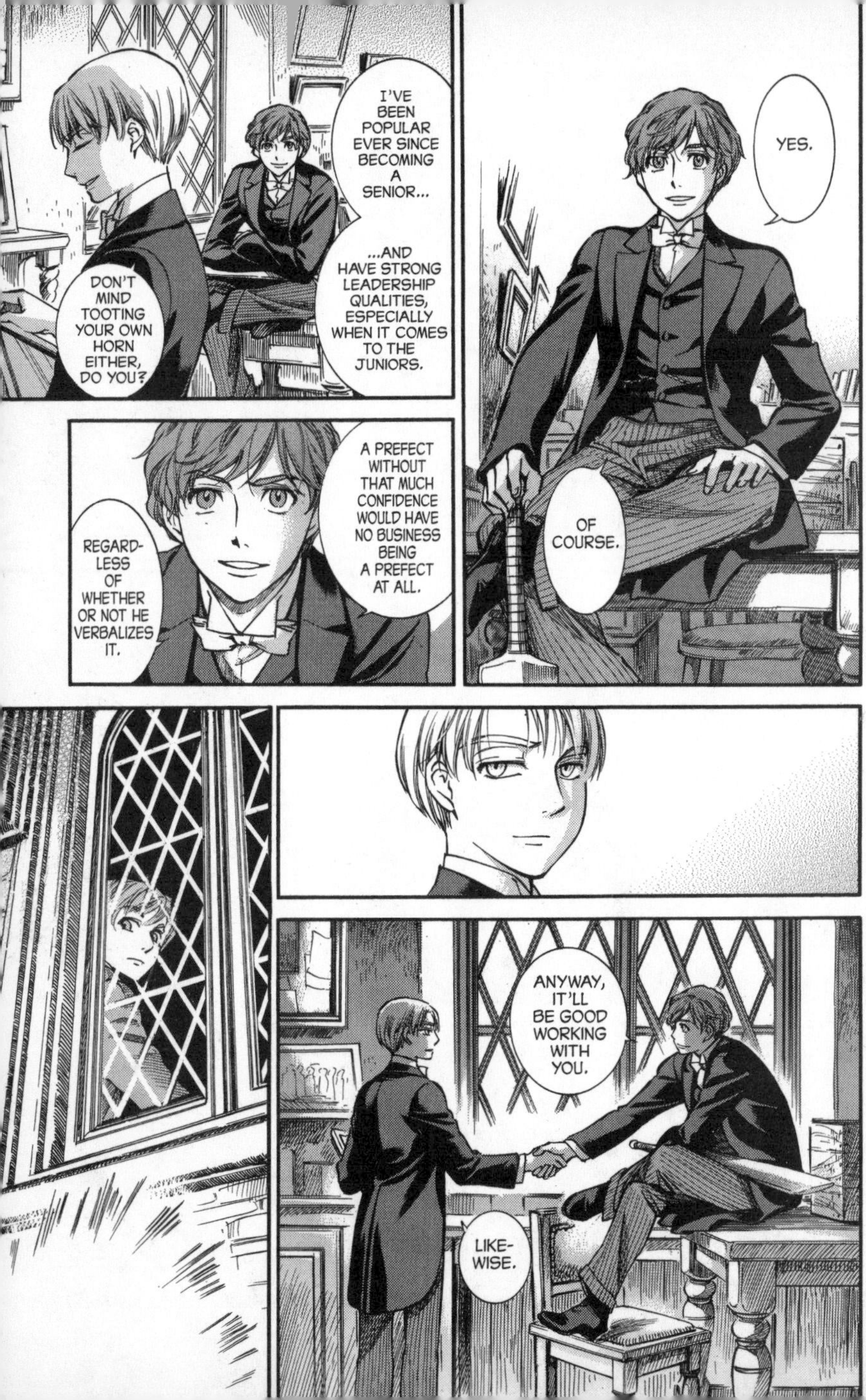
YES.
OF COURSE.
I'VE BEEN POPULAR EVER SINCE BECOMING A SENIOR...
...AND HAVE STRONG LEADERSHIP QUALITIES, ESPECIALLY WHEN IT COMES TO THE JUNIORS.
DON'T MIND TOOTING YOUR OWN HORN EITHER, DO YOU?
A PREFECT WITHOUT THAT MUCH CONFIDENCE WOULD HAVE NO BUSINESS BEING A PREFECT AT ALL.
REGARD-LESS OF WHETHER OR NOT HE VERBALIZES IT.
ANYWAY, IT'LL BE GOOD WORKING WITH YOU.
LIKE-WISE.

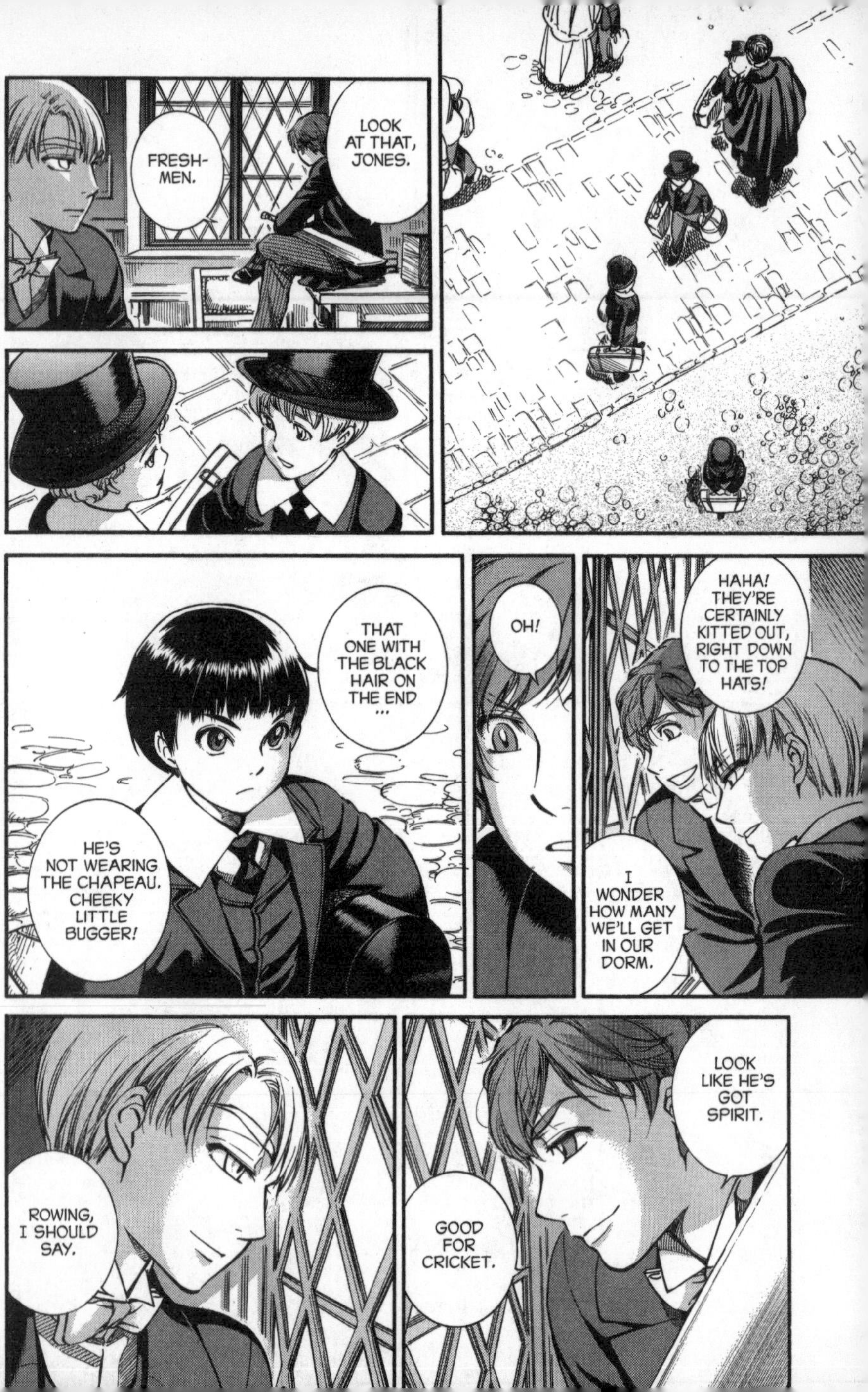
LOOK AT THAT, JONES.
FRESH-MEN.
HAHA! THEY'RE CERTAINLY KITTED OUT, RIGHT DOWN TO THE TOP HATS!
I WONDER HOW MANY WE'LL GET IN OUR DORM.
OH!
THAT ONE WITH THE BLACK HAIR ON THE END ...
HE'S NOT WEARING THE CHAPEAU. CHEEKY LITTLE BUGGER!
LOOK LIKE HE'S GOT SPIRIT.
GOOD FOR CRICKET.
ROWING, I SHOULD SAY.

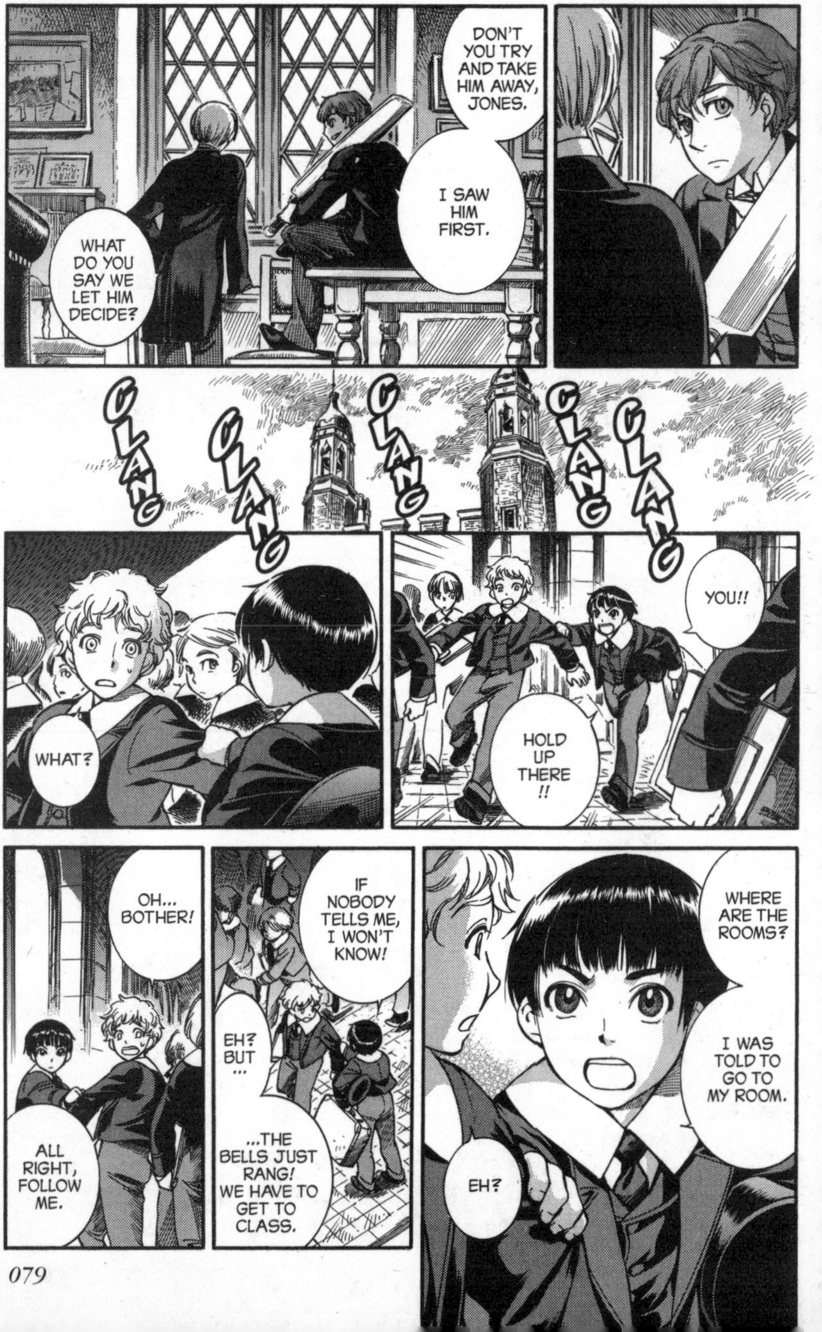
DON'T YOU TRY AND TAKE HIM AWAY, JONES.
I SAW HIM FIRST.
WHAT DO YOU SAY WE LET HIM DECIDE?
CLANG
CLANG
CLANG
CLANG
CLANG
YOU!!
HOLD UP THERE !!
WHAT?
WHERE ARE THE ROOMS?
I WAS TOLD TO GO TO MY ROOM.
EH?
IF NOBODY TELLS ME, I WON'T KNOW!
EH? BUT ...
...THE BELLS JUST RANG! WE HAVE TO GET TO CLASS.
OH... BOTHER!
ALL RIGHT, FOLLOW ME.

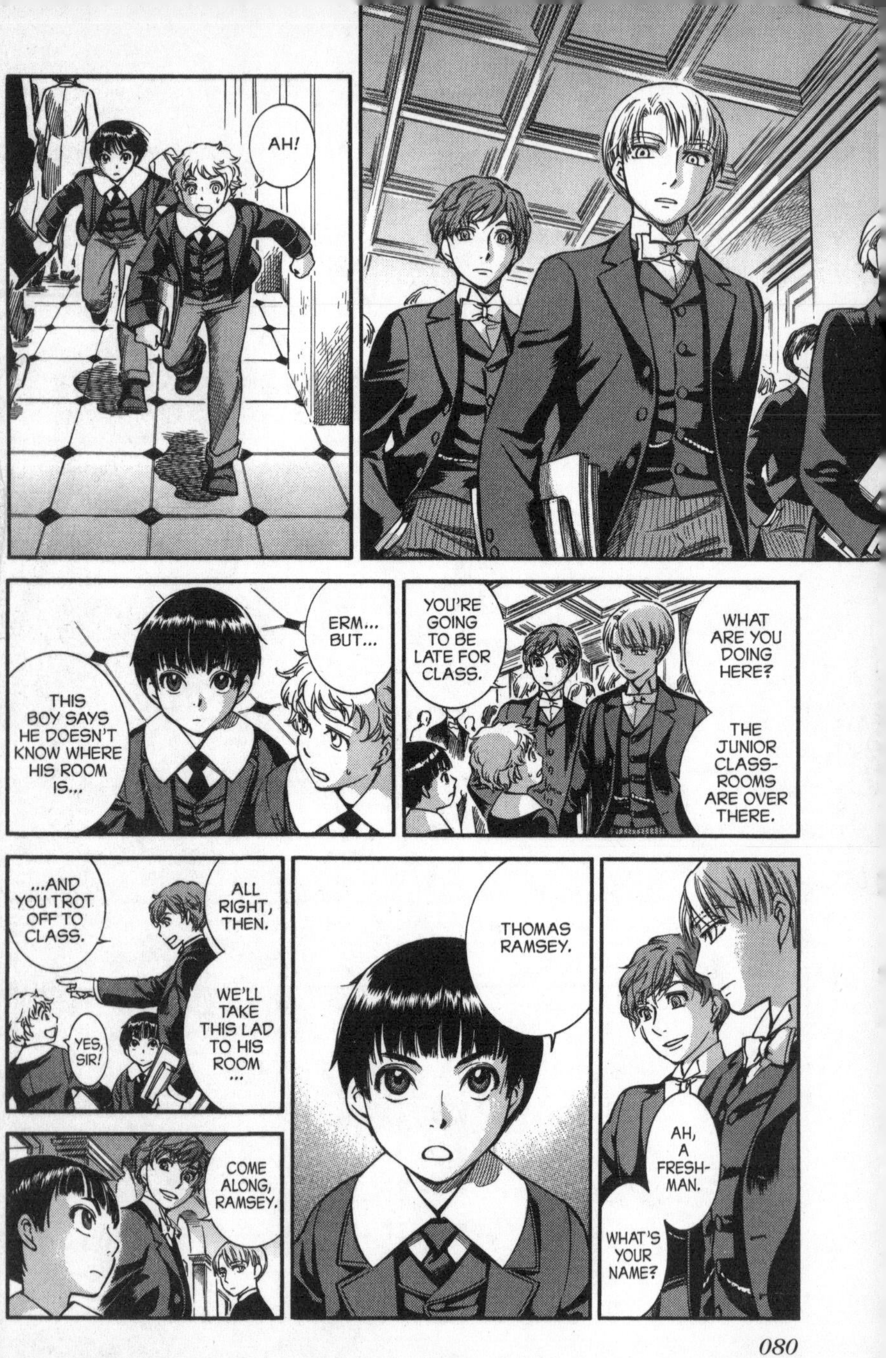
AH!
WHAT ARE YOU DOING HERE?
THE JUNIOR CLASS-ROOMS ARE OVER THERE.
YOU'RE GOING TO BE LATE FOR CLASS.
ERM... BUT...
THIS BOY SAYS HE DOESN'T KNOW WHERE HIS ROOM IS...
AH, A FRESH-MAN.
WHAT'S YOUR NAME?
THOMAS RAMSEY.
ALL RIGHT, THEN.
WE'LL TAKE THIS LAD TO HIS ROOM ...
...AND YOU TROT OFF TO CLASS.
YES, SIR!
COME ALONG, RAMSEY.

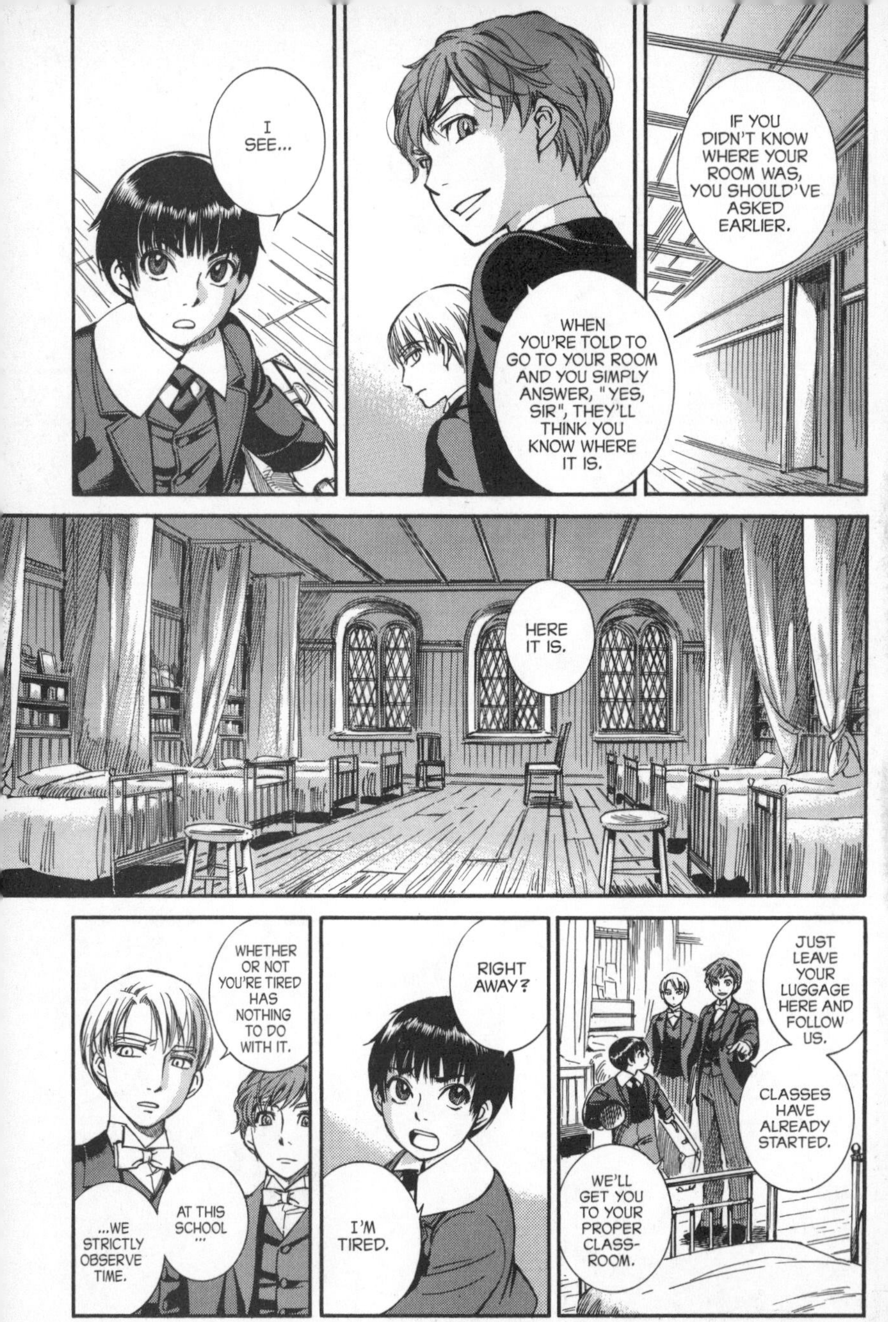
IF YOU DIDN'T KNOW WHERE YOUR ROOM WAS, YOU SHOULD'VE ASKED EARLIER.
WHEN YOU'RE TOLD TO GO TO YOUR ROOM AND YOU SIMPLY ANSWER, "YES, SIR", THEY'LL THINK YOU KNOW WHERE IT IS.
I SEE...
HERE IT IS.
JUST LEAVE YOUR LUGGAGE HERE AND FOLLOW US.
CLASSES HAVE ALREADY STARTED.
WE'LL GET YOU TO YOUR PROPER CLASS-ROOM.
RIGHT AWAY?
I'M TIRED.
WHETHER OR NOT YOU'RE TIRED HAS NOTHING TO DO WITH IT.
AT THIS SCHOOL ...
...WE STRICTLY OBSERVE TIME.

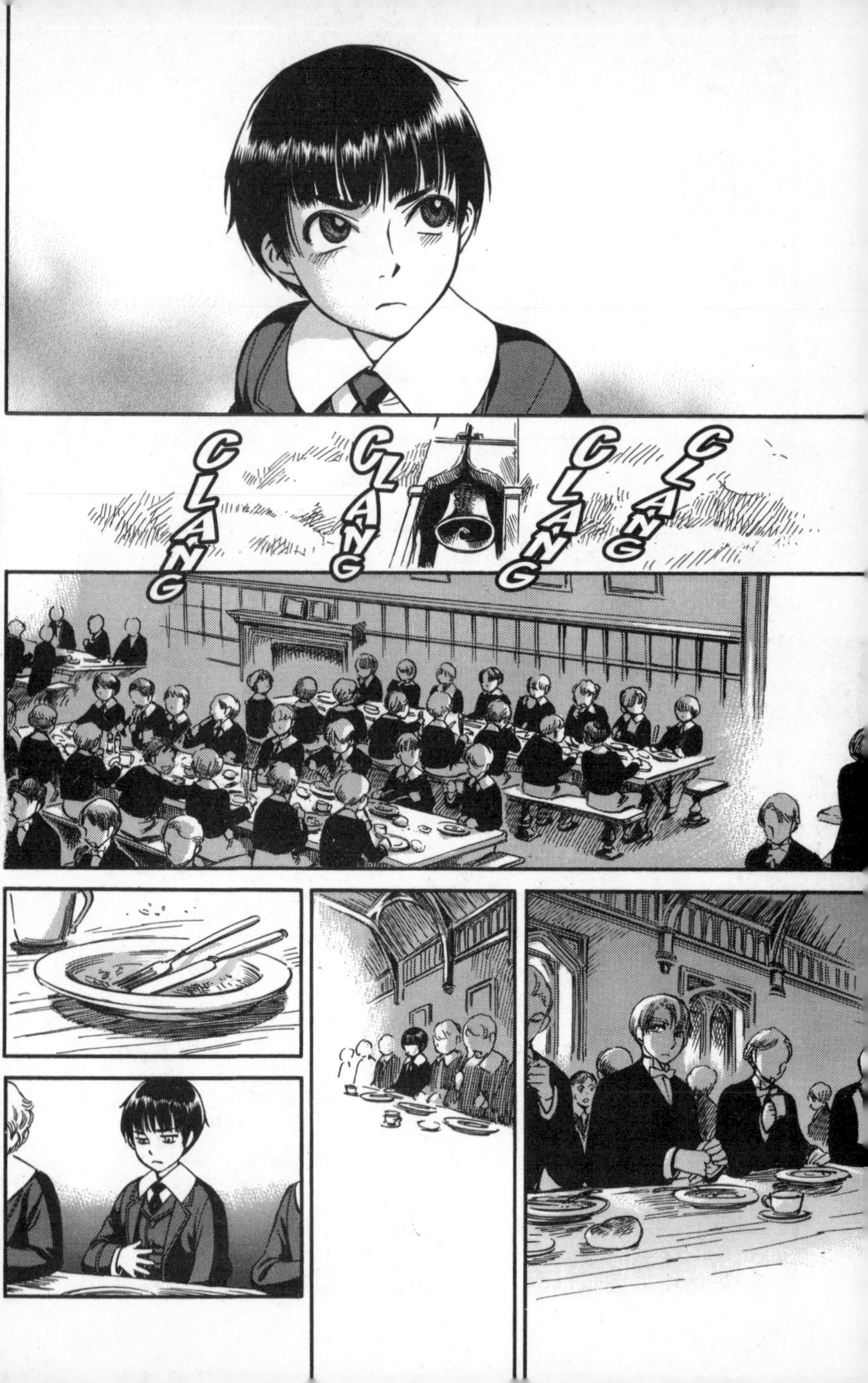
CLANG
CLANG
CLANG
CLANG

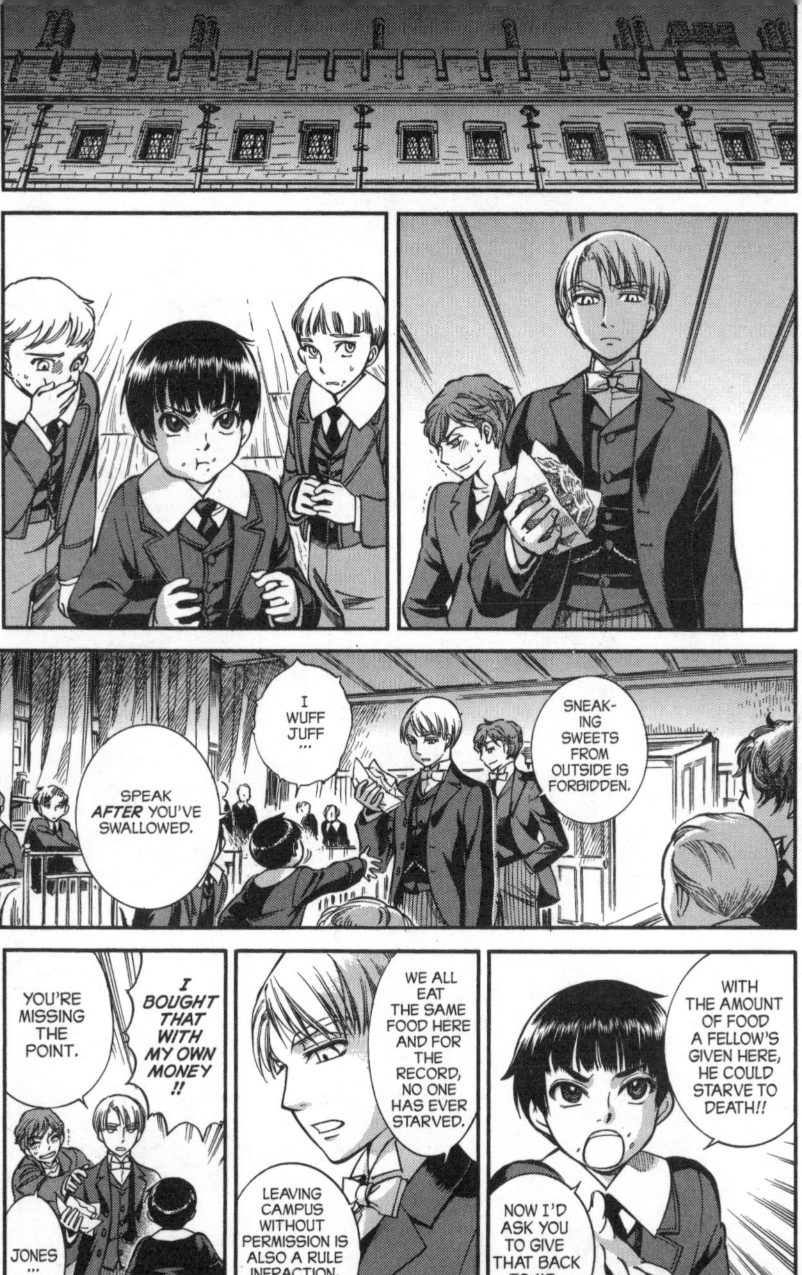
SNEAKING SWEETS FROM OUTSIDE IS FORBIDDEN.
I WUFF JUFF ...
SPEAK *AFTER* YOU'VE SWALLOWED.
WITH THE AMOUNT OF FOOD A FELLOW'S GIVEN HERE, HE COULD STARVE TO DEATH!!
NOW I'D ASK YOU TO GIVE THAT BACK TO ME, PLEASE!!
WE ALL EAT THE SAME FOOD HERE AND FOR THE RECORD, NO ONE HAS EVER STARVED.
LEAVING CAMPUS WITHOUT PERMISSION IS ALSO A RULE INFRACTION, BY THE WAY.
I BOUGHT THAT WITH MY OWN MONEY!!
YOU'RE MISSING THE POINT.
JONES ...

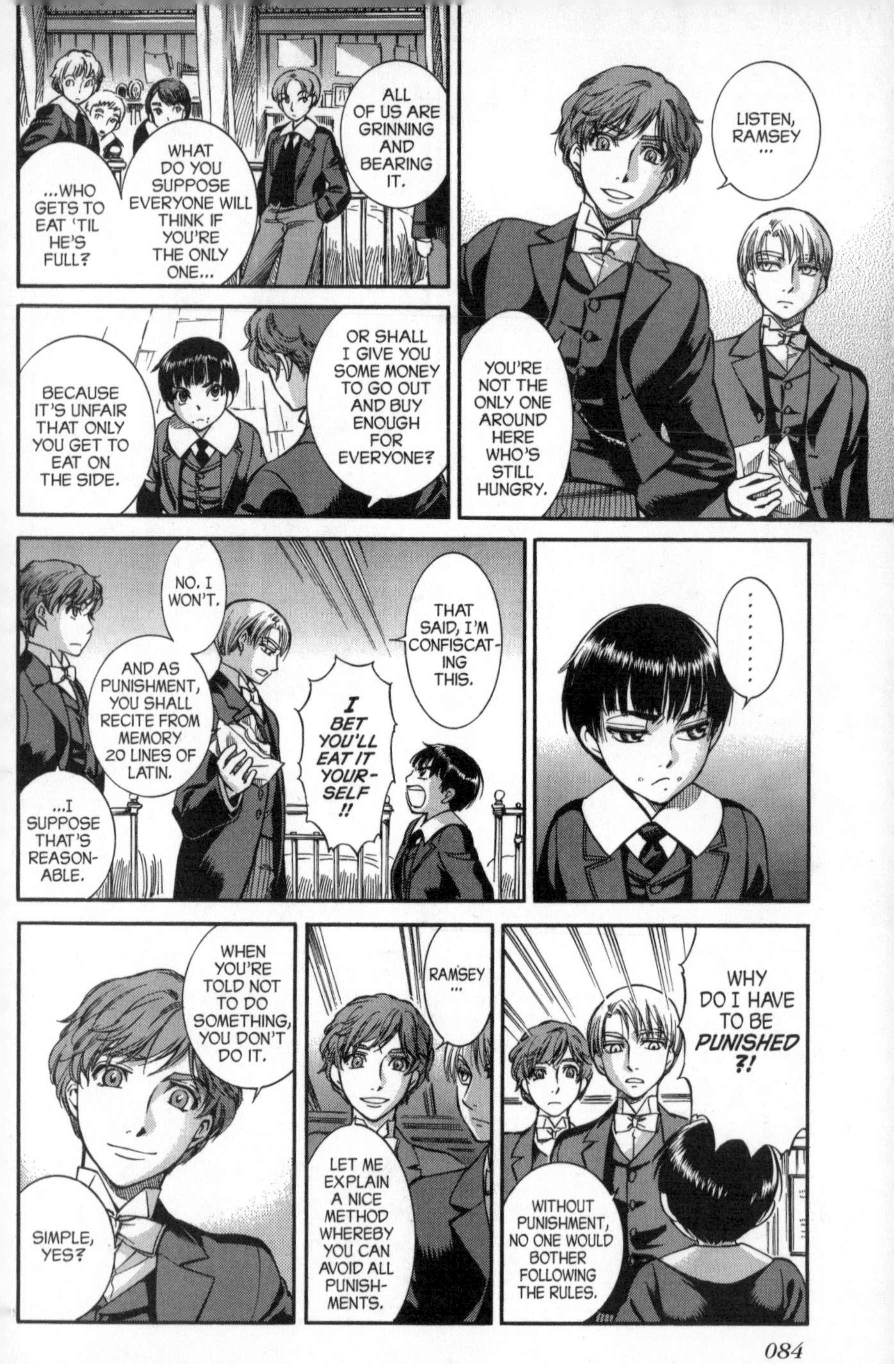

LISTEN, RAMSEY...
YOU'RE NOT THE ONLY ONE AROUND HERE WHO'S STILL HUNGRY.
ALL OF US ARE GRINNING AND BEARING IT.
WHAT DO YOU SUPPOSE EVERYONE WILL THINK IF YOU'RE THE ONLY ONE...
...WHO GETS TO EAT 'TIL HE'S FULL?
OR SHALL I GIVE YOU SOME MONEY TO GO OUT AND BUY ENOUGH FOR EVERYONE?
BECAUSE IT'S UNFAIR THAT ONLY YOU GET TO EAT ON THE SIDE.
......
THAT SAID, I'M CONFISCATING THIS.
I BET YOU'LL EAT IT YOURSELF!!
NO. I WON'T.
AND AS PUNISHMENT, YOU SHALL RECITE FROM MEMORY 20 LINES OF LATIN.
...I SUPPOSE THAT'S REASONABLE.
WHY DO I HAVE TO BE *PUNISHED*?!
WITHOUT PUNISHMENT, NO ONE WOULD BOTHER FOLLOWING THE RULES.
RAMSEY...
LET ME EXPLAIN A NICE METHOD WHEREBY YOU CAN AVOID ALL PUNISHMENTS.
WHEN YOU'RE TOLD NOT TO DO SOMETHING, YOU DON'T DO IT.
SIMPLE, YES?

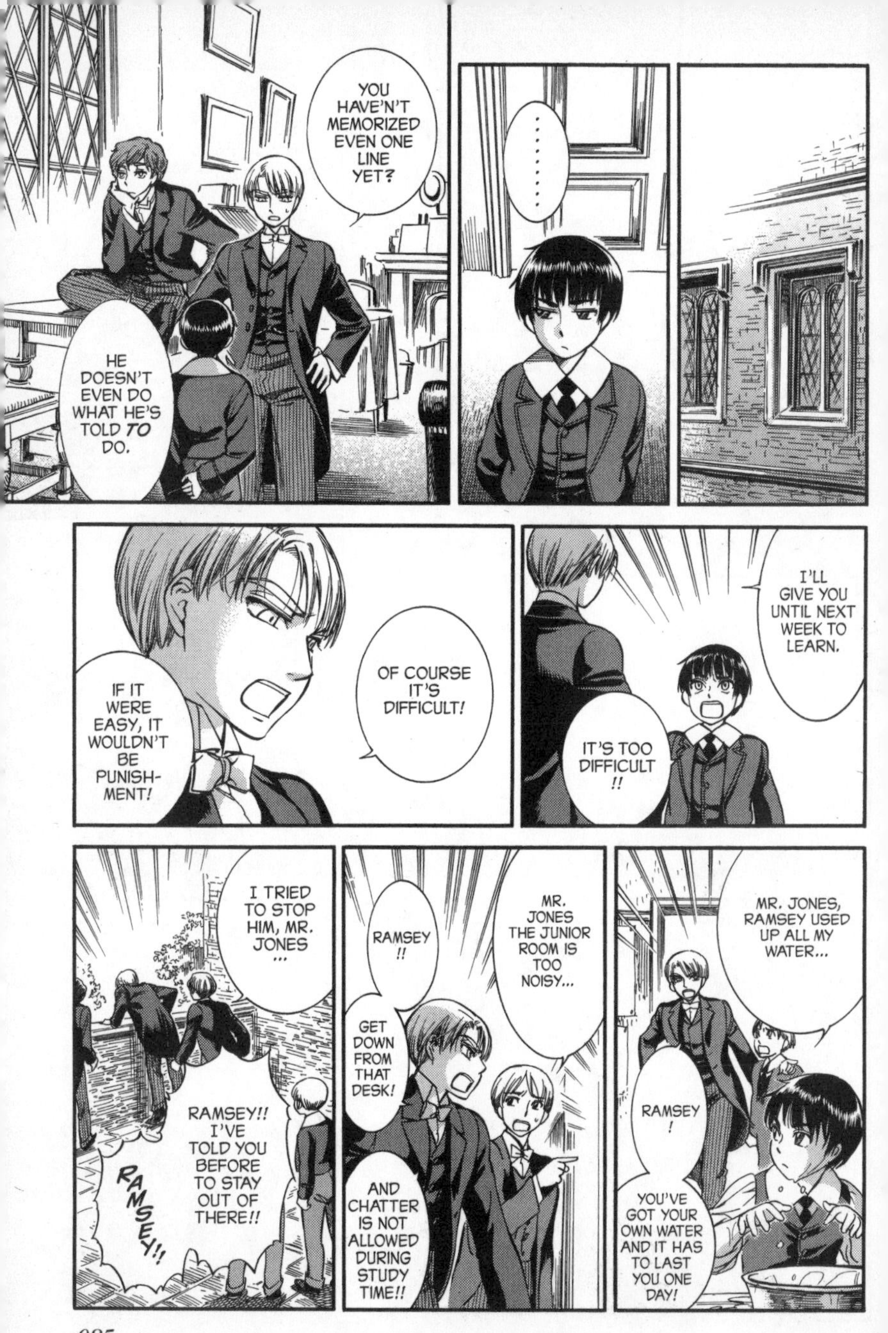

......
YOU HAVE'N'T MEMORIZED EVEN ONE LINE YET?
HE DOESN'T EVEN DO WHAT HE'S TOLD *TO* DO.
I'LL GIVE YOU UNTIL NEXT WEEK TO LEARN.
IT'S TOO DIFFICULT!!
OF COURSE IT'S DIFFICULT!
IF IT WERE EASY, IT WOULDN'T BE PUNISH-MENT!
MR. JONES, RAMSEY USED UP ALL MY WATER...
RAMSEY!
YOU'VE GOT YOUR OWN WATER AND IT HAS TO LAST YOU ONE DAY!
MR. JONES THE JUNIOR ROOM IS TOO NOISY...
RAMSEY!!
GET DOWN FROM THAT DESK!
AND CHATTER IS NOT ALLOWED DURING STUDY TIME!!
I TRIED TO STOP HIM, MR. JONES...
RAMSEY!! I'VE TOLD YOU BEFORE TO STAY OUT OF THERE!!
RAMSEY!!

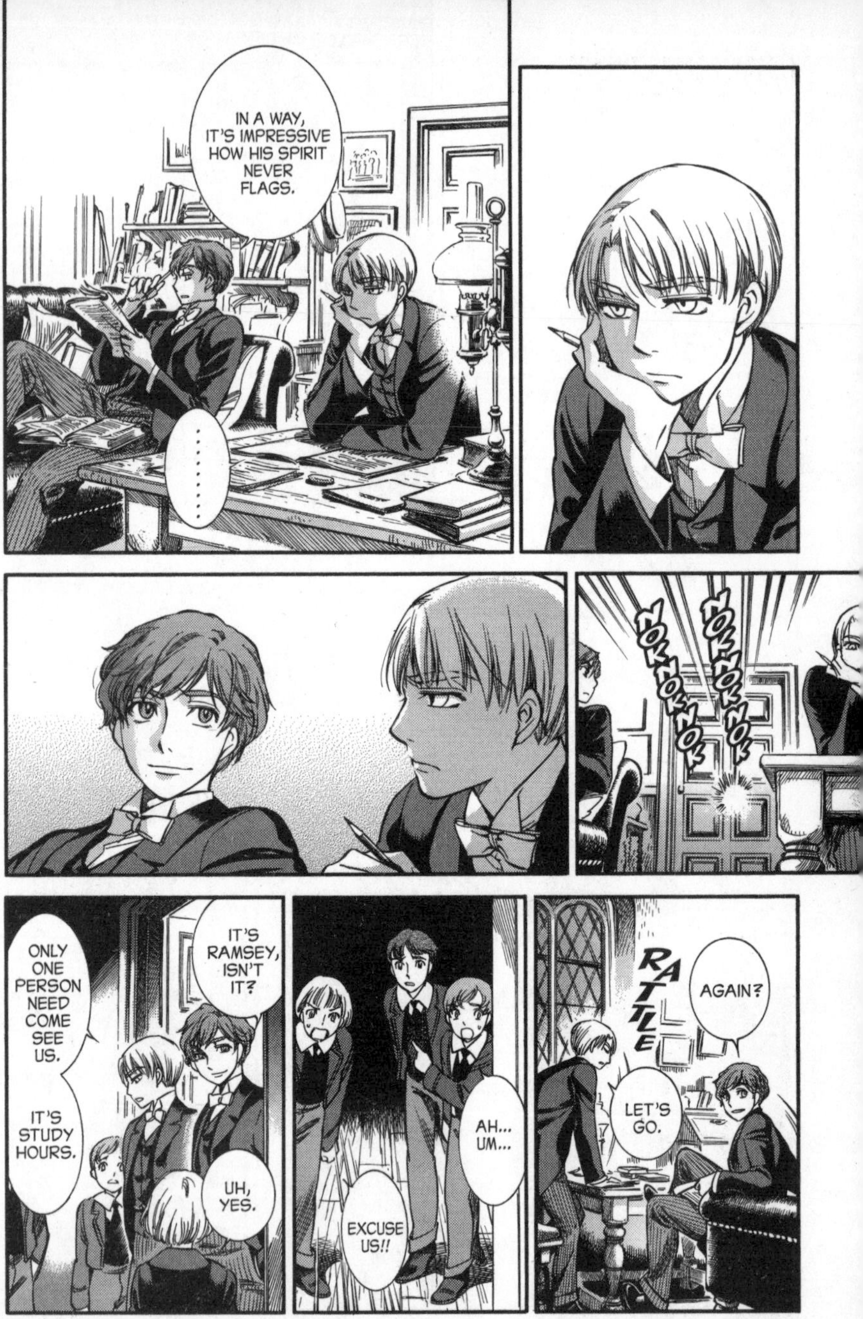
IN A WAY, IT'S IMPRESSIVE HOW HIS SPIRIT NEVER FLAGS.
......
NOKNOKNOK
NOKNOKNOK
AGAIN?
RATTLE
LET'S GO.
AH... UM...
EXCUSE US!!
IT'S RAMSEY, ISN'T IT?
ONLY ONE PERSON NEED COME SEE US.
IT'S STUDY HOURS.
UH, YES.

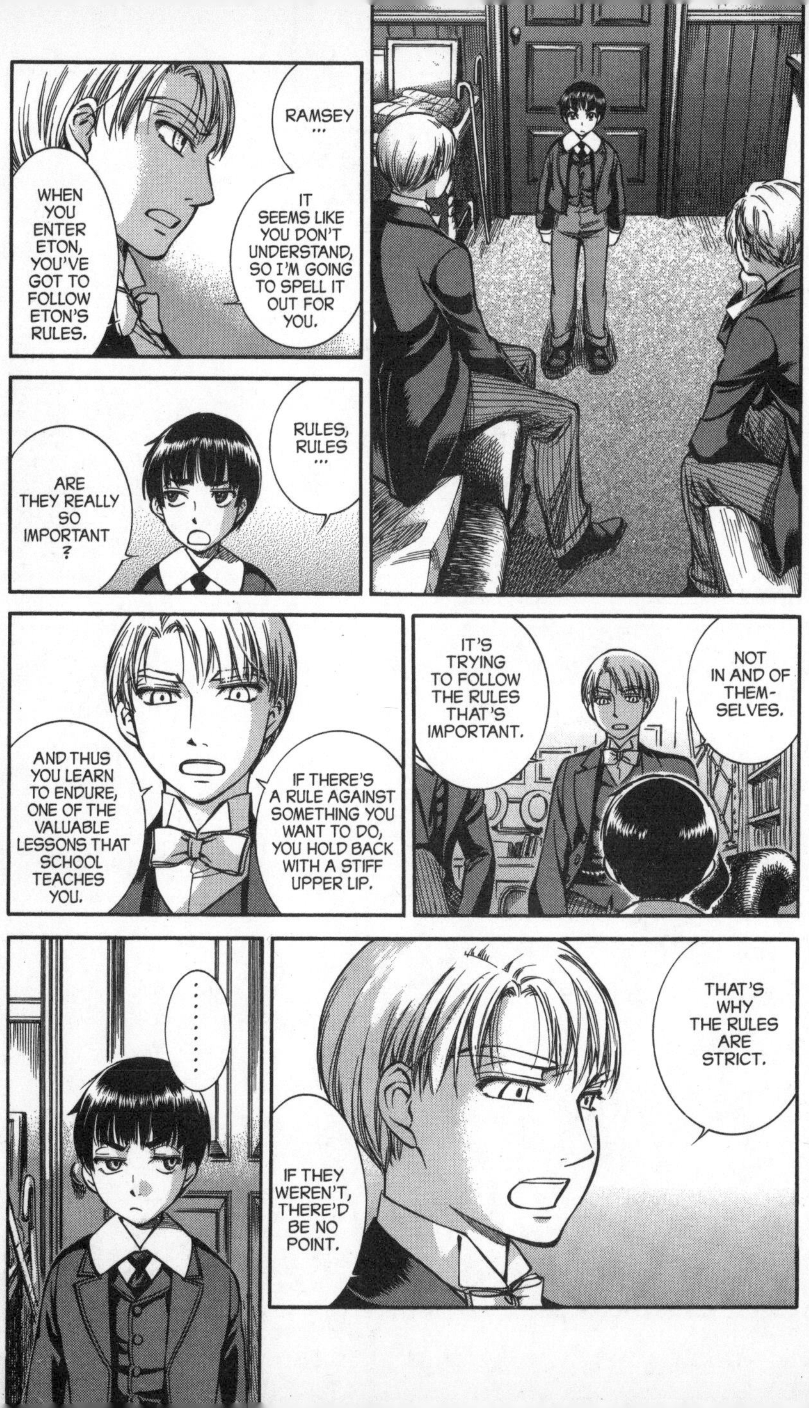
RAMSEY …
IT SEEMS LIKE YOU DON'T UNDERSTAND, SO I'M GOING TO SPELL IT OUT FOR YOU.
WHEN YOU ENTER ETON, YOU'VE GOT TO FOLLOW ETON'S RULES.
RULES, RULES …
ARE THEY REALLY SO IMPORTANT ?
NOT IN AND OF THEM-SELVES.
IT'S TRYING TO FOLLOW THE RULES THAT'S IMPORTANT.
IF THERE'S A RULE AGAINST SOMETHING YOU WANT TO DO, YOU HOLD BACK WITH A STIFF UPPER LIP.
AND THUS YOU LEARN TO ENDURE, ONE OF THE VALUABLE LESSONS THAT SCHOOL TEACHES YOU.
THAT'S WHY THE RULES ARE STRICT.
IF THEY WEREN'T, THERE'D BE NO POINT.
……

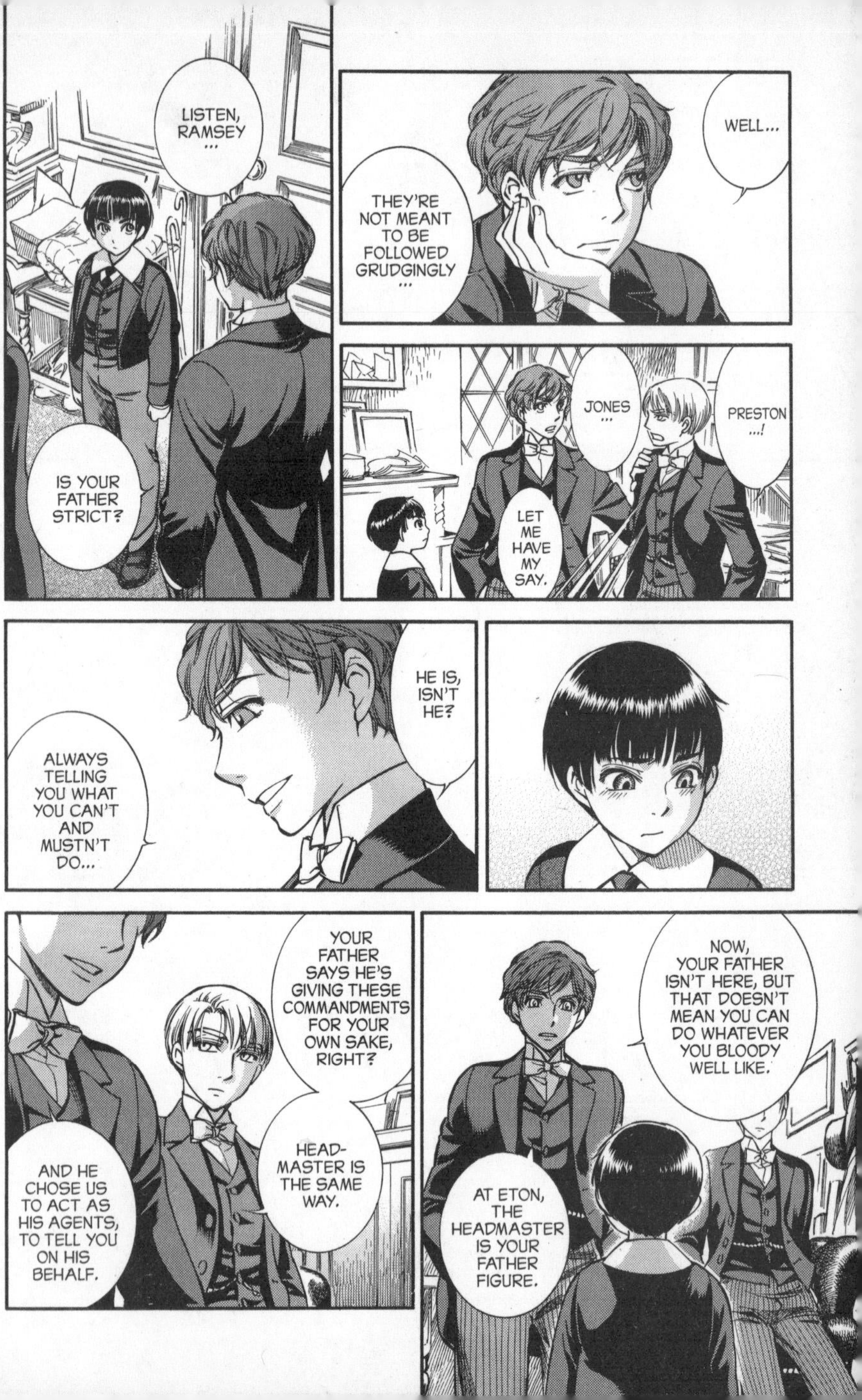
WELL...
THEY'RE NOT MEANT TO BE FOLLOWED GRUDGINGLY...
PRESTON...!
JONES...
LET ME HAVE MY SAY.
LISTEN, RAMSEY...
IS YOUR FATHER STRICT?
HE IS, ISN'T HE?
ALWAYS TELLING YOU WHAT YOU CAN'T AND MUSTN'T DO...
NOW, YOUR FATHER ISN'T HERE, BUT THAT DOESN'T MEAN YOU CAN DO WHATEVER YOU BLOODY WELL LIKE.
AT ETON, THE HEADMASTER IS YOUR FATHER FIGURE.
YOUR FATHER SAYS HE'S GIVING THESE COMMANDMENTS FOR YOUR OWN SAKE, RIGHT?
HEAD-MASTER IS THE SAME WAY.
AND HE CHOSE US TO ACT AS HIS AGENTS, TO TELL YOU ON HIS BEHALF.

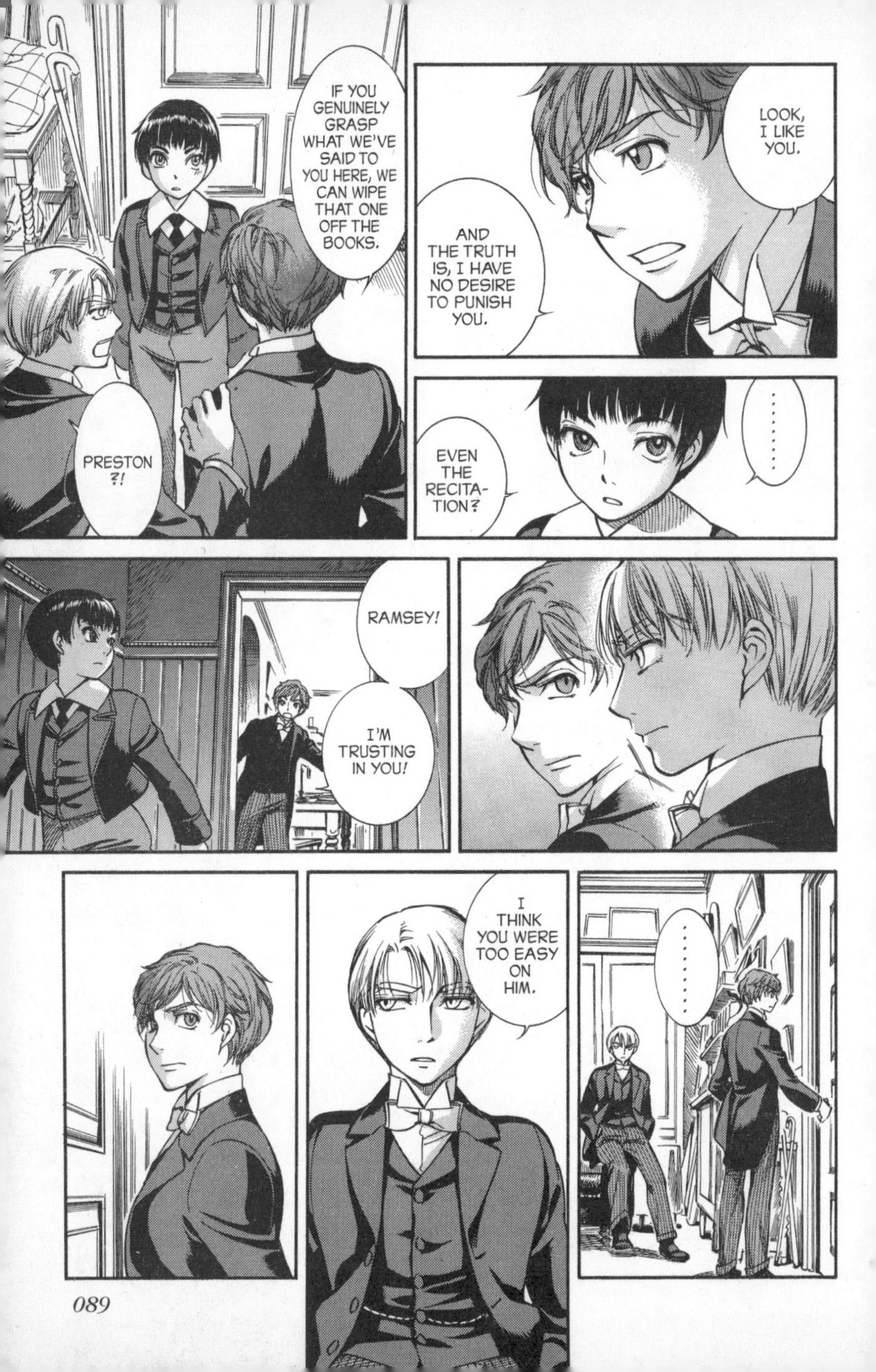
LOOK, I LIKE YOU.
AND THE TRUTH IS, I HAVE NO DESIRE TO PUNISH YOU.
. . . .
EVEN THE RECITA- TION?
IF YOU GENUINELY GRASP WHAT WE'VE SAID TO YOU HERE, WE CAN WIPE THAT ONE OFF THE BOOKS.
PRESTON ?!
RAMSEY!
I'M TRUSTING IN YOU!
. . . .
I THINK YOU WERE TOO EASY ON HIM.

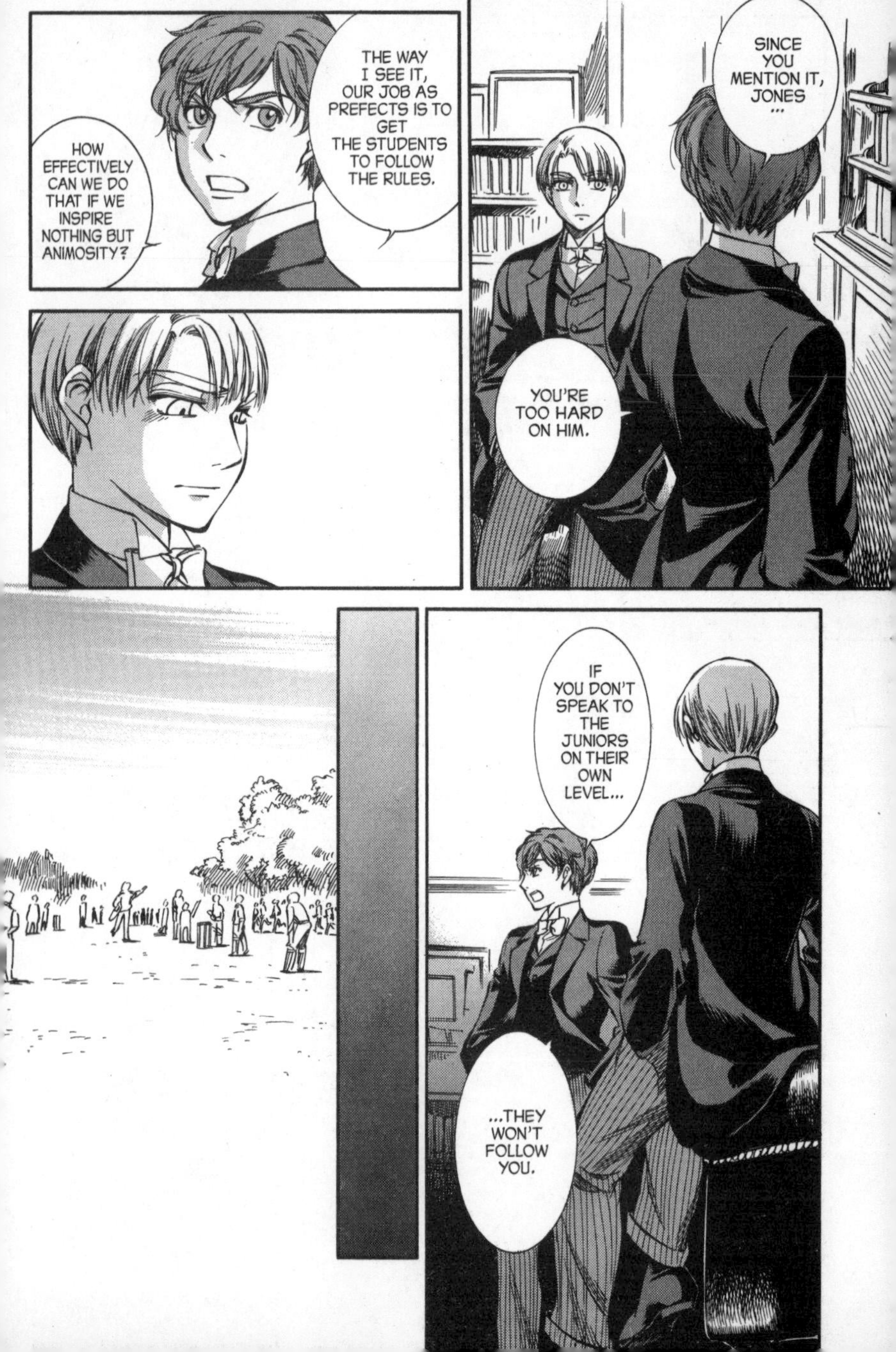
SINCE YOU MENTION IT, JONES...
YOU'RE TOO HARD ON HIM.
THE WAY I SEE IT, OUR JOB AS PREFECTS IS TO GET THE STUDENTS TO FOLLOW THE RULES.
HOW EFFECTIVELY CAN WE DO THAT IF WE INSPIRE NOTHING BUT ANIMOSITY?
IF YOU DON'T SPEAK TO THE JUNIORS ON THEIR OWN LEVEL...
...THEY WON'T FOLLOW YOU.

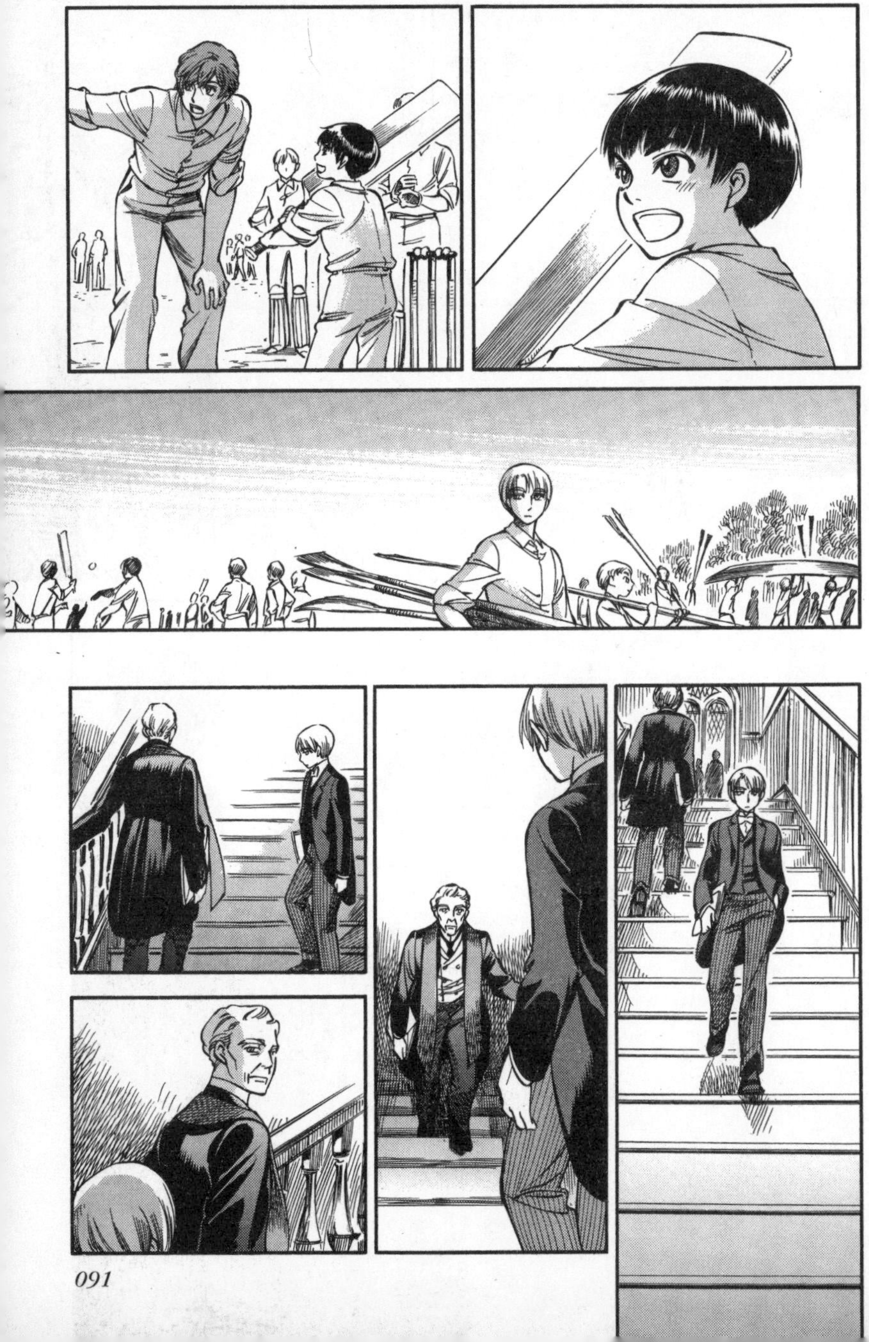

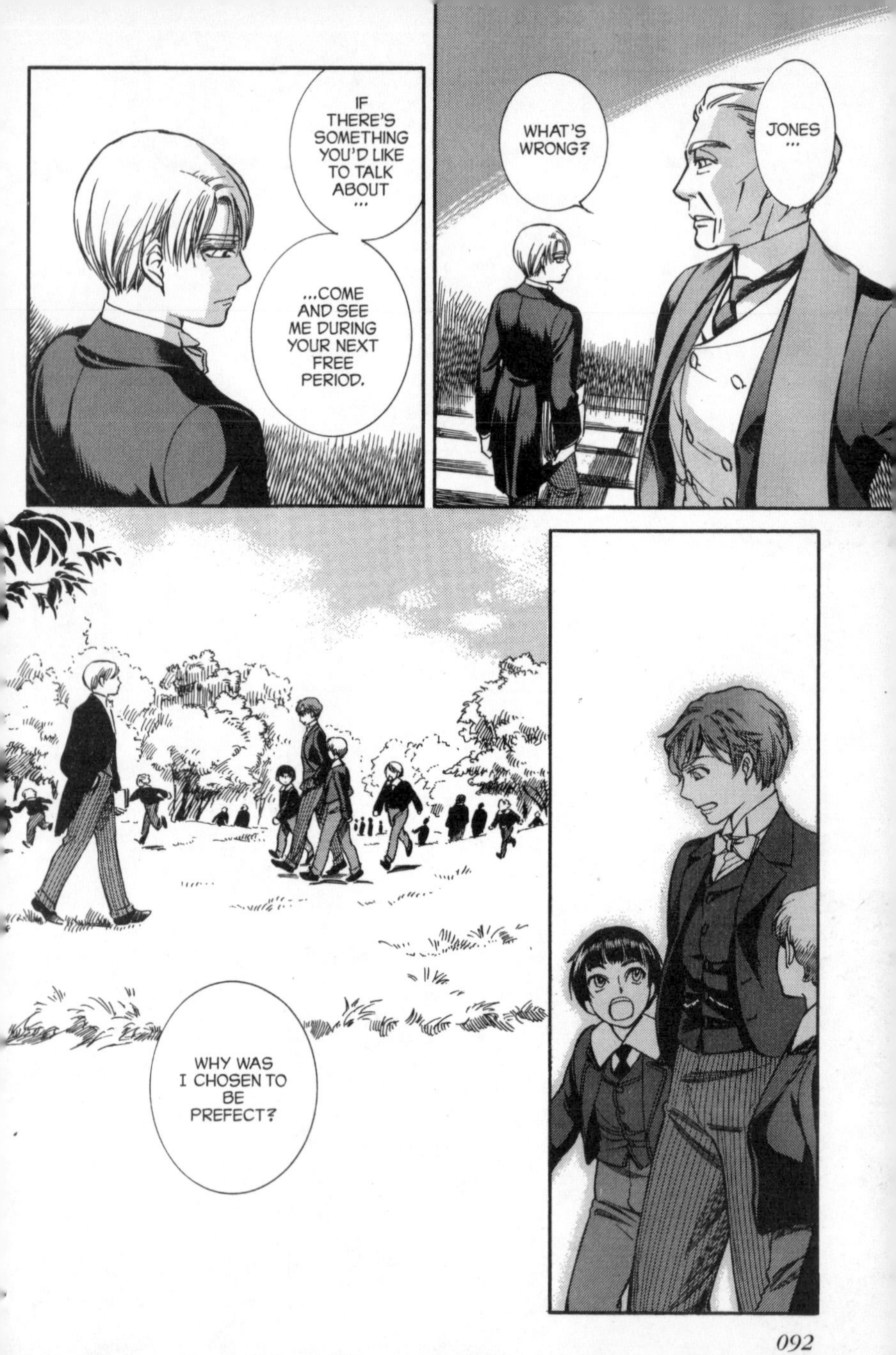
JONES ...
WHAT'S WRONG?
IF THERE'S SOMETHING YOU'D LIKE TO TALK ABOUT ...
...COME AND SEE ME DURING YOUR NEXT FREE PERIOD.
WHY WAS I CHOSEN TO BE PREFECT?

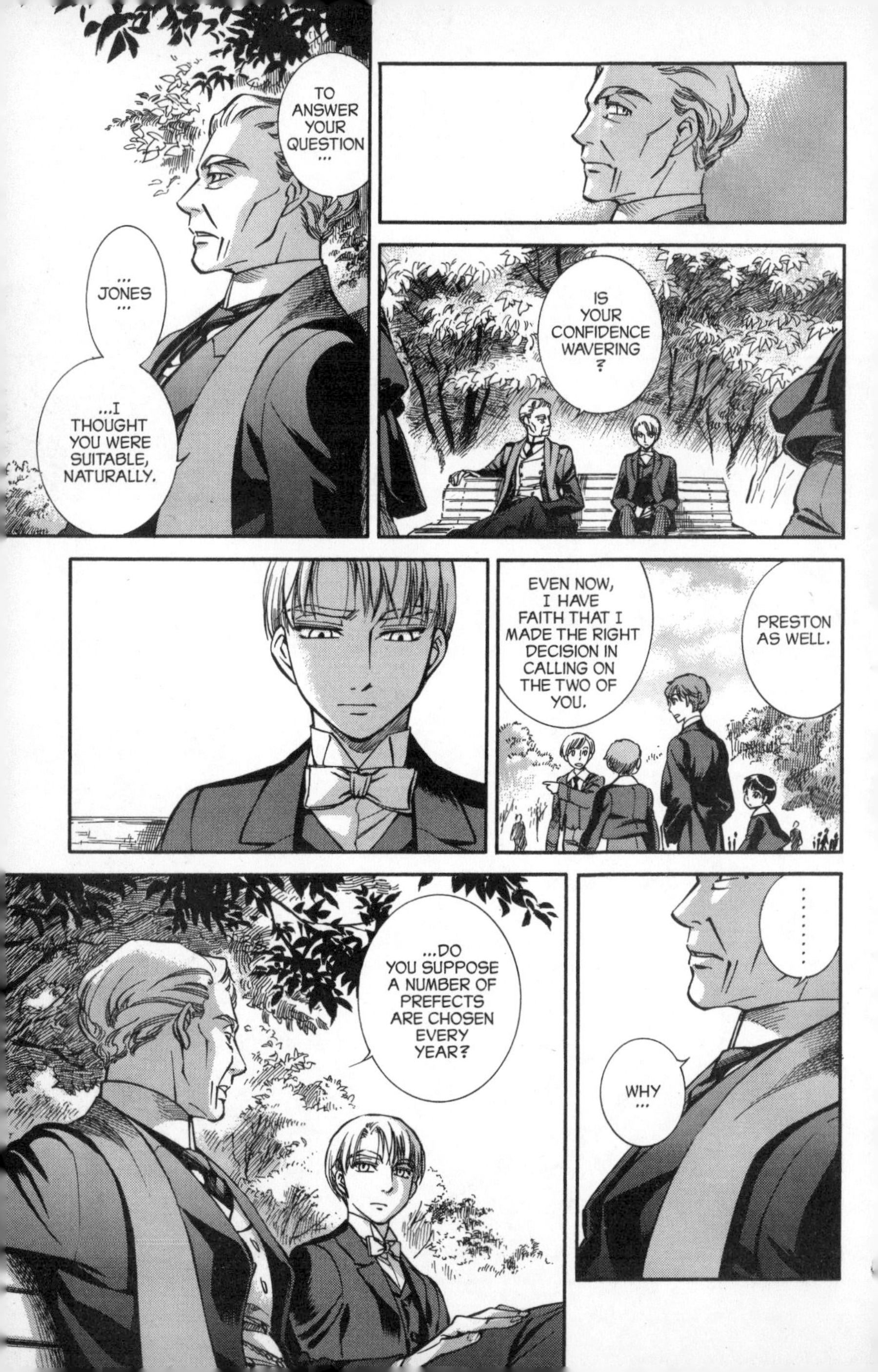
IS YOUR CONFIDENCE WAVERING?
TO ANSWER YOUR QUESTION...
...JONES...
...I THOUGHT YOU WERE SUITABLE, NATURALLY.
EVEN NOW, I HAVE FAITH THAT I MADE THE RIGHT DECISION IN CALLING ON THE TWO OF YOU.
PRESTON AS WELL.
......
WHY...
...DO YOU SUPPOSE A NUMBER OF PREFECTS ARE CHOSEN EVERY YEAR?

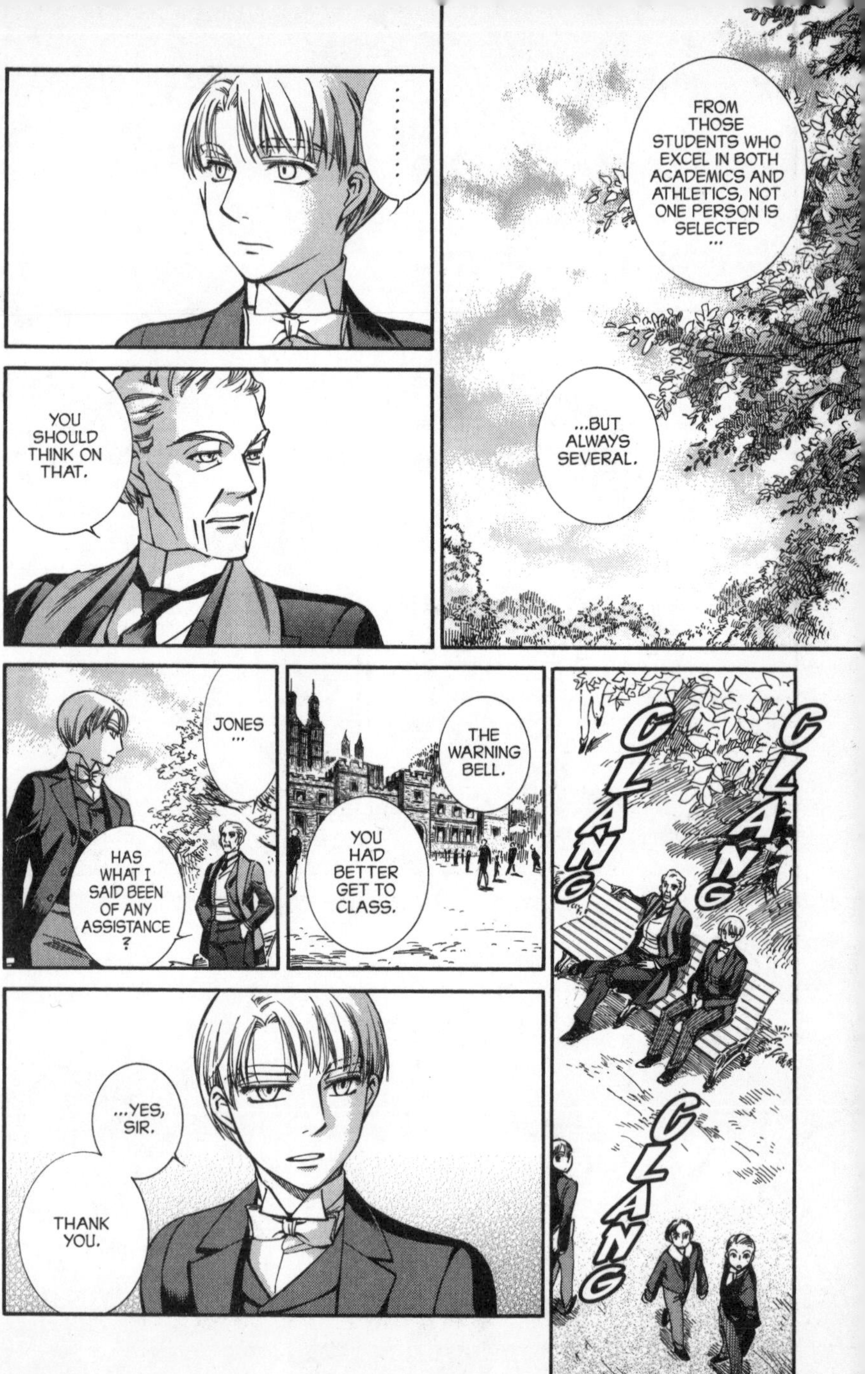
FROM THOSE STUDENTS WHO EXCEL IN BOTH ACADEMICS AND ATHLETICS, NOT ONE PERSON IS SELECTED ...
...BUT ALWAYS SEVERAL.
......
YOU SHOULD THINK ON THAT.
CLANG
CLANG
CLANG
THE WARNING BELL.
YOU HAD BETTER GET TO CLASS.
JONES ...
HAS WHAT I SAID BEEN OF ANY ASSISTANCE ?
...YES, SIR.
THANK YOU.

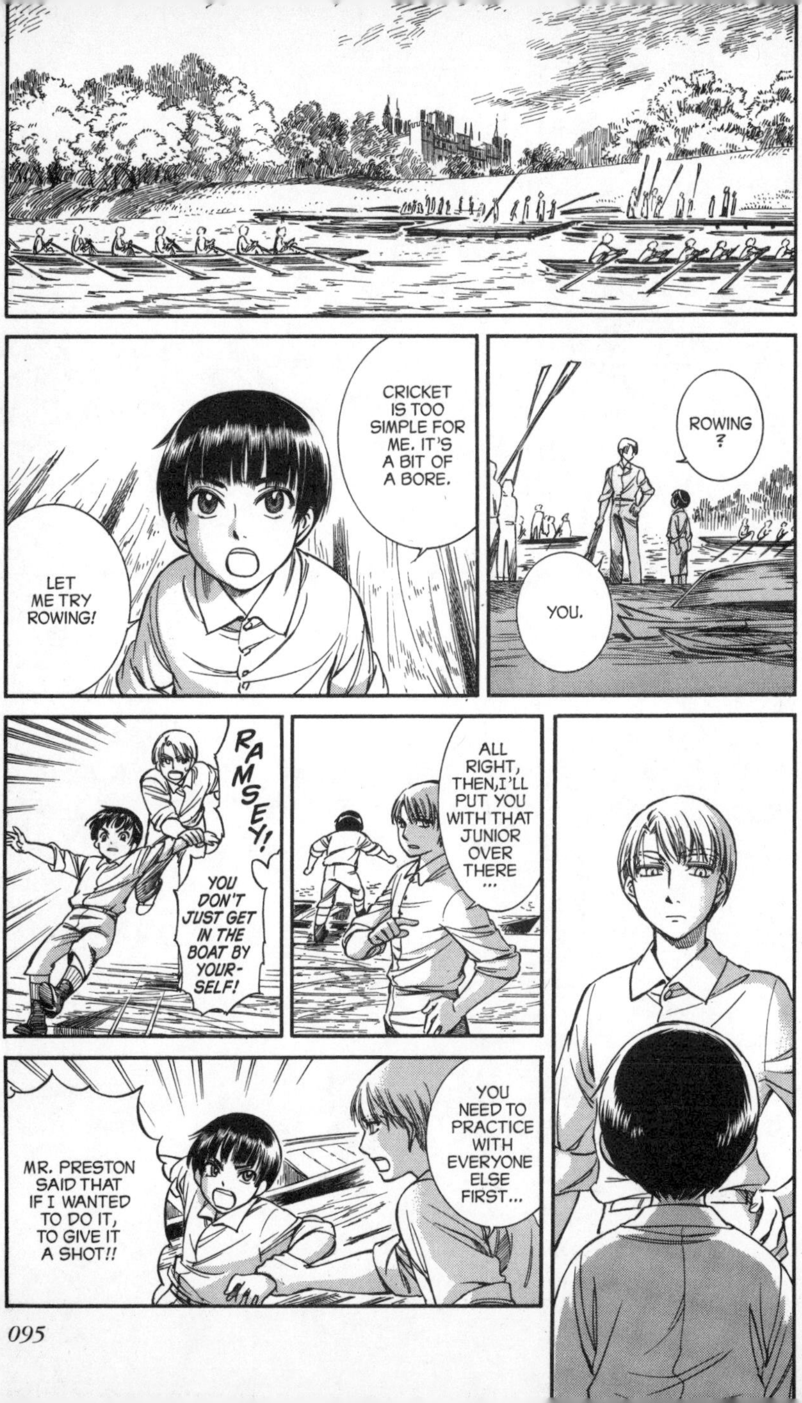
ROWING?
YOU.
CRICKET IS TOO SIMPLE FOR ME. IT'S A BIT OF A BORE.
LET ME TRY ROWING!
ALL RIGHT, THEN, I'LL PUT YOU WITH THAT JUNIOR OVER THERE...
RAMSEY!!
YOU DON'T JUST GET IN THE BOAT BY YOURSELF!
YOU NEED TO PRACTICE WITH EVERYONE ELSE FIRST...
MR. PRESTON SAID THAT IF I WANTED TO DO IT, TO GIVE IT A SHOT!!

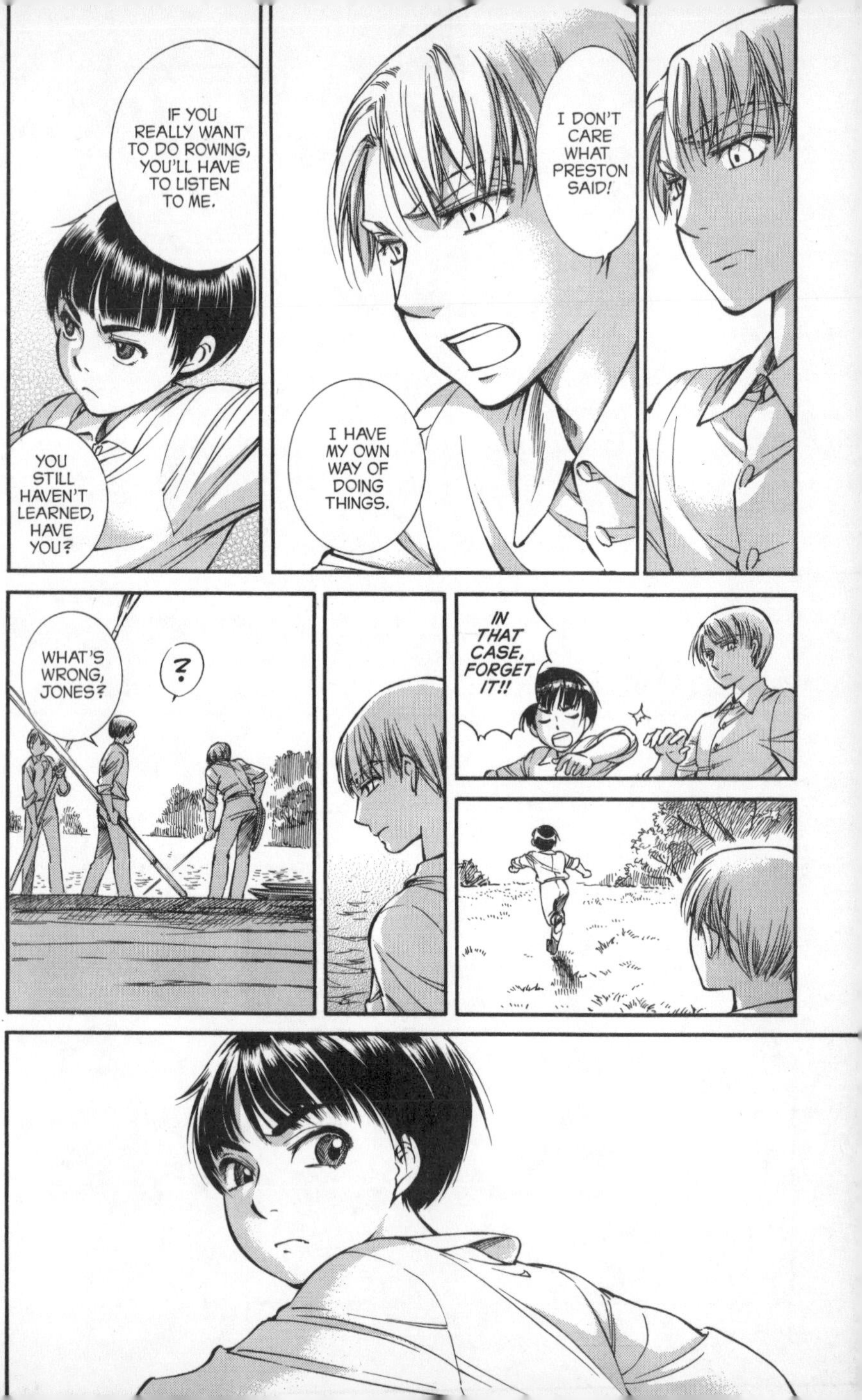
I DON'T CARE WHAT PRESTON SAID!
I HAVE MY OWN WAY OF DOING THINGS.
IF YOU REALLY WANT TO DO ROWING, YOU'LL HAVE TO LISTEN TO ME.
YOU STILL HAVEN'T LEARNED, HAVE YOU?
IN THAT CASE, FORGET IT!!
WHAT'S WRONG, JONES?
?

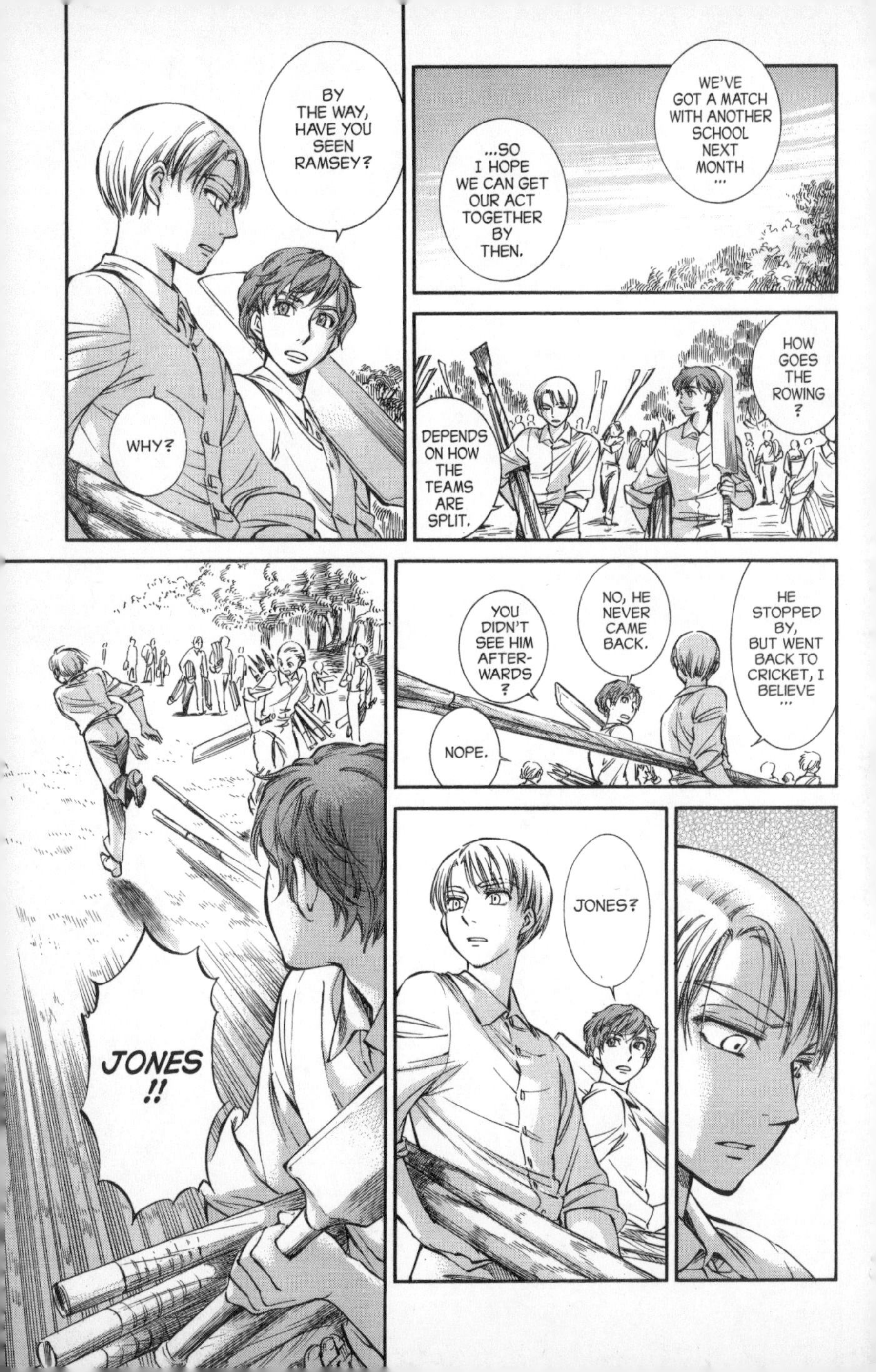
WE'VE GOT A MATCH WITH ANOTHER SCHOOL NEXT MONTH ...
...SO I HOPE WE CAN GET OUR ACT TOGETHER BY THEN.
HOW GOES THE ROWING ?
DEPENDS ON HOW THE TEAMS ARE SPLIT.
BY THE WAY, HAVE YOU SEEN RAMSEY?
WHY?
HE STOPPED BY, BUT WENT BACK TO CRICKET, I BELIEVE ...
NO, HE NEVER CAME BACK.
YOU DIDN'T SEE HIM AFTER-WARDS ?
NOPE.
JONES?
JONES !!

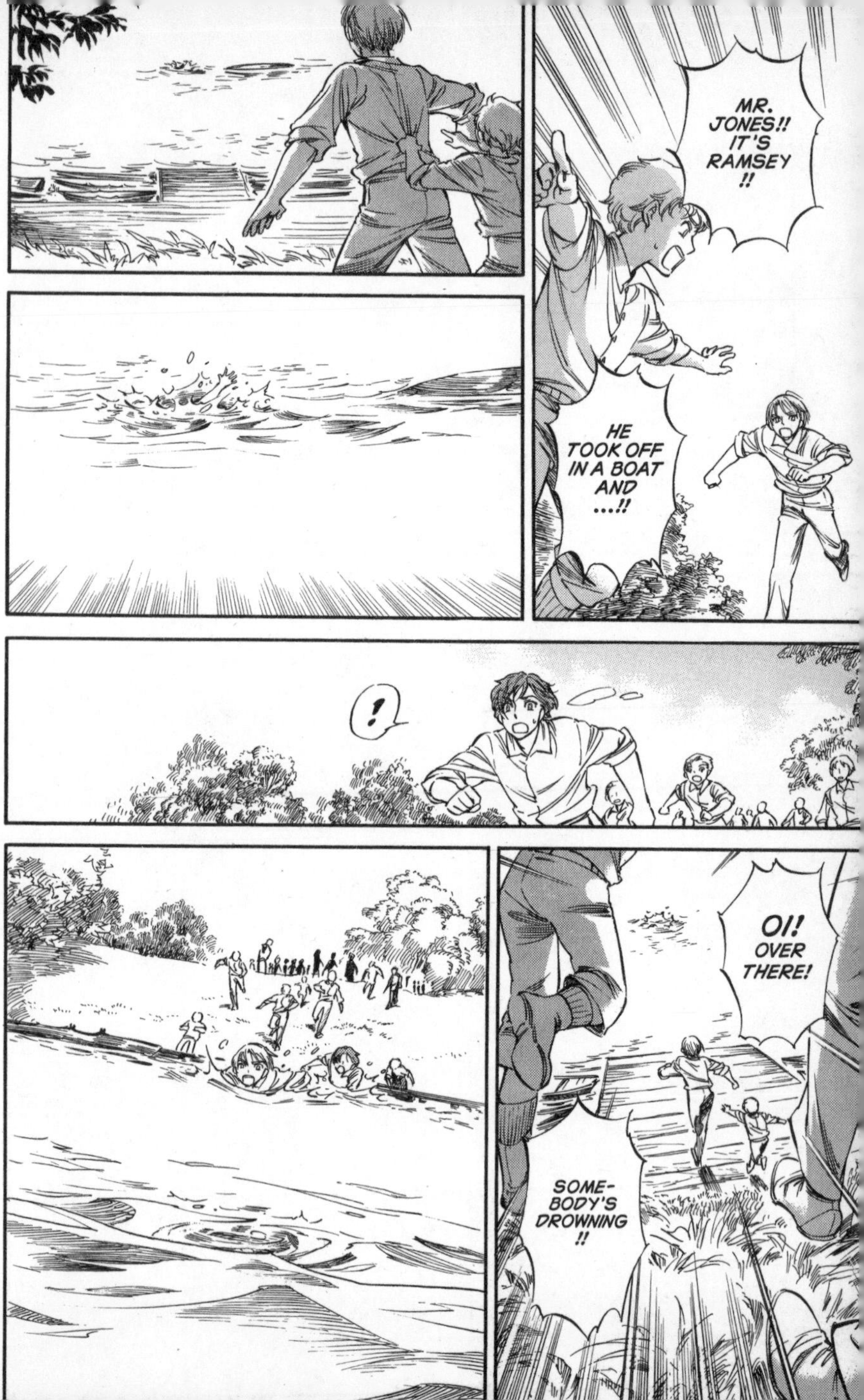
MR. JONES!! IT'S RAMSEY !!
HE TOOK OFF IN A BOAT AND ...!!
!
OI! OVER THERE!
SOME-BODY'S DROWNING !!

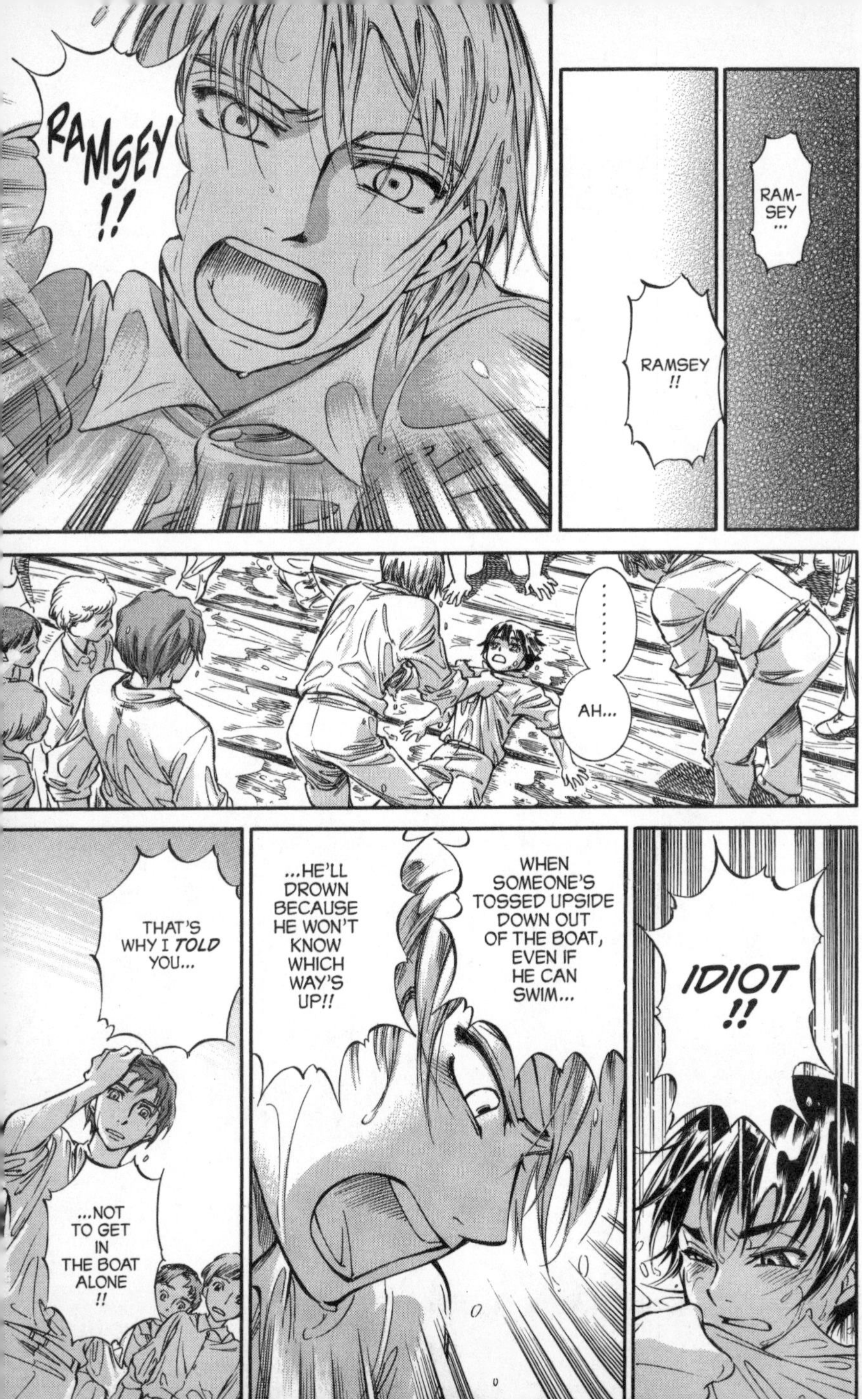
RAM-SEY...
RAMSEY!!
RAMSEY!!
......
AH...
IDIOT!!
WHEN SOMEONE'S TOSSED UPSIDE DOWN OUT OF THE BOAT, EVEN IF HE CAN SWIM...
...HE'LL DROWN BECAUSE HE WON'T KNOW WHICH WAY'S UP!!
THAT'S WHY I *TOLD* YOU...
...NOT TO GET IN THE BOAT ALONE!!

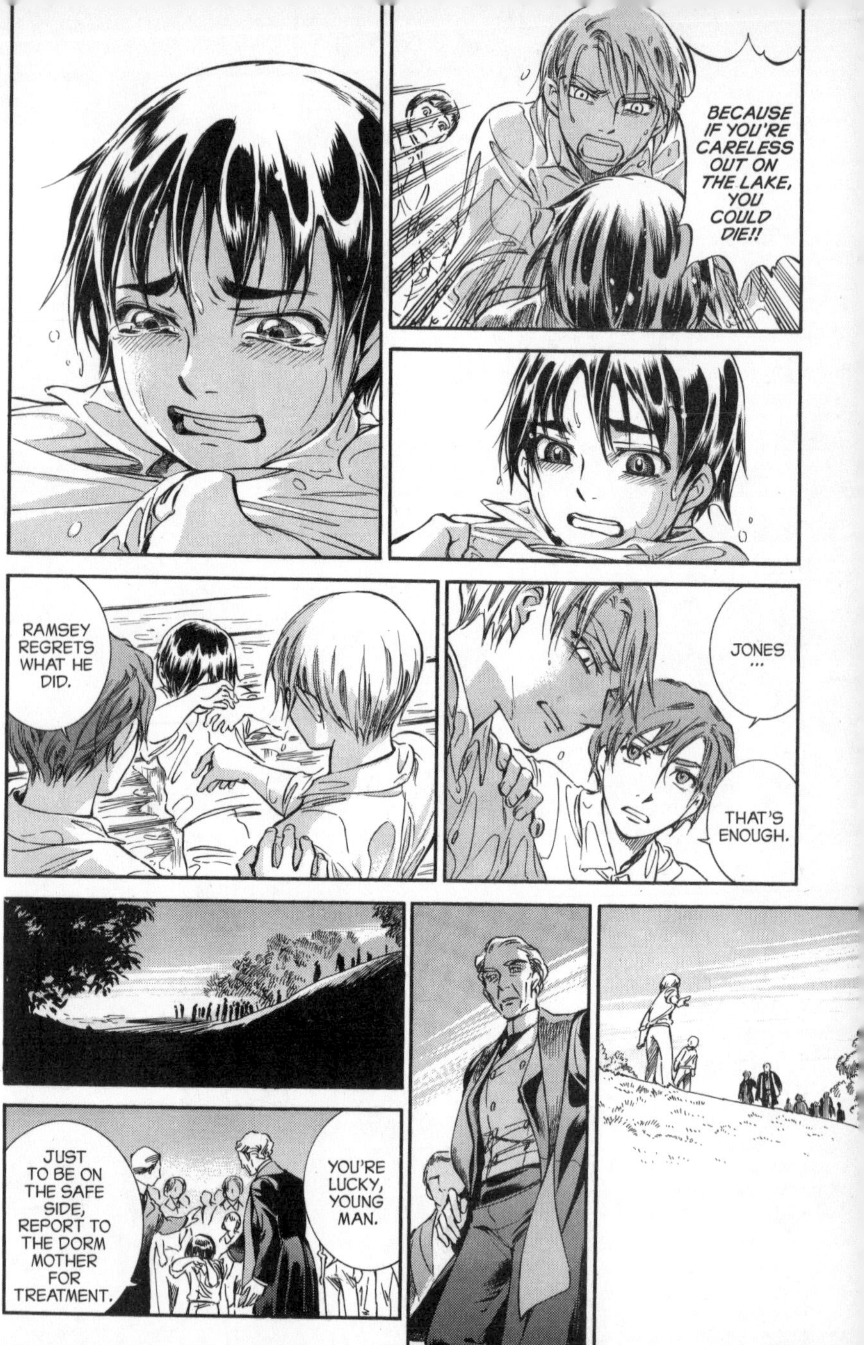
BECAUSE IF YOU'RE CARELESS OUT ON THE LAKE, YOU COULD DIE!!
JONES ...
THAT'S ENOUGH.
RAMSEY REGRETS WHAT HE DID.
YOU'RE LUCKY, YOUNG MAN.
JUST TO BE ON THE SAFE SIDE, REPORT TO THE DORM MOTHER FOR TREATMENT.

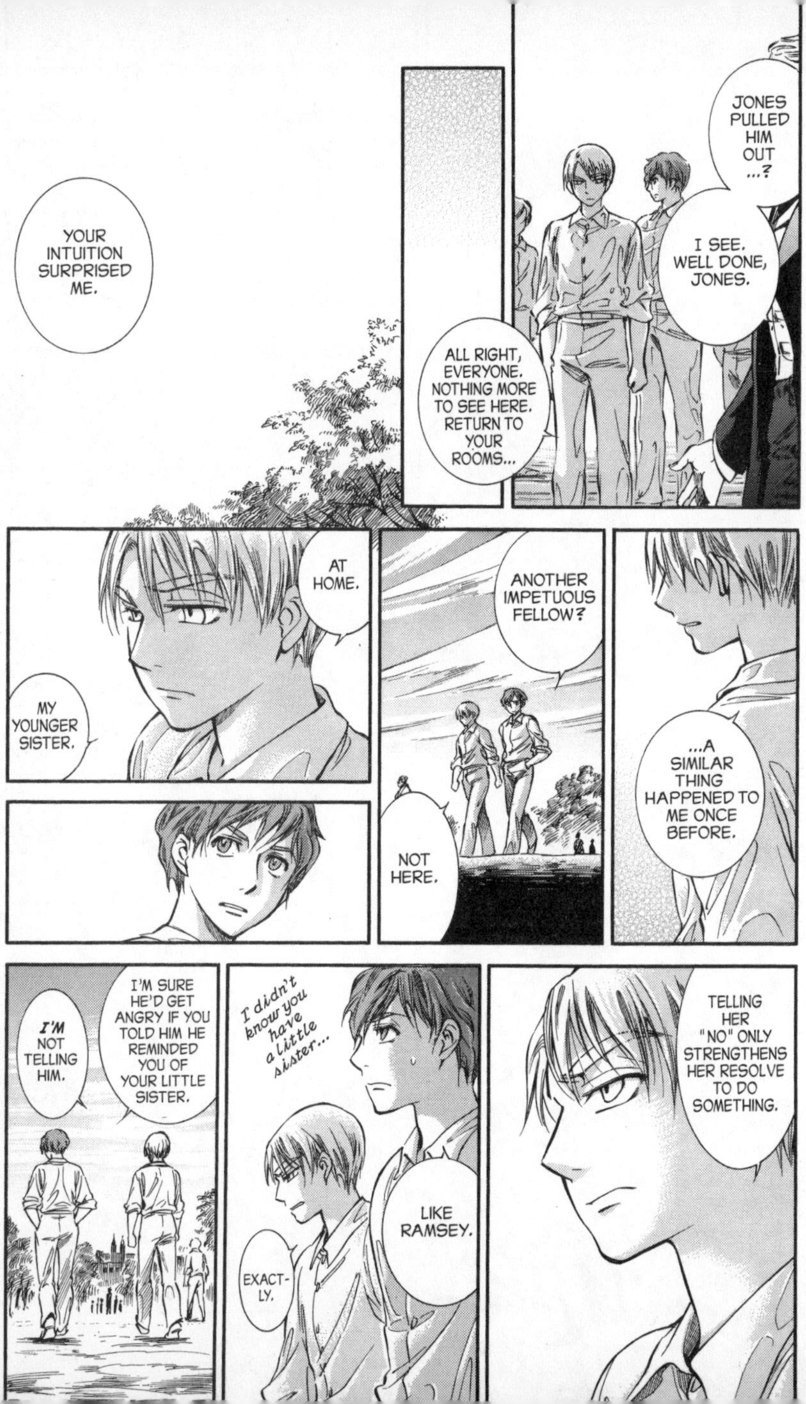
JONES PULLED HIM OUT ...?
I SEE. WELL DONE, JONES.
ALL RIGHT, EVERYONE. NOTHING MORE TO SEE HERE. RETURN TO YOUR ROOMS...
YOUR INTUITION SURPRISED ME.
...A SIMILAR THING HAPPENED TO ME ONCE BEFORE.
ANOTHER IMPETUOUS FELLOW?
NOT HERE.
AT HOME.
MY YOUNGER SISTER.
TELLING HER "NO" ONLY STRENGTHENS HER RESOLVE TO DO SOMETHING.
LIKE RAMSEY.
EXACTLY.
I didn't know you have a little sister...
I'M SURE HE'D GET ANGRY IF YOU TOLD HIM HE REMINDED YOU OF YOUR LITTLE SISTER.
I'M NOT TELLING HIM.

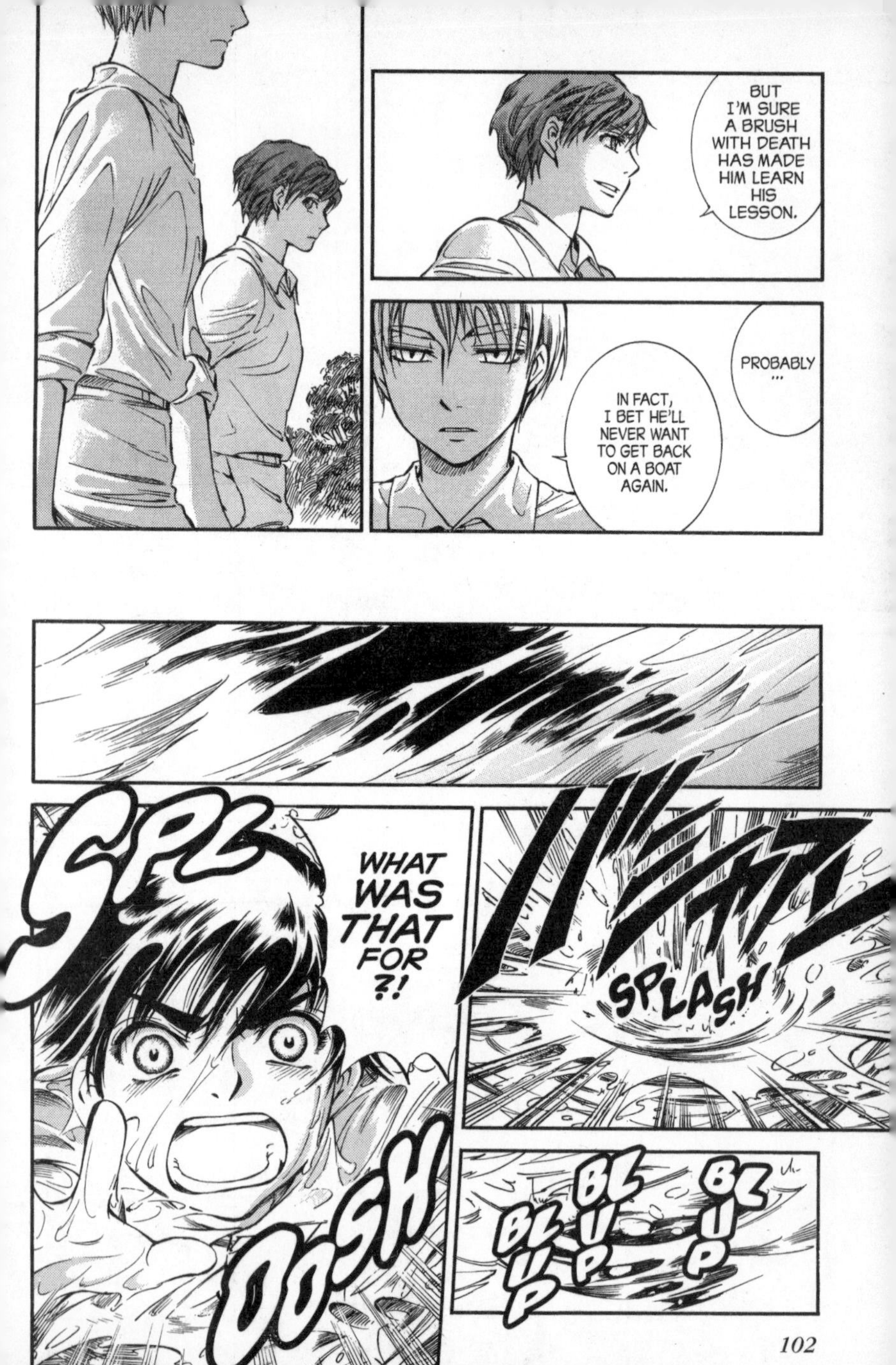
BUT I'M SURE A BRUSH WITH DEATH HAS MADE HIM LEARN HIS LESSON.
PROBABLY ...
IN FACT, I BET HE'LL NEVER WANT TO GET BACK ON A BOAT AGAIN.
SPLASH
BLUP
BLUP.
BLUP
WHAT WAS THAT FOR?!
SPLOOSH

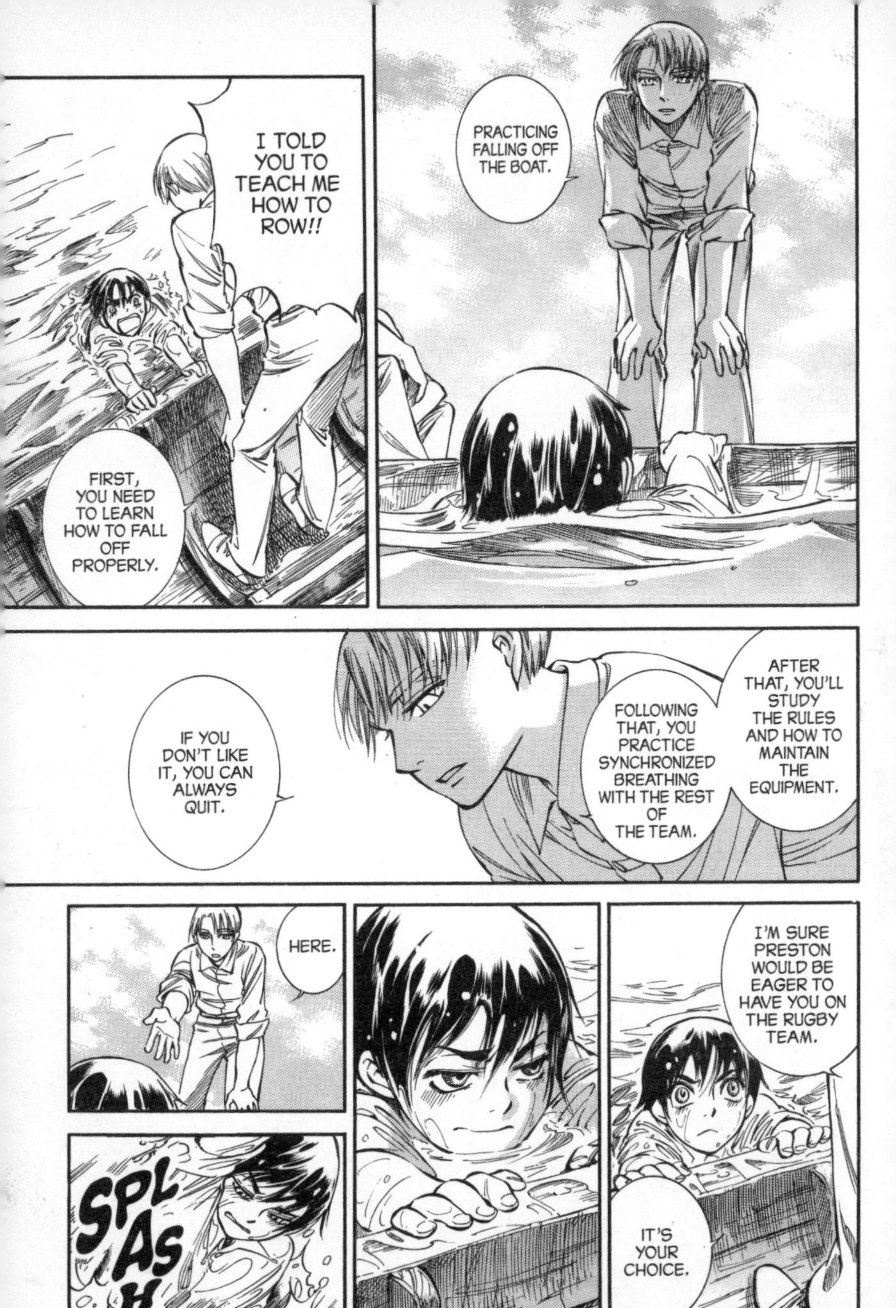
PRACTICING FALLING OFF THE BOAT.
I TOLD YOU TO TEACH ME HOW TO ROW!!
FIRST, YOU NEED TO LEARN HOW TO FALL OFF PROPERLY.
AFTER THAT, YOU'LL STUDY THE RULES AND HOW TO MAINTAIN THE EQUIPMENT.
FOLLOWING THAT, YOU PRACTICE SYNCHRONIZED BREATHING WITH THE REST OF THE TEAM.
IF YOU DON'T LIKE IT, YOU CAN ALWAYS QUIT.
I'M SURE PRESTON WOULD BE EAGER TO HAVE YOU ON THE RUGBY TEAM.
IT'S YOUR CHOICE.
HERE.
SPLASH

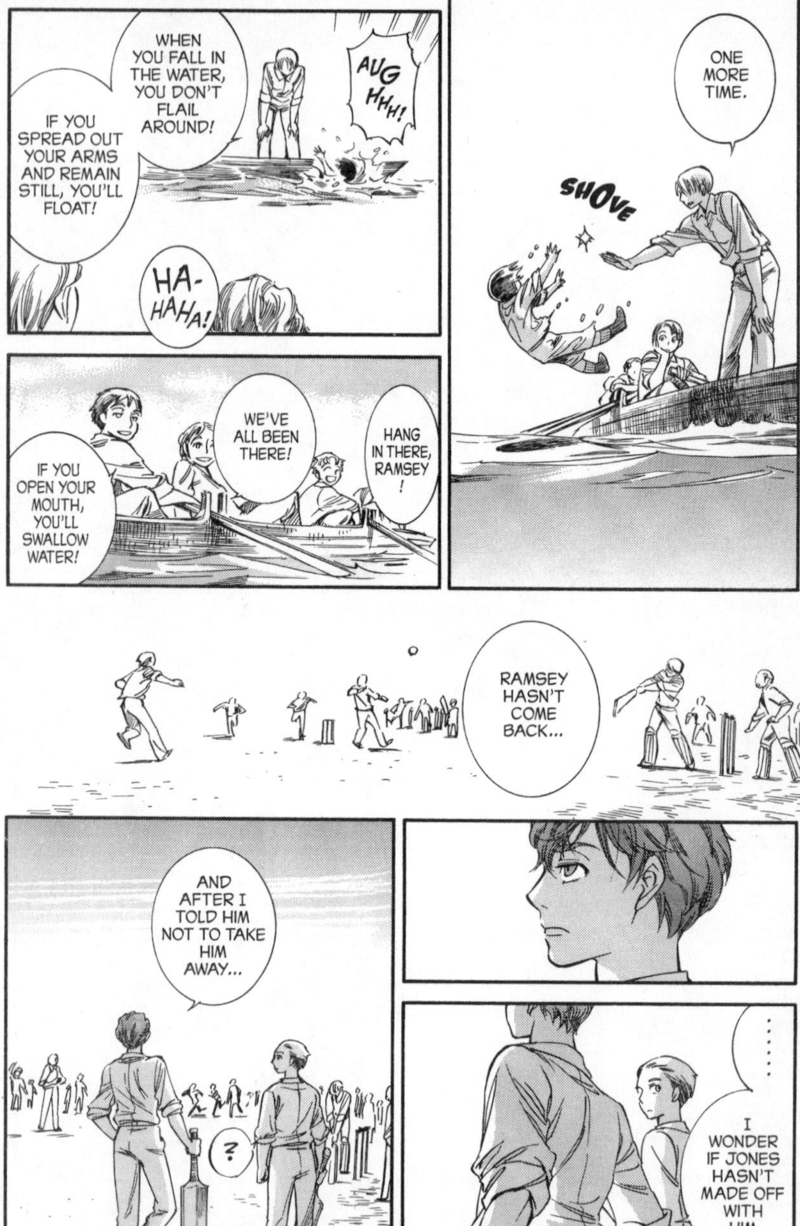
ONE MORE TIME.
SHOVE
AUGHHH!
WHEN YOU FALL IN THE WATER, YOU DON'T FLAIL AROUND!
IF YOU SPREAD OUT YOUR ARMS AND REMAIN STILL, YOU'LL FLOAT!
HA-HAHA!
HANG IN THERE, RAMSEY!
WE'VE ALL BEEN THERE!
IF YOU OPEN YOUR MOUTH, YOU'LL SWALLOW WATER!
RAMSEY HASN'T COME BACK...
......
I WONDER IF JONES HASN'T MADE OFF WITH HIM.
AND AFTER I TOLD HIM NOT TO TAKE HIM AWAY...
?

CHAPTER 16: THE FOLLOWING DAY

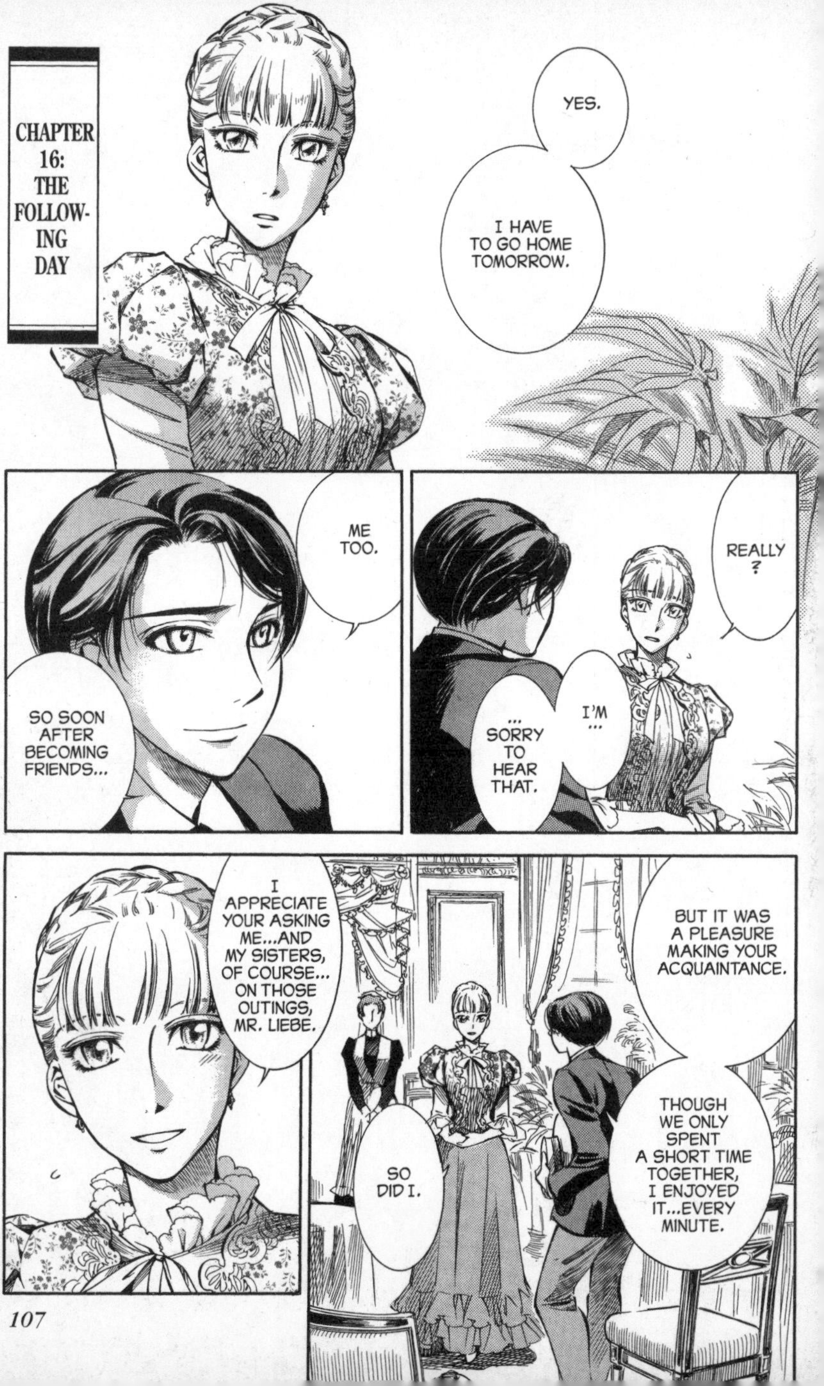
CHAPTER 16: THE FOLLOWING DAY
YES.
I HAVE TO GO HOME TOMORROW.
REALLY?
I'M...
...SORRY TO HEAR THAT.
ME TOO.
SO SOON AFTER BECOMING FRIENDS...
BUT IT WAS A PLEASURE MAKING YOUR ACQUAINTANCE.
THOUGH WE ONLY SPENT A SHORT TIME TOGETHER, I ENJOYED IT...EVERY MINUTE.
SO DID I.
I APPRECIATE YOUR ASKING ME...AND MY SISTERS, OF COURSE... ON THOSE OUTINGS, MR. LIEBE.

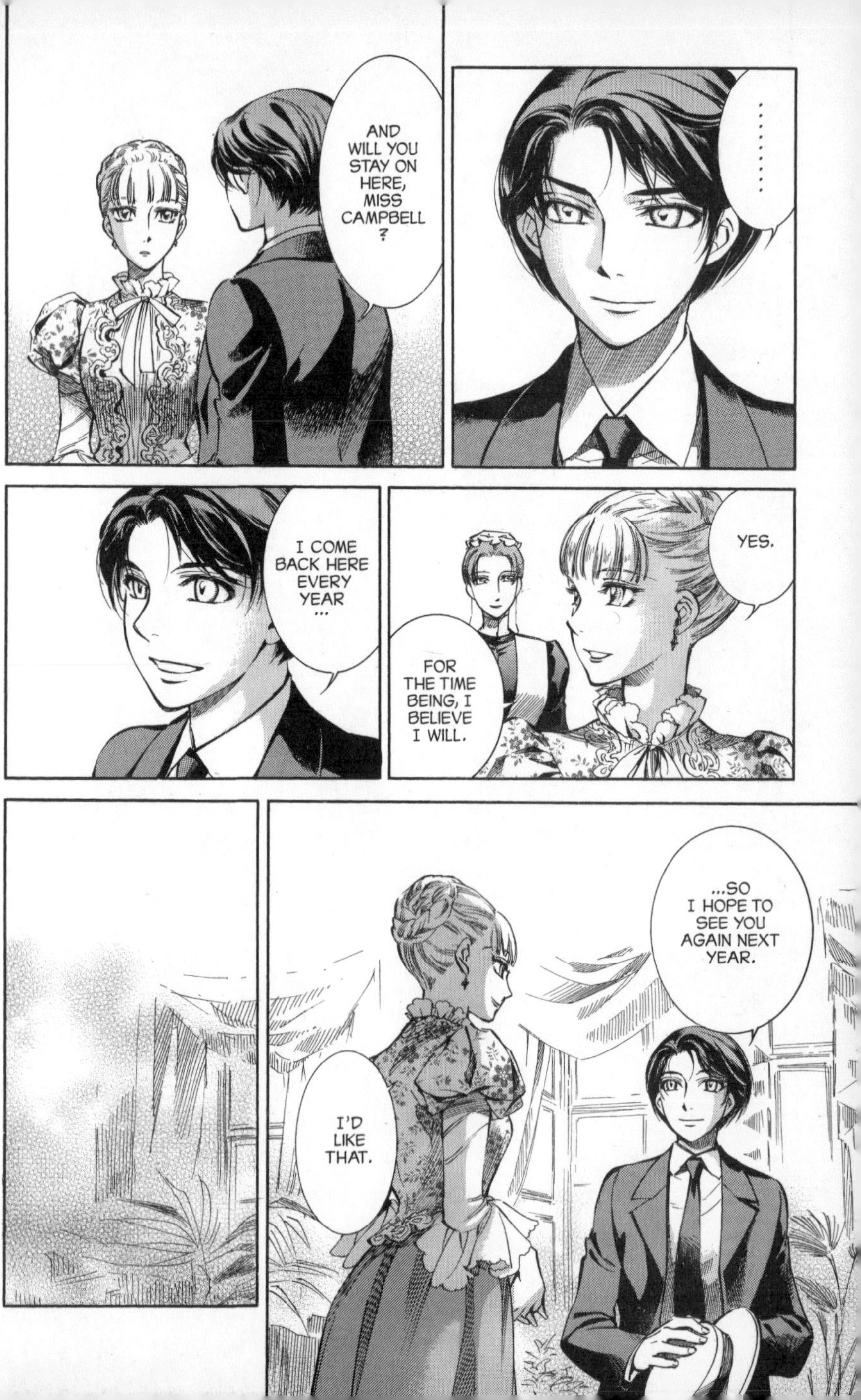
......
AND WILL YOU STAY ON HERE, MISS CAMPBELL?
YES.
FOR THE TIME BEING, I BELIEVE I WILL.
I COME BACK HERE EVERY YEAR...
...SO I HOPE TO SEE YOU AGAIN NEXT YEAR.
I'D LIKE THAT.

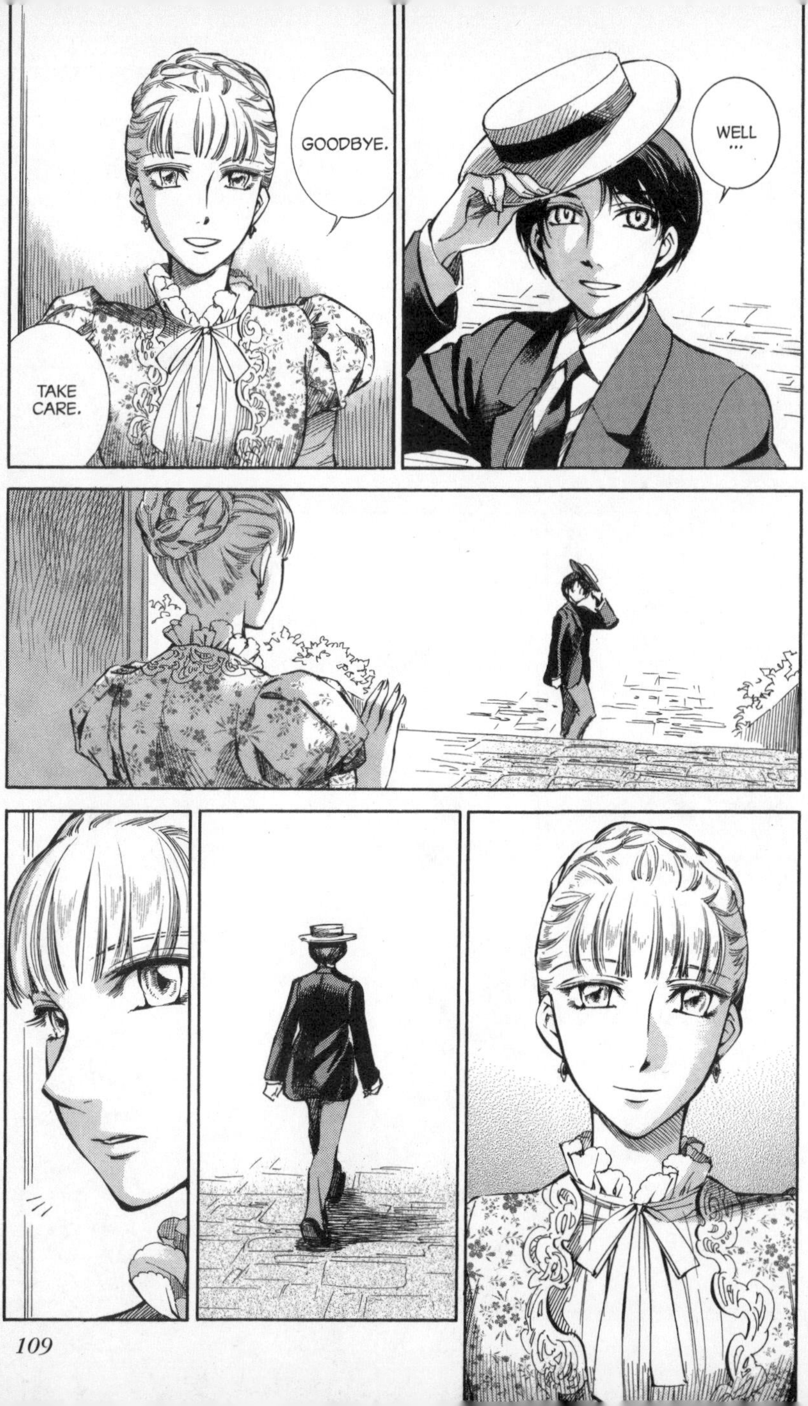
WELL ...
GOODBYE.
TAKE CARE.

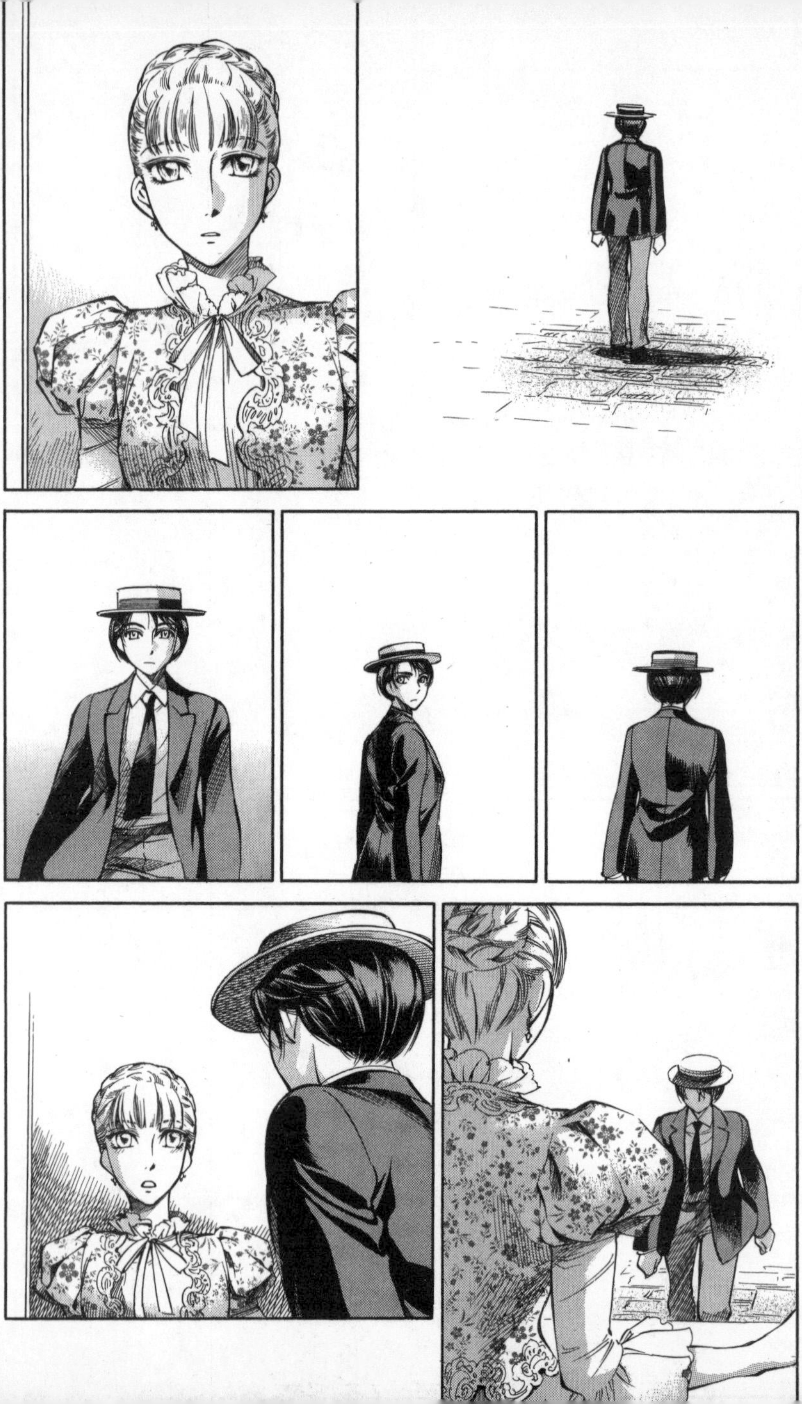

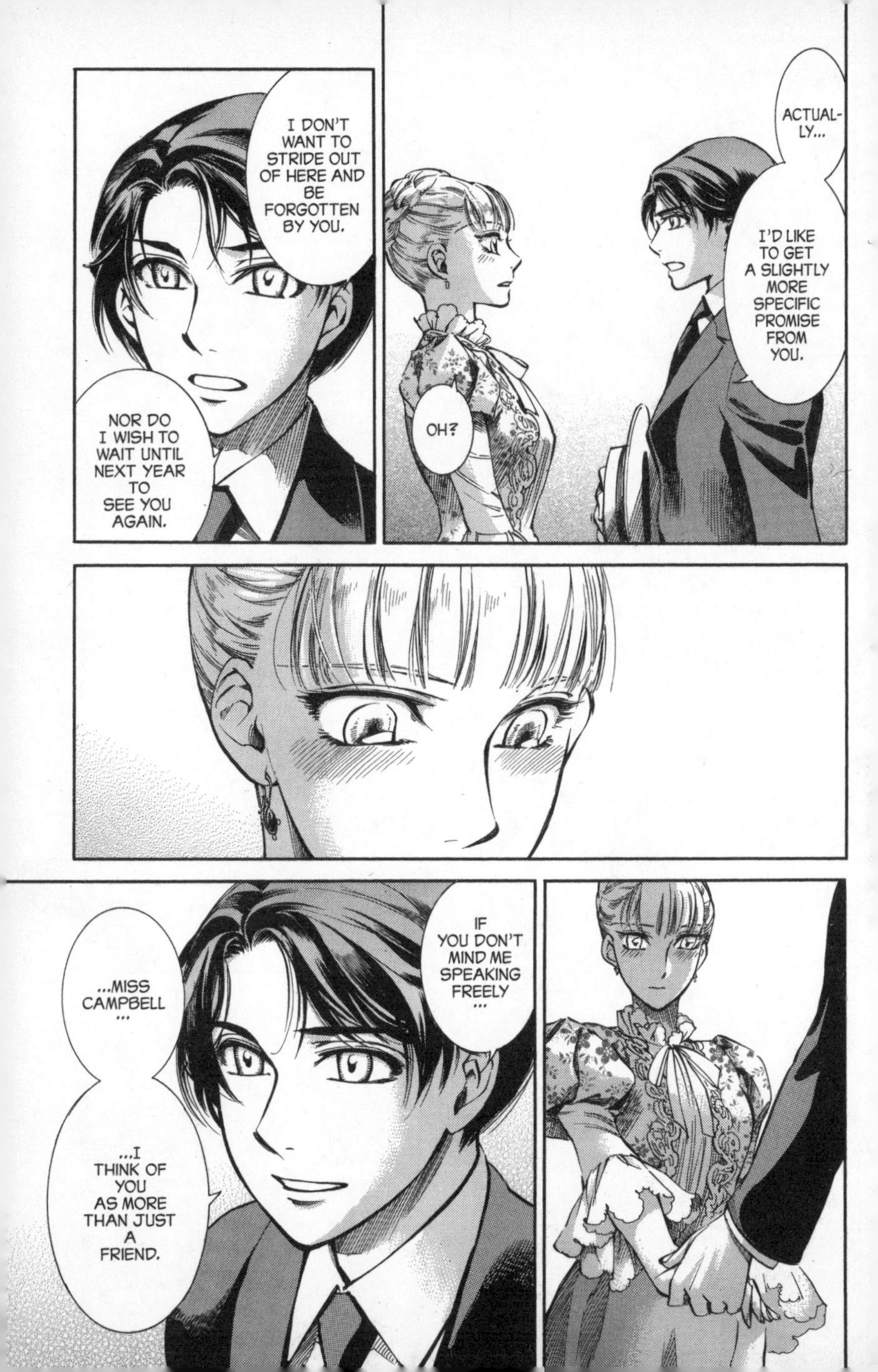
ACTUAL-LY...
I'D LIKE TO GET A SLIGHTLY MORE SPECIFIC PROMISE FROM YOU.
OH?
I DON'T WANT TO STRIDE OUT OF HERE AND BE FORGOTTEN BY YOU.
NOR DO I WISH TO WAIT UNTIL NEXT YEAR TO SEE YOU AGAIN.
IF YOU DON'T MIND ME SPEAKING FREELY...
...MISS CAMPBELL...
...I THINK OF YOU AS MORE THAN JUST A FRIEND.

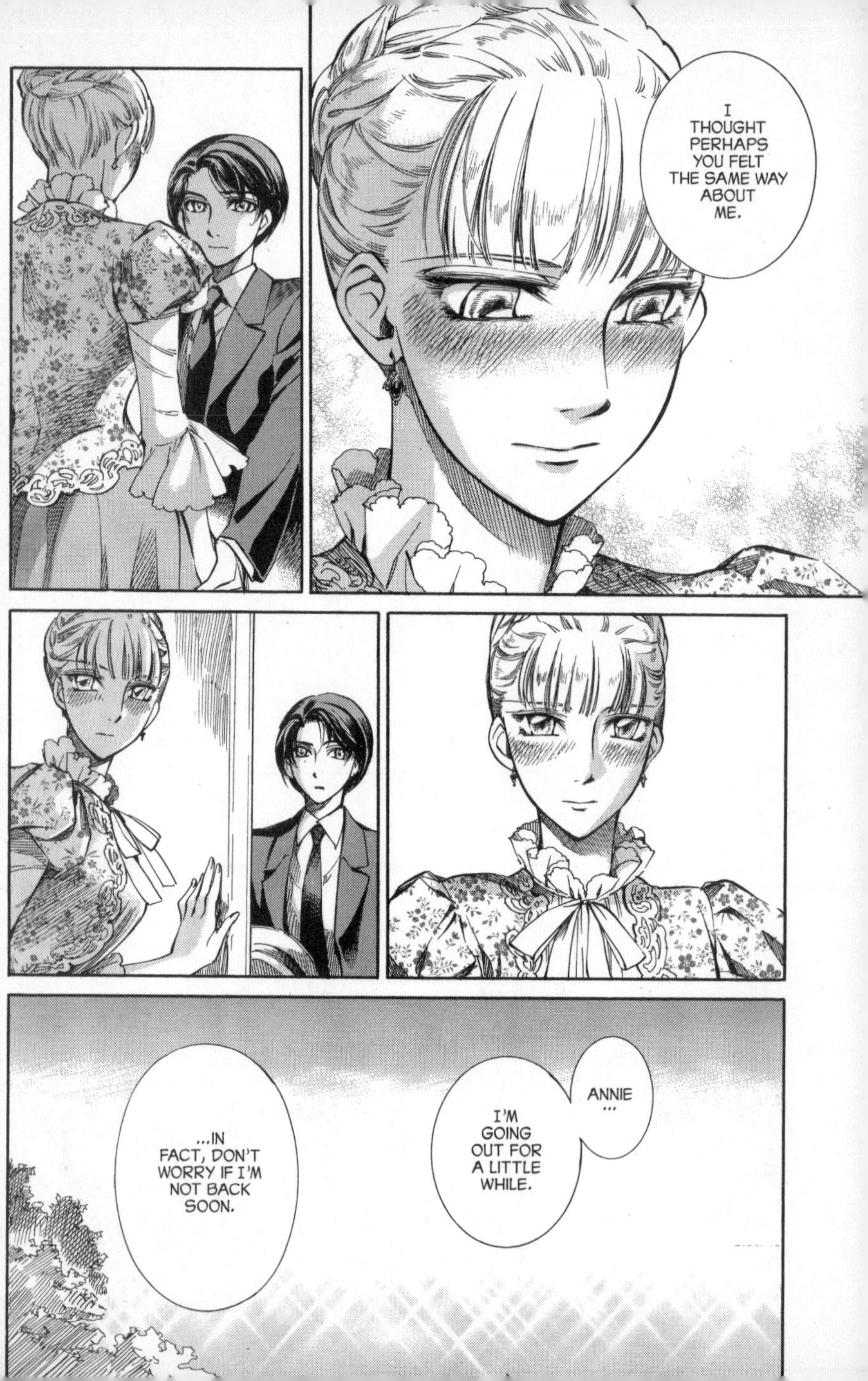
I THOUGHT PERHAPS YOU FELT THE SAME WAY ABOUT ME.
ANNIE ...
I'M GOING OUT FOR A LITTLE WHILE.
...IN FACT, DON'T WORRY IF I'M NOT BACK SOON.

CHAPTER
17:
HAPPY
DAYS
FOREVER

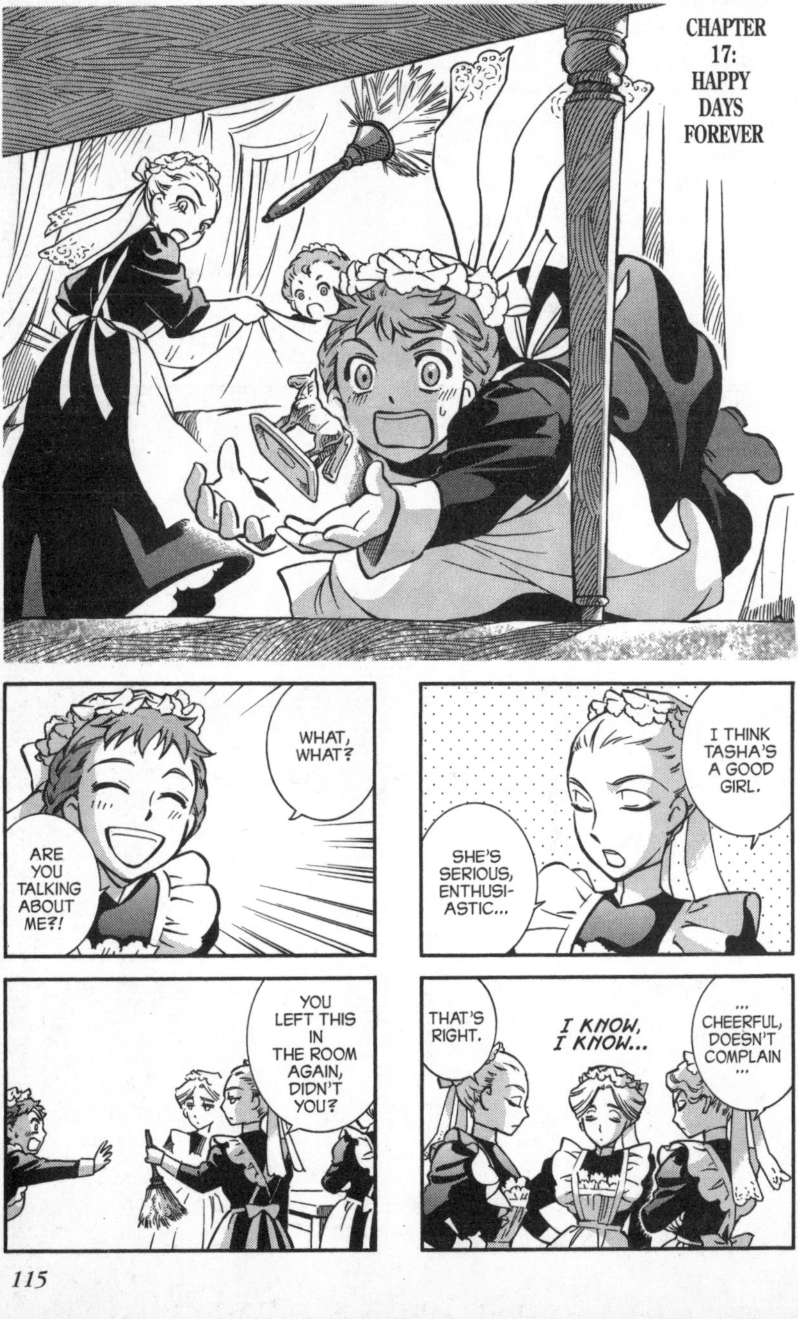
CHAPTER 17: HAPPY DAYS FOREVER
I THINK TASHA'S A GOOD GIRL.
SHE'S SERIOUS, ENTHUSI-ASTIC...
WHAT, WHAT?
ARE YOU TALKING ABOUT ME?!
... CHEERFUL, DOESN'T COMPLAIN ...
I KNOW, I KNOW...
THAT'S RIGHT.
YOU LEFT THIS IN THE ROOM AGAIN, DIDN'T YOU?

....

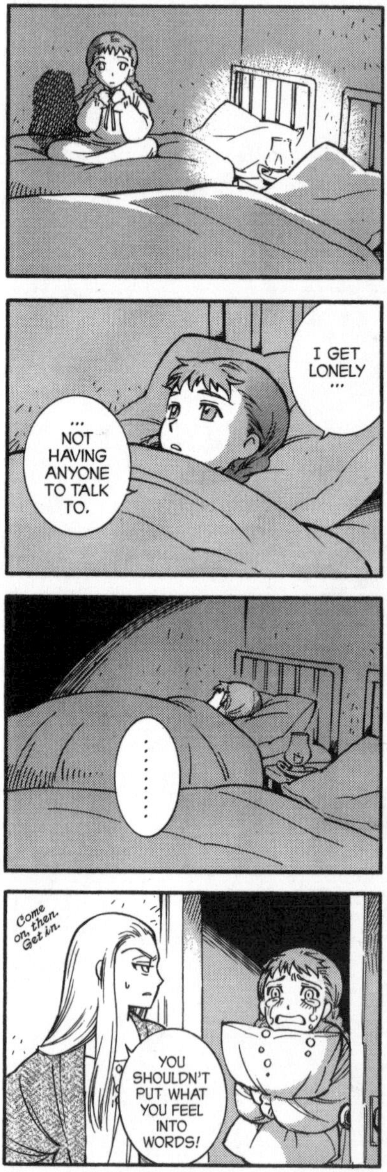
I GET LONELY ...
... NOT HAVING ANYONE TO TALK TO.
....
Come on, then. Get in.
YOU SHOULDN'T PUT WHAT YOU FEEL INTO WORDS!

I'M SORRY...

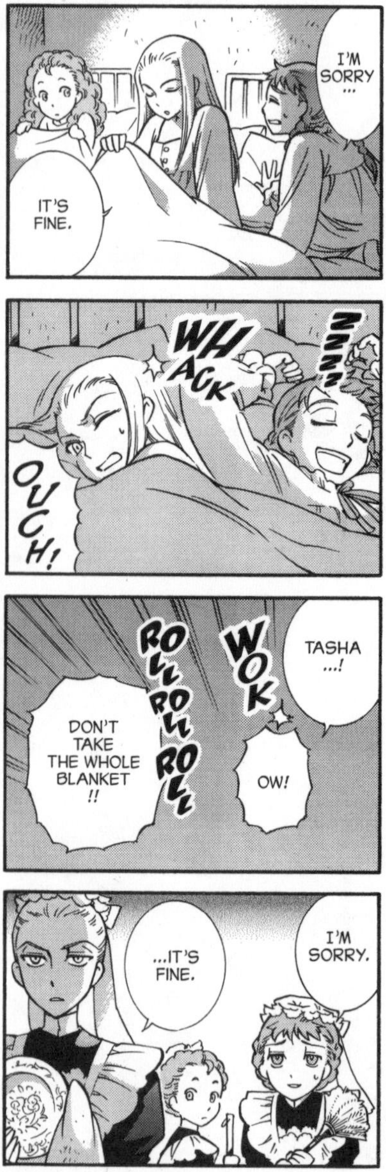
I'M SORRY ...
IT'S FINE.
ZZZZ
WHACK
OUCH!
TASHA ...!
WOK
OW!
ROLL ROLL ROLL
DON'T TAKE THE WHOLE BLANKET !!
I'M SORRY.
...IT'S FINE.

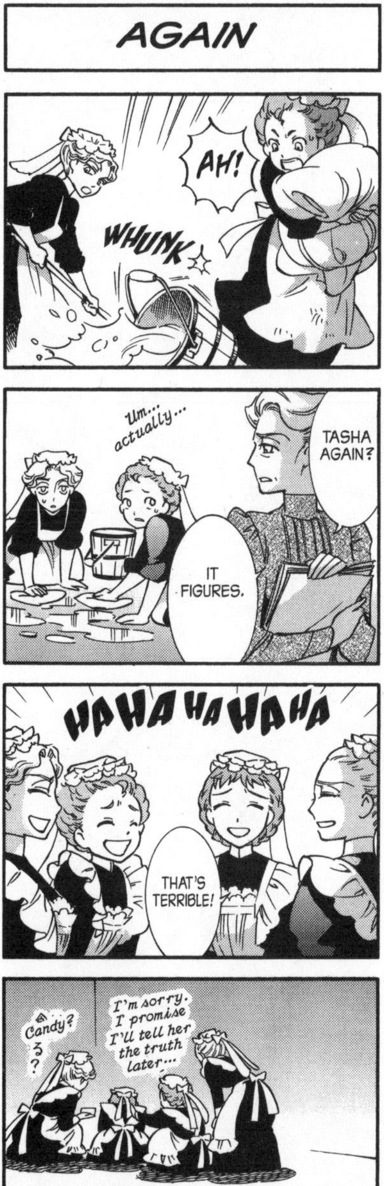
AGAIN
AH!
WHUNK
TASHA AGAIN?
Um... actually...
IT FIGURES.
HAHA HA HAHA
THAT'S TERRIBLE!
I'm sorry. I promise I'll tell her the truth later...
Candy?

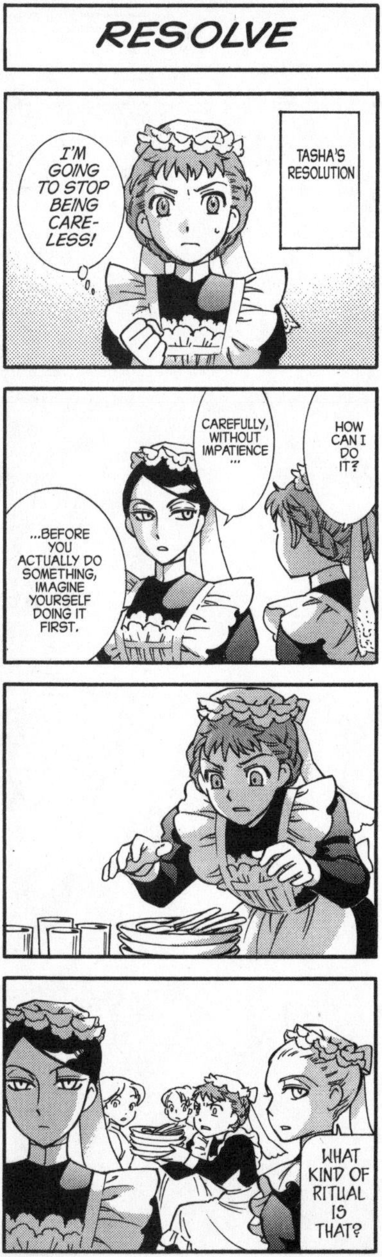
RESOLVE
TASHA'S RESOLUTION
I'M GOING TO STOP BEING CARE-LESS!
HOW CAN I DO IT?
CAREFULLY, WITHOUT IMPATIENCE...
...BEFORE YOU ACTUALLY DO SOMETHING, IMAGINE YOURSELF DOING IT FIRST.
WHAT KIND OF RITUAL IS THAT?

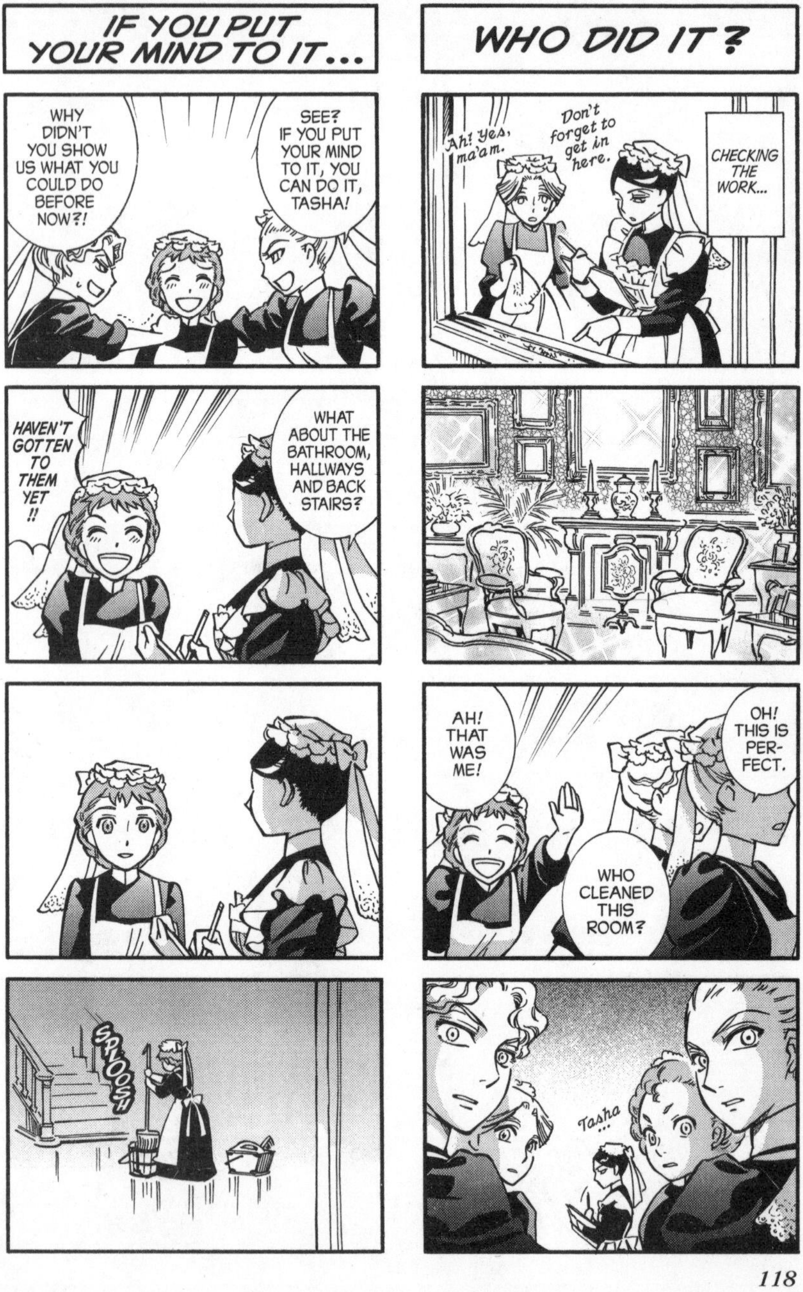
WHO DID IT?
CHECKING THE WORK...
Don't forget to get in here.
Ah! yes, ma'am.
OH! THIS IS PERFECT.
WHO CLEANED THIS ROOM?
AH! THAT WAS ME!
Tasha...
IF YOU PUT YOUR MIND TO IT...
SEE? IF YOU PUT YOUR MIND TO IT, YOU CAN DO IT, TASHA!
WHY DIDN'T YOU SHOW US WHAT YOU COULD DO BEFORE NOW?!
WHAT ABOUT THE BATHROOM, HALLWAYS AND BACK STAIRS?
HAVEN'T GOTTEN TO THEM YET!!
SPLOOSH

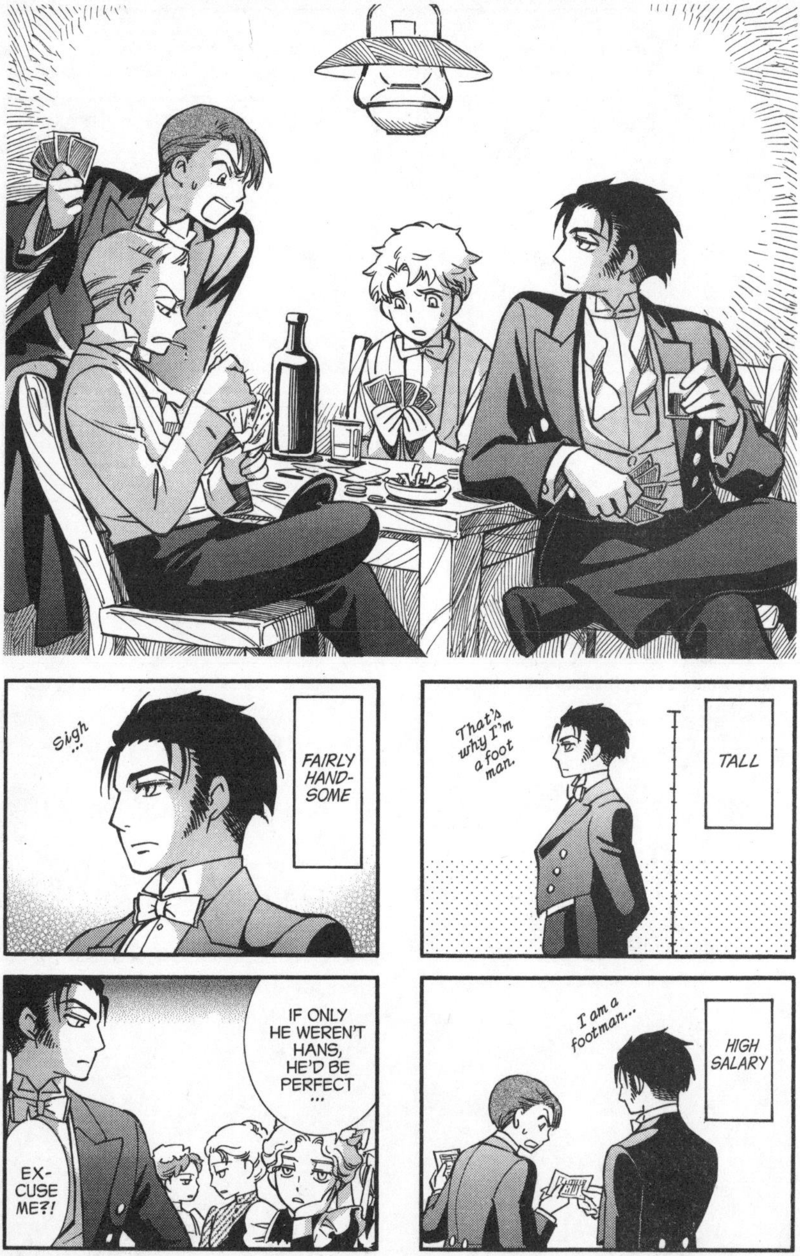
TALL
That's why I'm a foot man.
FAIRLY HAND-SOME
Sigh ...
HIGH SALARY
I am a footman...
IF ONLY HE WEREN'T HANS, HE'D BE PERFECT ...
EX-CUSE ME?!

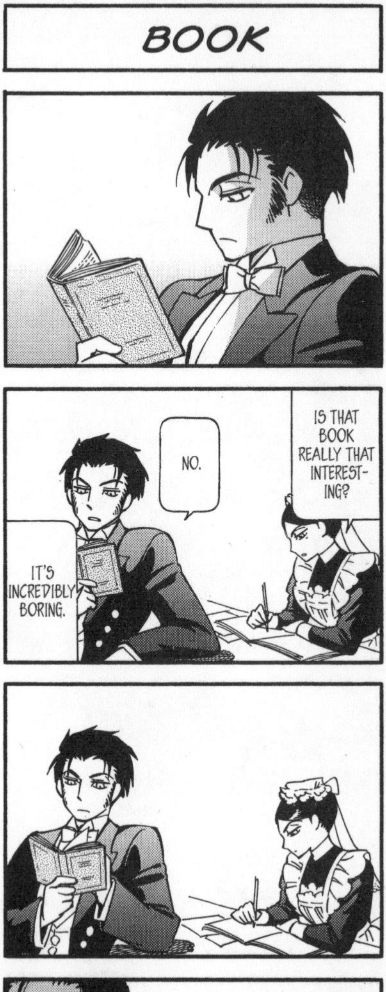
BOOK
IS THAT BOOK REALLY THAT INTEREST-ING?
NO.
IT'S INCREDIBLY BORING.
RUSTLE

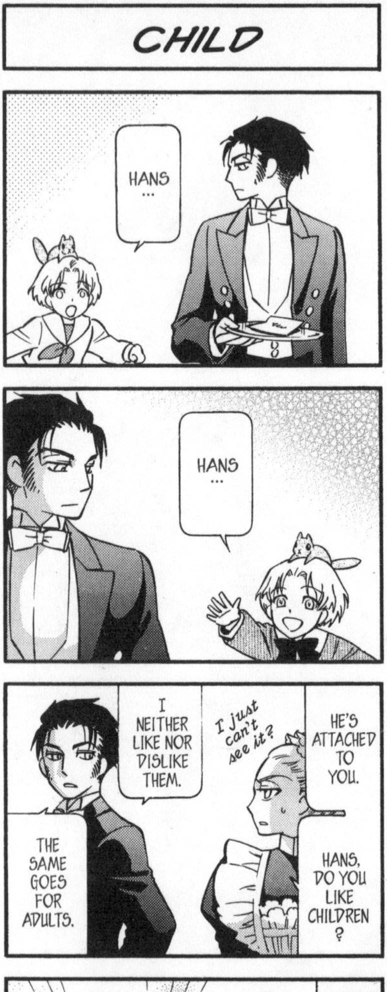
CHILD
HANS ...
HANS ...
HE'S ATTACHED TO YOU.
HANS, DO YOU LIKE CHILDREN?
I NEITHER LIKE NOR DISLIKE THEM.
THE SAME GOES FOR ADULTS.
I just can't see it?
I THINK I SEE WHY HE LIKES HANS...
What's wrong, Master Erich?
What are you angry about?

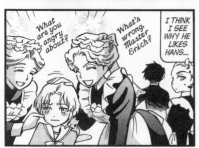

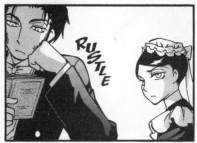

INSURANCE

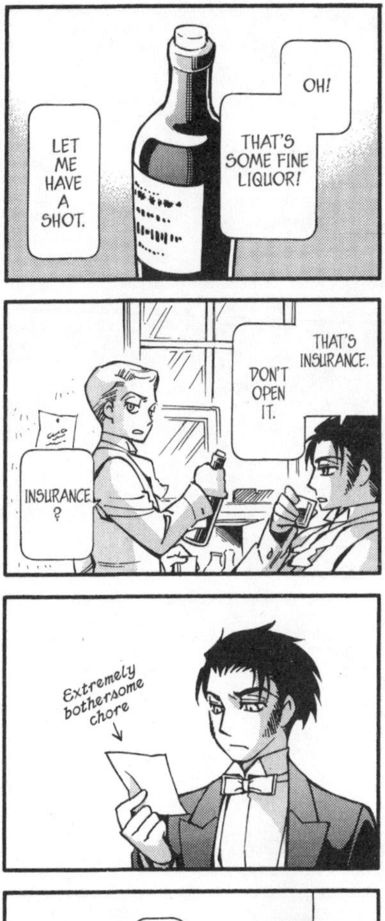
OH!
THAT'S SOME FINE LIQUOR!
LET ME HAVE A SHOT.
THAT'S INSURANCE.
DON'T OPEN IT.
INSURANCE?
Extremely bothersome chore
PLEASE.
....
THAT'LL COST YOU ONE BOTTLE.

NOTHING

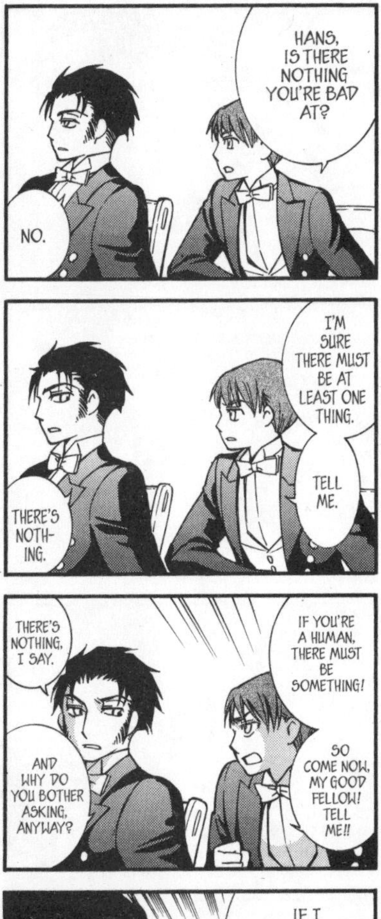
HANS, IS THERE NOTHING YOU'RE BAD AT?
NO.
I'M SURE THERE MUST BE AT LEAST ONE THING.
TELL ME.
THERE'S NOTHING.
IF YOU'RE A HUMAN, THERE MUST BE SOMETHING!
SO COME NOW, MY GOOD FELLOW! TELL ME!!
THERE'S NOTHING, I SAY.
AND WHY DO YOU BOTHER ASKING, ANYWAY?
IF I FIND YOUR WEAKNESS, I CAN EXPLOIT IT LATER! OF COURSE!
AND I TELL YOU, I HAVE NO WEAKNESS!

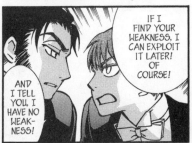

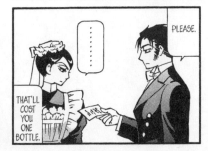

TELL ME

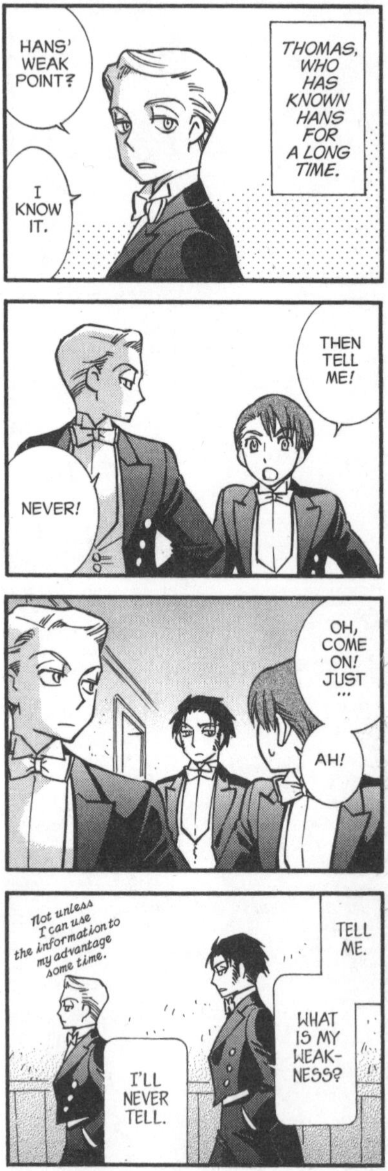
THOMAS, WHO HAS KNOWN HANS FOR A LONG TIME.
HANS' WEAK POINT?
I KNOW IT.
THEN TELL ME!
NEVER!
OH, COME ON! JUST ...
AH!
TELL ME.
WHAT IS MY WEAKNESS?
Not unless I can use the information to my advantage some time.
I'LL NEVER TELL.

WEAKNESS

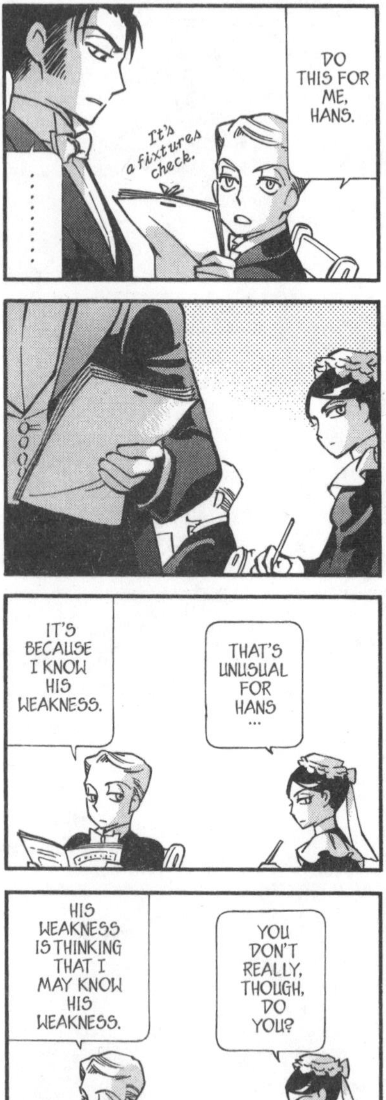
DO THIS FOR ME, HANS.
It's a fixtures check.
......
THAT'S UNUSUAL FOR HANS ...
IT'S BECAUSE I KNOW HIS WEAKNESS.
YOU DON'T REALLY, THOUGH, DO YOU?
HIS WEAKNESS IS THINKING THAT I MAY KNOW HIS WEAKNESS.

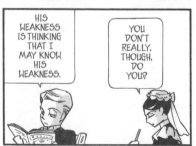

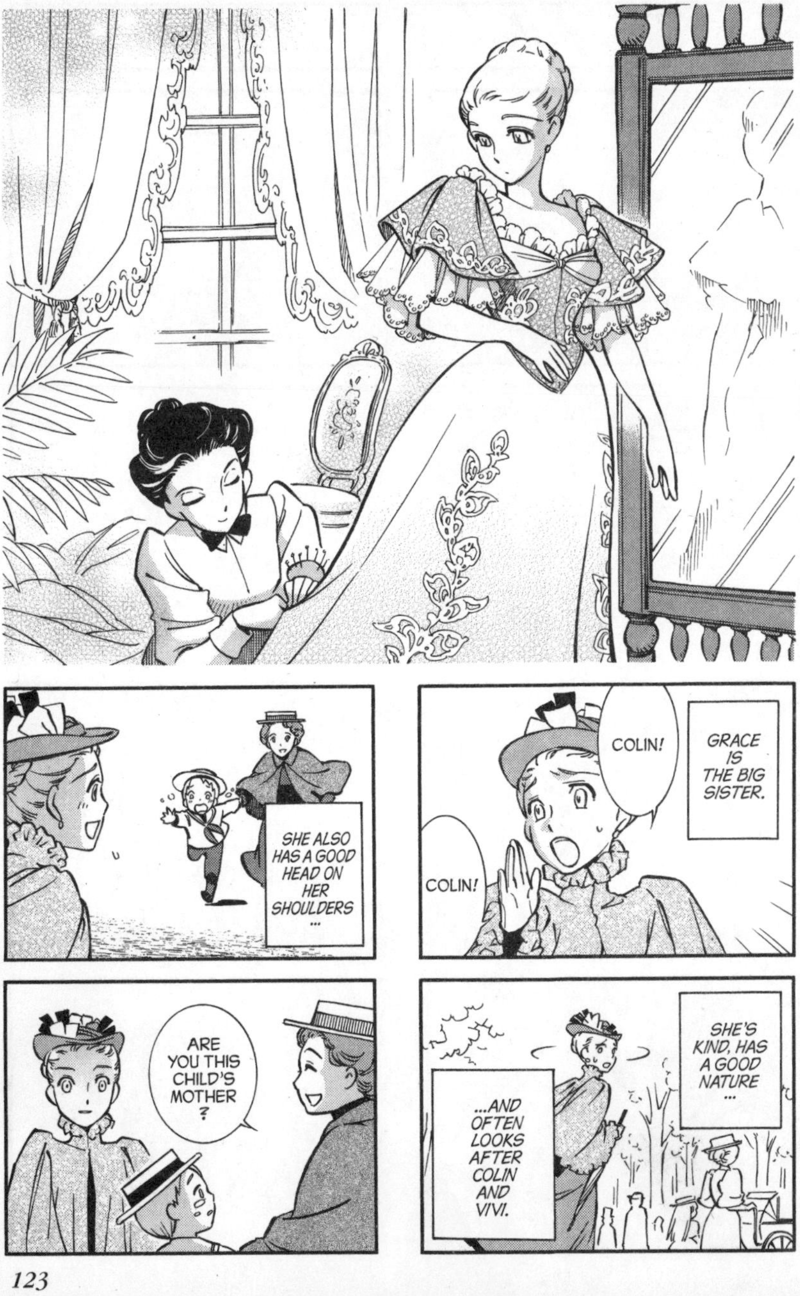
GRACE IS THE BIG SISTER.
COLIN!
COLIN!
SHE ALSO HAS A GOOD HEAD ON HER SHOULDERS ...
SHE'S KIND, HAS A GOOD NATURE ...
...AND OFTEN LOOKS AFTER COLIN AND VIVI.
ARE YOU THIS CHILD'S MOTHER?

HAIRSTYLE

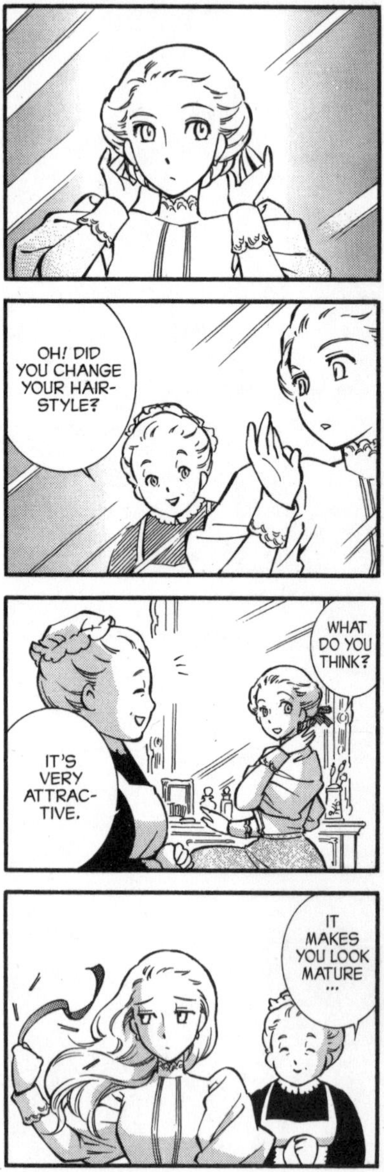
OH! DID YOU CHANGE YOUR HAIR-STYLE?
WHAT DO YOU THINK?
IT'S VERY ATTRACTIVE.
IT MAKES YOU LOOK MATURE ...

NOT THE WAY YOU LOOK

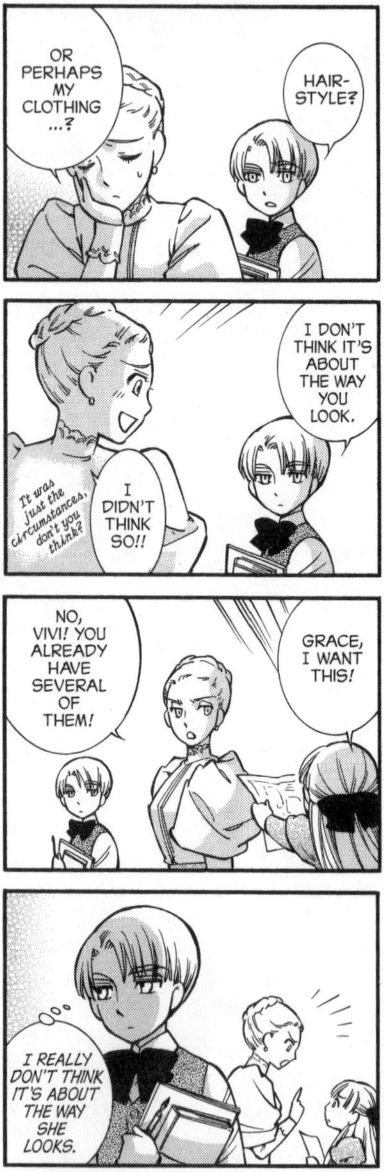
HAIR-STYLE?
OR PERHAPS MY CLOTHING ...?
I DON'T THINK IT'S ABOUT THE WAY YOU LOOK.
I DIDN'T THINK SO!!
It was just the circumstances, don't you think?
GRACE, I WANT THIS!
NO, VIVI! YOU ALREADY HAVE SEVERAL OF THEM!
I REALLY DON'T THINK IT'S ABOUT THE WAY SHE LOOKS.

DRAW

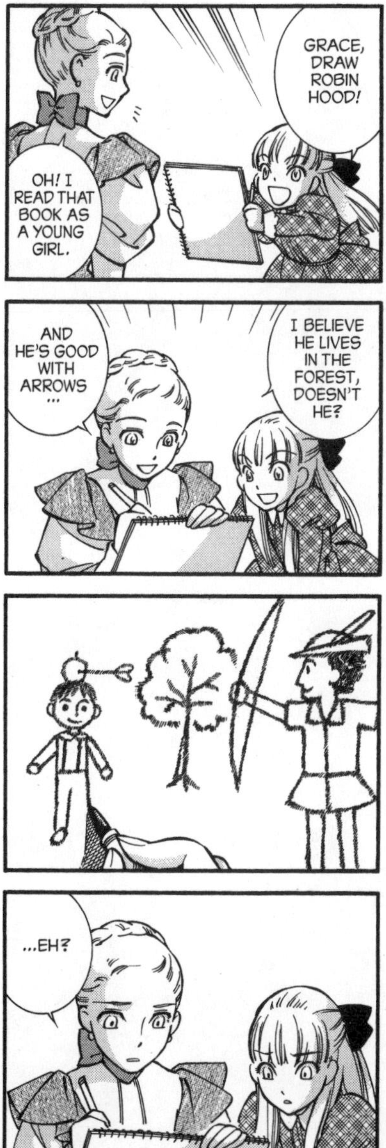
GRACE, DRAW ROBIN HOOD!
OH! I READ THAT BOOK AS A YOUNG GIRL.
I BELIEVE HE LIVES IN THE FOREST, DOESN'T HE?
AND HE'S GOOD WITH ARROWS ...
...EH?

BIRDCAGE

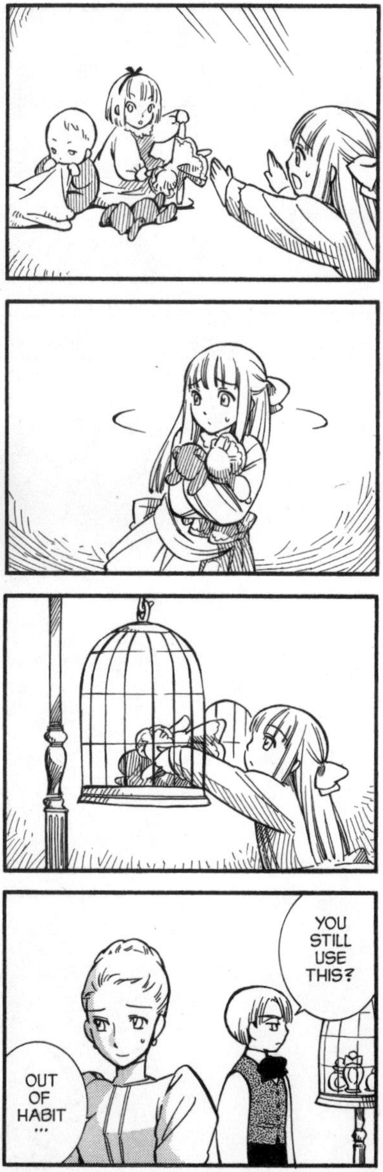
YOU STILL USE THIS?
OUT OF HABIT ...

EH?

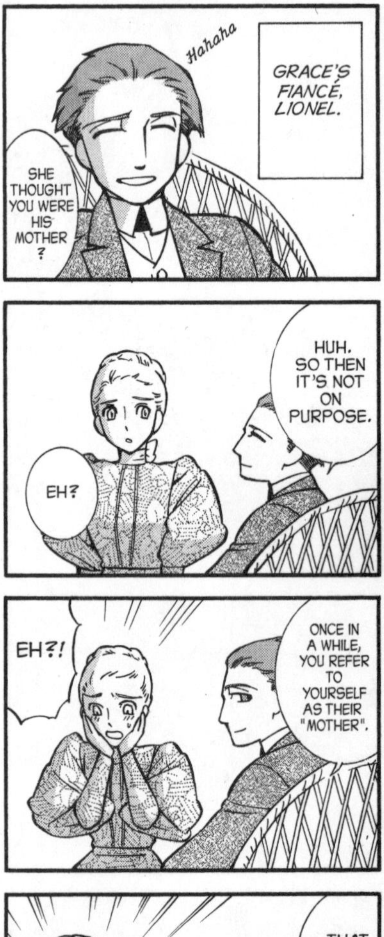
GRACE'S FIANCÉ, LIONEL.
Hahaha
SHE THOUGHT YOU WERE HIS MOTHER?
HUH. SO THEN IT'S NOT ON PURPOSE.
EH?
ONCE IN A WHILE, YOU REFER TO YOURSELF AS THEIR "MOTHER".
EH?!
...THAT WAS A JOKE.
EH?!

WHY?

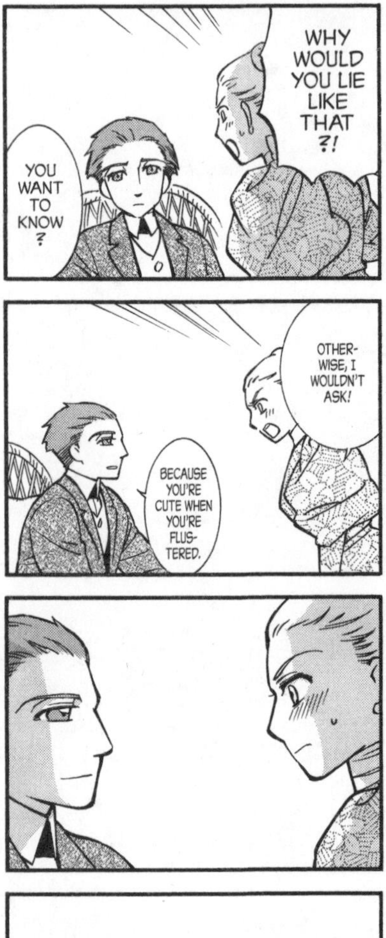
WHY WOULD YOU LIE LIKE THAT?!
YOU WANT TO KNOW?
OTHER-WISE, I WOULDN'T ASK!
BECAUSE YOU'RE CUTE WHEN YOU'RE FLUS-TERED.

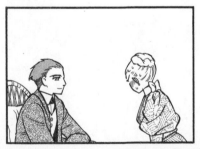

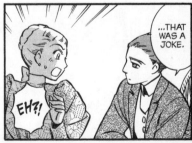

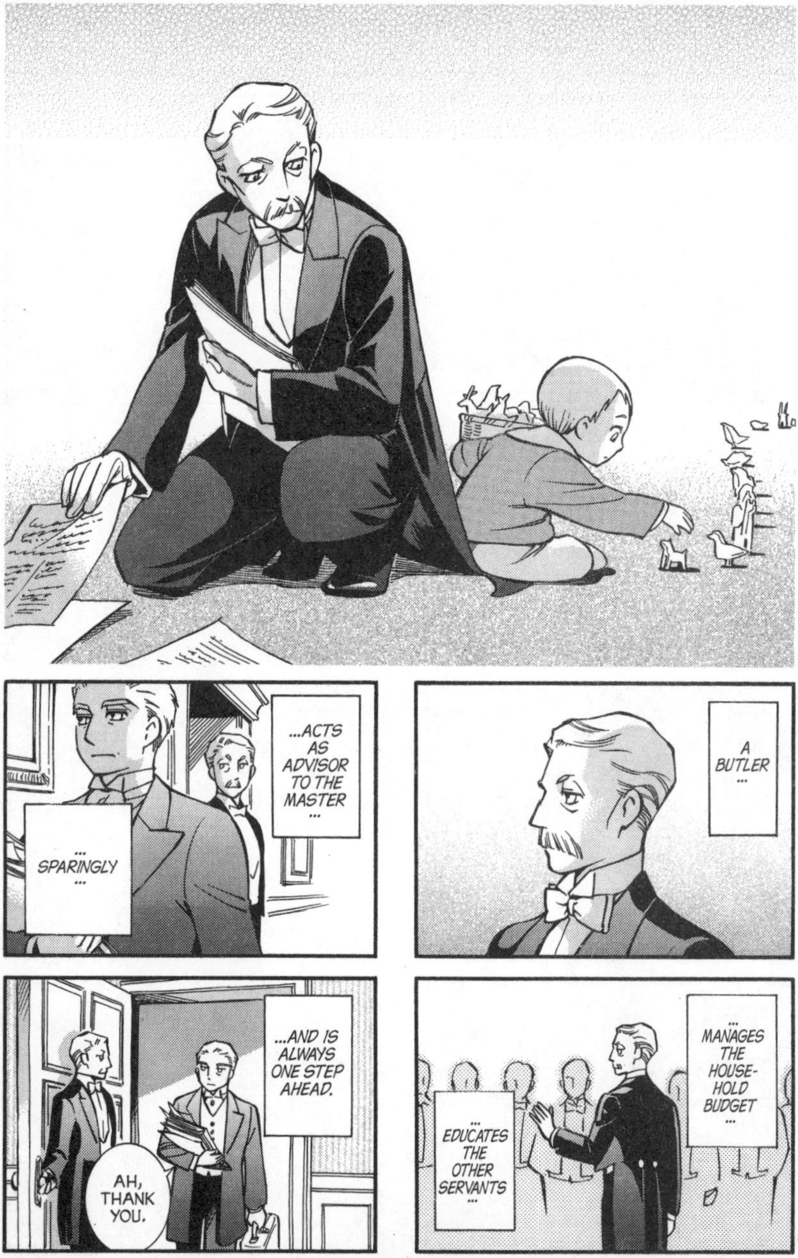
A BUTLER ...
...ACTS AS ADVISOR TO THE MASTER ...
... SPARINGLY ...
... MANAGES THE HOUSE-HOLD BUDGET ...
... EDUCATES THE OTHER SERVANTS ...
...AND IS ALWAYS ONE STEP AHEAD.
AH, THANK YOU.

CHAIR

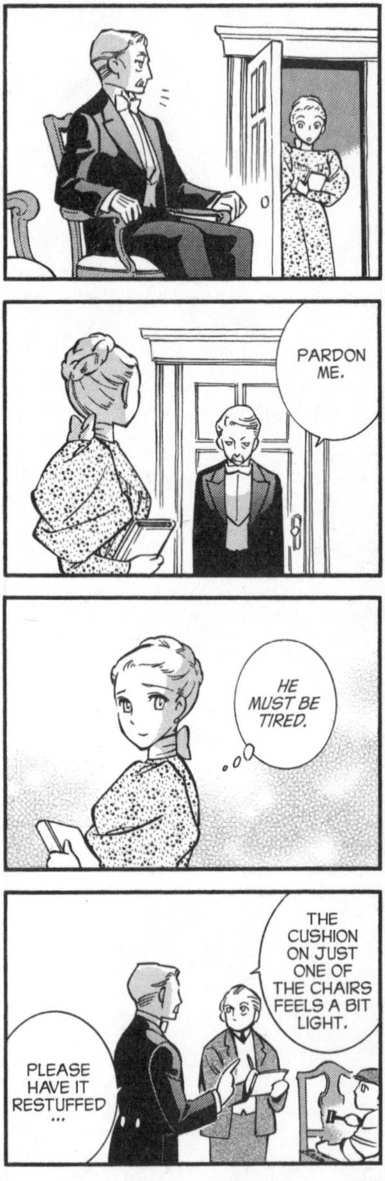
PARDON ME.
HE MUST BE TIRED.
THE CUSHION ON JUST ONE OF THE CHAIRS FEELS A BIT LIGHT.
PLEASE HAVE IT RESTUFFED ...

STEPHENS

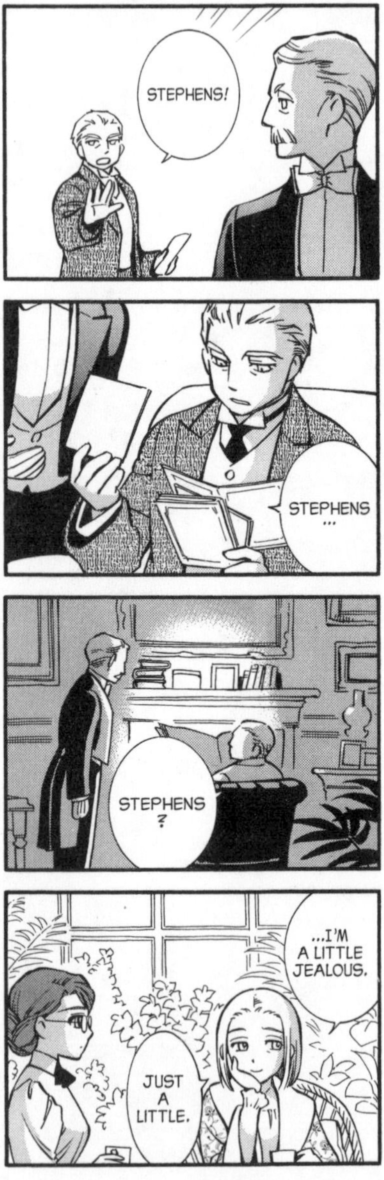
STEPHENS!
STEPHENS ...
STEPHENS ?
...I'M A LITTLE JEALOUS.
JUST A LITTLE.

BABY

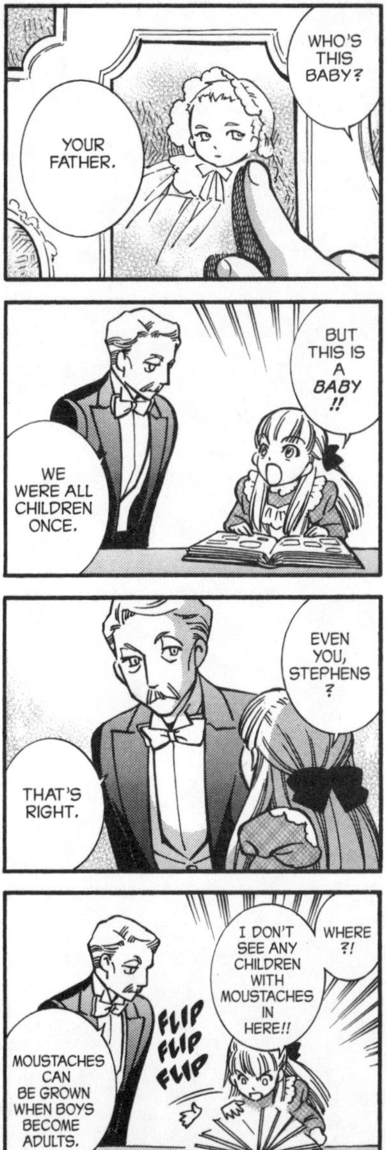
WHO'S THIS BABY?
YOUR FATHER.
BUT THIS IS A BABY!!
WE WERE ALL CHILDREN ONCE.
EVEN YOU, STEPHENS?
THAT'S RIGHT.
WHERE?!
I DON'T SEE ANY CHILDREN WITH MOUSTACHES IN HERE!!
FLIP FLIP FLIP
MOUSTACHES CAN BE GROWN WHEN BOYS BECOME ADULTS.

DRAWING

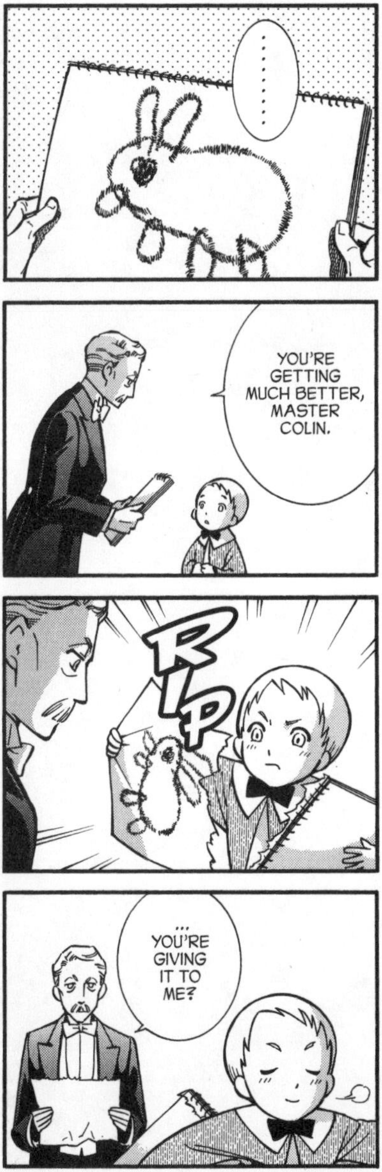
......
YOU'RE GETTING MUCH BETTER, MASTER COLIN.
RIP
... YOU'RE GIVING IT TO ME?

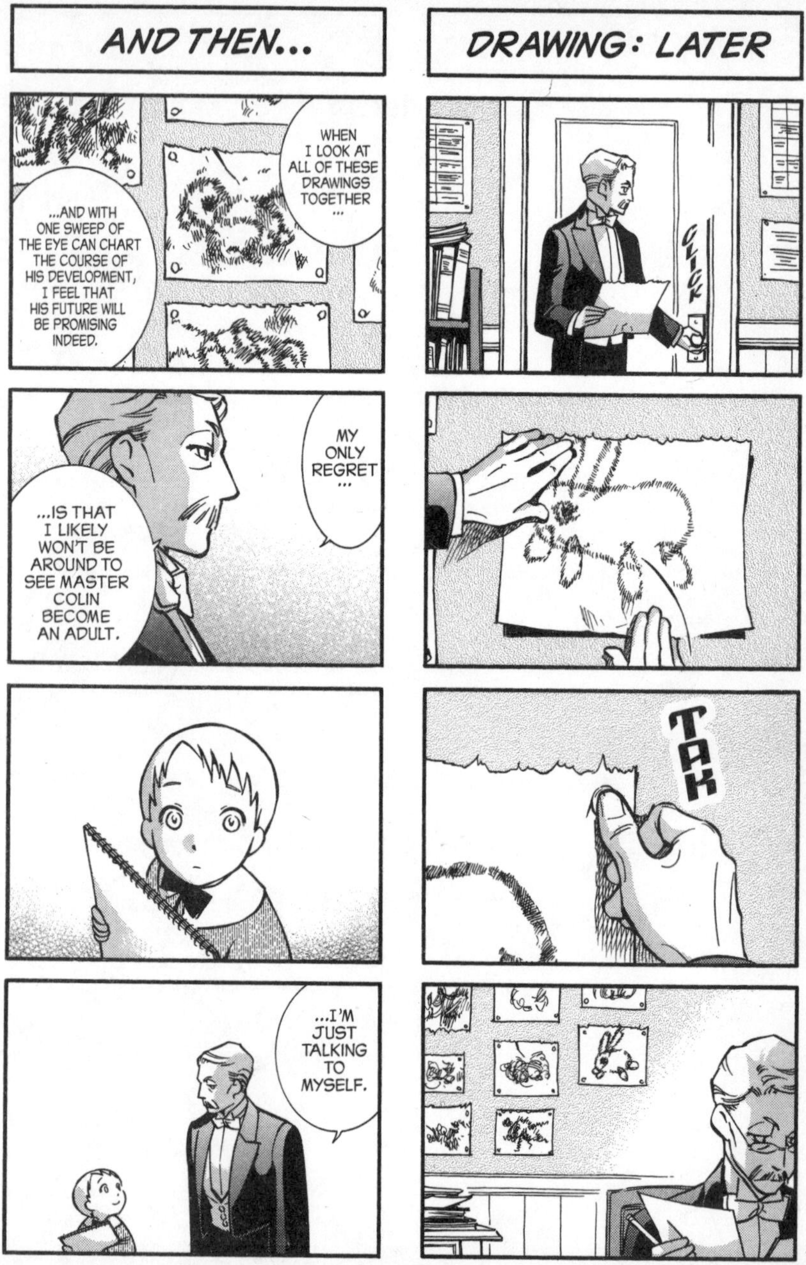
DRAWING : LATER
CLICK
TAK
AND THEN...
WHEN I LOOK AT ALL OF THESE DRAWINGS TOGETHER ...
...AND WITH ONE SWEEP OF THE EYE CAN CHART THE COURSE OF HIS DEVELOPMENT, I FEEL THAT HIS FUTURE WILL BE PROMISING INDEED.
MY ONLY REGRET ...
...IS THAT I LIKELY WON'T BE AROUND TO SEE MASTER COLIN BECOME AN ADULT.
...I'M JUST TALKING TO MYSELF.

**CHAPTER
18:
A
NEW
AGE
(part one)**

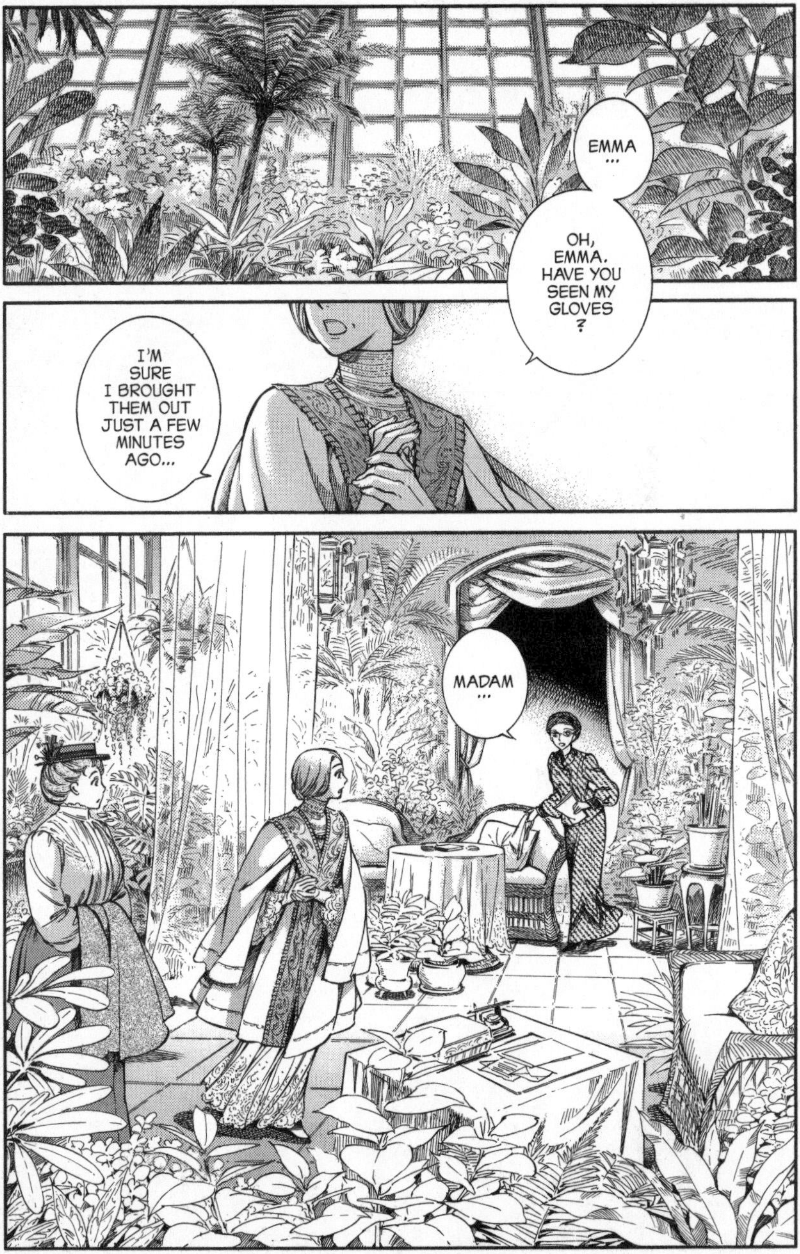
EMMA...
OH, EMMA. HAVE YOU SEEN MY GLOVES?
I'M SURE I BROUGHT THEM OUT JUST A FEW MINUTES AGO...
MADAM...

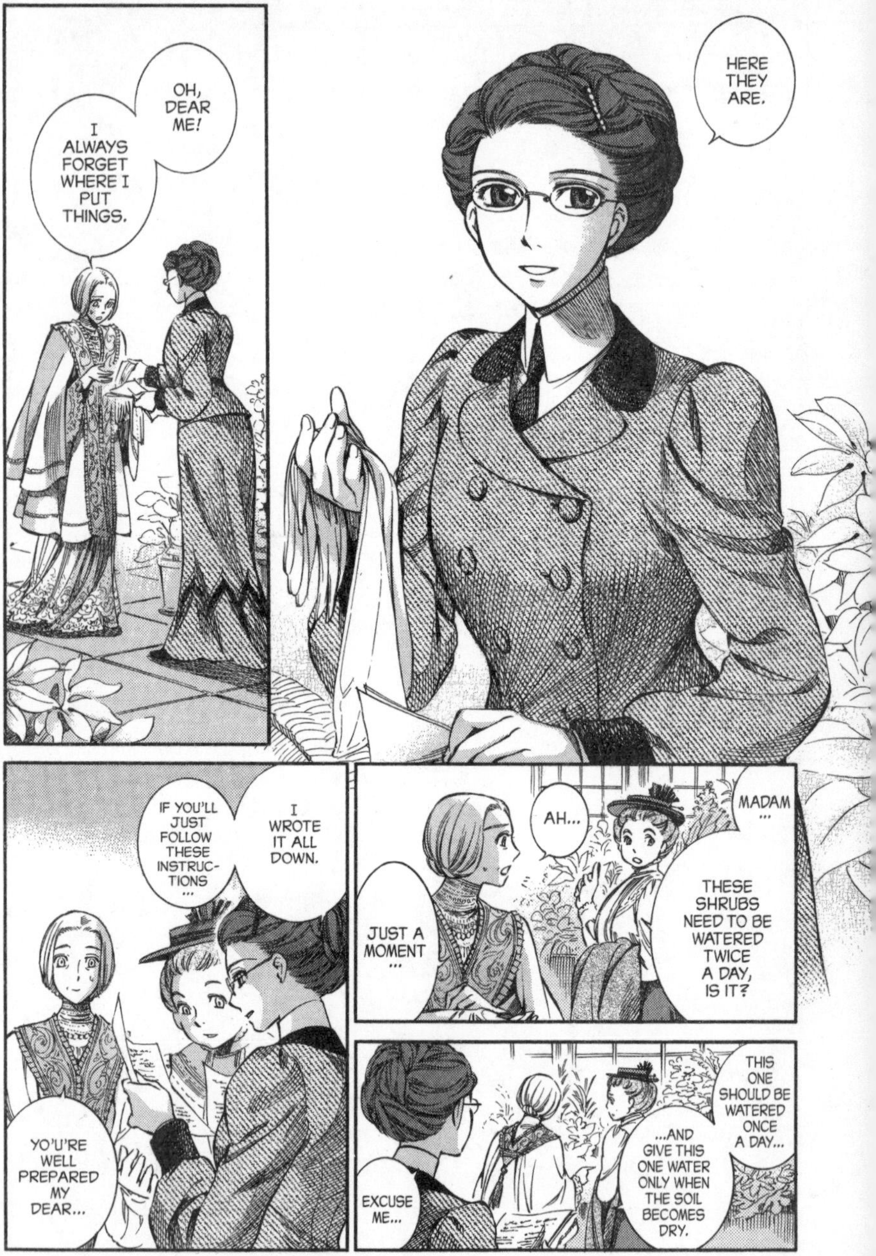
HERE THEY ARE.
OH, DEAR ME!
I ALWAYS FORGET WHERE I PUT THINGS.
MADAM...
THESE SHRUBS NEED TO BE WATERED TWICE A DAY, IS IT?
AH...
JUST A MOMENT...
THIS ONE SHOULD BE WATERED ONCE A DAY...
...AND GIVE THIS ONE WATER ONLY WHEN THE SOIL BECOMES DRY.
EXCUSE ME...
I WROTE IT ALL DOWN.
IF YOU'LL JUST FOLLOW THESE INSTRUC-TIONS...
YO'U'RE WELL PREPARED MY DEAR...

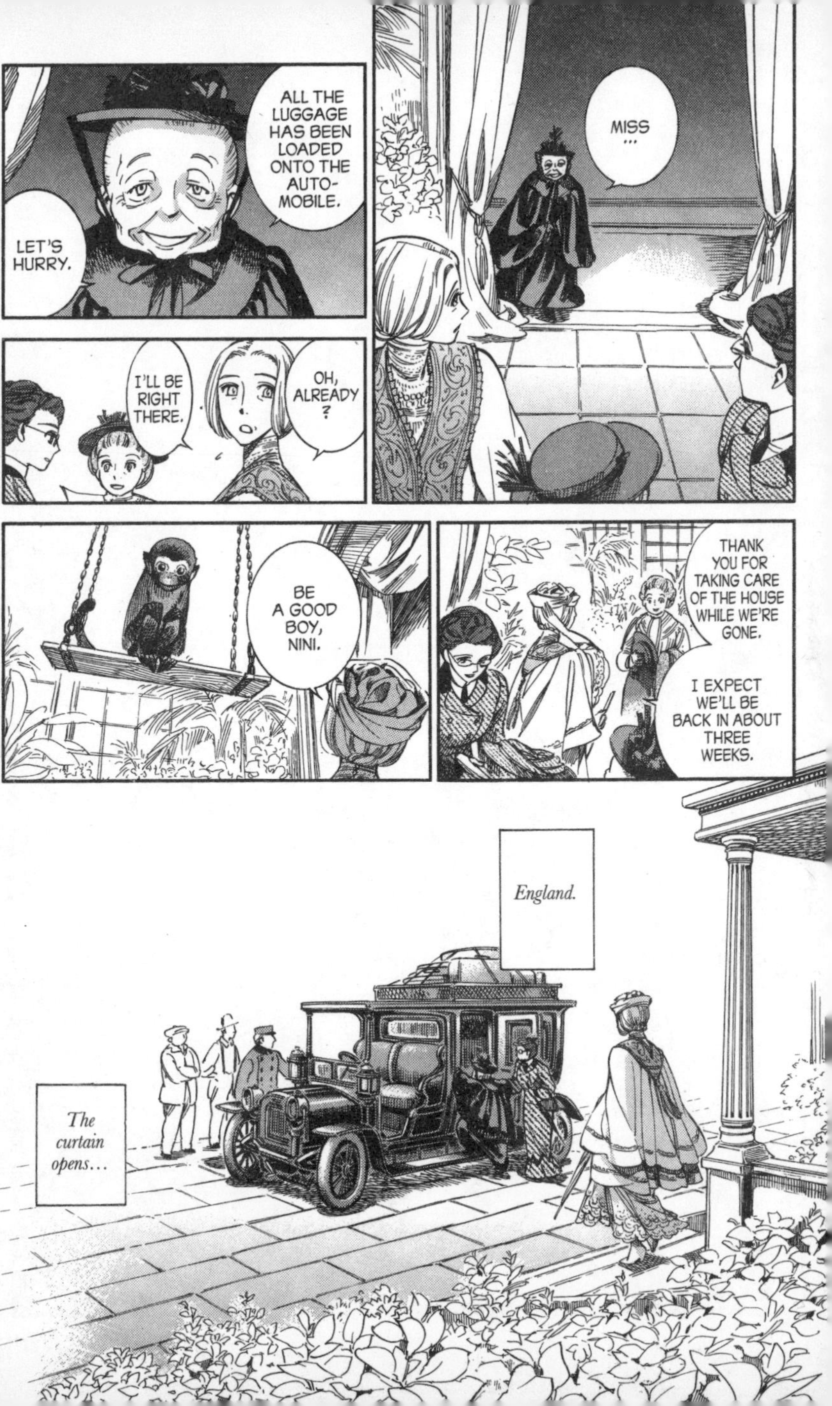
MISS ...
ALL THE LUGGAGE HAS BEEN LOADED ONTO THE AUTO-MOBILE.
LET'S HURRY.
OH, ALREADY?
I'LL BE RIGHT THERE.
THANK YOU FOR TAKING CARE OF THE HOUSE WHILE WE'RE GONE.
I EXPECT WE'LL BE BACK IN ABOUT THREE WEEKS.
BE A GOOD BOY, NINI.
England.
The curtain opens...

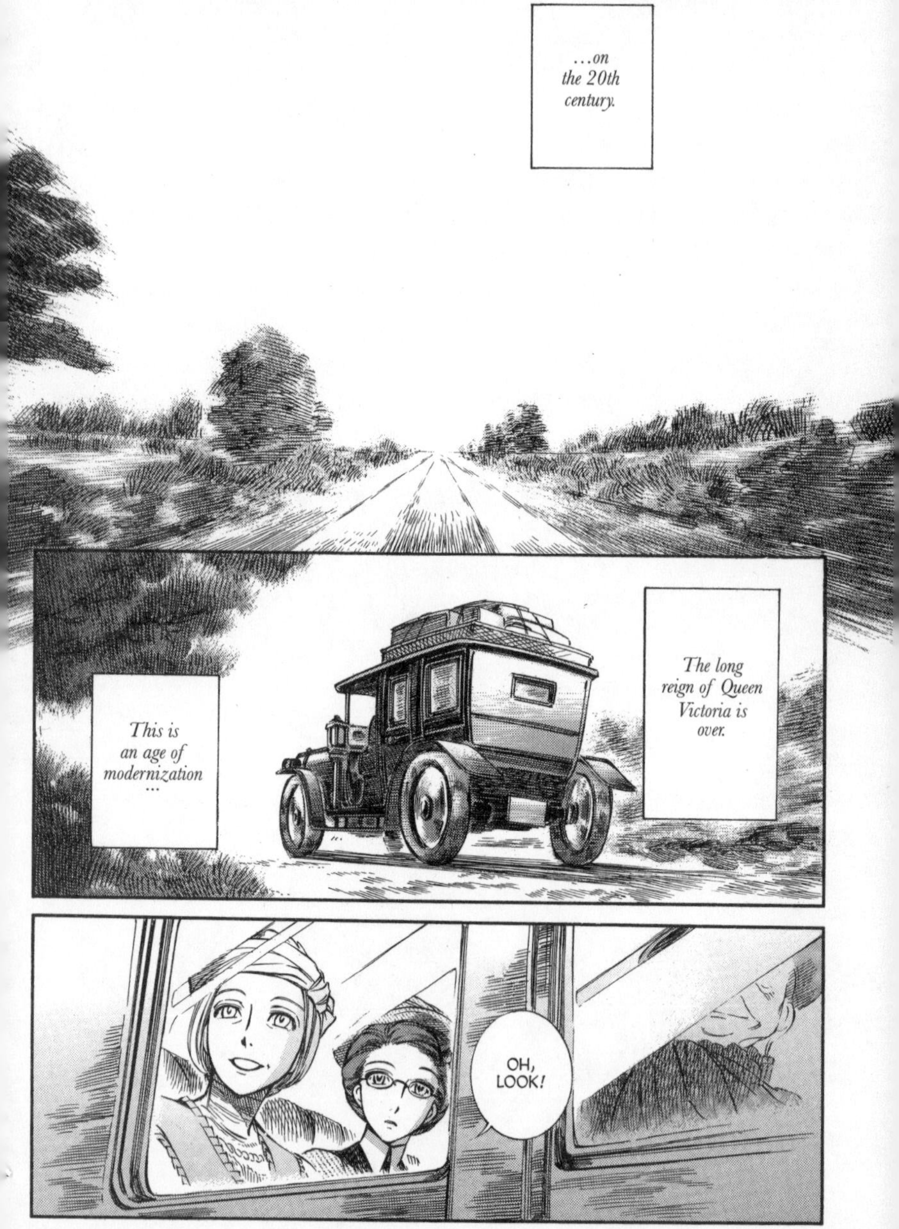
...on the 20th century.
The long reign of Queen Victoria is over.
This is an age of modernization ...
OH, LOOK!

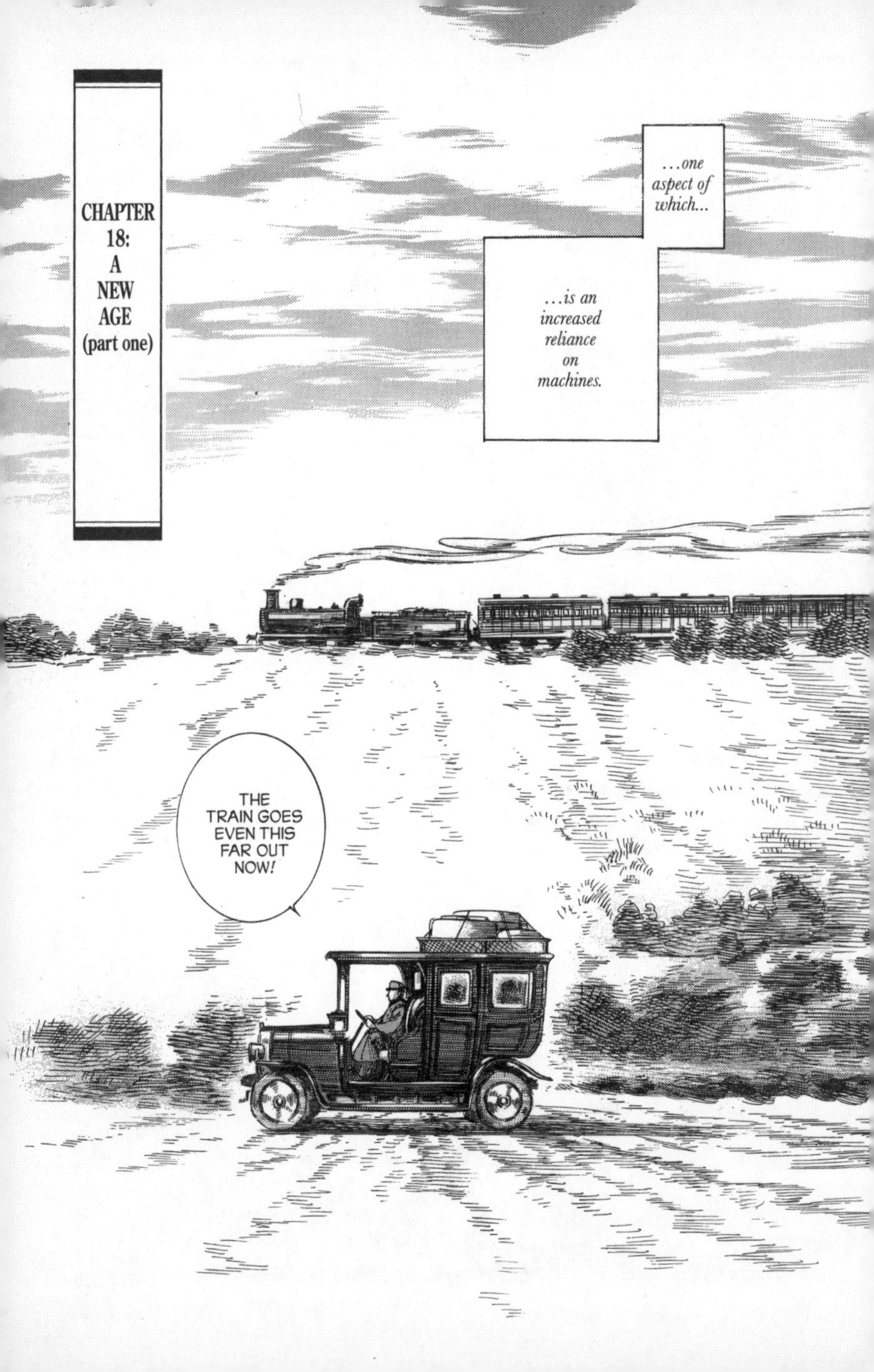
...one aspect of which...
...is an increased reliance on machines.
CHAPTER 18: A NEW AGE (part one)
THE TRAIN GOES EVEN THIS FAR OUT NOW!

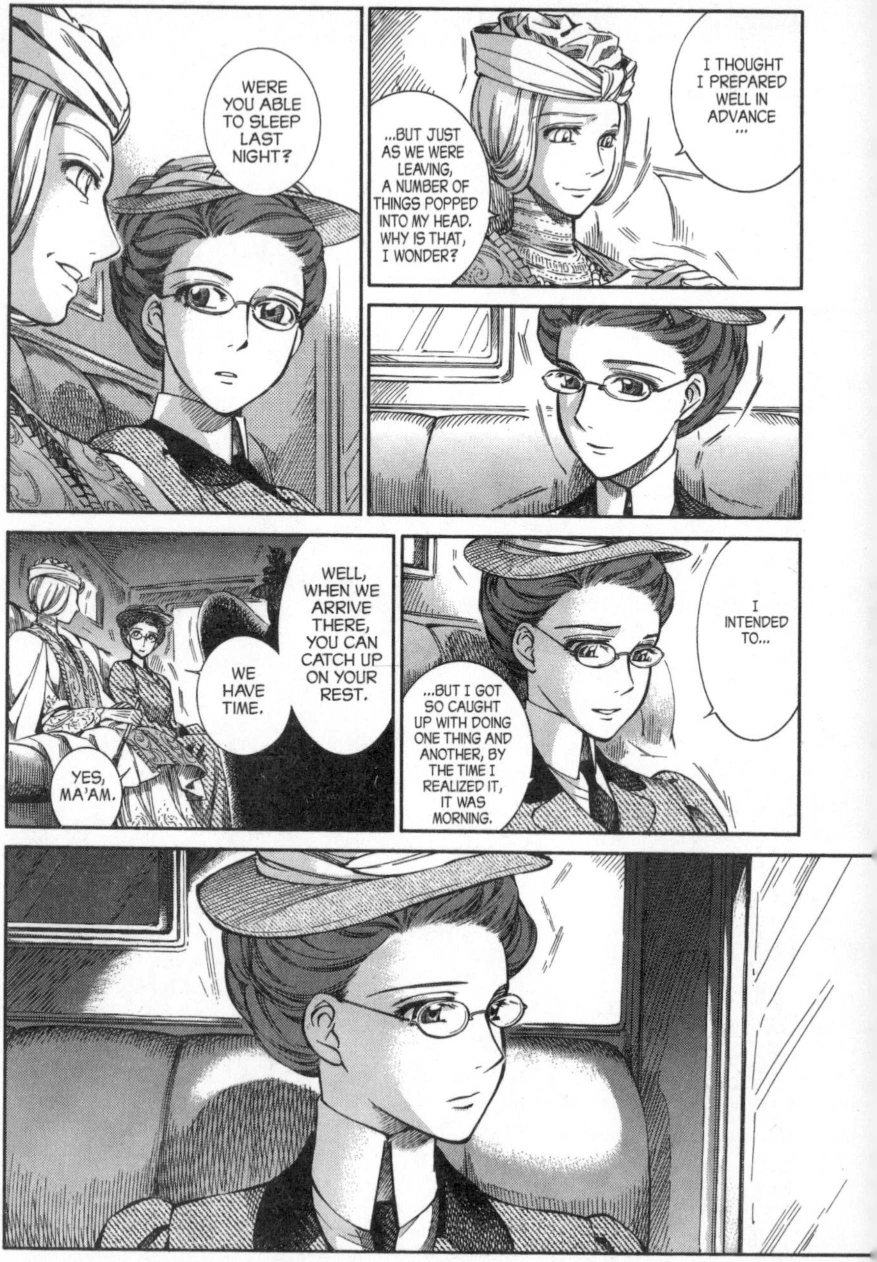
I THOUGHT I PREPARED WELL IN ADVANCE ...
...BUT JUST AS WE WERE LEAVING, A NUMBER OF THINGS POPPED INTO MY HEAD. WHY IS THAT, I WONDER?
WERE YOU ABLE TO SLEEP LAST NIGHT?
I INTENDED TO...
...BUT I GOT SO CAUGHT UP WITH DOING ONE THING AND ANOTHER, BY THE TIME I REALIZED IT, IT WAS MORNING.
WELL, WHEN WE ARRIVE THERE, YOU CAN CATCH UP ON YOUR REST.
WE HAVE TIME.
YES, MA'AM.

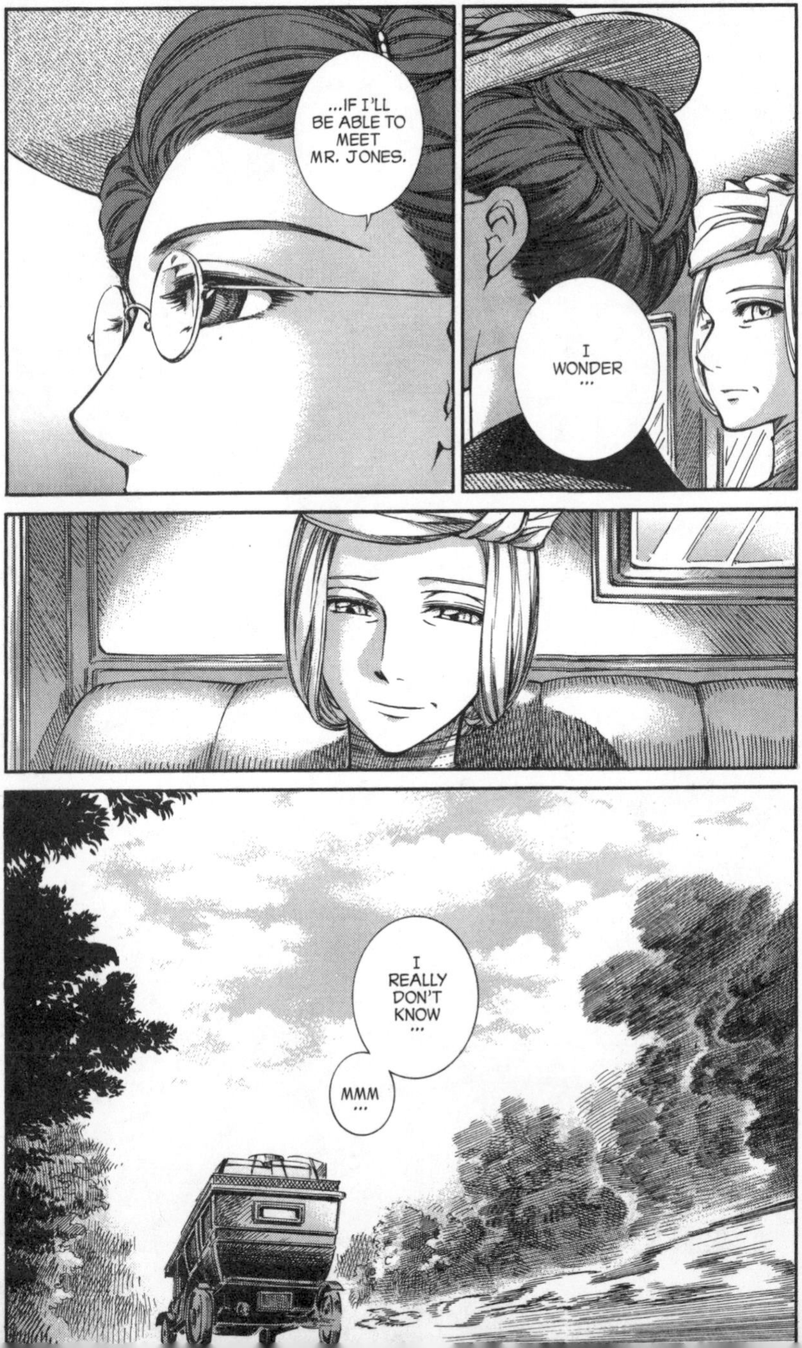
I WONDER...
...IF I'LL BE ABLE TO MEET MR. JONES.
I REALLY DON'T KNOW...
MMM...

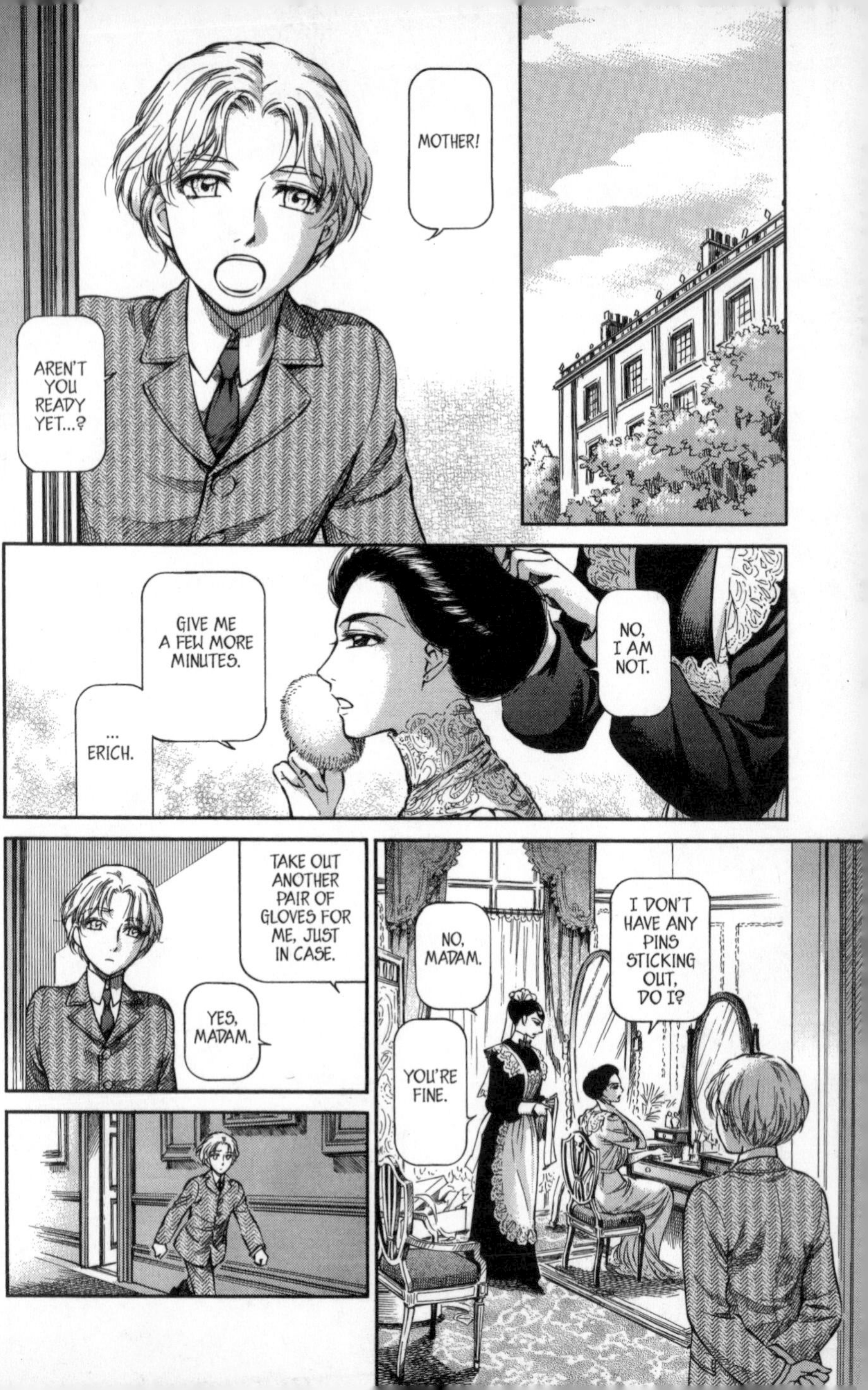
MOTHER!
AREN'T YOU READY YET...?
NO, I AM NOT.
GIVE ME A FEW MORE MINUTES.
... ERICH.
I DON'T HAVE ANY PINS STICKING OUT, DO I?
NO, MADAM.
YOU'RE FINE.
TAKE OUT ANOTHER PAIR OF GLOVES FOR ME, JUST IN CASE.
YES, MADAM.

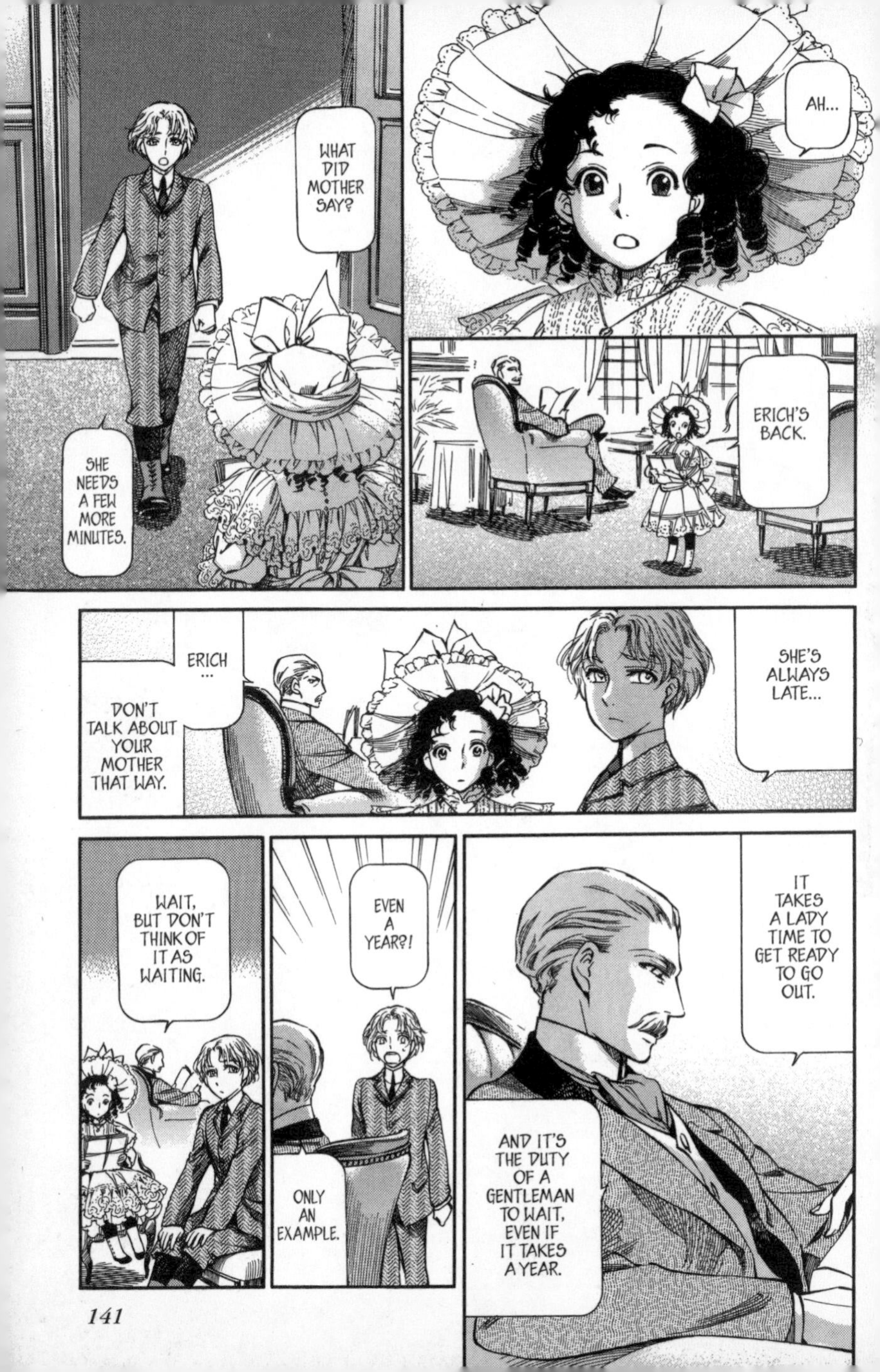
AH...
ERICH'S BACK.
WHAT DID MOTHER SAY?
SHE NEEDS A FEW MORE MINUTES.
SHE'S ALWAYS LATE...
ERICH...
DON'T TALK ABOUT YOUR MOTHER THAT WAY.
IT TAKES A LADY TIME TO GET READY TO GO OUT.
AND IT'S THE DUTY OF A GENTLEMAN TO WAIT, EVEN IF IT TAKES A YEAR.
EVEN A YEAR?!
ONLY AN EXAMPLE.
WAIT, BUT DON'T THINK OF IT AS WAITING.

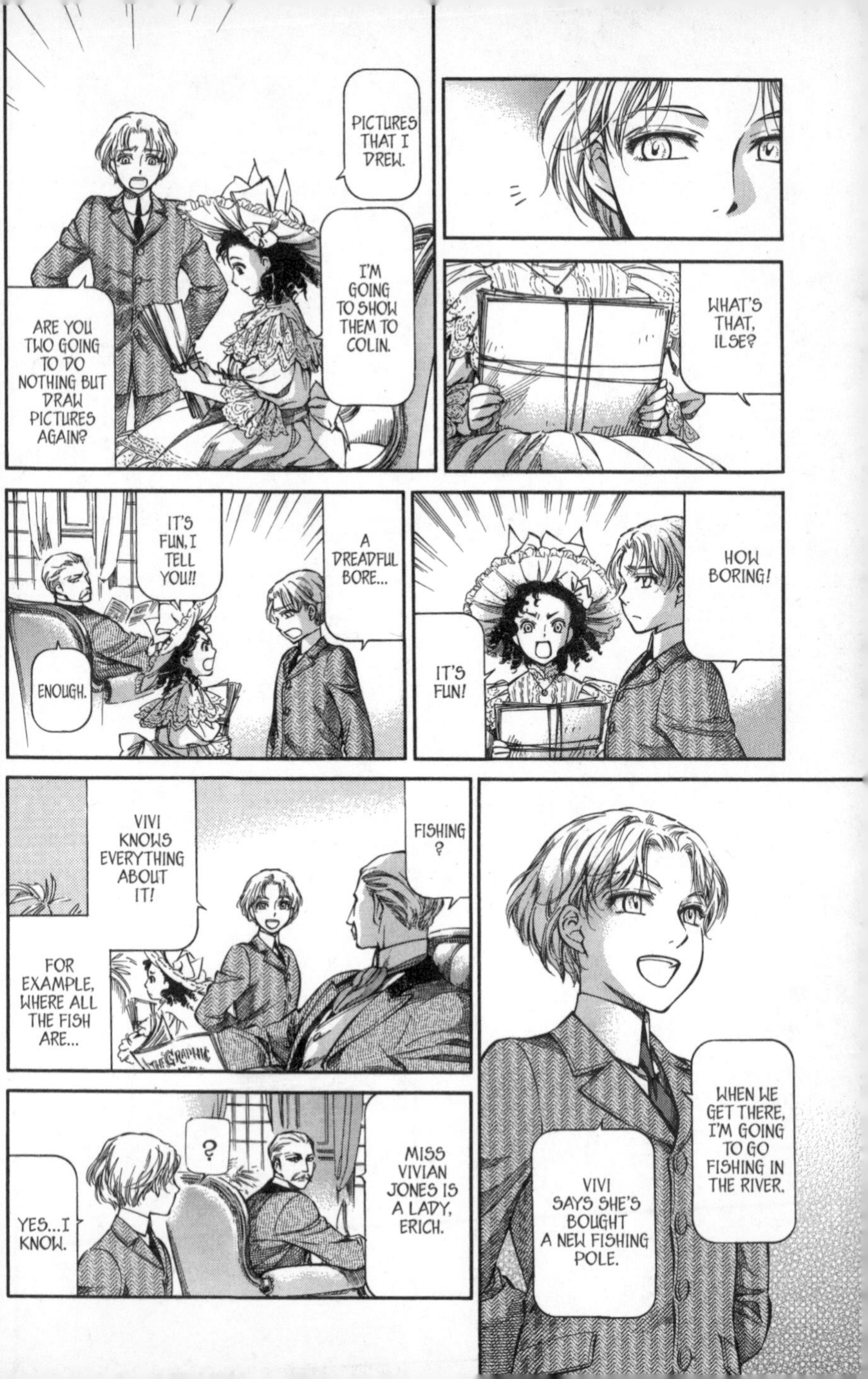
WHAT'S THAT, ILSE?
PICTURES THAT I DREW.
I'M GOING TO SHOW THEM TO COLIN.
ARE YOU TWO GOING TO DO NOTHING BUT DRAW PICTURES AGAIN?
HOW BORING!
IT'S FUN!
A DREADFUL BORE...
IT'S FUN, I TELL YOU!!
ENOUGH.
WHEN WE GET THERE, I'M GOING TO GO FISHING IN THE RIVER.
VIVI SAYS SHE'S BOUGHT A NEW FISHING POLE.
FISHING?
VIVI KNOWS EVERYTHING ABOUT IT!
FOR EXAMPLE, WHERE ALL THE FISH ARE...
MISS VIVIAN JONES IS A LADY, ERICH.
?
YES...I KNOW.

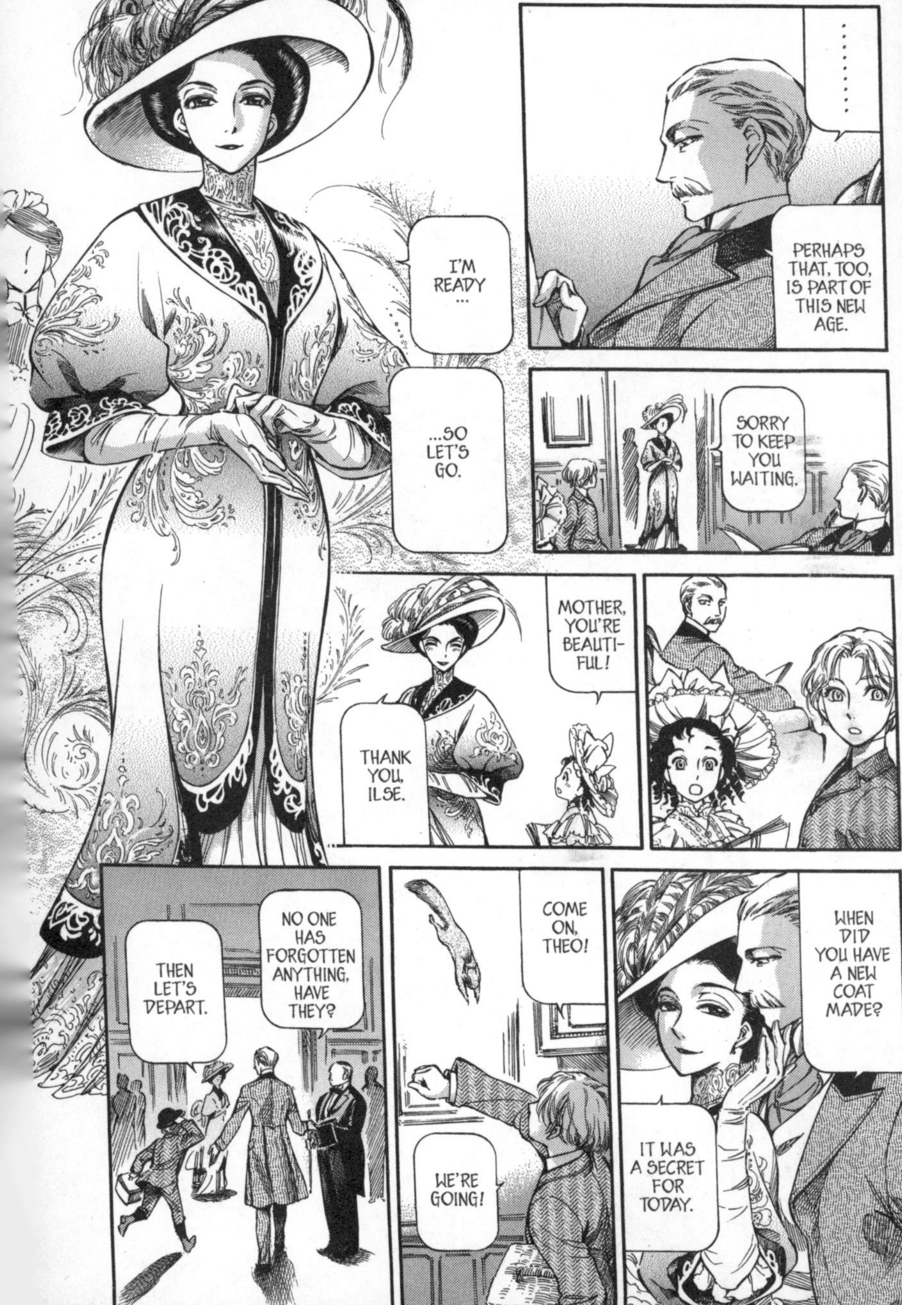
......
PERHAPS THAT, TOO, IS PART OF THIS NEW AGE.
SORRY TO KEEP YOU WAITING.
MOTHER, YOU'RE BEAUTI-FUL!
THANK YOU, ILSE.
I'M READY ...
...SO LET'S GO.
WHEN DID YOU HAVE A NEW COAT MADE?
IT WAS A SECRET FOR TODAY.
COME ON, THEO!
WE'RE GOING!
NO ONE HAS FORGOTTEN ANYTHING, HAVE THEY?
THEN LET'S DEPART.

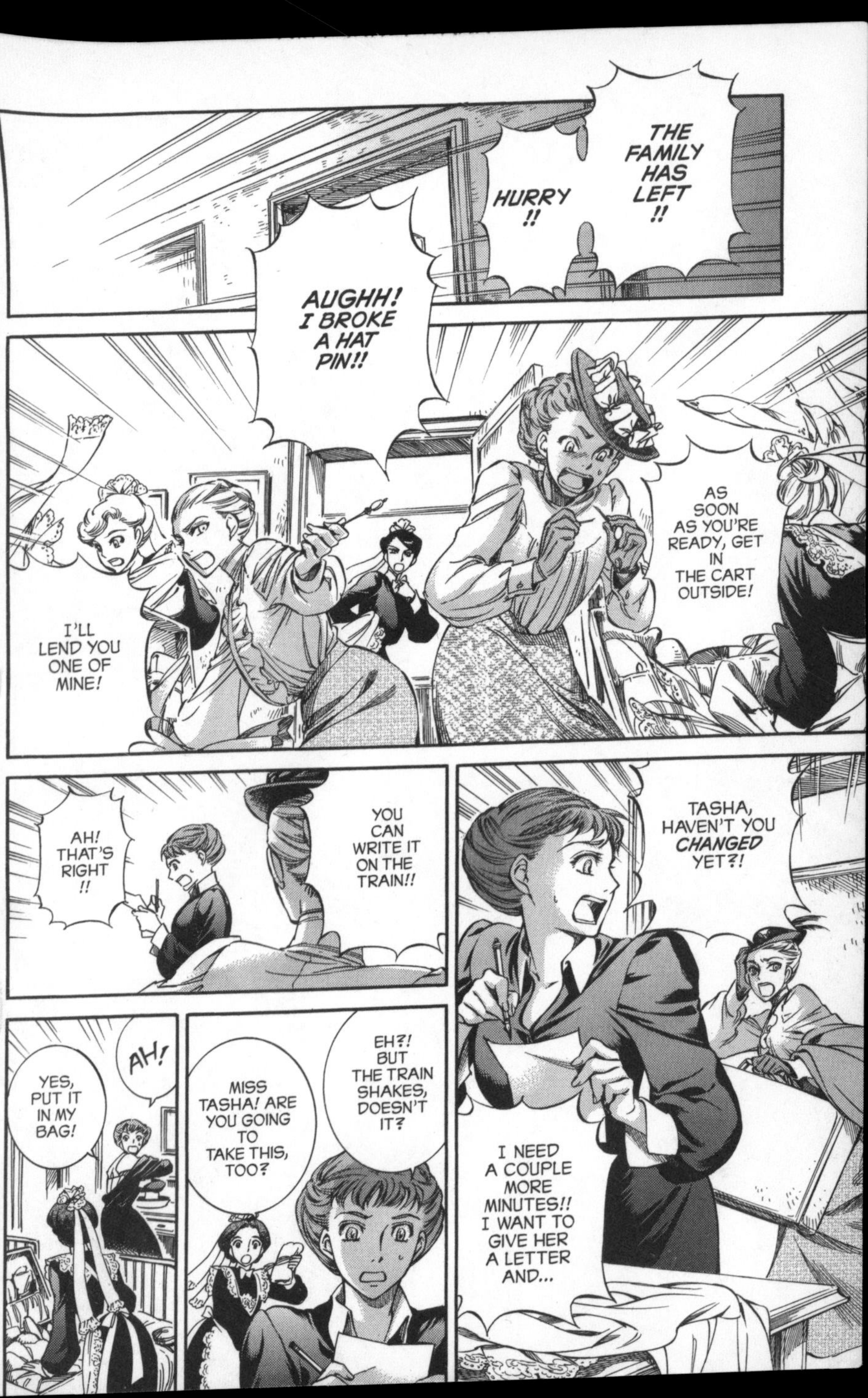
THE FAMILY HAS LEFT!!
HURRY!!
AUGHH! I BROKE A HAT PIN!!
AS SOON AS YOU'RE READY, GET IN THE CART OUTSIDE!
I'LL LEND YOU ONE OF MINE!
TASHA, HAVEN'T YOU *CHANGED* YET?!
I NEED A COUPLE MORE MINUTES!! I WANT TO GIVE HER A LETTER AND...
YOU CAN WRITE IT ON THE TRAIN!!
AH! THAT'S RIGHT!!
EH?! BUT THE TRAIN SHAKES, DOESN'T IT?
MISS TASHA! ARE YOU GOING TO TAKE THIS, TOO?
AH!
YES, PUT IT IN MY BAG!

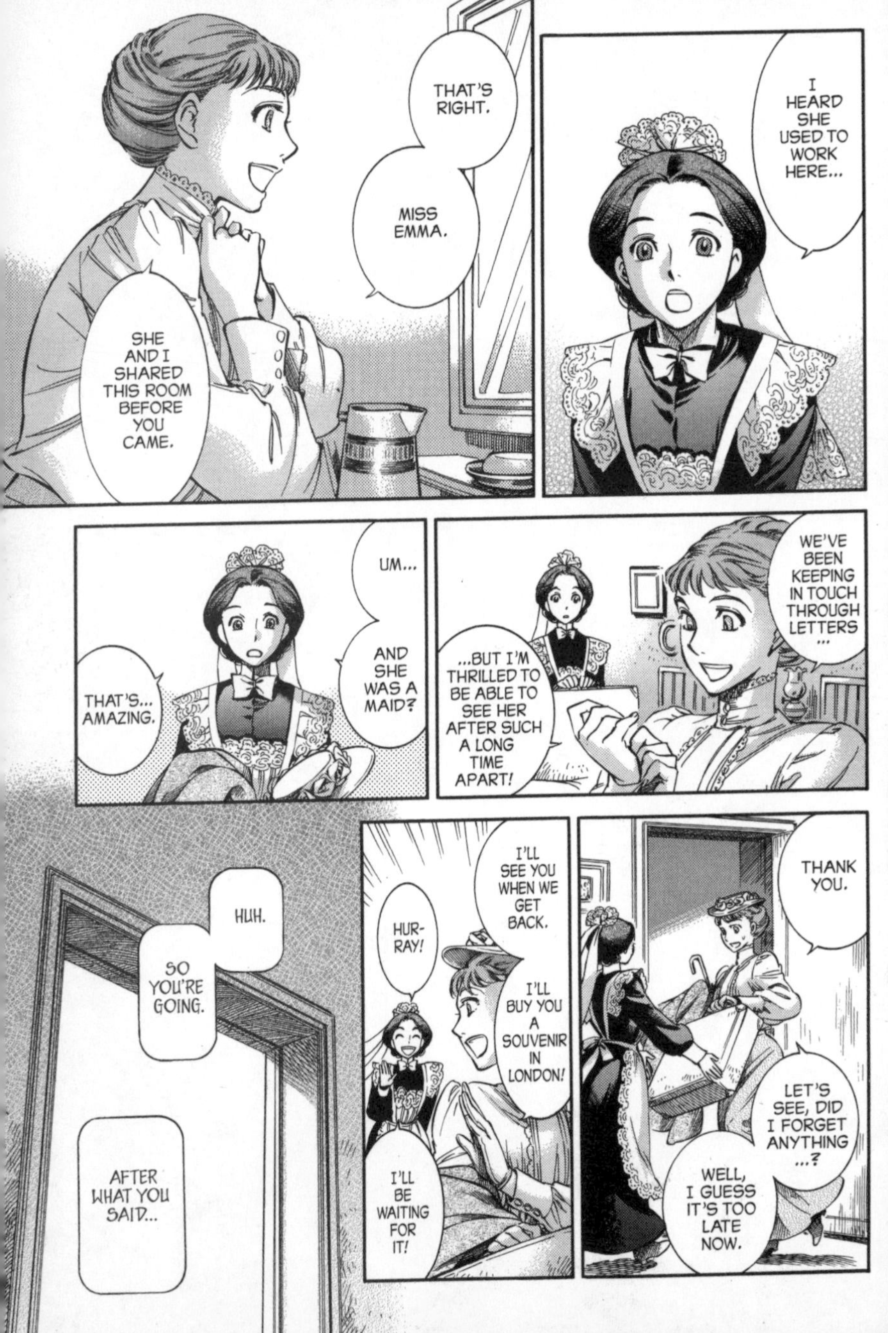
I HEARD SHE USED TO WORK HERE...
THAT'S RIGHT.
MISS EMMA.
SHE AND I SHARED THIS ROOM BEFORE YOU CAME.
WE'VE BEEN KEEPING IN TOUCH THROUGH LETTERS...
...BUT I'M THRILLED TO BE ABLE TO SEE HER AFTER SUCH A LONG TIME APART!
UM...
AND SHE WAS A MAID?
THAT'S... AMAZING.
THANK YOU.
LET'S SEE, DID I FORGET ANYTHING...?
WELL, I GUESS IT'S TOO LATE NOW.
I'LL SEE YOU WHEN WE GET BACK.
HUR-RAY!
I'LL BUY YOU A SOUVENIR IN LONDON!
I'LL BE WAITING FOR IT!
HUH.
SO YOU'RE GOING.
AFTER WHAT YOU SAID...

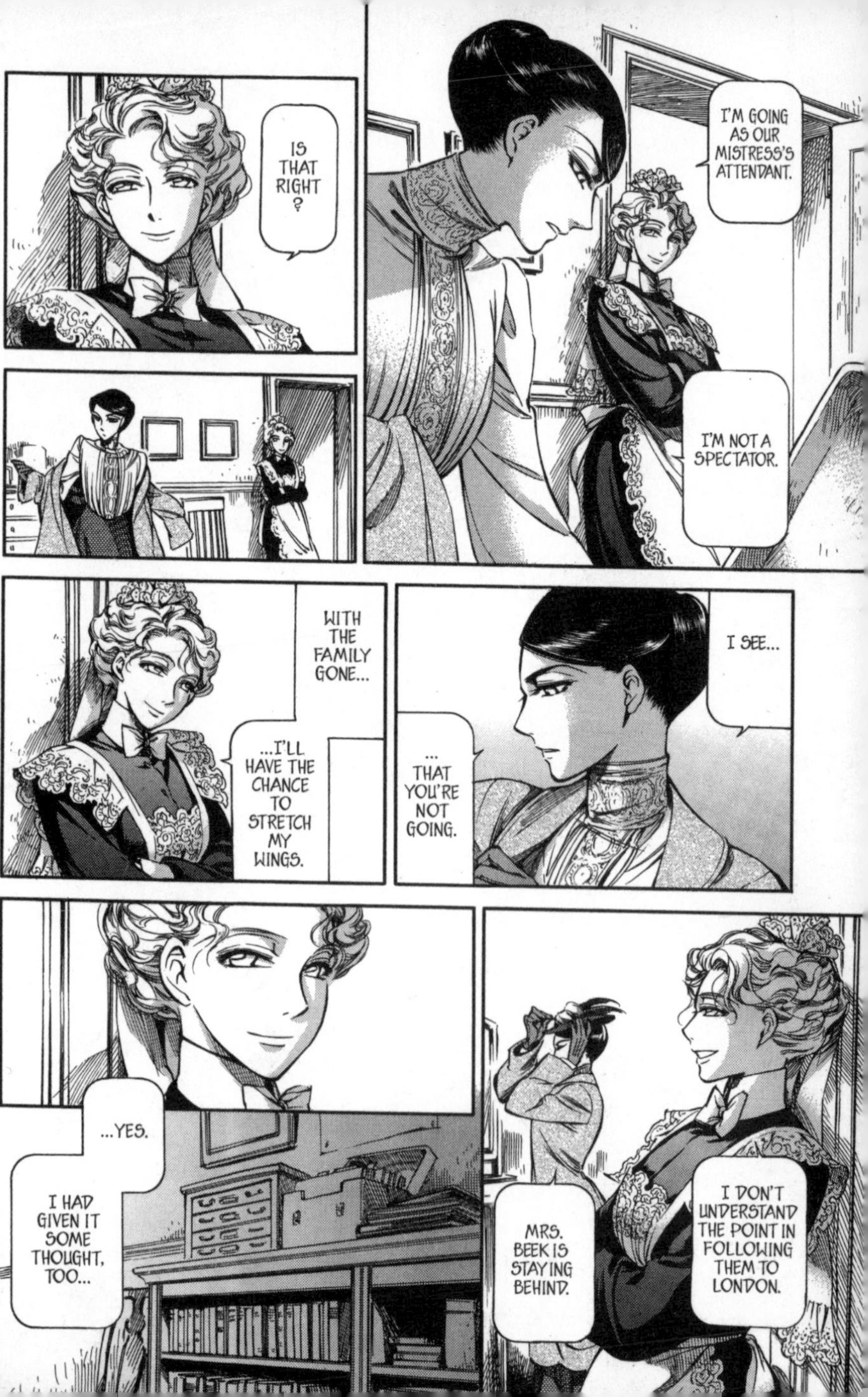
I'M GOING AS OUR MISTRESS'S ATTENDANT.
I'M NOT A SPECTATOR.
IS THAT RIGHT?
I SEE...
...THAT YOU'RE NOT GOING.
WITH THE FAMILY GONE...
...I'LL HAVE THE CHANCE TO STRETCH MY WINGS.
I DON'T UNDERSTAND THE POINT IN FOLLOWING THEM TO LONDON.
MRS. BEEK IS STAYING BEHIND.
...YES.
I HAD GIVEN IT SOME THOUGHT, TOO...

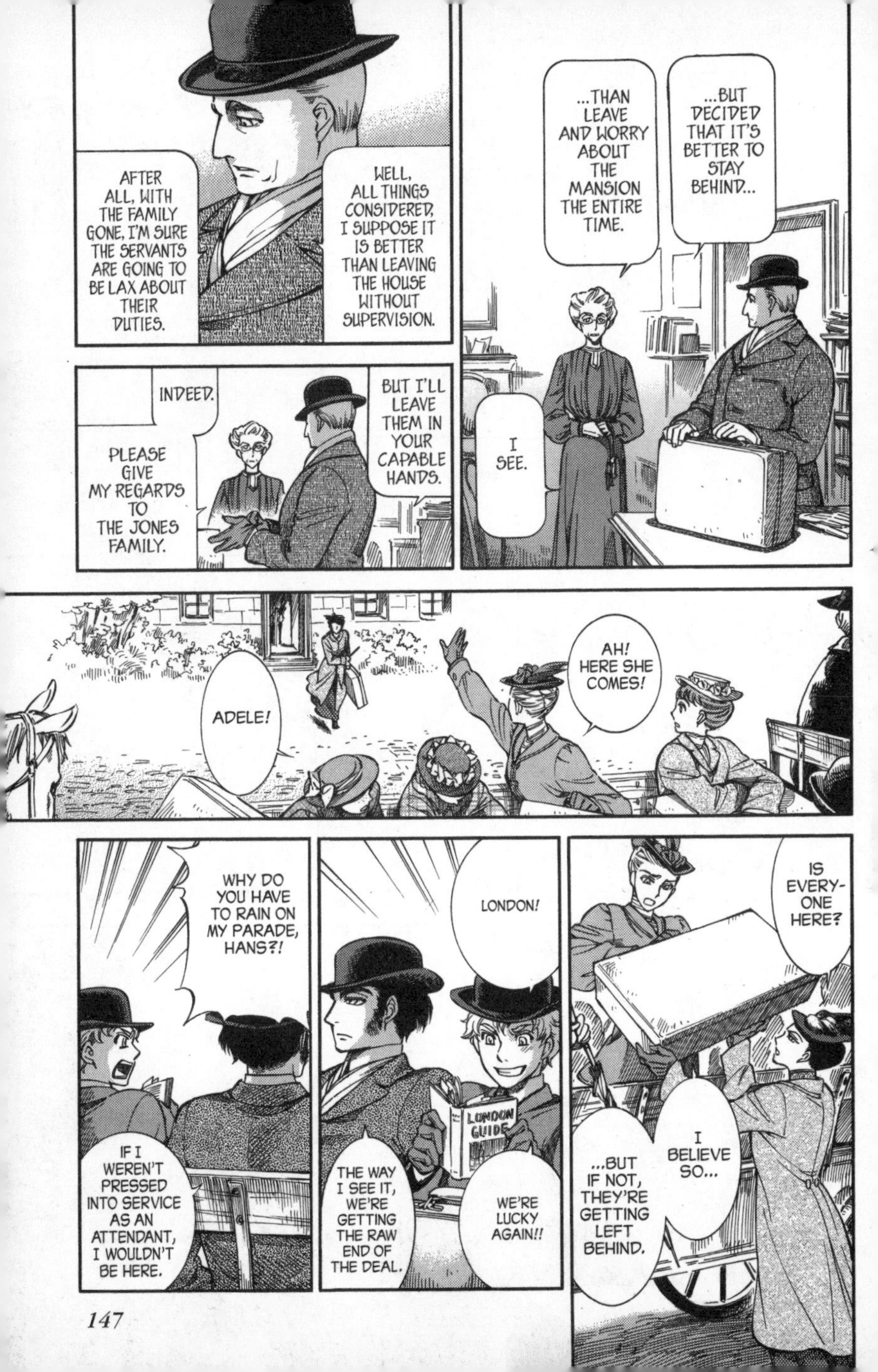
...BUT DECIDED THAT IT'S BETTER TO STAY BEHIND...
...THAN LEAVE AND WORRY ABOUT THE MANSION THE ENTIRE TIME.
I SEE.
WELL, ALL THINGS CONSIDERED, I SUPPOSE IT IS BETTER THAN LEAVING THE HOUSE WITHOUT SUPERVISION.
AFTER ALL, WITH THE FAMILY GONE, I'M SURE THE SERVANTS ARE GOING TO BE LAX ABOUT THEIR DUTIES.
BUT I'LL LEAVE THEM IN YOUR CAPABLE HANDS.
INDEED.
PLEASE GIVE MY REGARDS TO THE JONES FAMILY.
AH! HERE SHE COMES!
ADELE!
IS EVERY-ONE HERE?
I BELIEVE SO...
...BUT IF NOT, THEY'RE GETTING LEFT BEHIND.
LONDON!
LONDON GUIDE
WE'RE LUCKY AGAIN!!
THE WAY I SEE IT, WE'RE GETTING THE RAW END OF THE DEAL.
WHY DO YOU HAVE TO RAIN ON MY PARADE, HANS?!
IF I WEREN'T PRESSED INTO SERVICE AS AN ATTENDANT, I WOULDN'T BE HERE.

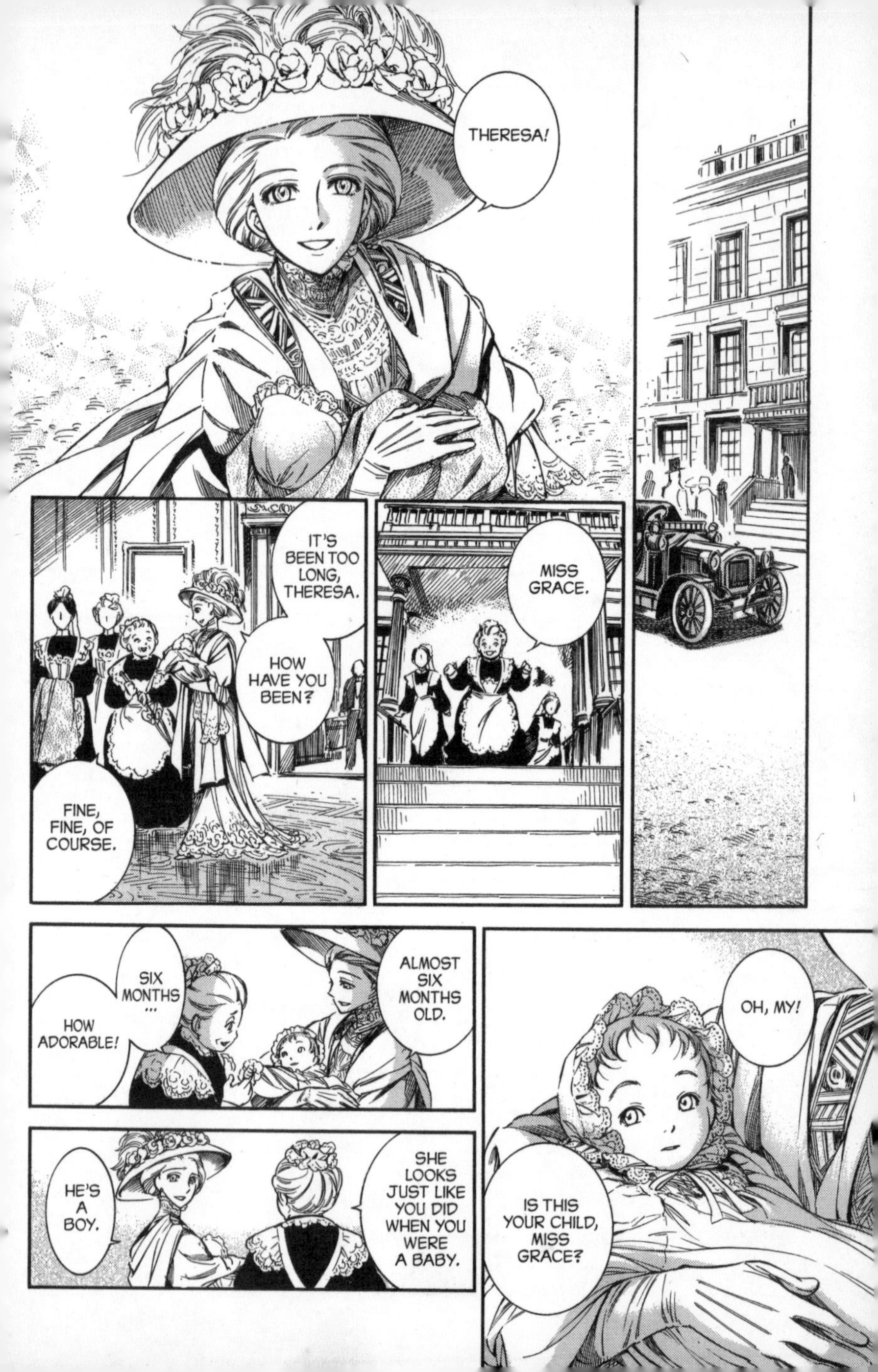
THERESA!
MISS GRACE.
IT'S BEEN TOO LONG, THERESA.
HOW HAVE YOU BEEN?
FINE, FINE, OF COURSE.
OH, MY!
IS THIS YOUR CHILD, MISS GRACE?
ALMOST SIX MONTHS OLD.
SIX MONTHS...
HOW ADORABLE!
SHE LOOKS JUST LIKE YOU DID WHEN YOU WERE A BABY.
HE'S A BOY.

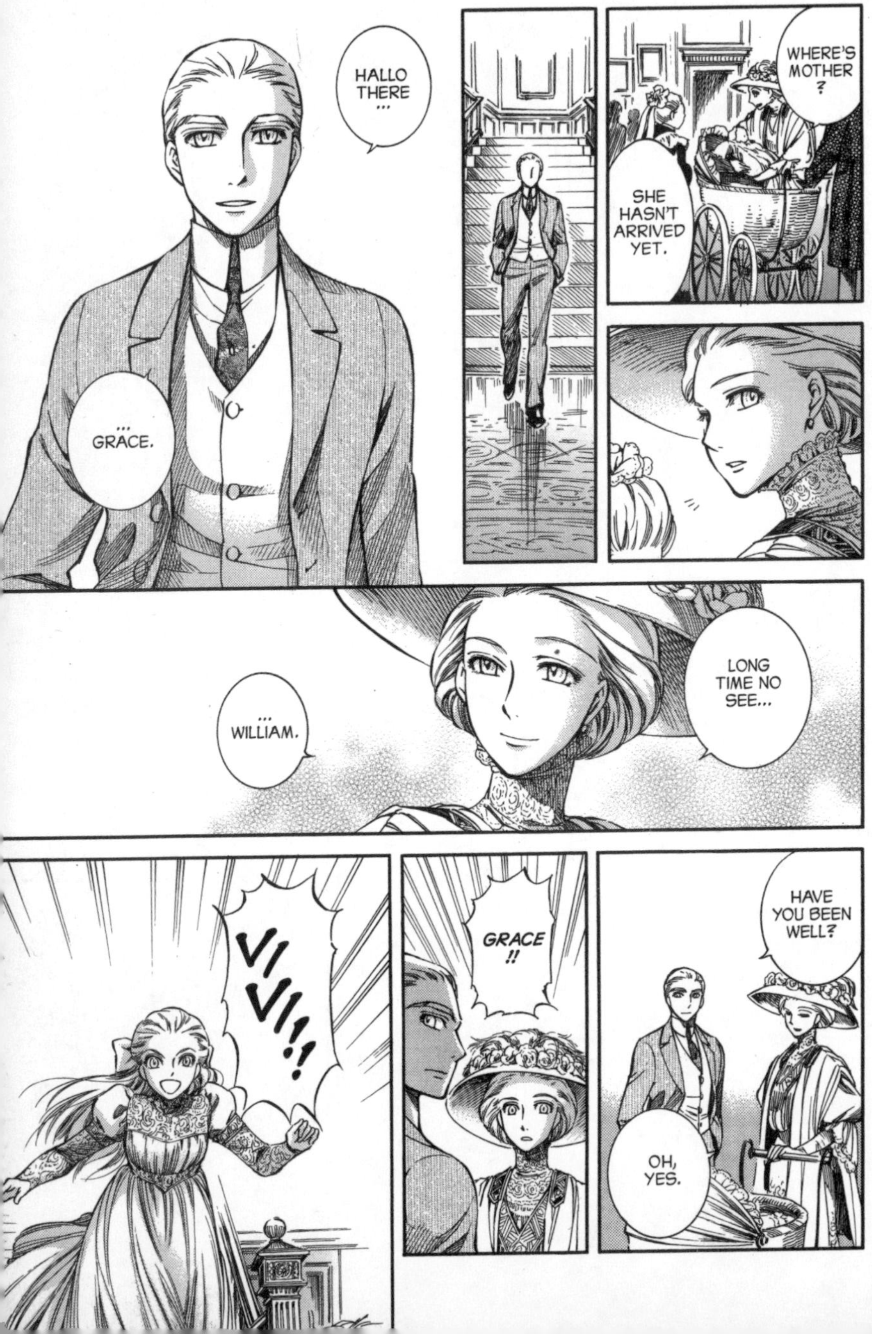
WHERE'S MOTHER?
SHE HASN'T ARRIVED YET.
HALLO THERE ...
... GRACE.
LONG TIME NO SEE...
... WILLIAM.
HAVE YOU BEEN WELL?
OH, YES.
GRACE !!
VI VI!!

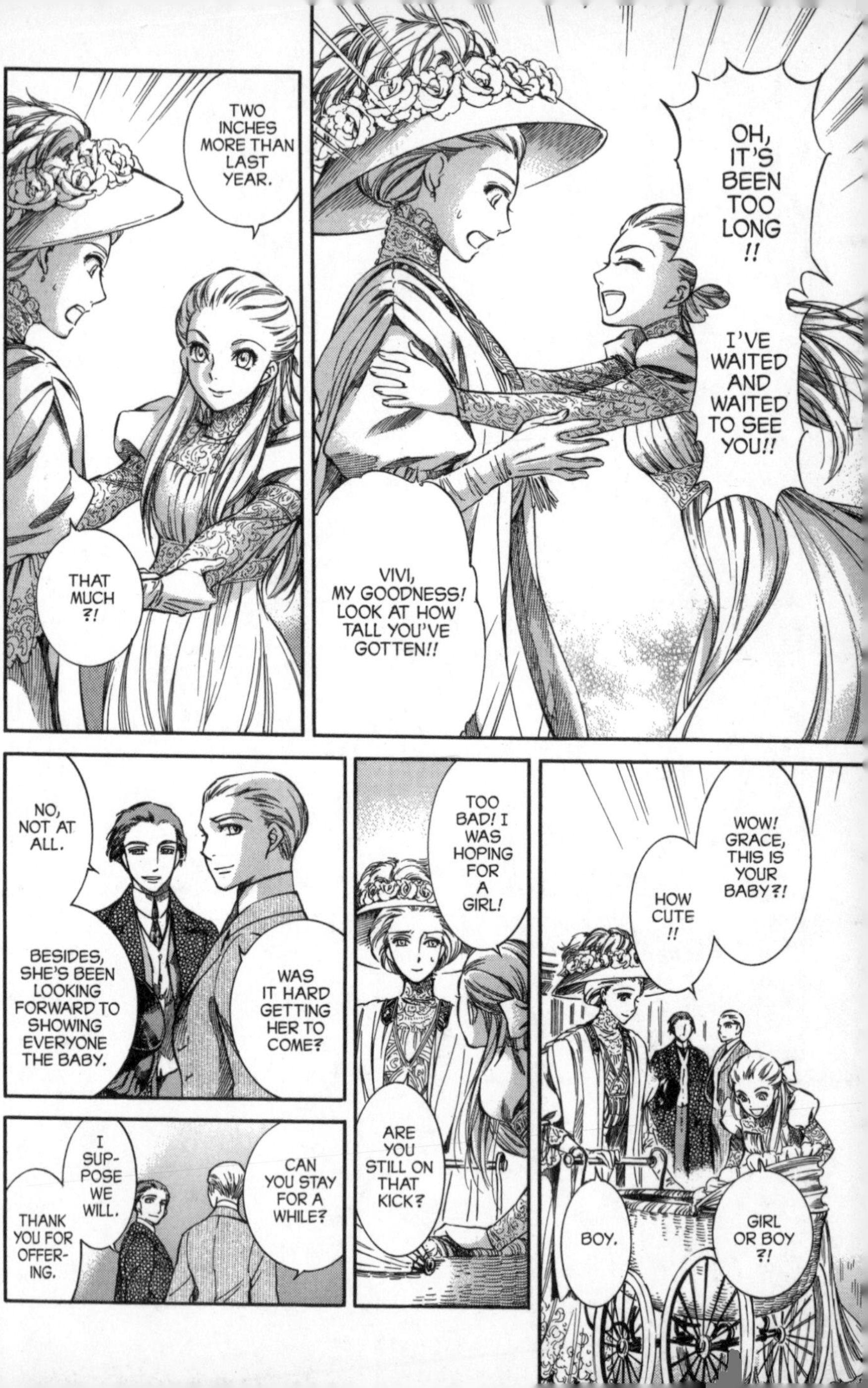

OH, IT'S BEEN TOO LONG!!
I'VE WAITED AND WAITED TO SEE YOU!!
VIVI, MY GOODNESS! LOOK AT HOW TALL YOU'VE GOTTEN!!
TWO INCHES MORE THAN LAST YEAR.
THAT MUCH?!
WOW! GRACE, THIS IS YOUR BABY?!
HOW CUTE!!
GIRL OR BOY?!
BOY.
TOO BAD! I WAS HOPING FOR A GIRL!
ARE YOU STILL ON THAT KICK?
WAS IT HARD GETTING HER TO COME?
NO, NOT AT ALL.
BESIDES, SHE'S BEEN LOOKING FORWARD TO SHOWING EVERYONE THE BABY.
CAN YOU STAY FOR A WHILE?
I SUPPOSE WE WILL.
THANK YOU FOR OFFERING.

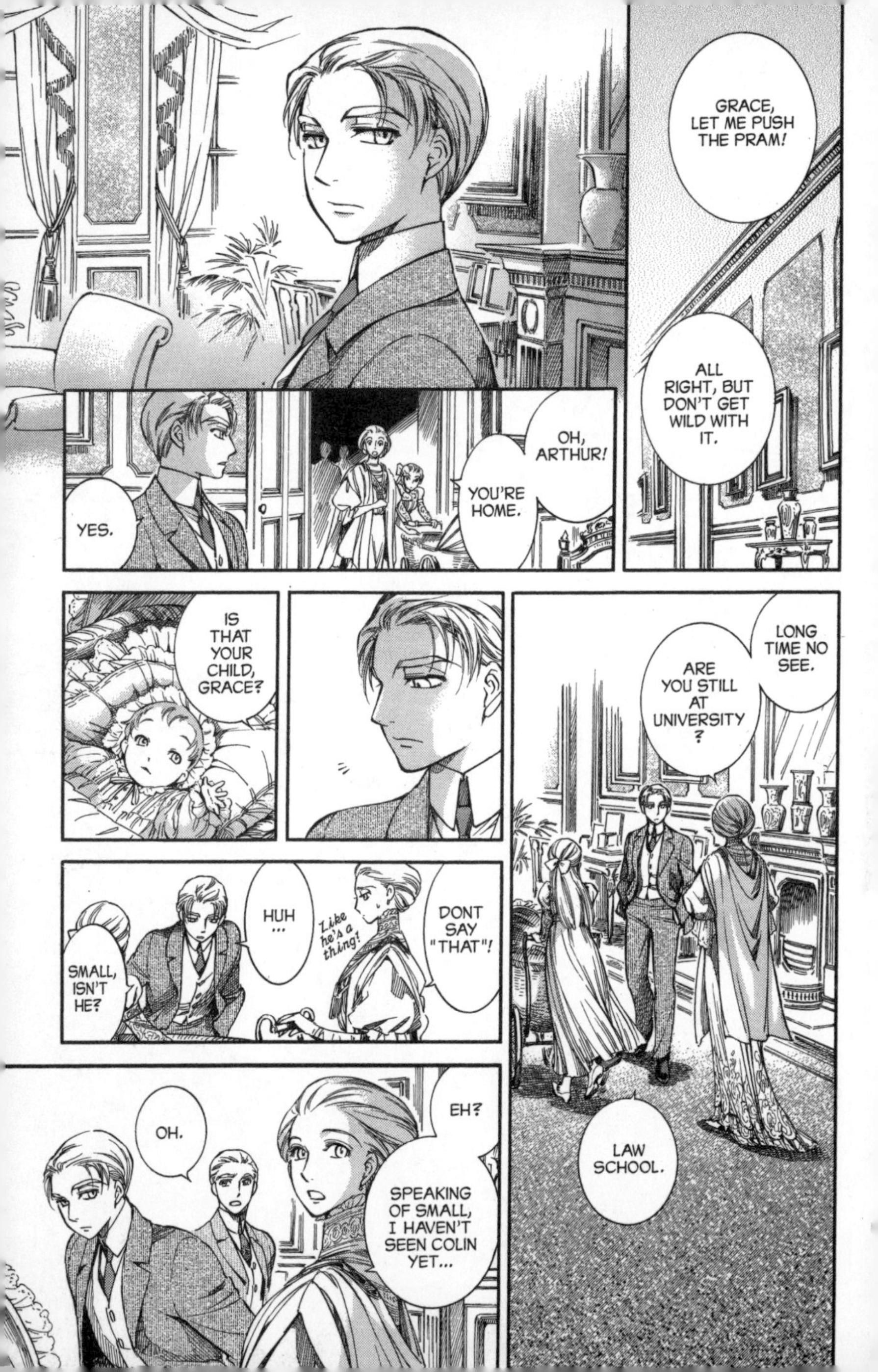
GRACE, LET ME PUSH THE PRAM!
ALL RIGHT, BUT DON'T GET WILD WITH IT.
OH, ARTHUR!
YOU'RE HOME.
YES.
LONG TIME NO SEE.
ARE YOU STILL AT UNIVERSITY?
LAW SCHOOL.
IS THAT YOUR CHILD, GRACE?
DONT SAY "THAT"!
Like he's a thing!
HUH...
SMALL, ISN'T HE?
EH?
SPEAKING OF SMALL, I HAVEN'T SEEN COLIN YET...
OH.

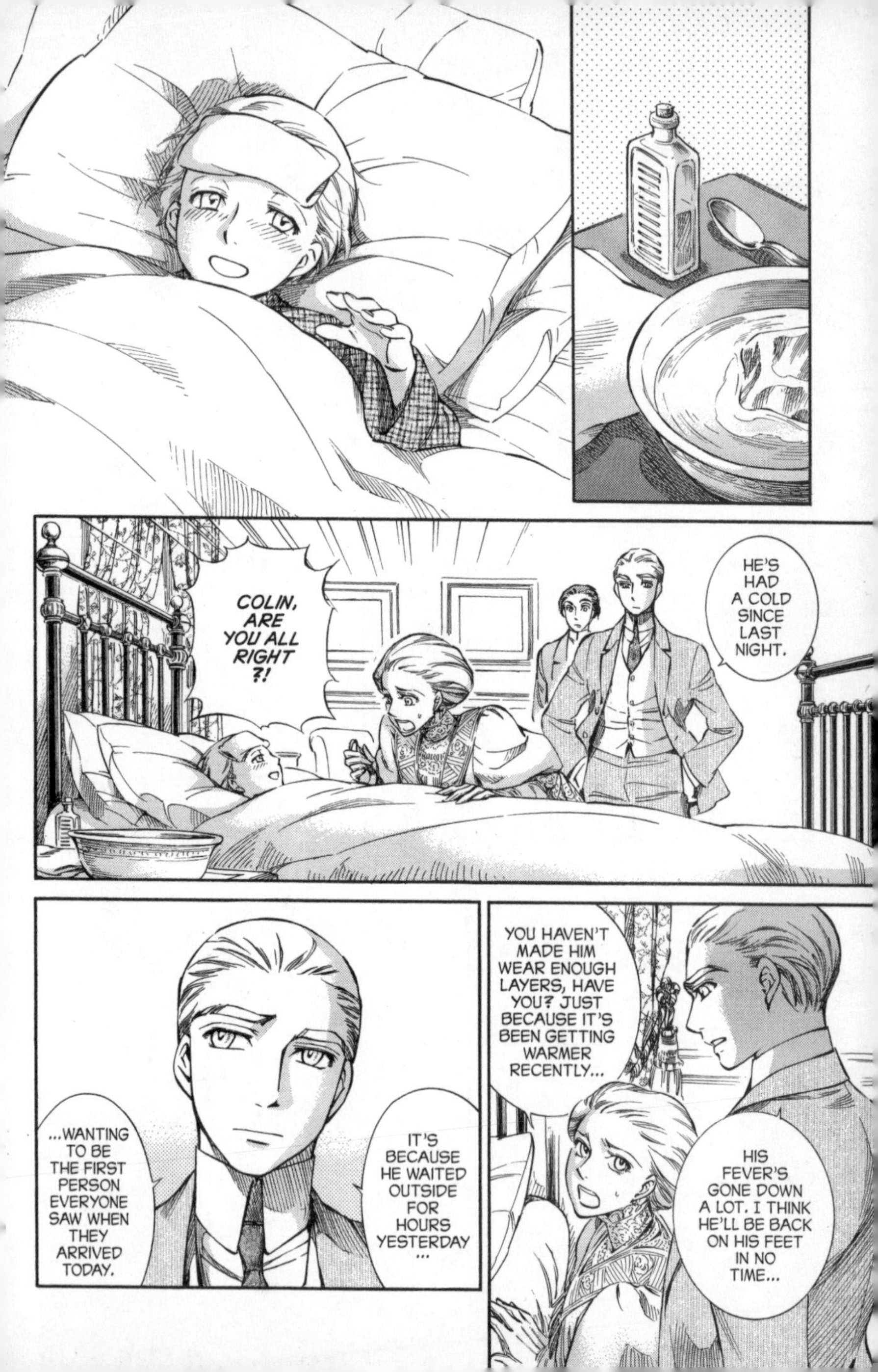
HE'S HAD A COLD SINCE LAST NIGHT.
COLIN, ARE YOU ALL RIGHT?!
YOU HAVEN'T MADE HIM WEAR ENOUGH LAYERS, HAVE YOU? JUST BECAUSE IT'S BEEN GETTING WARMER RECENTLY...
HIS FEVER'S GONE DOWN A LOT. I THINK HE'LL BE BACK ON HIS FEET IN NO TIME...
IT'S BECAUSE HE WAITED OUTSIDE FOR HOURS YESTERDAY...
...WANTING TO BE THE FIRST PERSON EVERYONE SAW WHEN THEY ARRIVED TODAY.

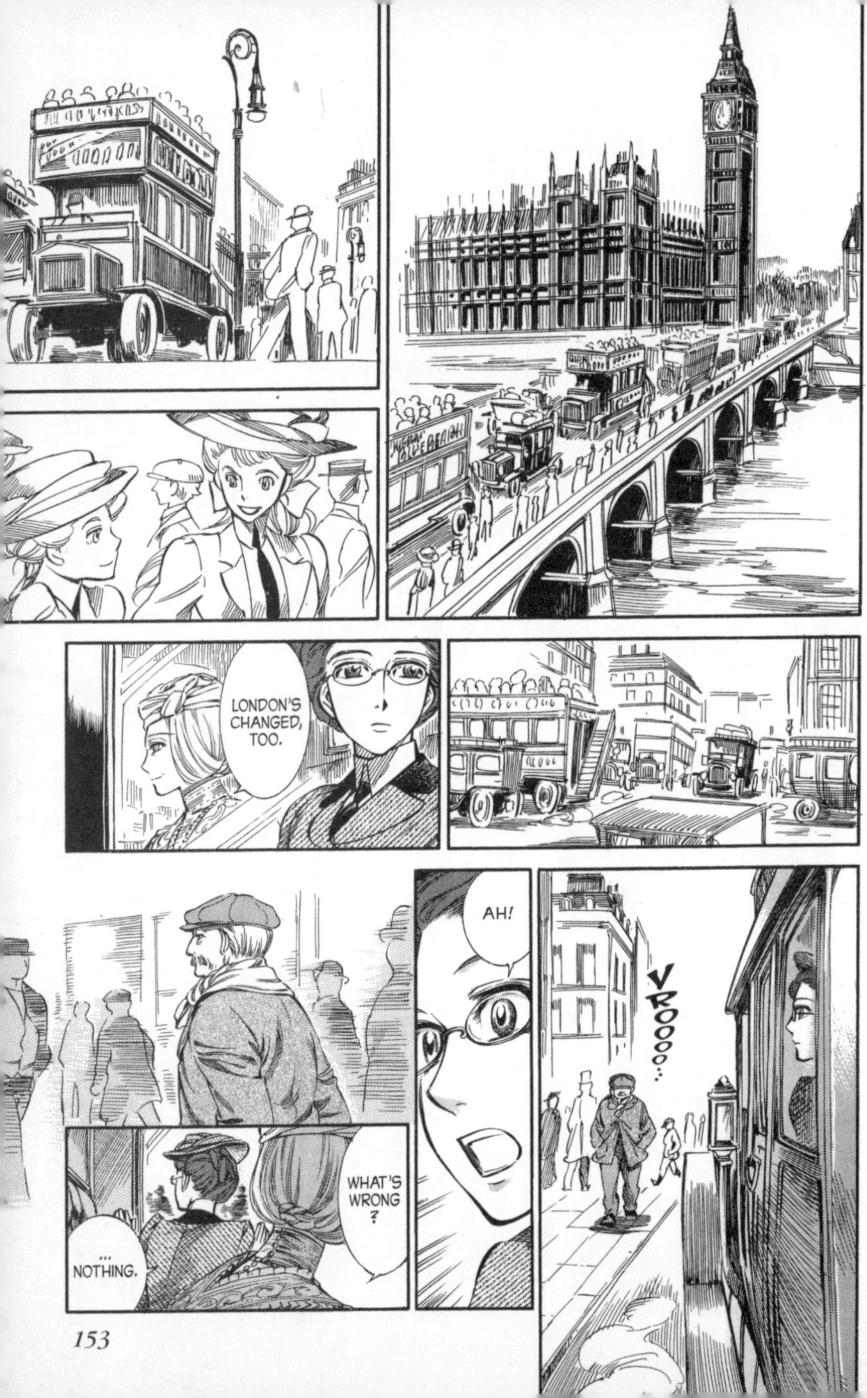
LONDON'S CHANGED, TOO.
VROOOO...
AH!
WHAT'S WRONG?
... NOTHING.

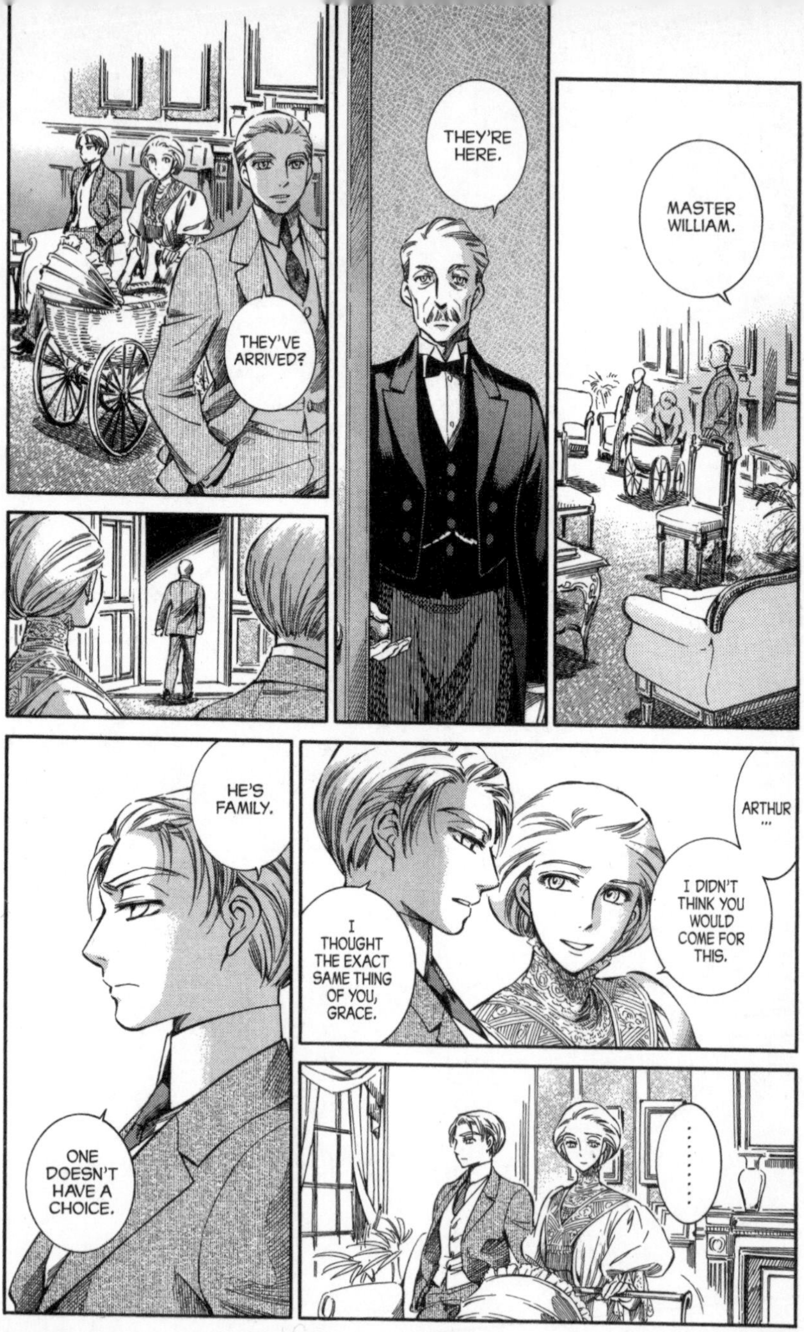

MASTER WILLIAM.
THEY'RE HERE.
THEY'VE ARRIVED?
ARTHUR ...
I DIDN'T THINK YOU WOULD COME FOR THIS.
I THOUGHT THE EXACT SAME THING OF YOU, GRACE.
......
HE'S FAMILY.
ONE DOESN'T HAVE A CHOICE.

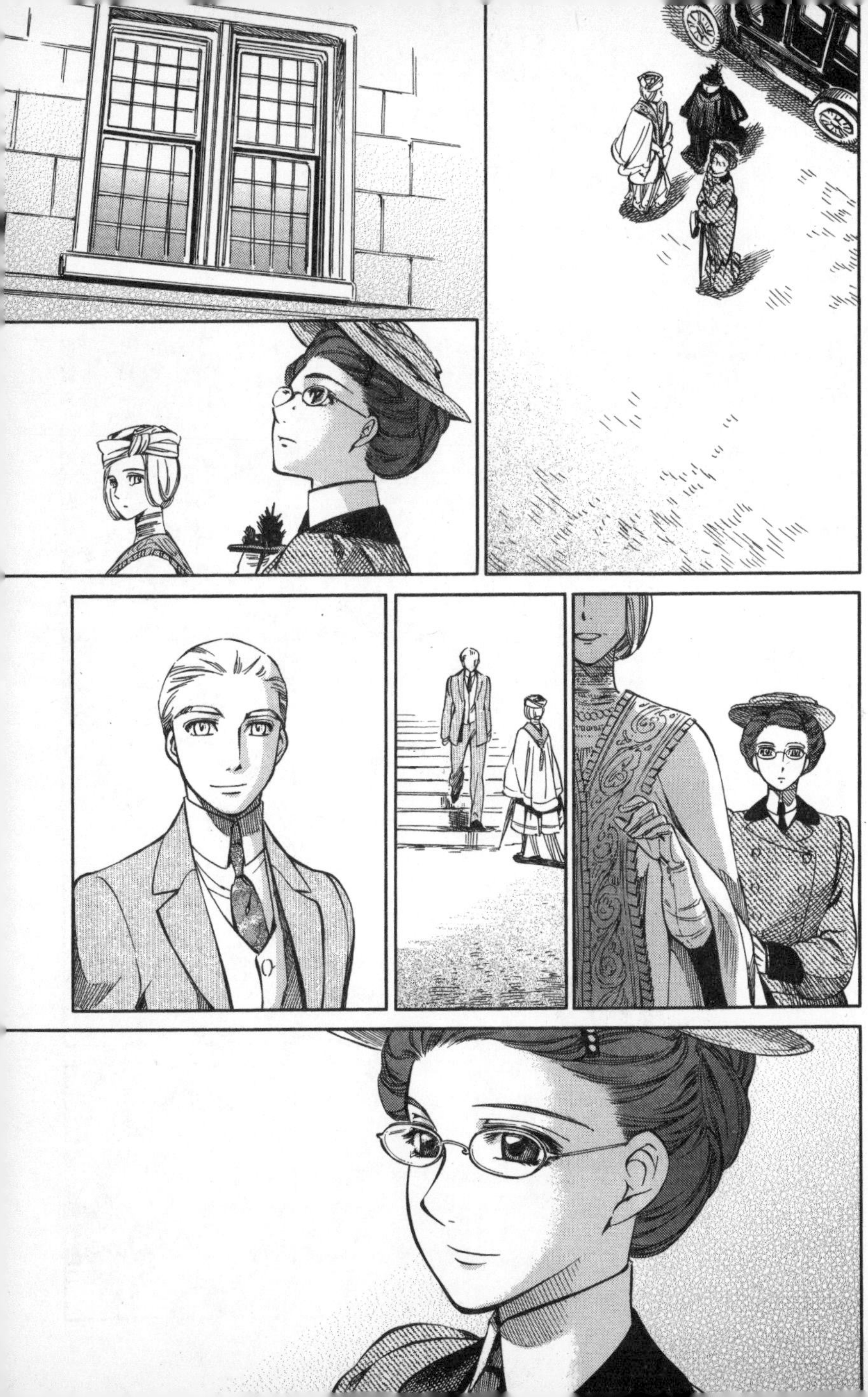

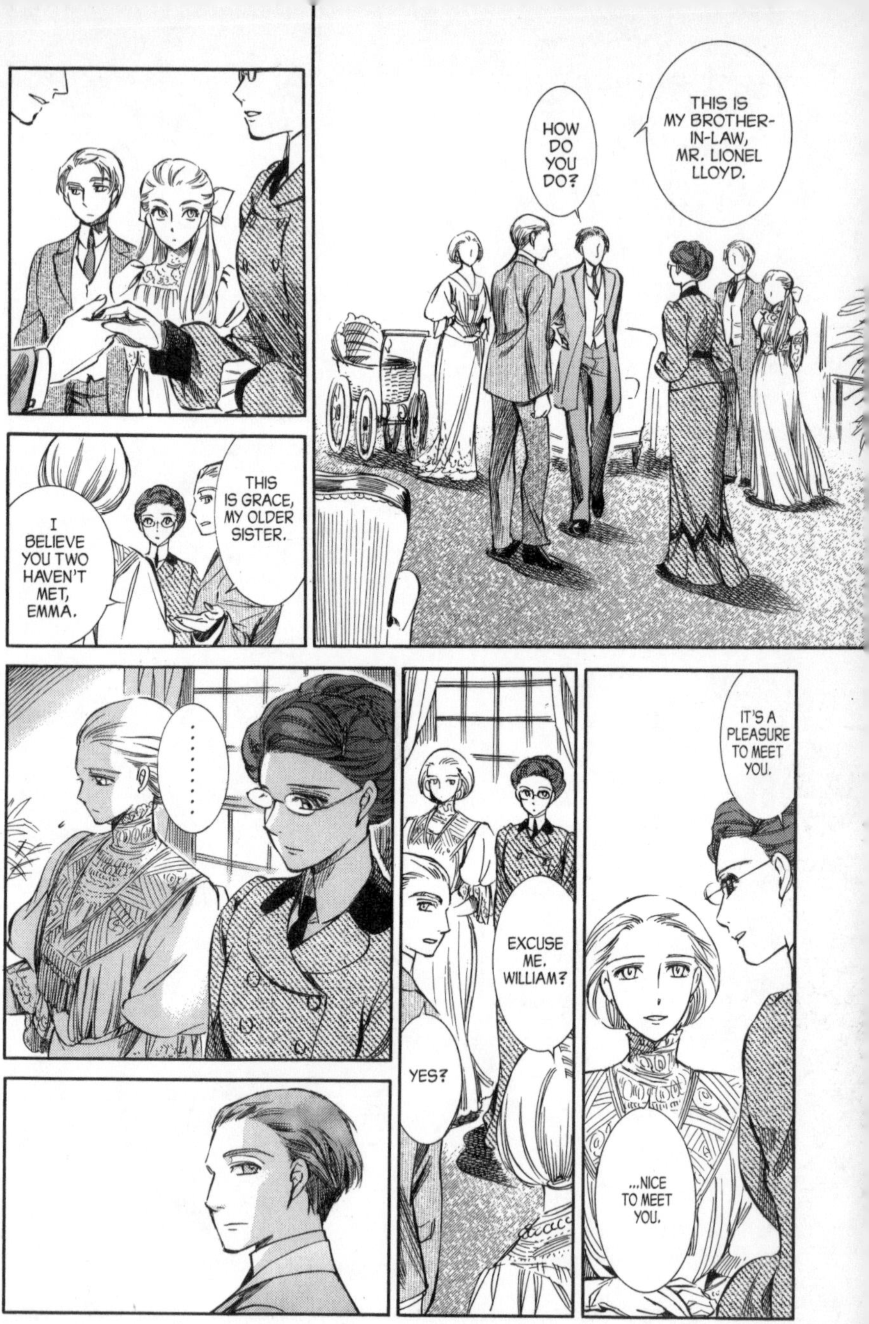
THIS IS MY BROTHER-IN-LAW, MR. LIONEL LLOYD.
HOW DO YOU DO?
THIS IS GRACE, MY OLDER SISTER.
I BELIEVE YOU TWO HAVEN'T MET, EMMA.
IT'S A PLEASURE TO MEET YOU.
...NICE TO MEET YOU.
EXCUSE ME. WILLIAM?
YES?
......

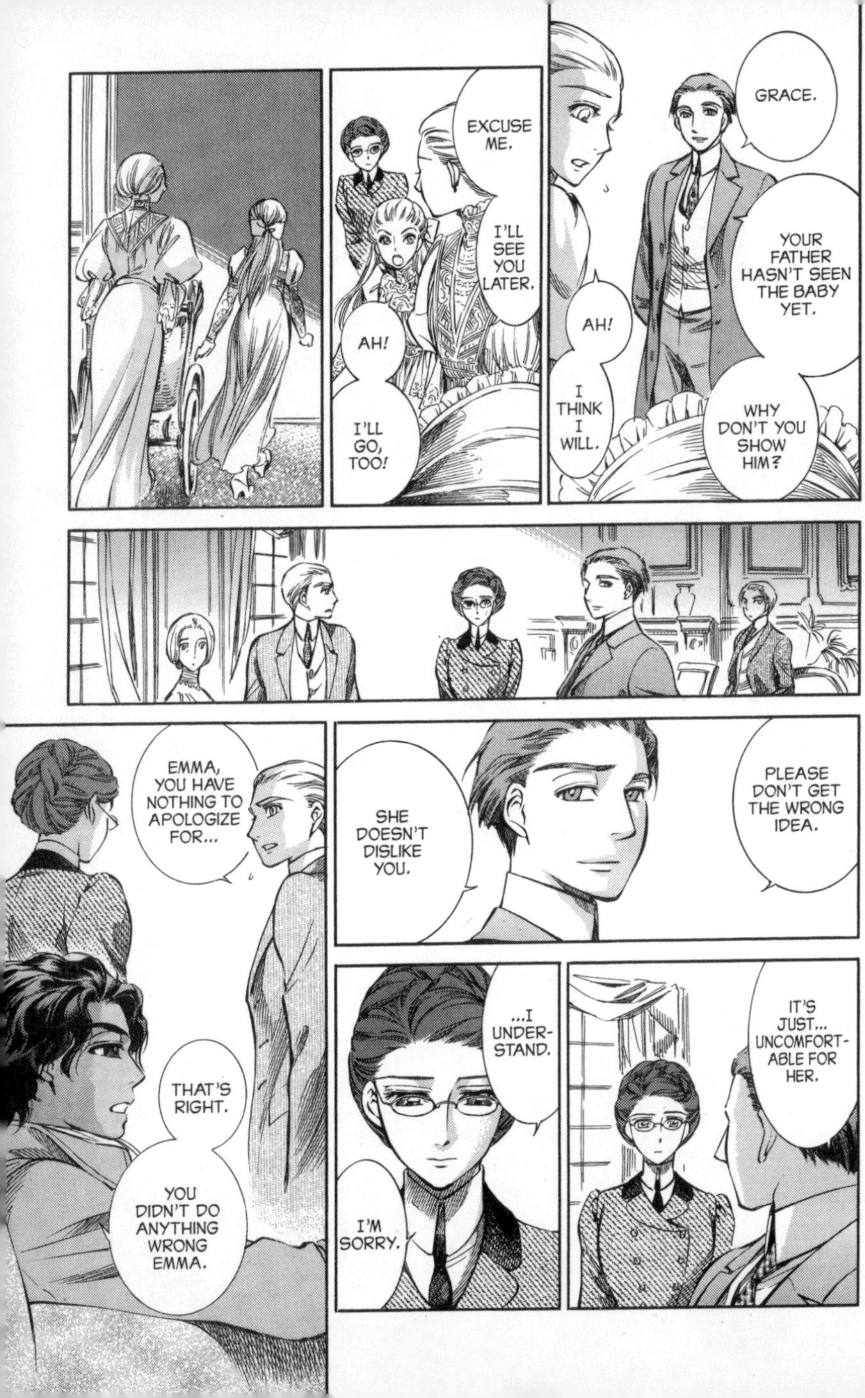
GRACE.
YOUR FATHER HASN'T SEEN THE BABY YET.
WHY DON'T YOU SHOW HIM?
AH!
I THINK I WILL.
EXCUSE ME.
I'LL SEE YOU LATER.
AH!
I'LL GO, TOO!
PLEASE DON'T GET THE WRONG IDEA.
SHE DOESN'T DISLIKE YOU.
IT'S JUST... UNCOMFORTABLE FOR HER.
...I UNDERSTAND.
I'M SORRY.
EMMA, YOU HAVE NOTHING TO APOLOGIZE FOR...
THAT'S RIGHT.
YOU DIDN'T DO ANYTHING WRONG EMMA.

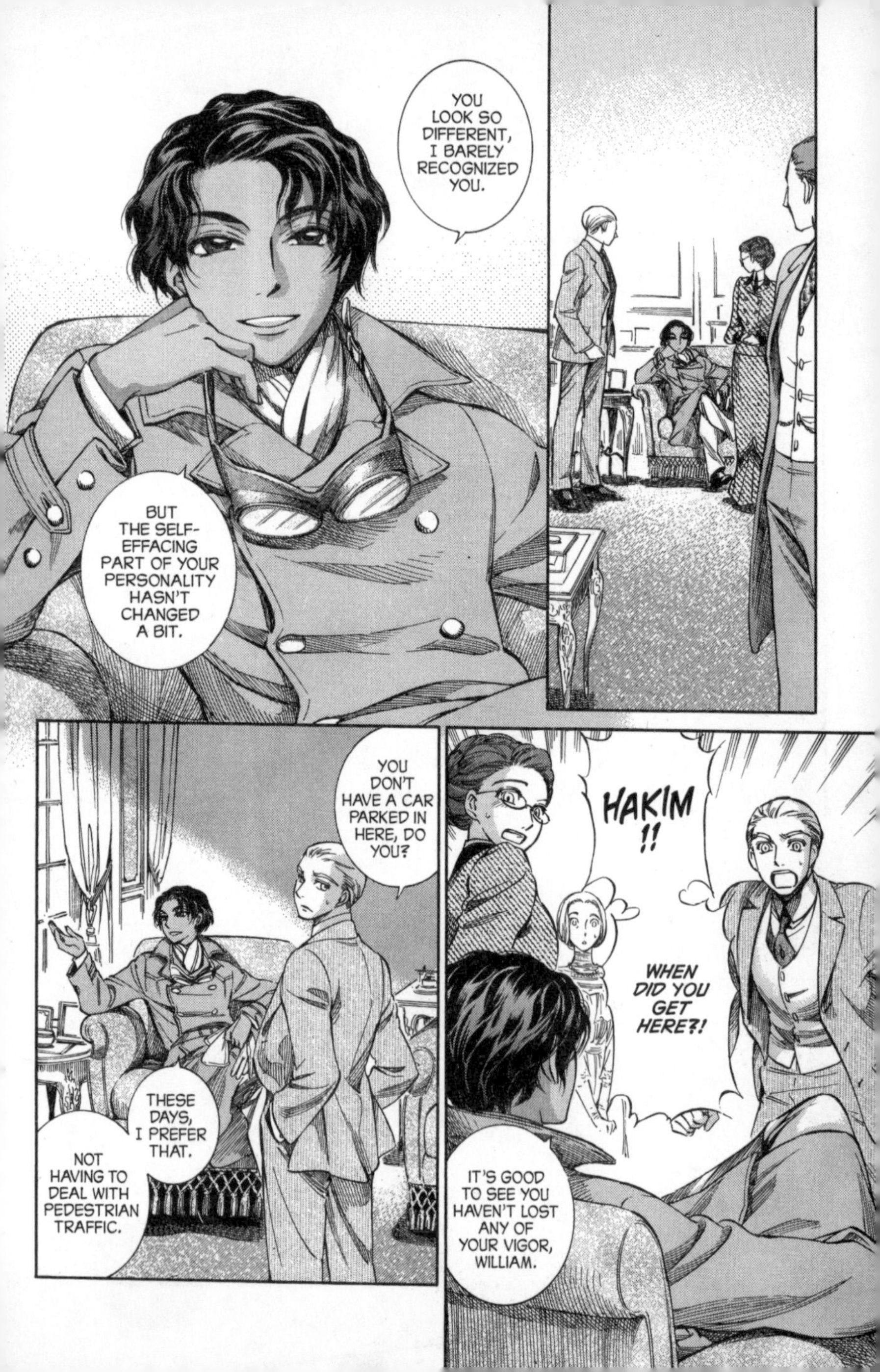
YOU LOOK SO DIFFERENT, I BARELY RECOGNIZED YOU.
BUT THE SELF-EFFACING PART OF YOUR PERSONALITY HASN'T CHANGED A BIT.
HAKIM !!
WHEN DID YOU GET HERE?!
IT'S GOOD TO SEE YOU HAVEN'T LOST ANY OF YOUR VIGOR, WILLIAM.
YOU DON'T HAVE A CAR PARKED IN HERE, DO YOU?
THESE DAYS, I PREFER THAT.
NOT HAVING TO DEAL WITH PEDESTRIAN TRAFFIC.

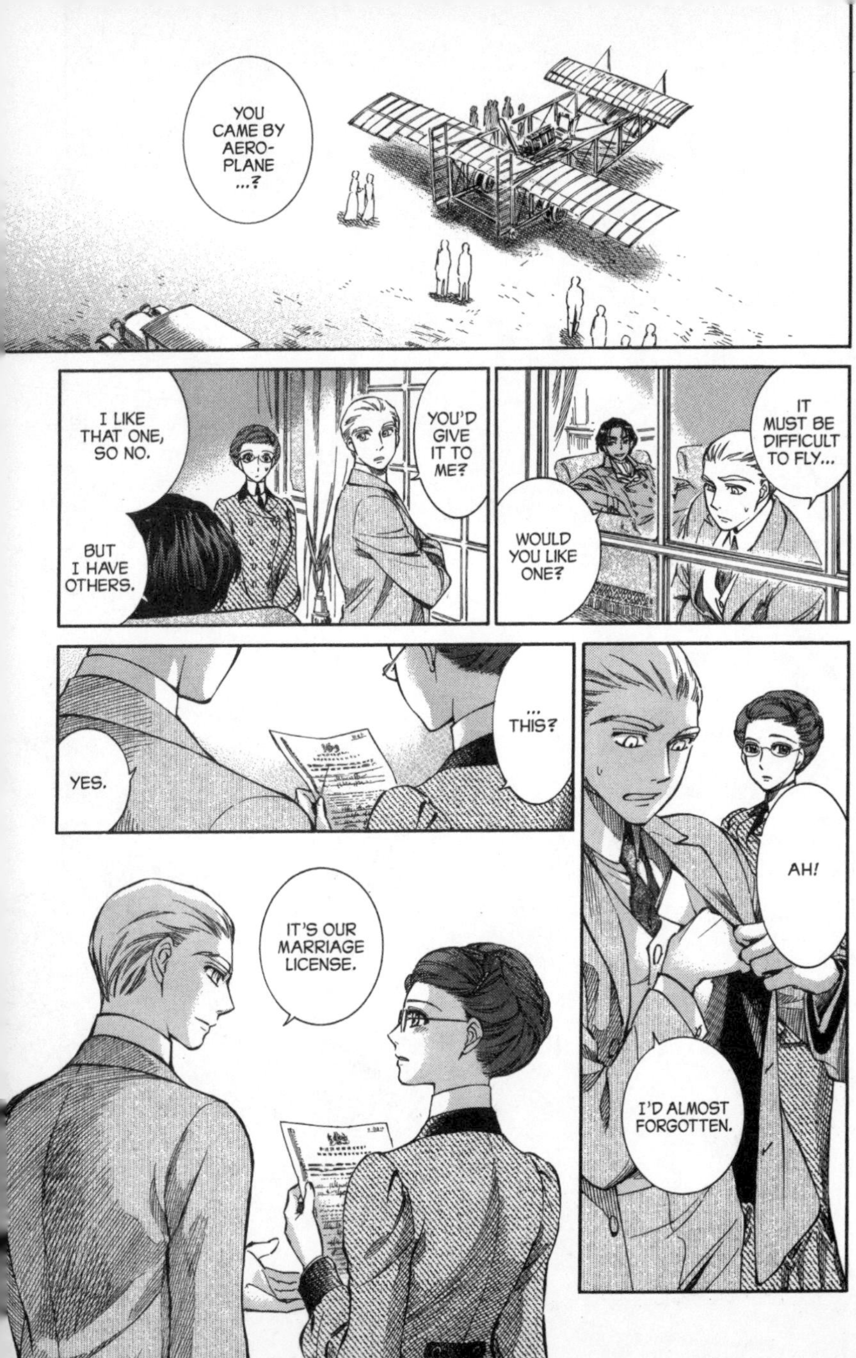
YOU CAME BY AERO-PLANE ...?
IT MUST BE DIFFICULT TO FLY...
WOULD YOU LIKE ONE?
YOU'D GIVE IT TO ME?
I LIKE THAT ONE, SO NO.
BUT I HAVE OTHERS.
AH!
I'D ALMOST FORGOTTEN.
... THIS?
YES.
IT'S OUR MARRIAGE LICENSE.

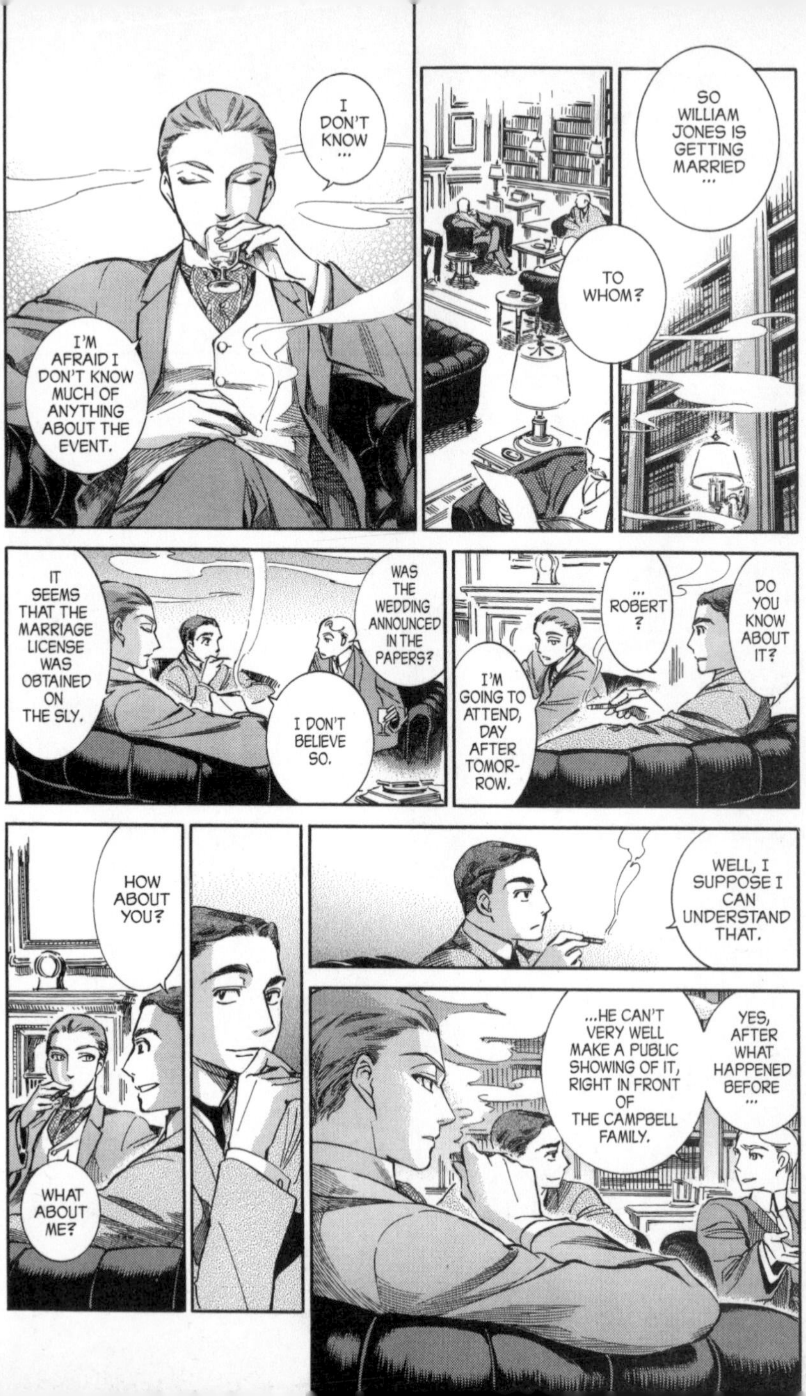
SO WILLIAM JONES IS GETTING MARRIED ...
TO WHOM?
I DON'T KNOW ...
I'M AFRAID I DON'T KNOW MUCH OF ANYTHING ABOUT THE EVENT.
DO YOU KNOW ABOUT IT?
... ROBERT?
I'M GOING TO ATTEND, DAY AFTER TOMORROW.
WAS THE WEDDING ANNOUNCED IN THE PAPERS?
I DON'T BELIEVE SO.
IT SEEMS THAT THE MARRIAGE LICENSE WAS OBTAINED ON THE SLY.
WELL, I SUPPOSE I CAN UNDERSTAND THAT.
YES, AFTER WHAT HAPPENED BEFORE ...
...HE CAN'T VERY WELL MAKE A PUBLIC SHOWING OF IT, RIGHT IN FRONT OF THE CAMPBELL FAMILY.
HOW ABOUT YOU?
WHAT ABOUT ME?

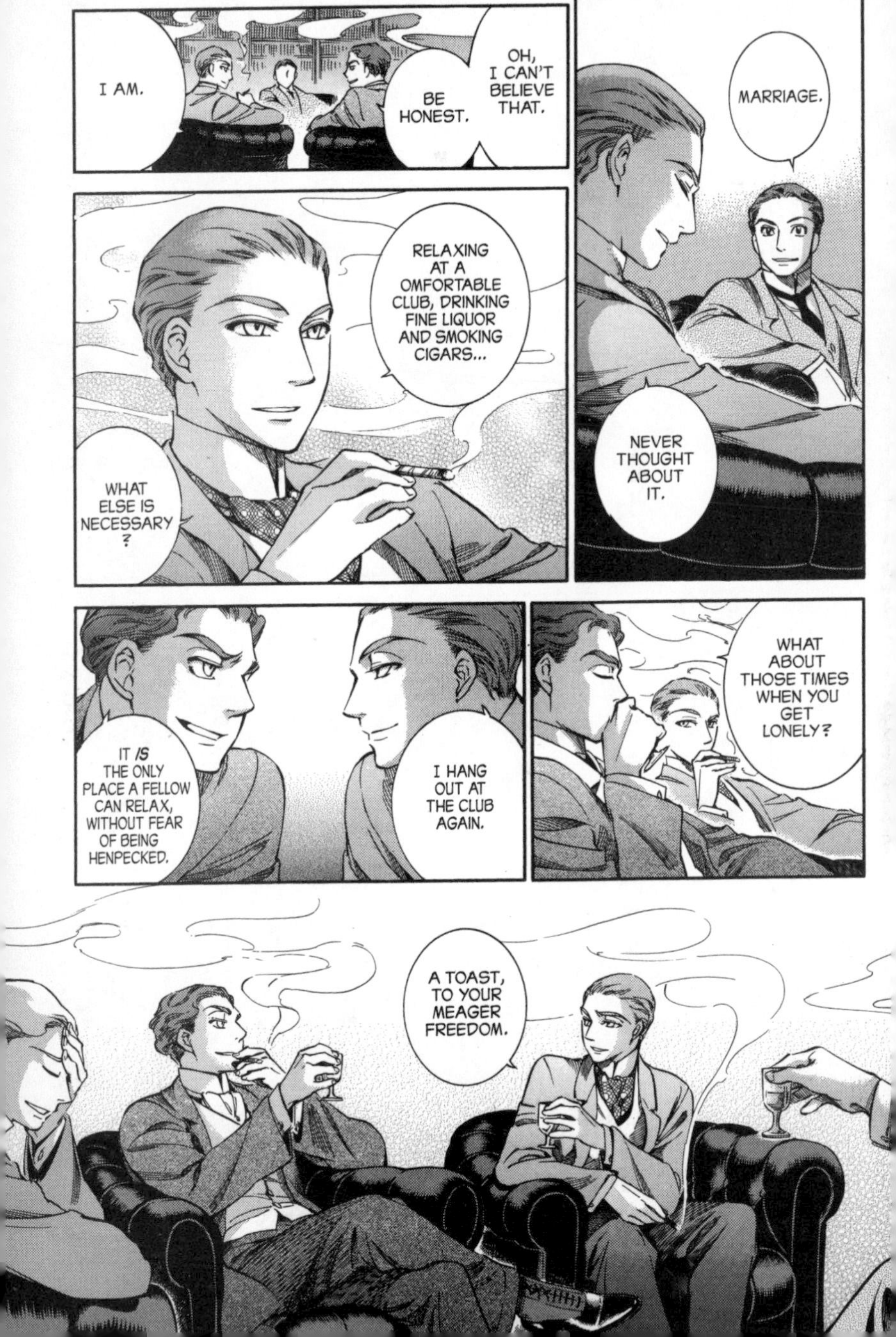
MARRIAGE.
NEVER THOUGHT ABOUT IT.
OH, I CAN'T BELIEVE THAT.
BE HONEST.
I AM.
RELAXING AT A OMFORTABLE CLUB, DRINKING FINE LIQUOR AND SMOKING CIGARS...
WHAT ELSE IS NECESSARY?
WHAT ABOUT THOSE TIMES WHEN YOU GET LONELY?
I HANG OUT AT THE CLUB AGAIN.
IT *IS* THE ONLY PLACE A FELLOW CAN RELAX, WITHOUT FEAR OF BEING HENPECKED.
A TOAST, TO YOUR MEAGER FREEDOM.

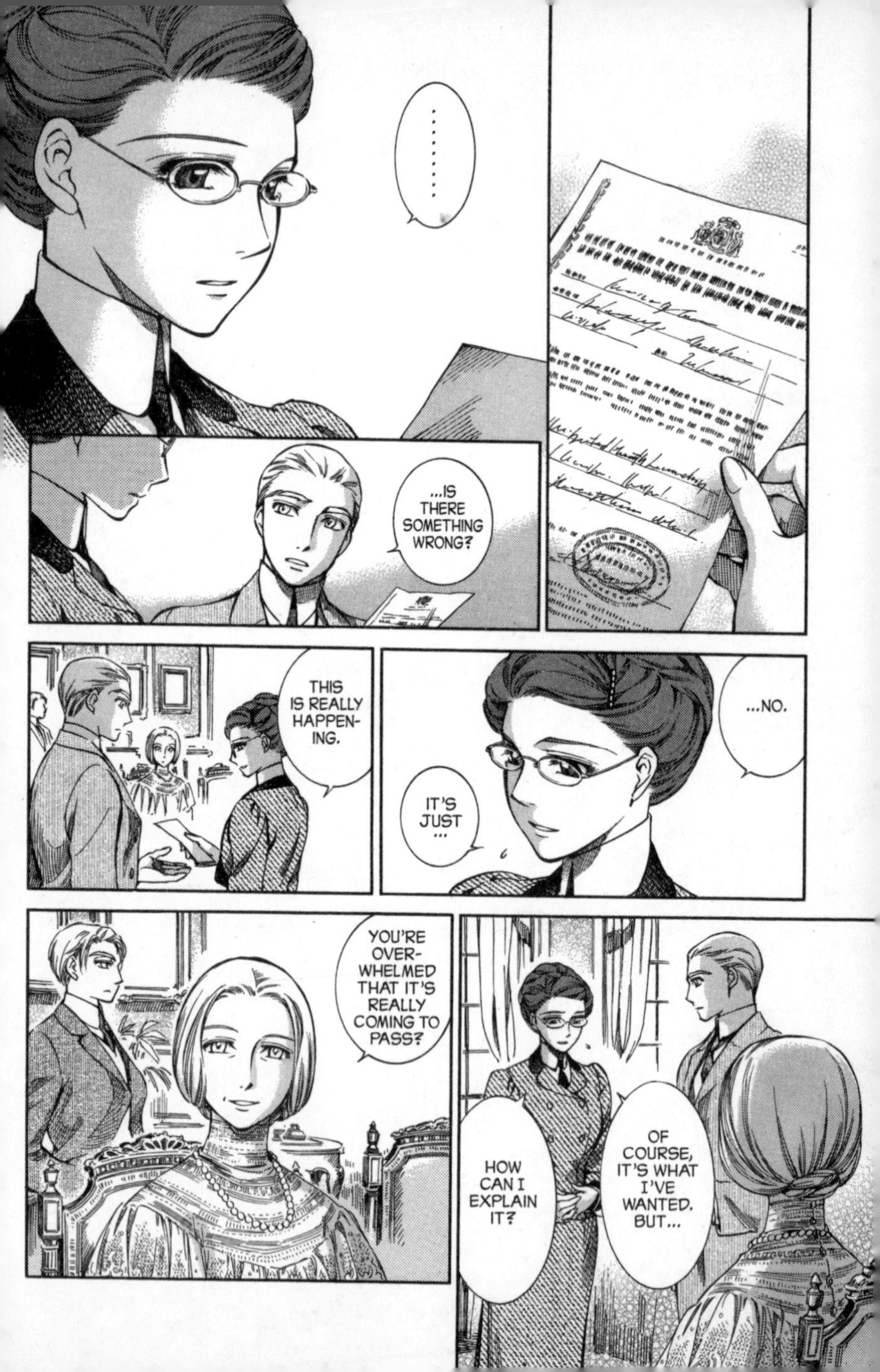
......
...IS THERE SOMETHING WRONG?
...NO.
IT'S JUST ...
THIS IS REALLY HAPPEN-ING.
OF COURSE, IT'S WHAT I'VE WANTED. BUT...
HOW CAN I EXPLAIN IT?
YOU'RE OVER-WHELMED THAT IT'S REALLY COMING TO PASS?

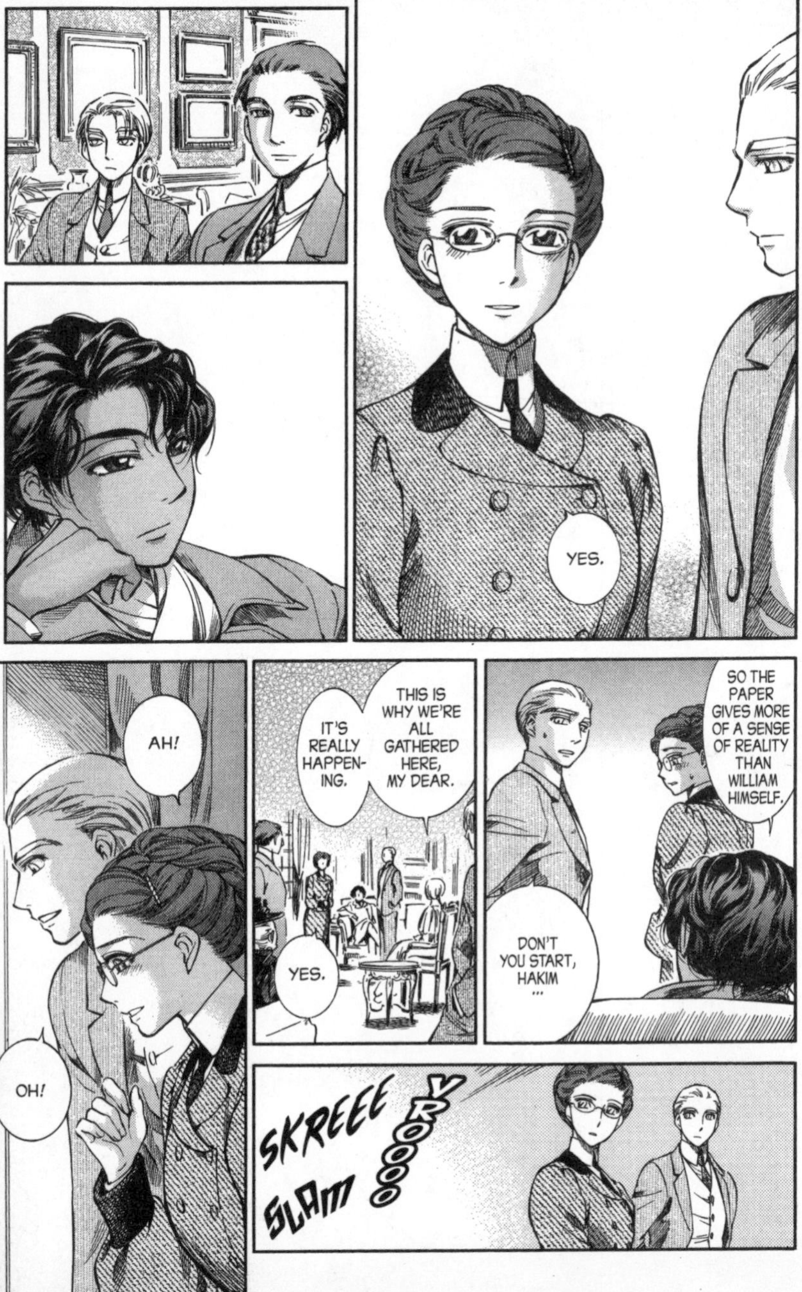
YES.
SO THE PAPER GIVES MORE OF A SENSE OF REALITY THAN WILLIAM HIMSELF.
DON'T YOU START, HAKIM ...
THIS IS WHY WE'RE ALL GATHERED HERE, MY DEAR.
IT'S REALLY HAPPEN-ING.
YES.
VROOOOO
SKREEE
SLAM
AH!
OH!

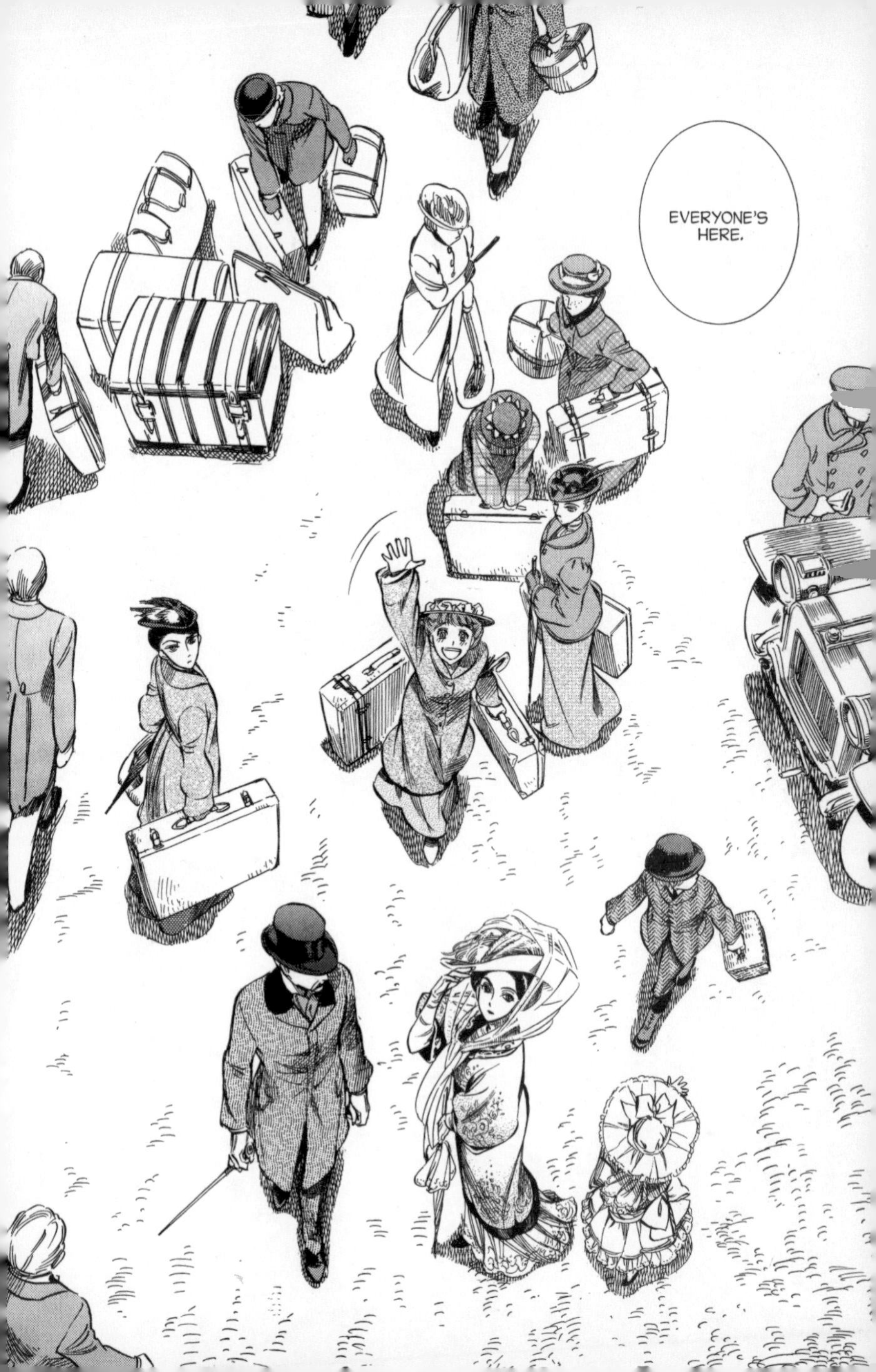
EVERYONE'S HERE.

**CHAPTER
19:
A NEW
AGE
(part two)**

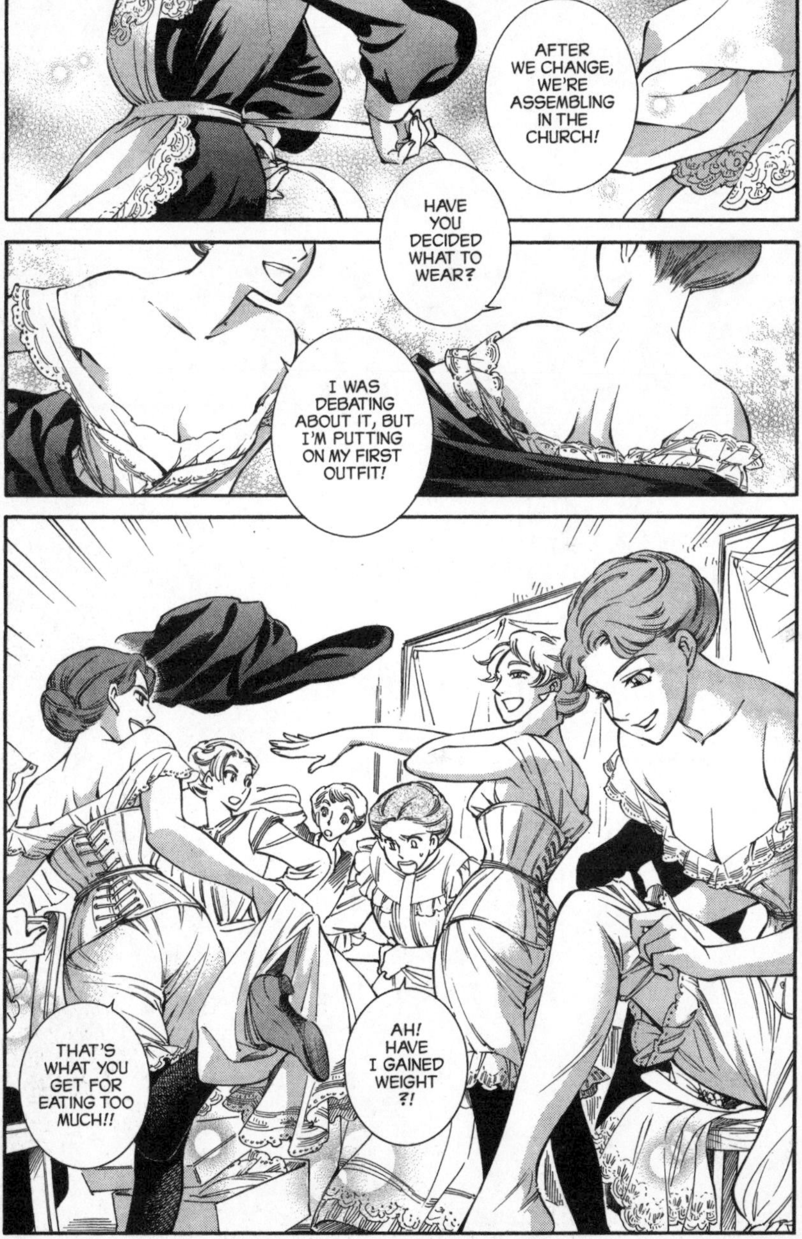
AFTER WE CHANGE, WE'RE ASSEMBLING IN THE CHURCH!
HAVE YOU DECIDED WHAT TO WEAR?
I WAS DEBATING ABOUT IT, BUT I'M PUTTING ON MY FIRST OUTFIT!
AH! HAVE I GAINED WEIGHT?!
THAT'S WHAT YOU GET FOR EATING TOO MUCH!!

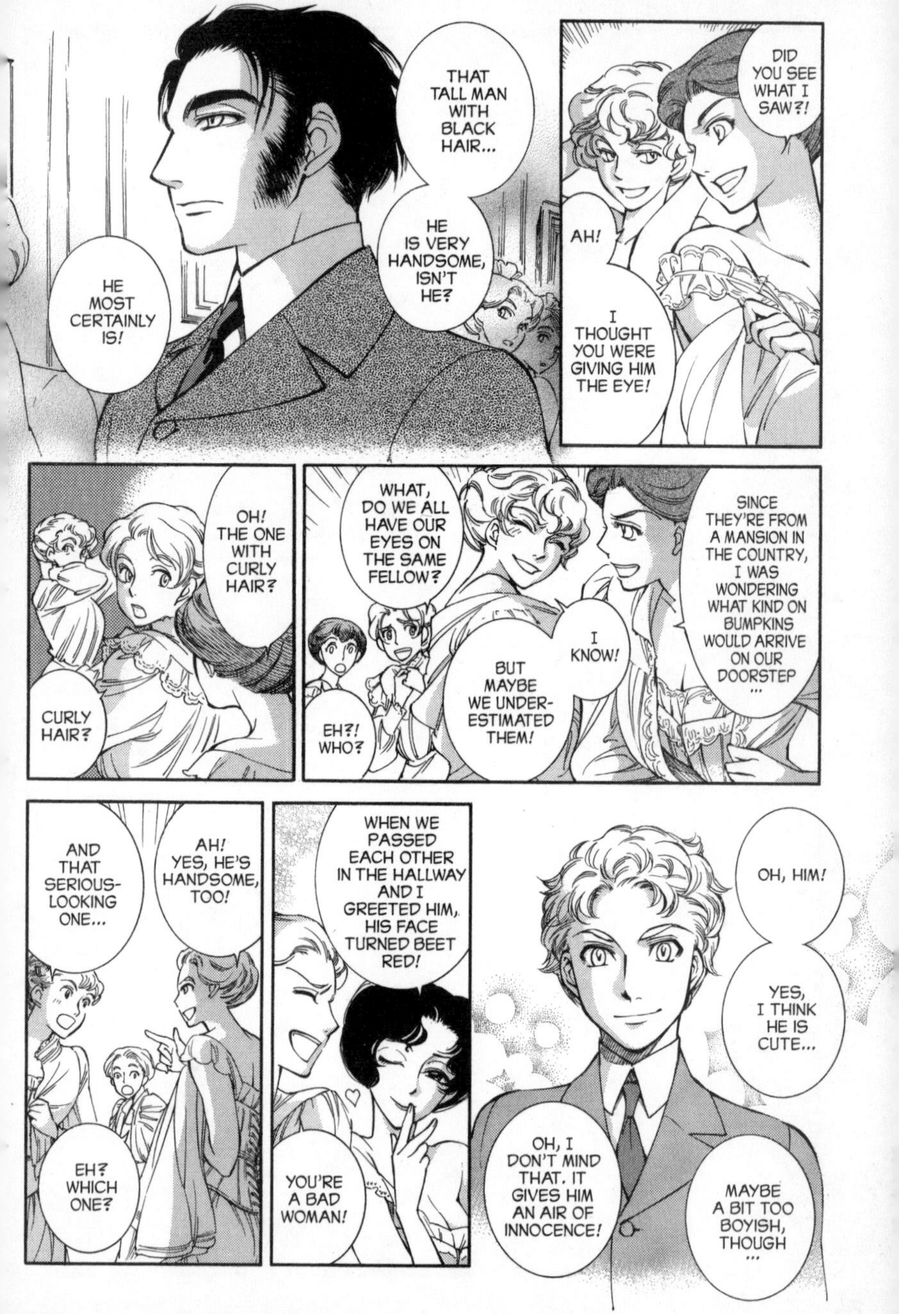
DID YOU SEE WHAT I SAW?!
AH!
I THOUGHT YOU WERE GIVING HIM THE EYE!
THAT TALL MAN WITH BLACK HAIR...
HE IS VERY HANDSOME, ISN'T HE?
HE MOST CERTAINLY IS!
SINCE THEY'RE FROM A MANSION IN THE COUNTRY, I WAS WONDERING WHAT KIND ON BUMPKINS WOULD ARRIVE ON OUR DOORSTEP...
I KNOW!
BUT MAYBE WE UNDER-ESTIMATED THEM!
WHAT, DO WE ALL HAVE OUR EYES ON THE SAME FELLOW?
EH?! WHO?
OH! THE ONE WITH CURLY HAIR?
CURLY HAIR?
OH, HIM!
YES, I THINK HE IS CUTE...
MAYBE A BIT TOO BOYISH, THOUGH...
OH, I DON'T MIND THAT. IT GIVES HIM AN AIR OF INNOCENCE!
WHEN WE PASSED EACH OTHER IN THE HALLWAY AND I GREETED HIM, HIS FACE TURNED BEET RED!
YOU'RE A BAD WOMAN!
AH! YES, HE'S HANDSOME, TOO!
AND THAT SERIOUS-LOOKING ONE...
EH? WHICH ONE?

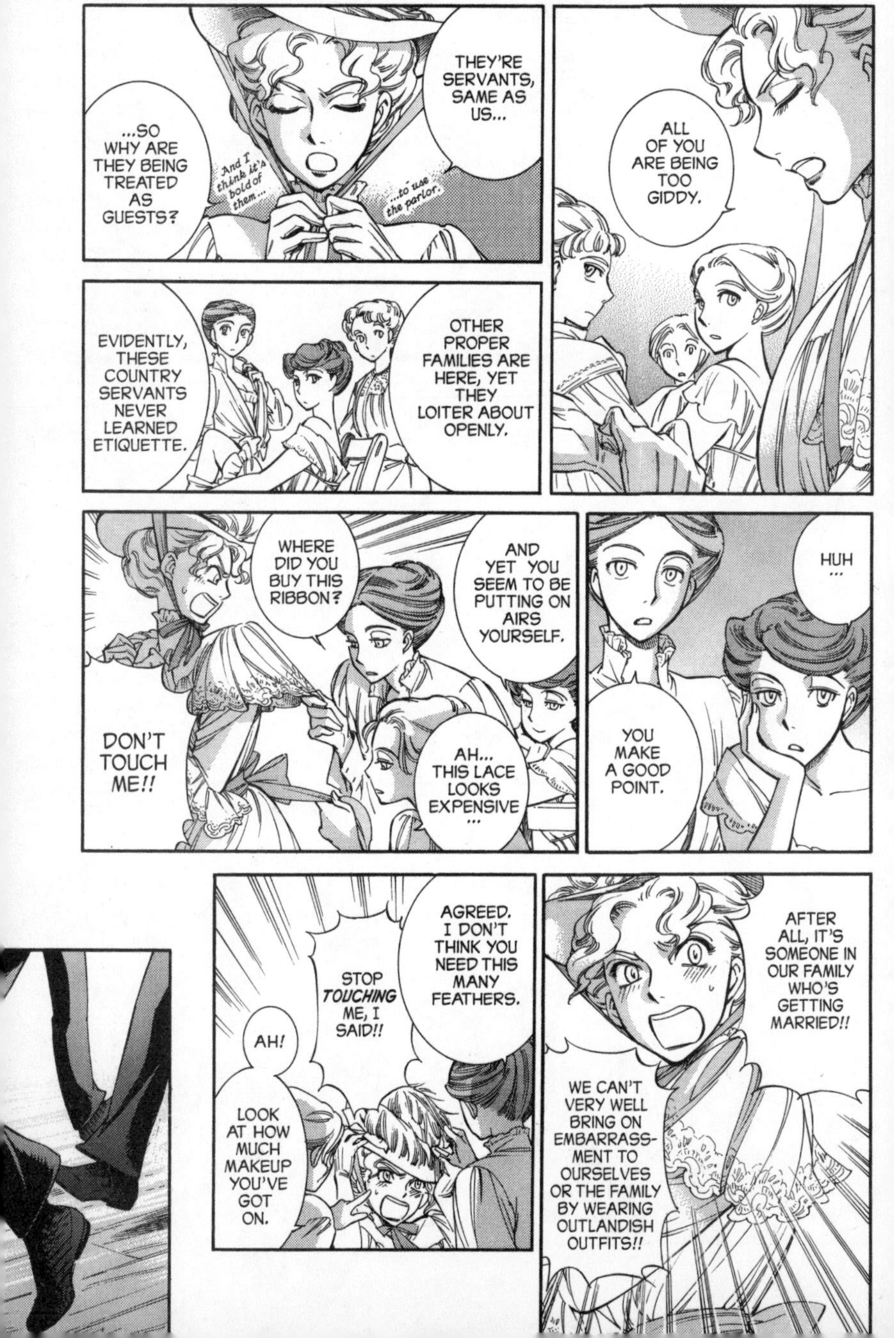
ALL OF YOU ARE BEING TOO GIDDY.
THEY'RE SERVANTS, SAME AS US...
...SO WHY ARE THEY BEING TREATED AS GUESTS?
And I think it's bold of them...
...to use the parlor.
OTHER PROPER FAMILIES ARE HERE, YET THEY LOITER ABOUT OPENLY.
EVIDENTLY, THESE COUNTRY SERVANTS NEVER LEARNED ETIQUETTE.
HUH...
YOU MAKE A GOOD POINT.
AND YET YOU SEEM TO BE PUTTING ON AIRS YOURSELF.
WHERE DID YOU BUY THIS RIBBON?
AH... THIS LACE LOOKS EXPENSIVE...
DON'T TOUCH ME!!
AFTER ALL, IT'S SOMEONE IN OUR FAMILY WHO'S GETTING MARRIED!!
WE CAN'T VERY WELL BRING ON EMBARRASS-MENT TO OURSELVES OR THE FAMILY BY WEARING OUTLANDISH OUTFITS!!
AGREED. I DON'T THINK YOU NEED THIS MANY FEATHERS.
STOP TOUCHING ME, I SAID!!
AH!
LOOK AT HOW MUCH MAKEUP YOU'VE GOT ON.

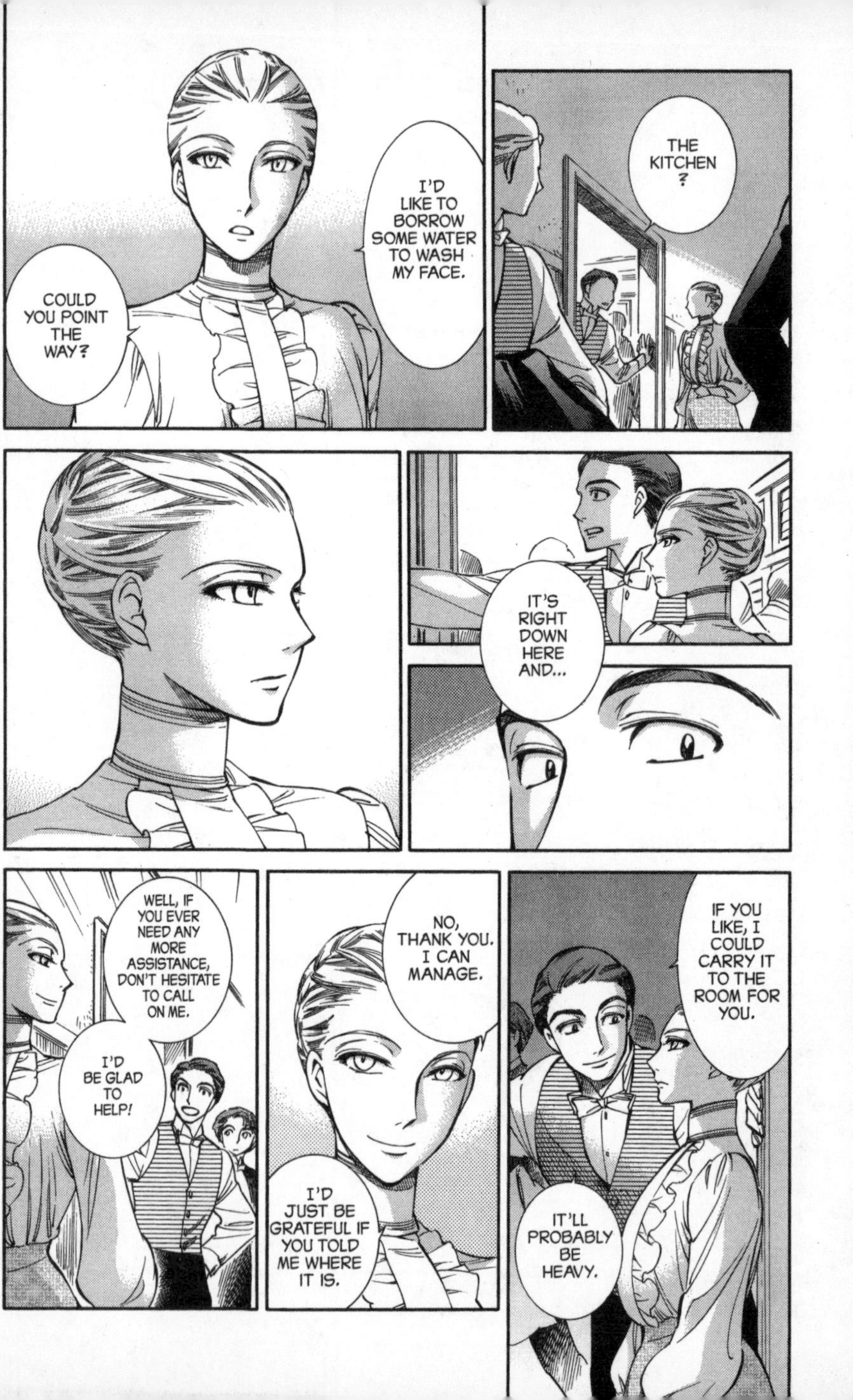
THE KITCHEN?
I'D LIKE TO BORROW SOME WATER TO WASH MY FACE.
COULD YOU POINT THE WAY?
IT'S RIGHT DOWN HERE AND...
IF YOU LIKE, I COULD CARRY IT TO THE ROOM FOR YOU.
IT'LL PROBABLY BE HEAVY.
NO, THANK YOU. I CAN MANAGE.
I'D JUST BE GRATEFUL IF YOU TOLD ME WHERE IT IS.
WELL, IF YOU EVER NEED ANY MORE ASSISTANCE, DON'T HESITATE TO CALL ON ME.
I'D BE GLAD TO HELP!

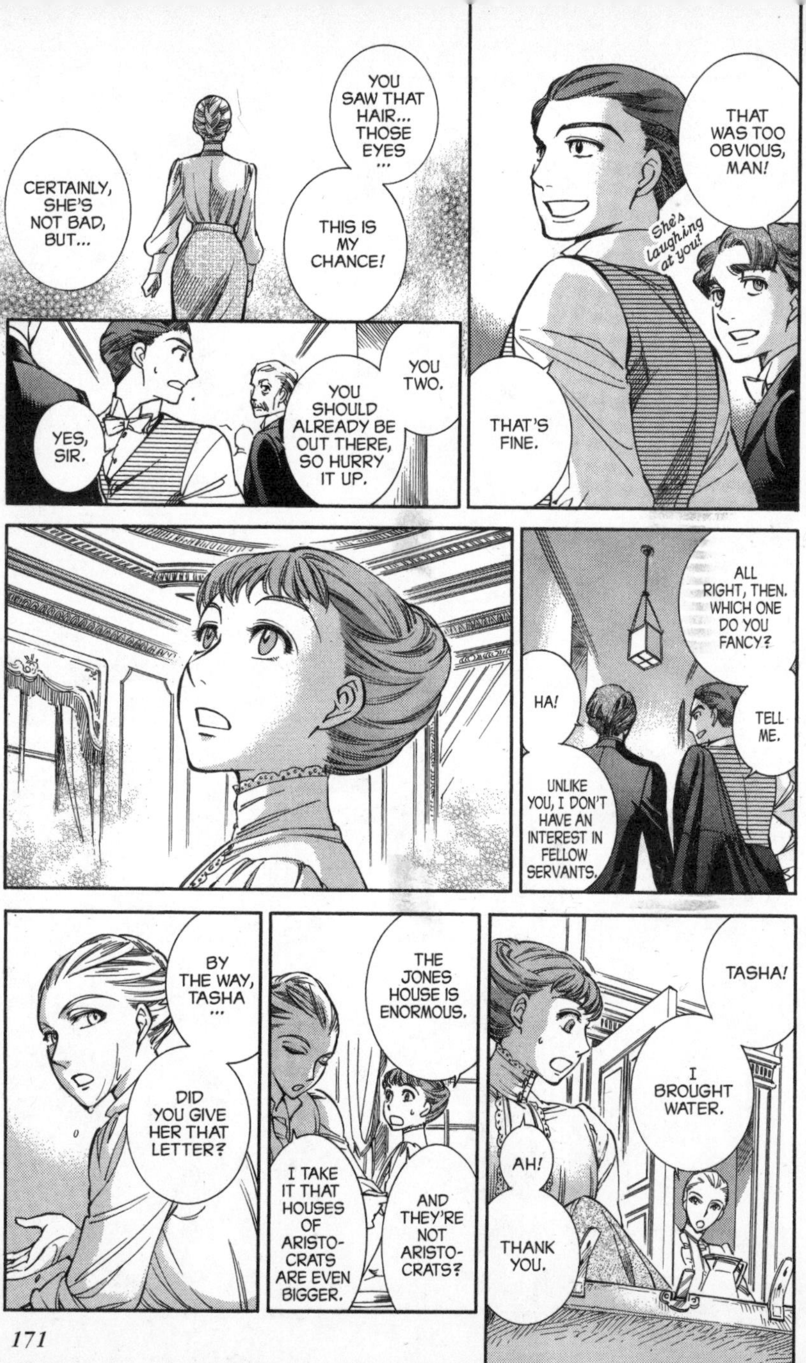
THAT WAS TOO OBVIOUS, MAN!
She's laughing at you!
THAT'S FINE.
YOU SAW THAT HAIR... THOSE EYES...
THIS IS MY CHANCE!
CERTAINLY, SHE'S NOT BAD, BUT...
YOU TWO.
YOU SHOULD ALREADY BE OUT THERE, SO HURRY IT UP.
YES, SIR.
ALL RIGHT, THEN. WHICH ONE DO YOU FANCY?
TELL ME.
HA!
UNLIKE YOU, I DON'T HAVE AN INTEREST IN FELLOW SERVANTS.
TASHA!
I BROUGHT WATER.
AH!
THANK YOU.
THE JONES HOUSE IS ENORMOUS.
AND THEY'RE NOT ARISTOCRATS?
I TAKE IT THAT HOUSES OF ARISTOCRATS ARE EVEN BIGGER.
BY THE WAY, TASHA...
DID YOU GIVE HER THAT LETTER?

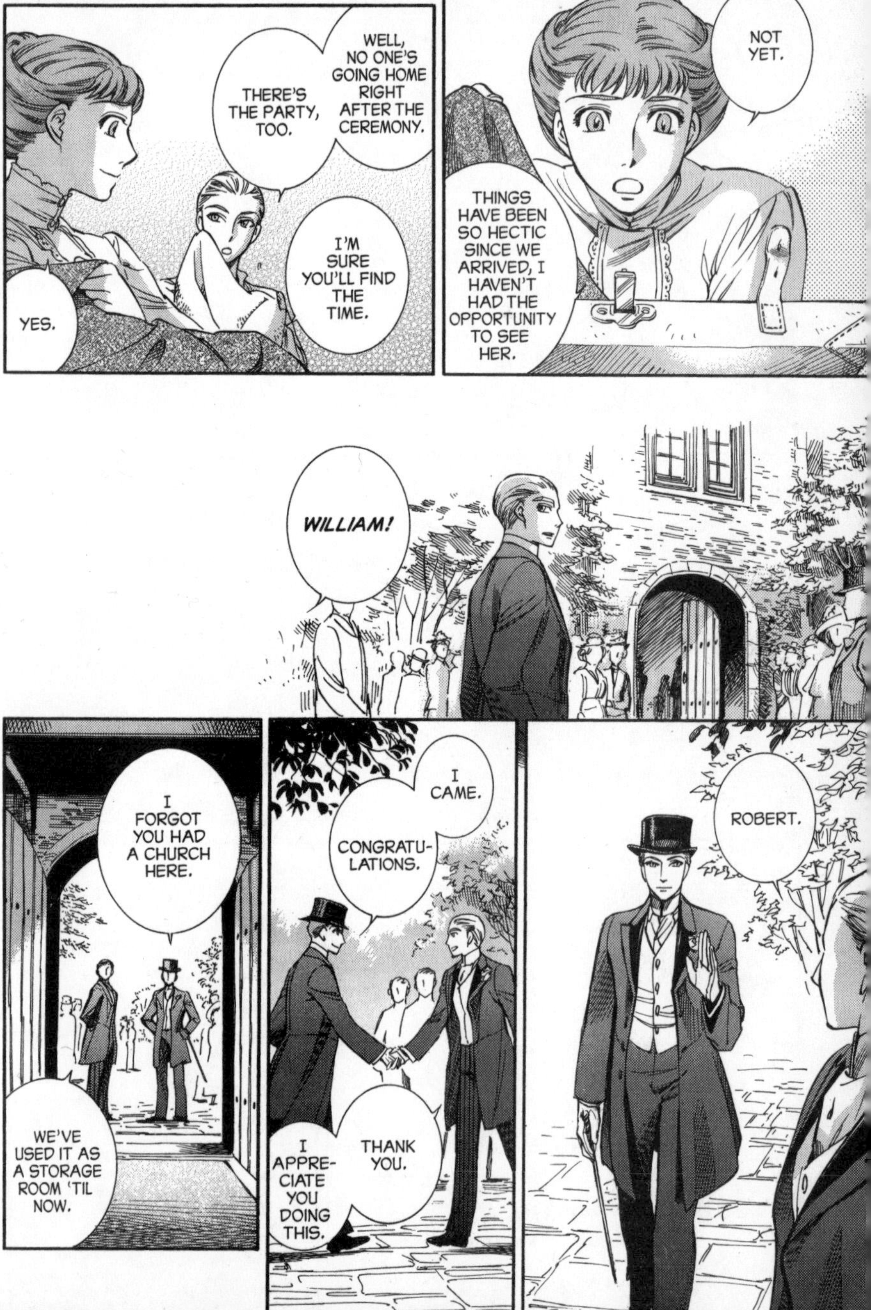
NOT YET.
THINGS HAVE BEEN SO HECTIC SINCE WE ARRIVED, I HAVEN'T HAD THE OPPORTUNITY TO SEE HER.
WELL, NO ONE'S GOING HOME RIGHT AFTER THE CEREMONY.
THERE'S THE PARTY, TOO.
I'M SURE YOU'LL FIND THE TIME.
YES.
WILLIAM!
ROBERT.
I CAME.
CONGRATULATIONS.
THANK YOU.
I APPRECIATE YOU DOING THIS.
I FORGOT YOU HAD A CHURCH HERE.
WE'VE USED IT AS A STORAGE ROOM 'TIL NOW.

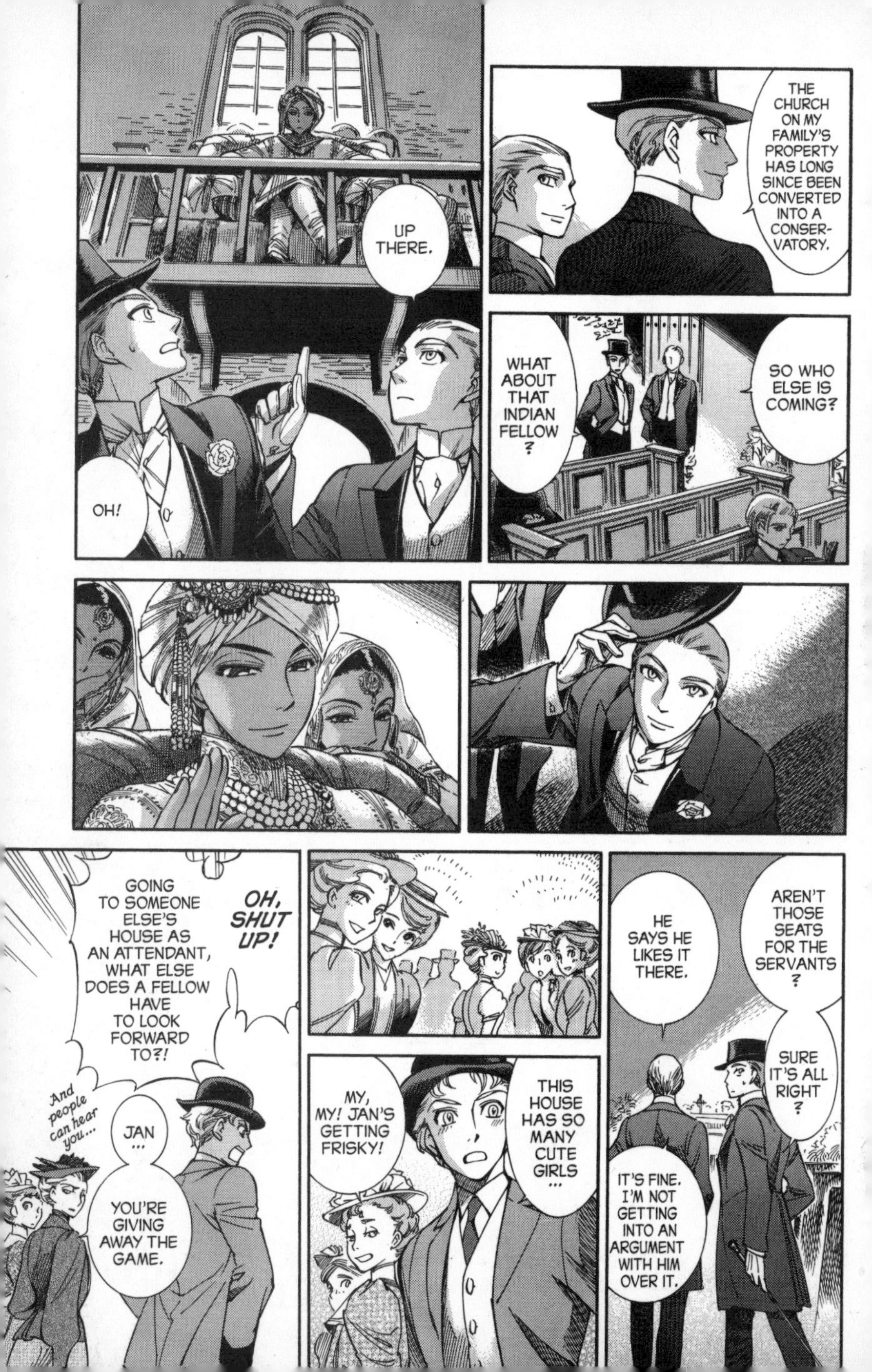
THE CHURCH ON MY FAMILY'S PROPERTY HAS LONG SINCE BEEN CONVERTED INTO A CONSER- VATORY.
SO WHO ELSE IS COMING?
WHAT ABOUT THAT INDIAN FELLOW?
UP THERE.
OH!
AREN'T THOSE SEATS FOR THE SERVANTS?
HE SAYS HE LIKES IT THERE.
SURE IT'S ALL RIGHT?
IT'S FINE. I'M NOT GETTING INTO AN ARGUMENT WITH HIM OVER IT.
THIS HOUSE HAS SO MANY CUTE GIRLS...
MY, MY! JAN'S GETTING FRISKY!
OH, SHUT UP!
GOING TO SOMEONE ELSE'S HOUSE AS AN ATTENDANT, WHAT ELSE DOES A FELLOW HAVE TO LOOK FORWARD TO?!
JAN...
YOU'RE GIVING AWAY THE GAME.
And people can hear you...

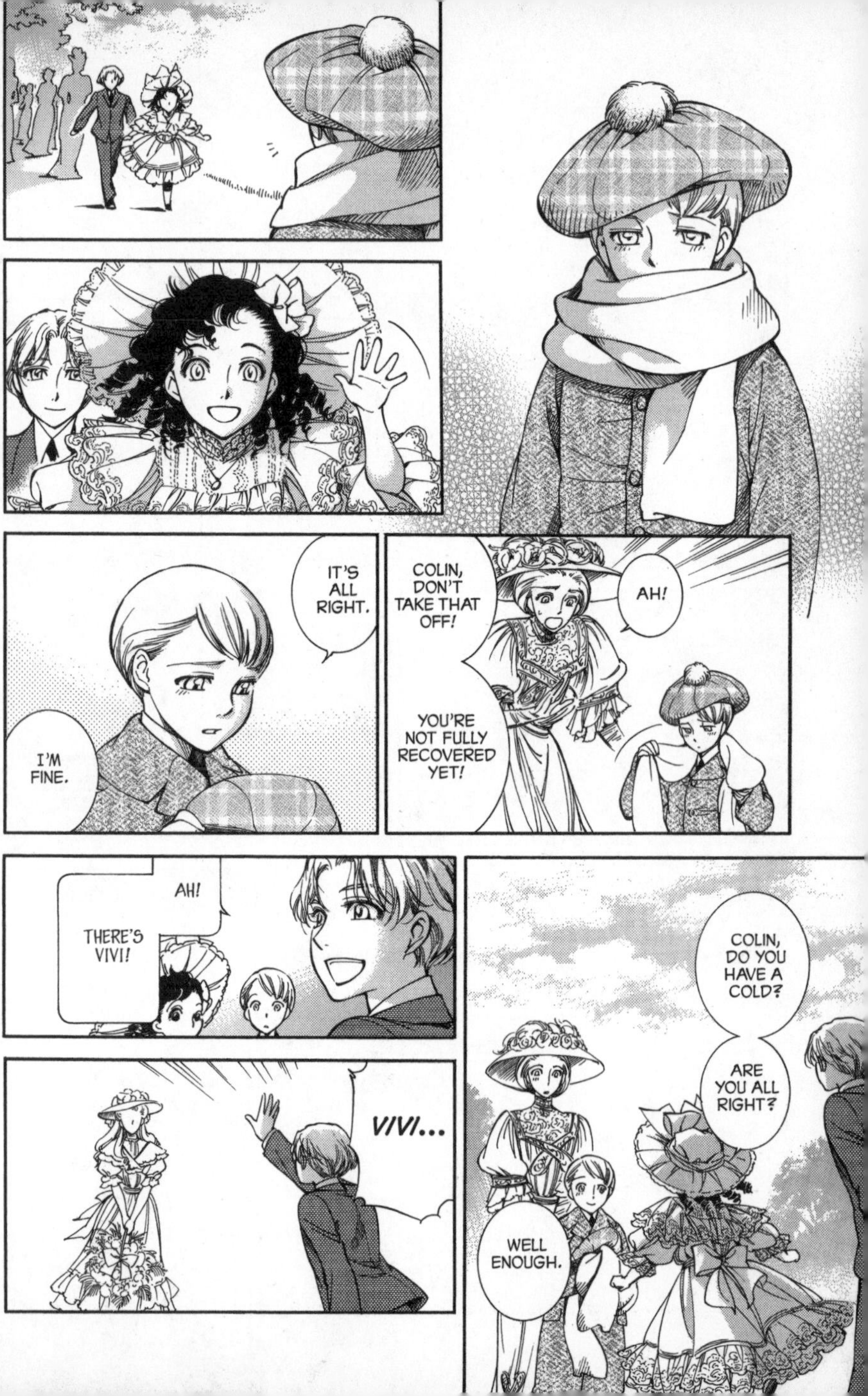
AH!
COLIN, DON'T TAKE THAT OFF!
YOU'RE NOT FULLY RECOVERED YET!
IT'S ALL RIGHT.
I'M FINE.
COLIN, DO YOU HAVE A COLD?
ARE YOU ALL RIGHT?
WELL ENOUGH.
AH!
THERE'S VIVI!
VIVI...

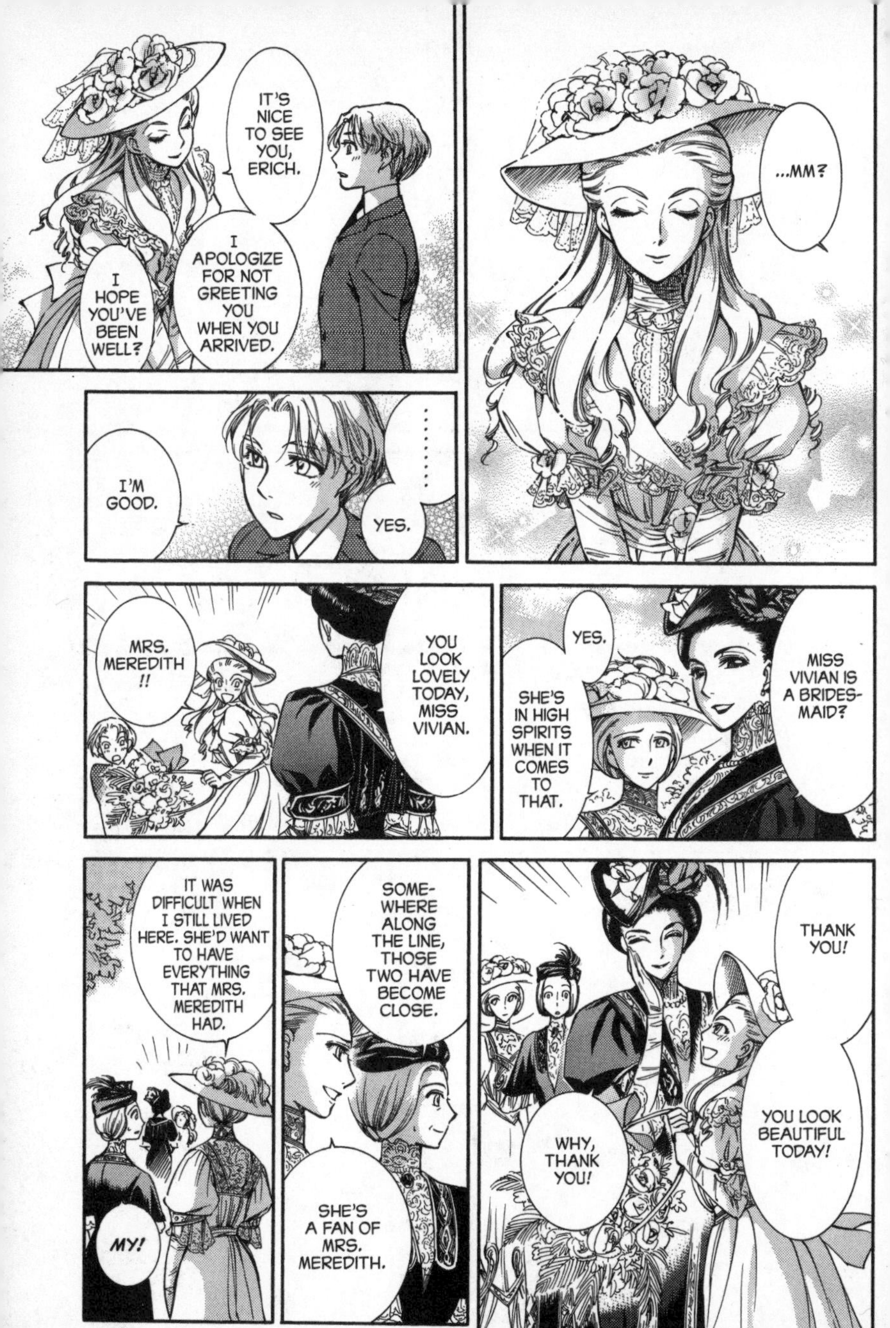
...MM?
IT'S NICE TO SEE YOU, ERICH.
I APOLOGIZE FOR NOT GREETING YOU WHEN YOU ARRIVED.
I HOPE YOU'VE BEEN WELL?
......
YES.
I'M GOOD.
MISS VIVIAN IS A BRIDES-MAID?
YES.
SHE'S IN HIGH SPIRITS WHEN IT COMES TO THAT.
YOU LOOK LOVELY TODAY, MISS VIVIAN.
MRS. MEREDITH!!
THANK YOU!
YOU LOOK BEAUTIFUL TODAY!
WHY, THANK YOU!
SOME-WHERE ALONG THE LINE, THOSE TWO HAVE BECOME CLOSE.
SHE'S A FAN OF MRS. MEREDITH.
IT WAS DIFFICULT WHEN I STILL LIVED HERE. SHE'D WANT TO HAVE EVERYTHING THAT MRS. MEREDITH HAD.
MY!

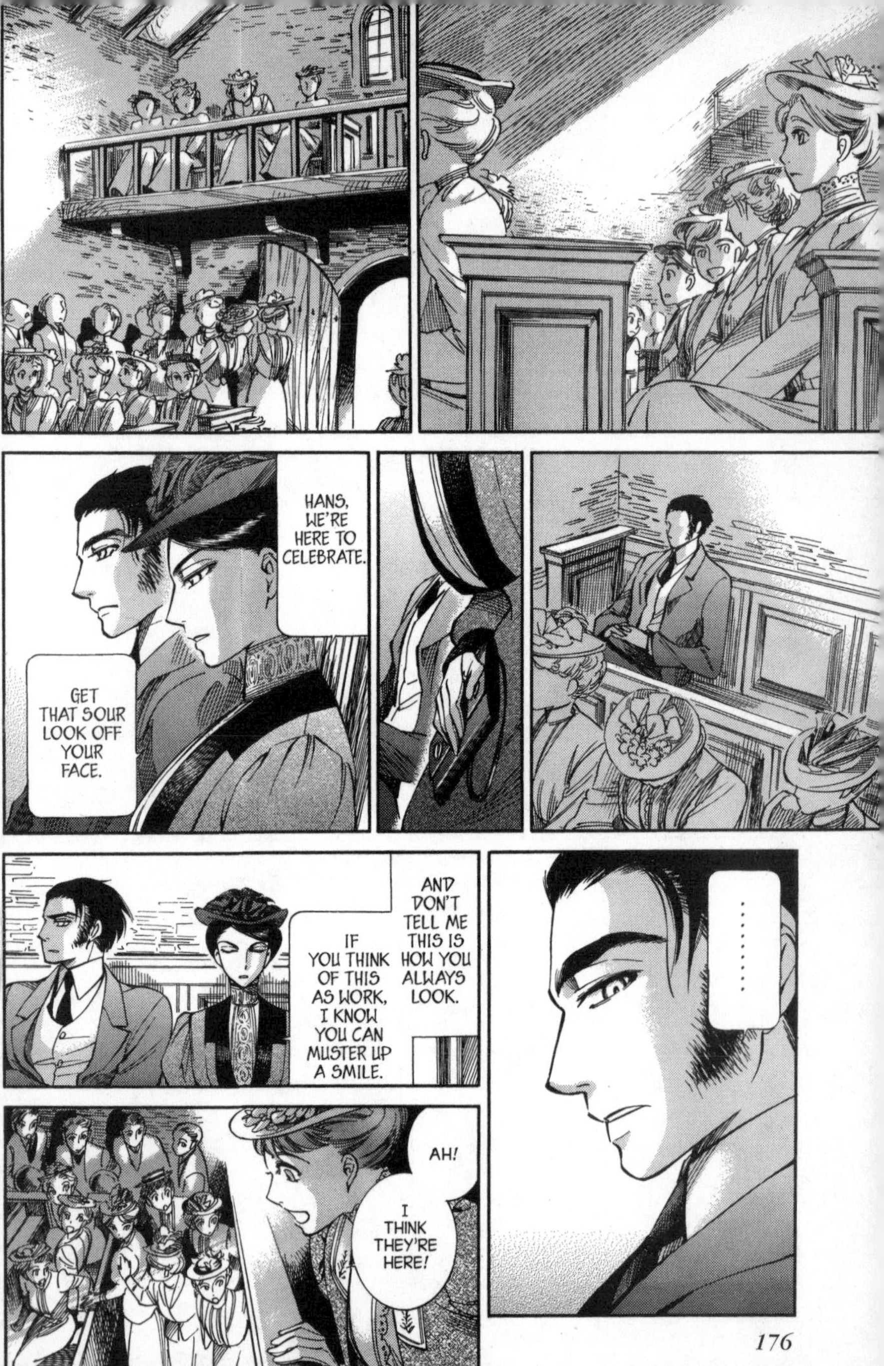
HANS, WE'RE HERE TO CELEBRATE.
GET THAT SOUR LOOK OFF YOUR FACE.
......
AND DON'T TELL ME THIS IS HOW YOU ALWAYS LOOK.
IF YOU THINK OF THIS AS WORK, I KNOW YOU CAN MUSTER UP A SMILE.
AH!
I THINK THEY'RE HERE!

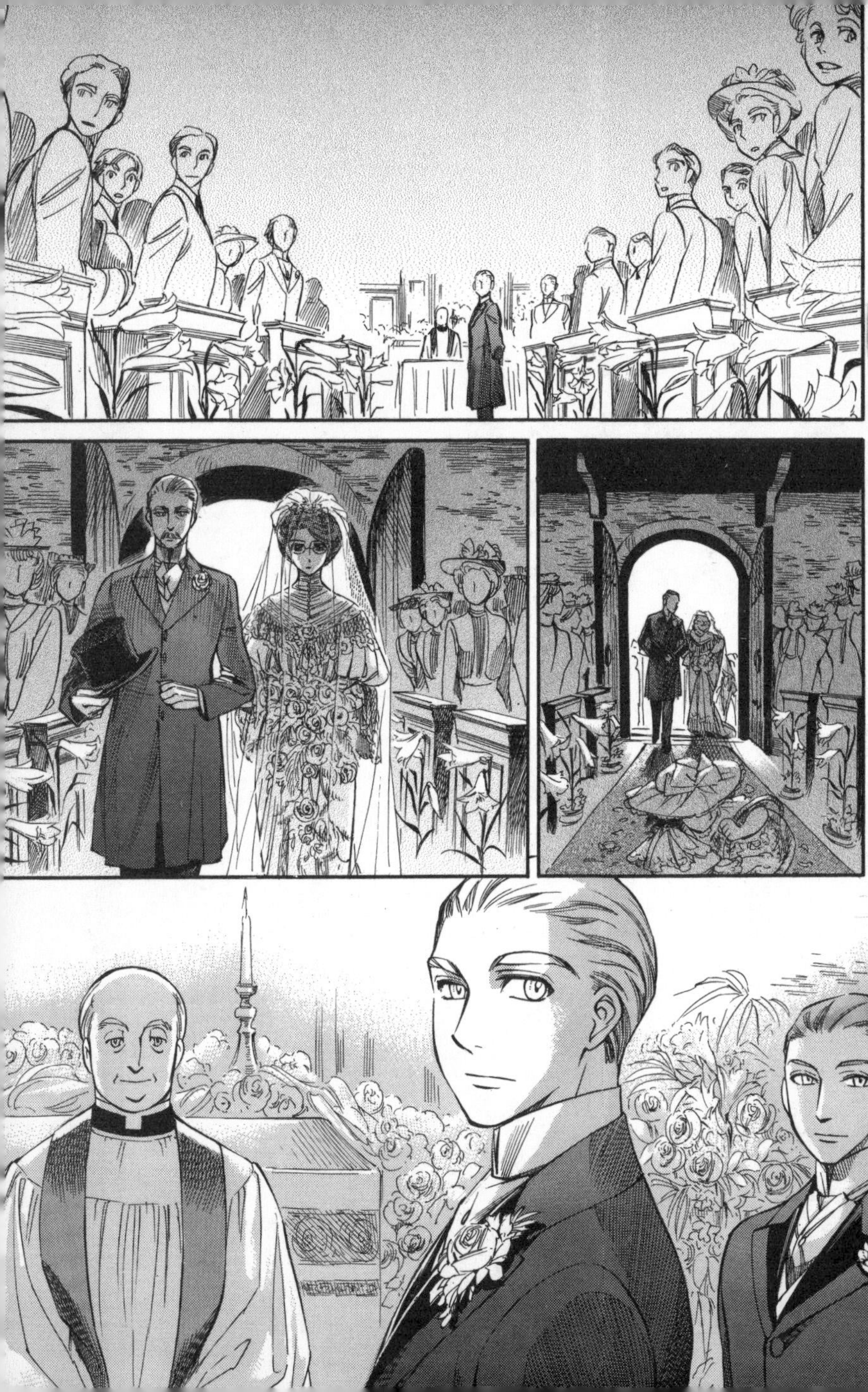

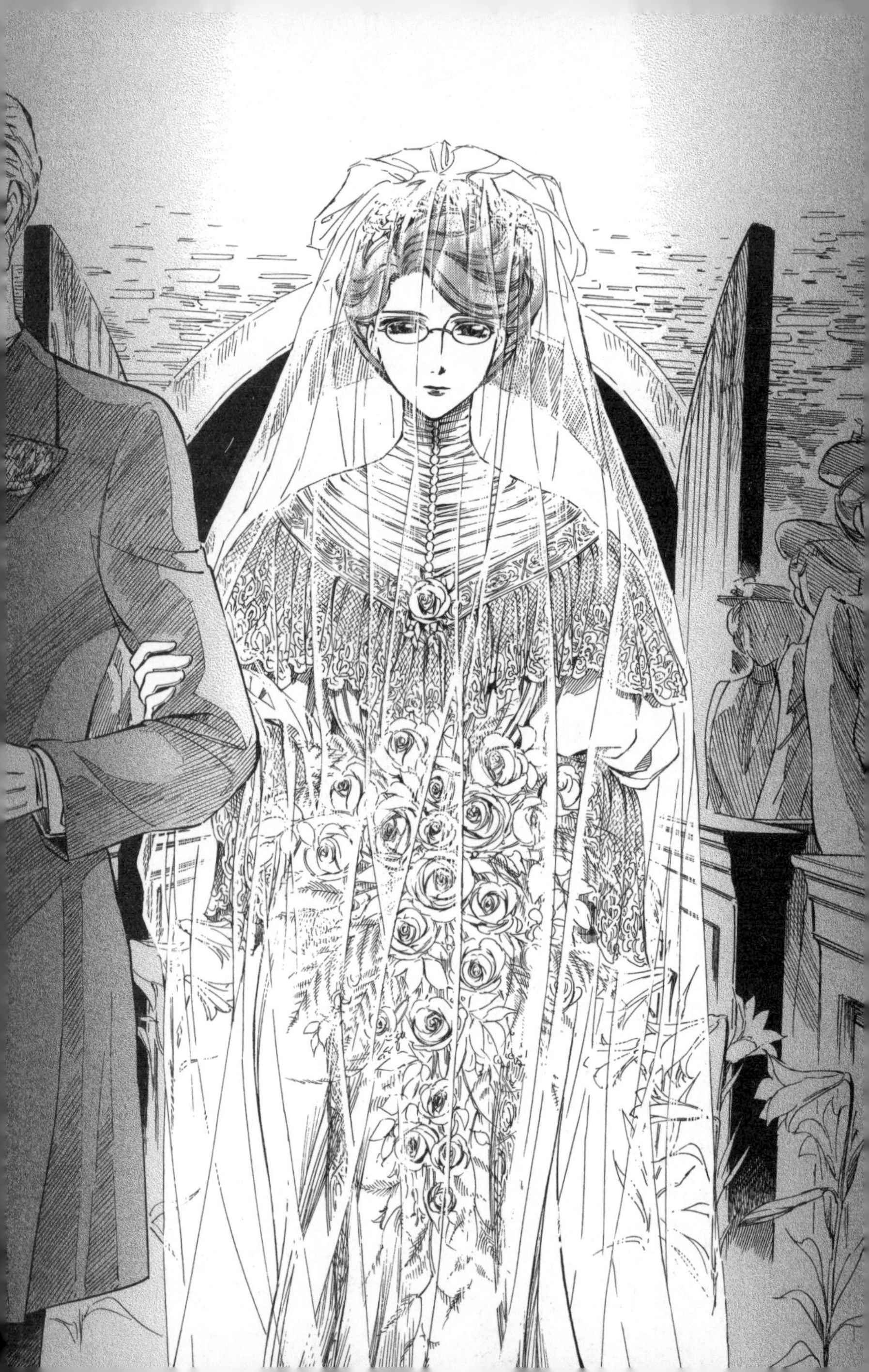

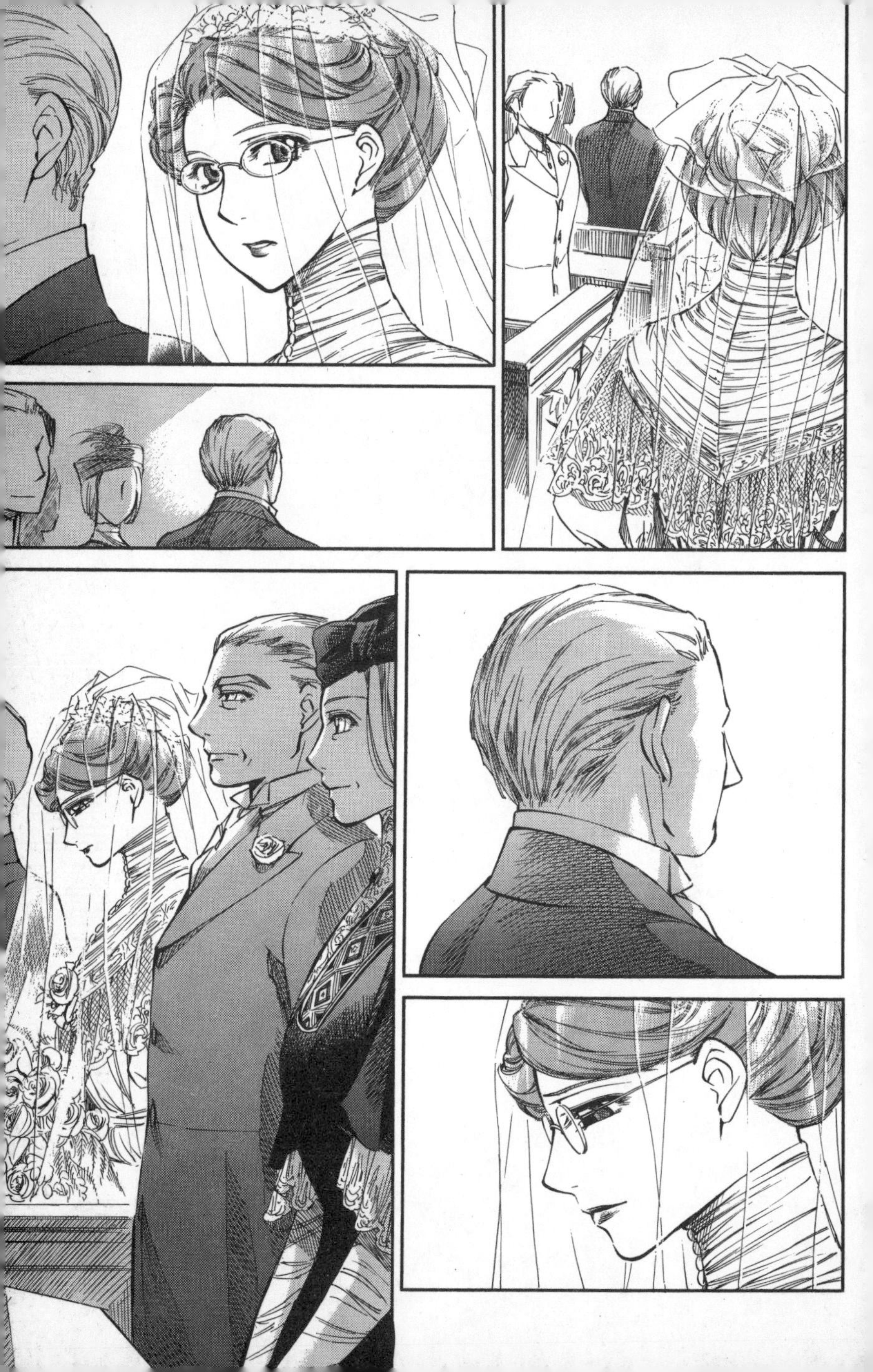

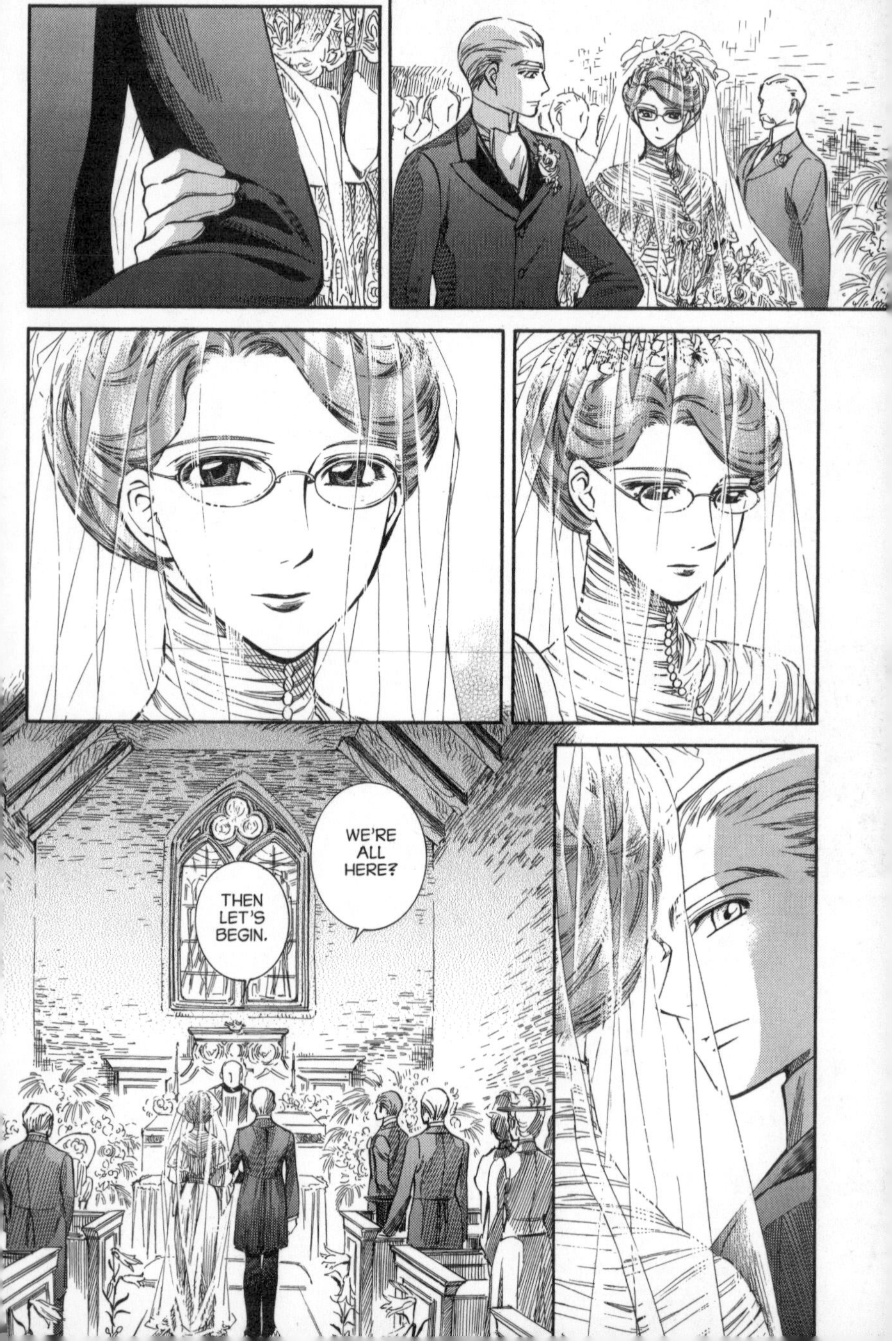
WE'RE ALL HERE?
THEN LET'S BEGIN.

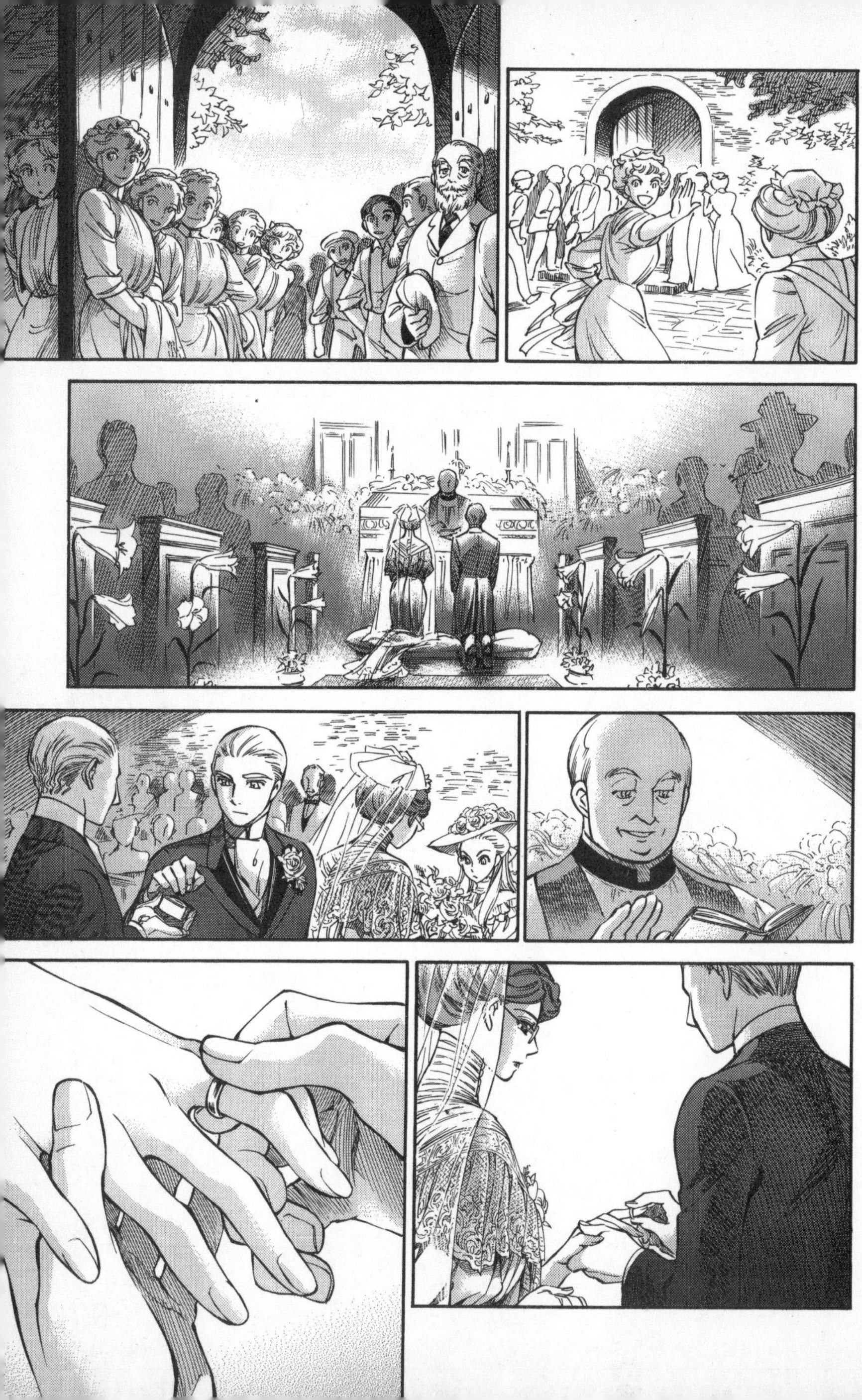

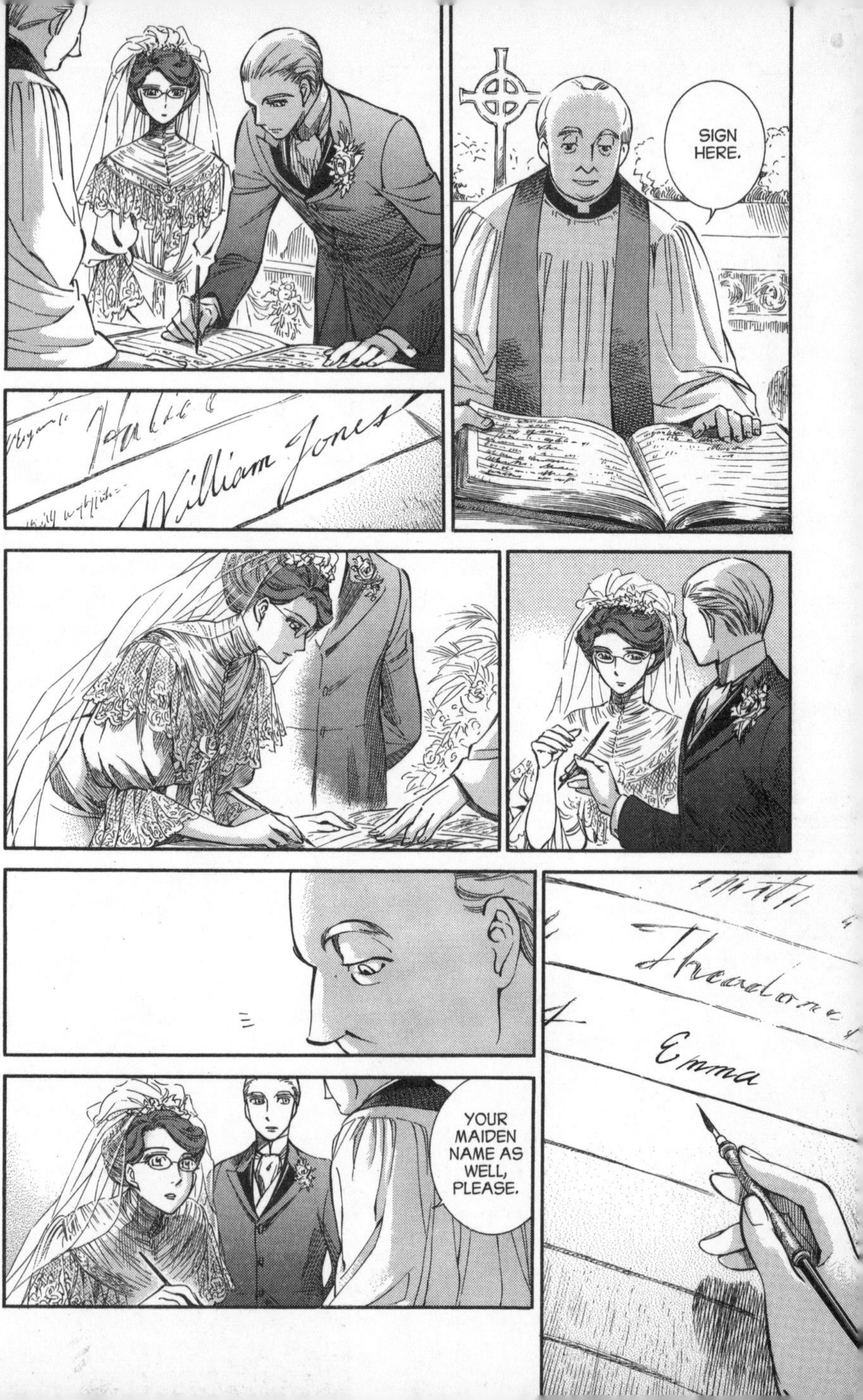
SIGN HERE.
William Jones
Emma
YOUR MAIDEN NAME AS WELL, PLEASE.

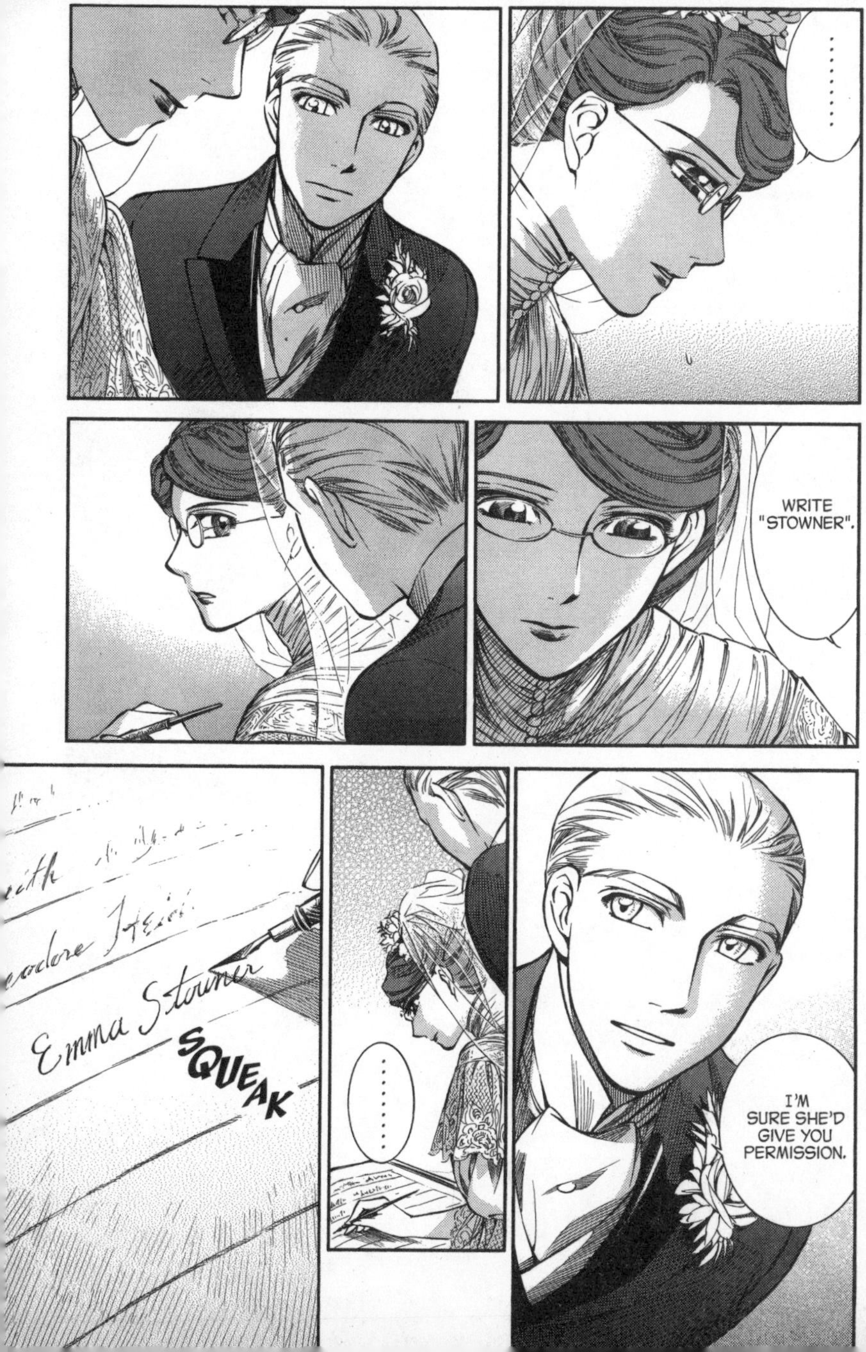
......
WRITE "STOWNER".
I'M SURE SHE'D GIVE YOU PERMISSION.
......
Emma Stowner
SQUEAK

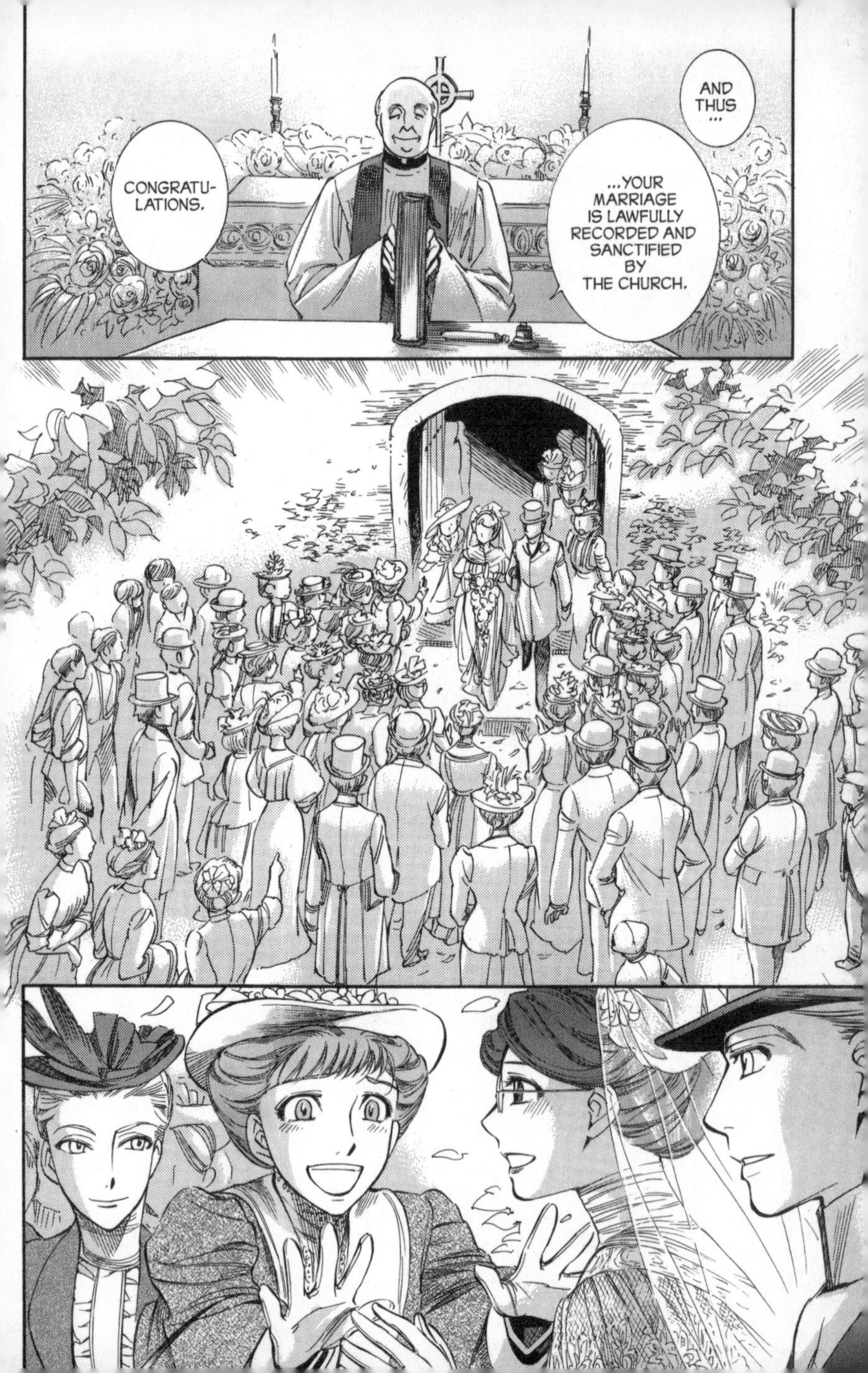
AND THUS ...
...YOUR MARRIAGE IS LAWFULLY RECORDED AND SANCTIFIED BY THE CHURCH.
CONGRATU-LATIONS.

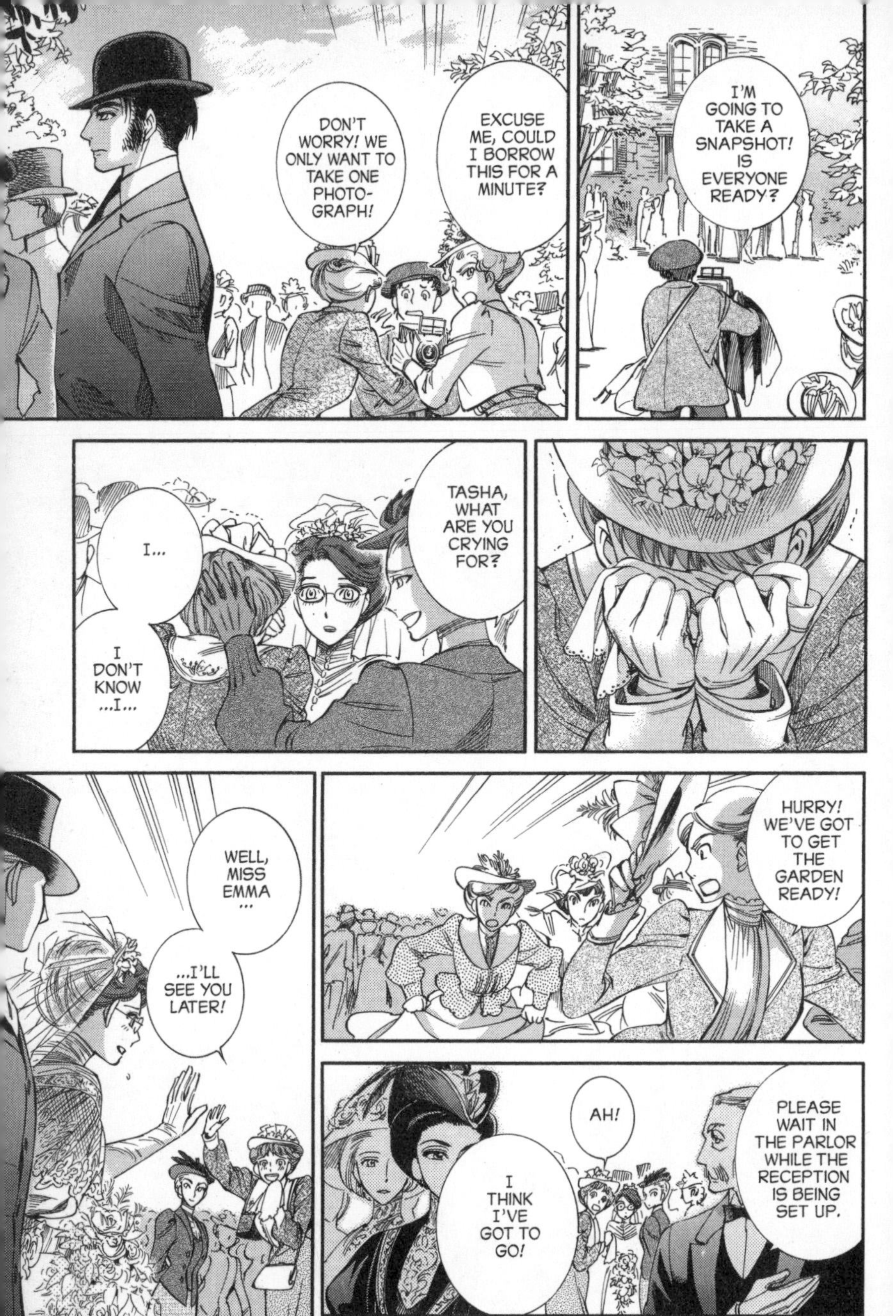
I'M GOING TO TAKE A SNAPSHOT! IS EVERYONE READY?
EXCUSE ME, COULD I BORROW THIS FOR A MINUTE?
DON'T WORRY! WE ONLY WANT TO TAKE ONE PHOTO-GRAPH!
TASHA, WHAT ARE YOU CRYING FOR?
I...
I DON'T KNOW ...I...
HURRY! WE'VE GOT TO GET THE GARDEN READY!
PLEASE WAIT IN THE PARLOR WHILE THE RECEPTION IS BEING SET UP.
AH!
I THINK I'VE GOT TO GO!
WELL, MISS EMMA ...
...I'LL SEE YOU LATER!

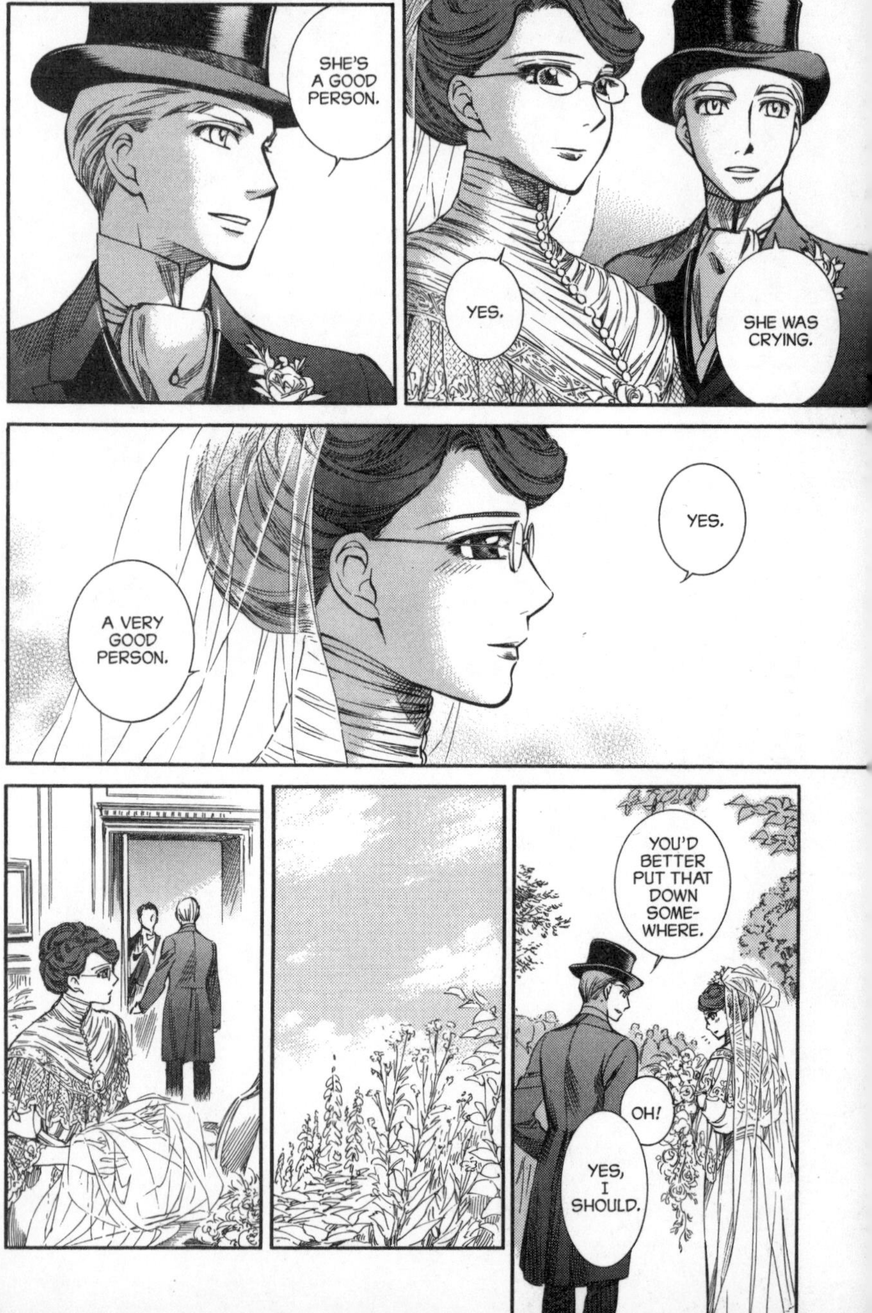
SHE WAS CRYING.
YES.
SHE'S A GOOD PERSON.
YES.
A VERY GOOD PERSON.
YOU'D BETTER PUT THAT DOWN SOME-WHERE.
OH!
YES, I SHOULD.

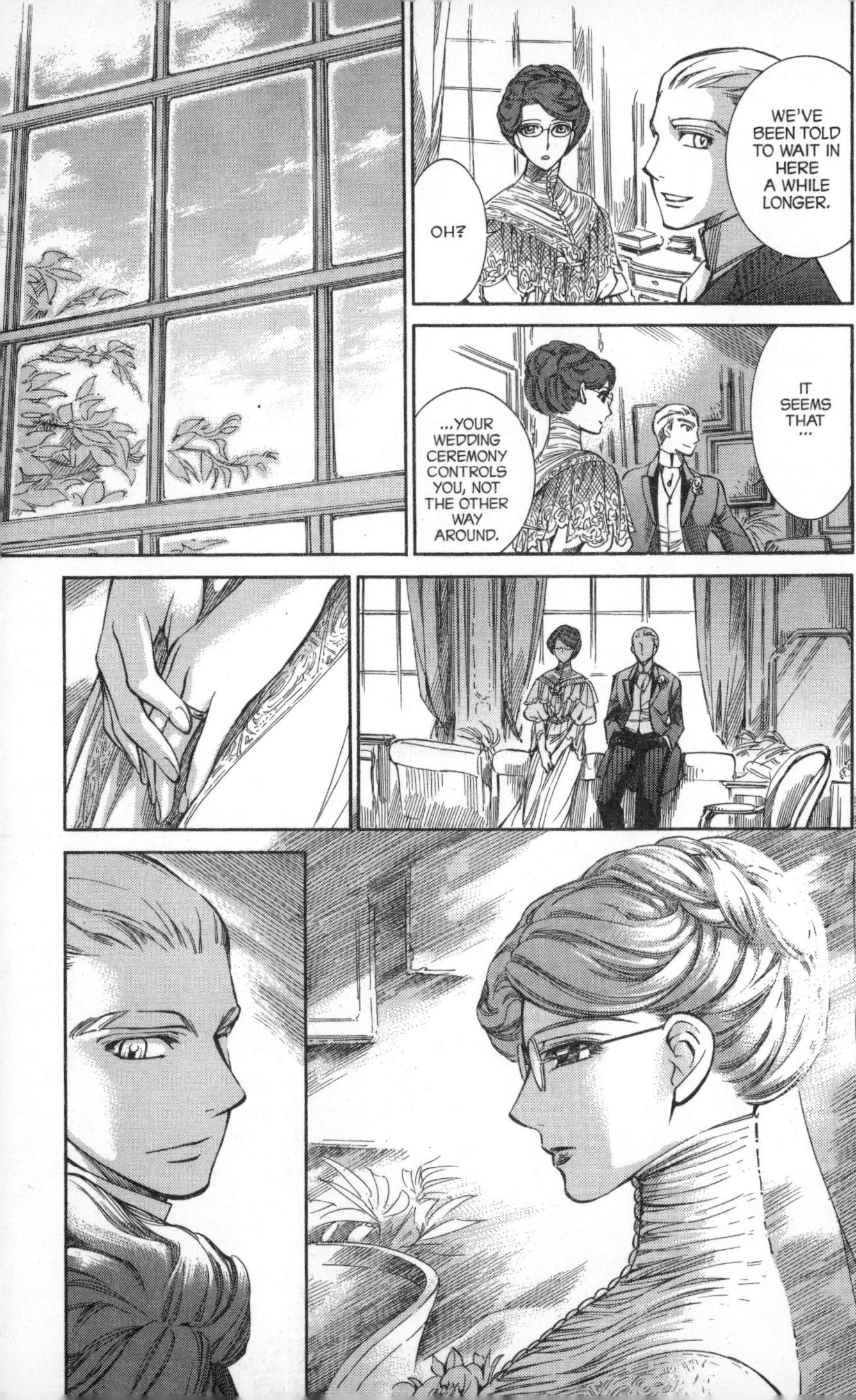
WE'VE BEEN TOLD TO WAIT IN HERE A WHILE LONGER.
OH?
IT SEEMS THAT ...
...YOUR WEDDING CEREMONY CONTROLS YOU, NOT THE OTHER WAY AROUND.

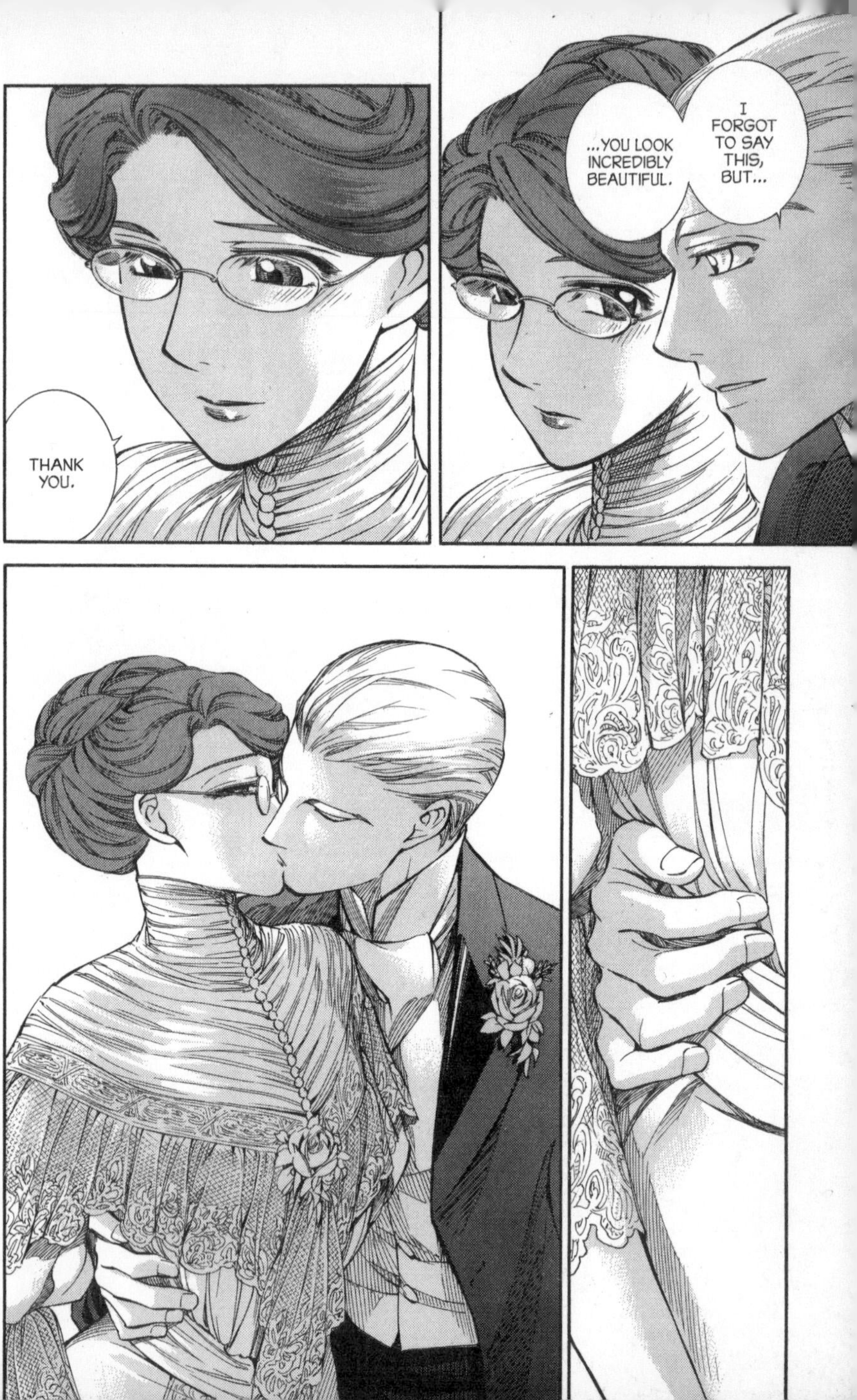
I FORGOT TO SAY THIS, BUT...
...YOU LOOK INCREDIBLY BEAUTIFUL.
THANK YOU.

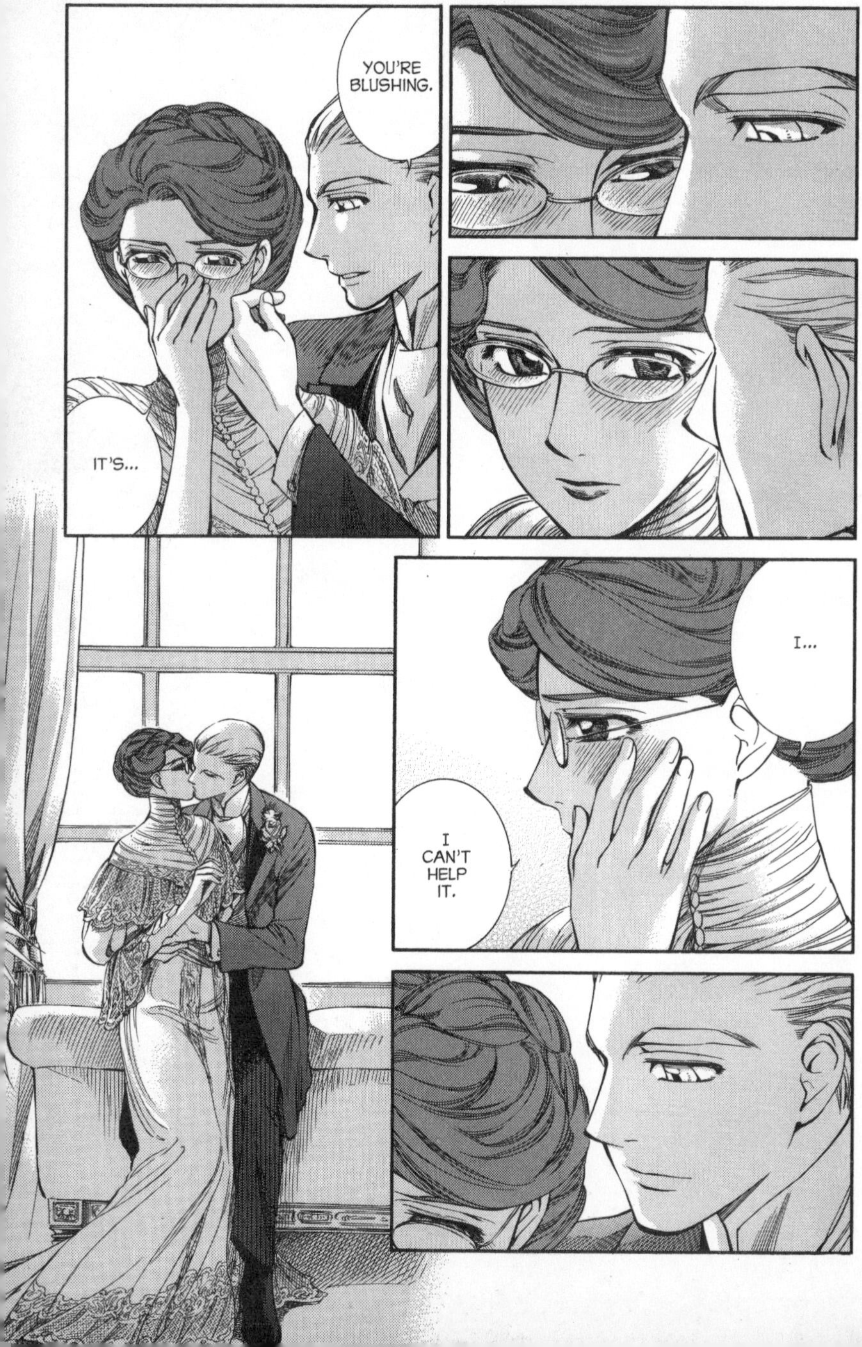
YOU'RE BLUSHING.
IT'S...
I...
I CAN'T HELP IT.

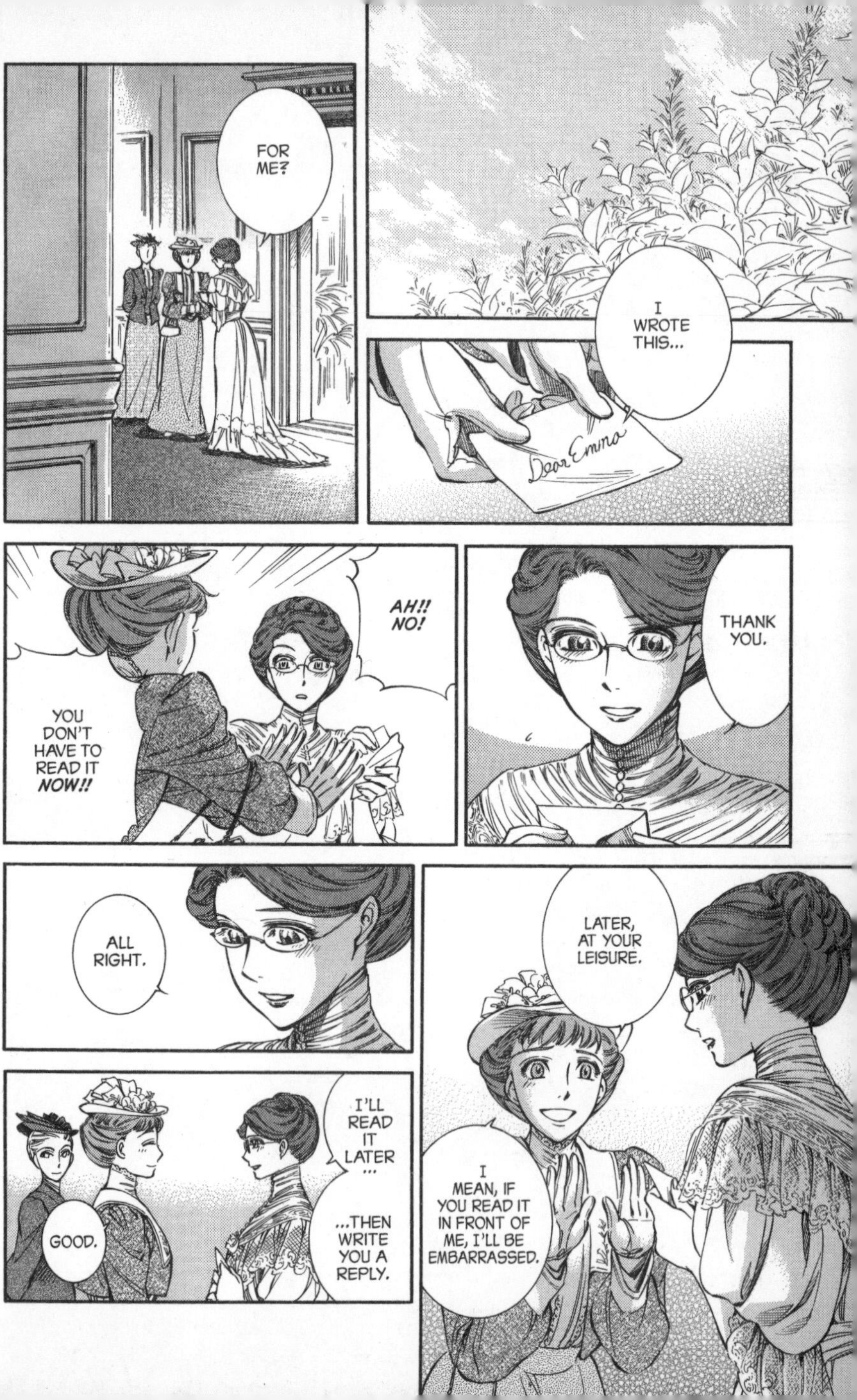
I WROTE THIS...
Dear Emma
FOR ME?
THANK YOU.
AH!! NO!
YOU DON'T HAVE TO READ IT *NOW!!*
LATER, AT YOUR LEISURE.
I MEAN, IF YOU READ IT IN FRONT OF ME, I'LL BE EMBARRASSED.
ALL RIGHT.
I'LL READ IT LATER...
...THEN WRITE YOU A REPLY.
GOOD.

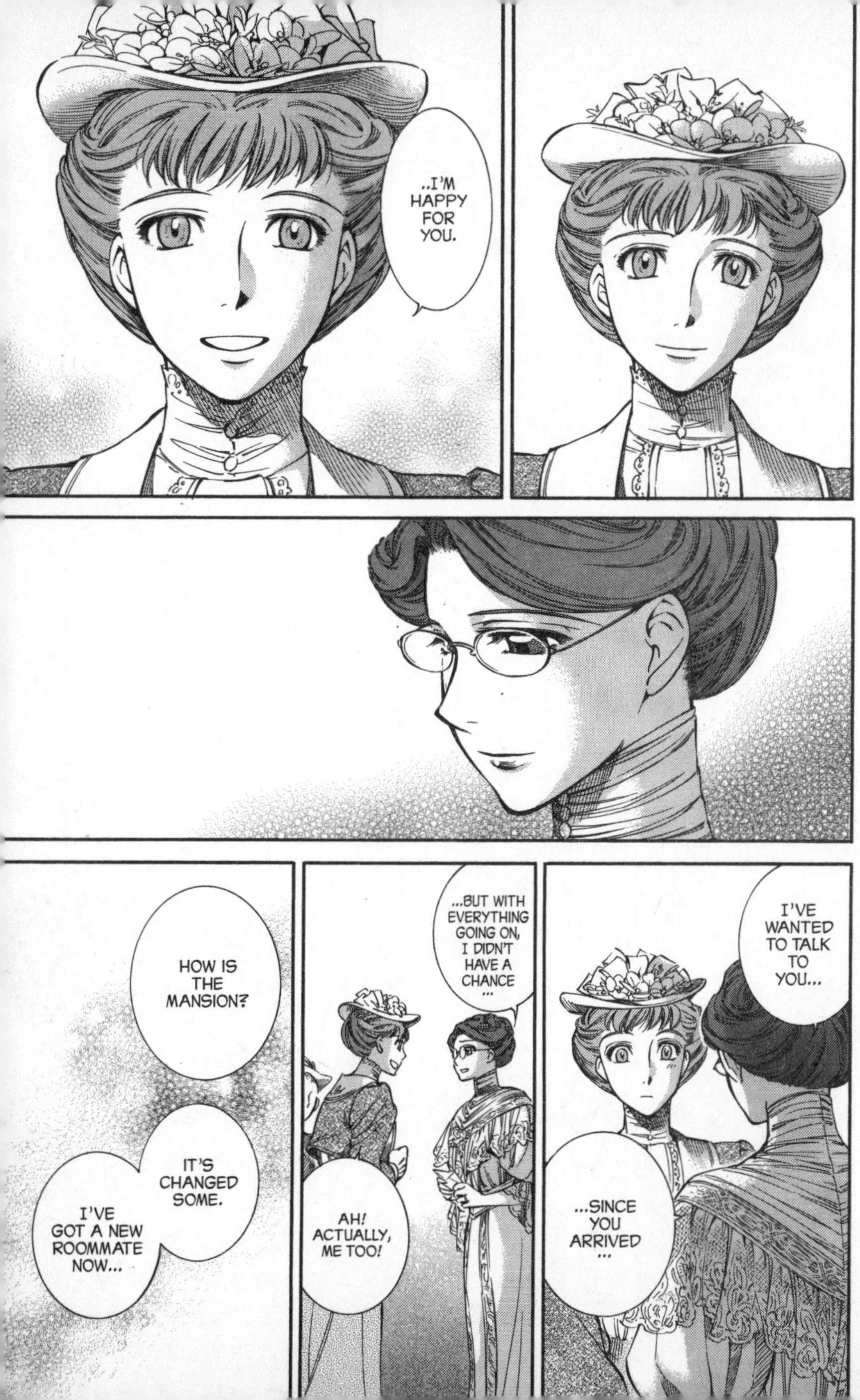
..I'M HAPPY FOR YOU.
I'VE WANTED TO TALK TO YOU...
...SINCE YOU ARRIVED ...
...BUT WITH EVERYTHING GOING ON, I DIDN'T HAVE A CHANCE ...
AH! ACTUALLY, ME TOO!
HOW IS THE MANSION?
IT'S CHANGED SOME.
I'VE GOT A NEW ROOMMATE NOW...

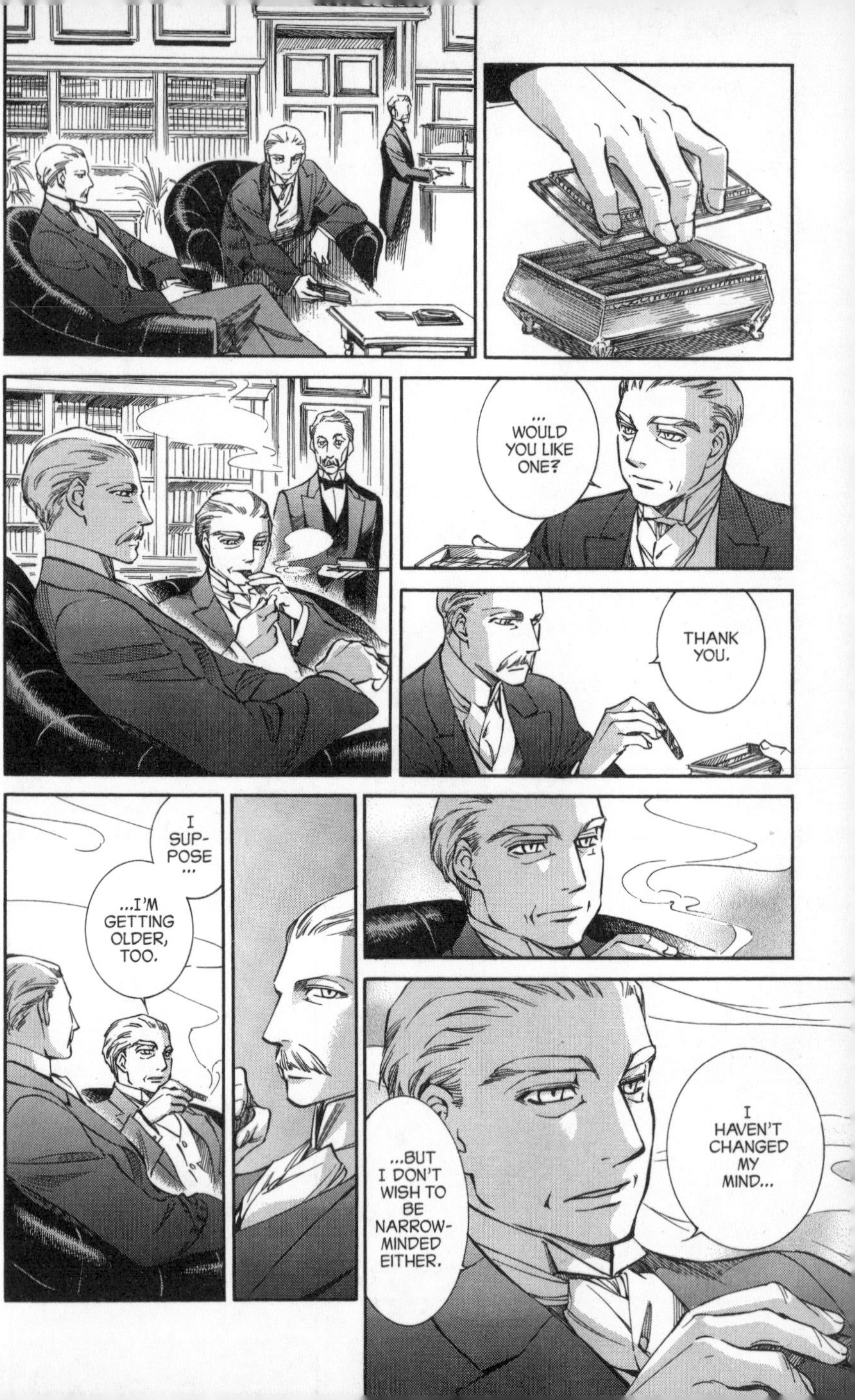
...WOULD YOU LIKE ONE?
THANK YOU.
I HAVEN'T CHANGED MY MIND...
...BUT I DON'T WISH TO BE NARROW-MINDED EITHER.
I SUPPOSE...
...I'M GETTING OLDER, TOO.

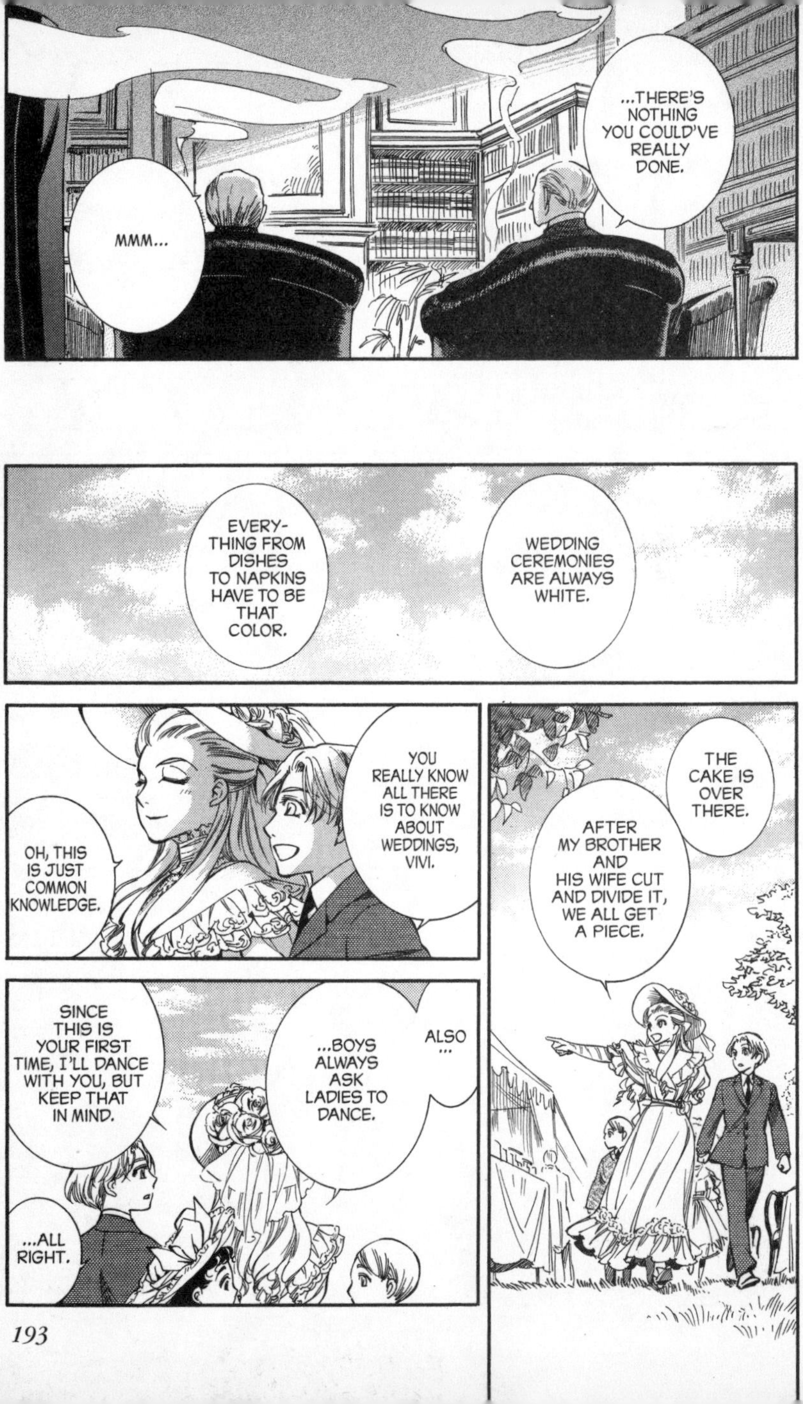
...THERE'S NOTHING YOU COULD'VE REALLY DONE.
MMM...
WEDDING CEREMONIES ARE ALWAYS WHITE.
EVERY-THING FROM DISHES TO NAPKINS HAVE TO BE THAT COLOR.
THE CAKE IS OVER THERE.
AFTER MY BROTHER AND HIS WIFE CUT AND DIVIDE IT, WE ALL GET A PIECE.
YOU REALLY KNOW ALL THERE IS TO KNOW ABOUT WEDDINGS, VIVI.
OH, THIS IS JUST COMMON KNOWLEDGE.
ALSO ...
...BOYS ALWAYS ASK LADIES TO DANCE.
SINCE THIS IS YOUR FIRST TIME, I'LL DANCE WITH YOU, BUT KEEP THAT IN MIND.
...ALL RIGHT.

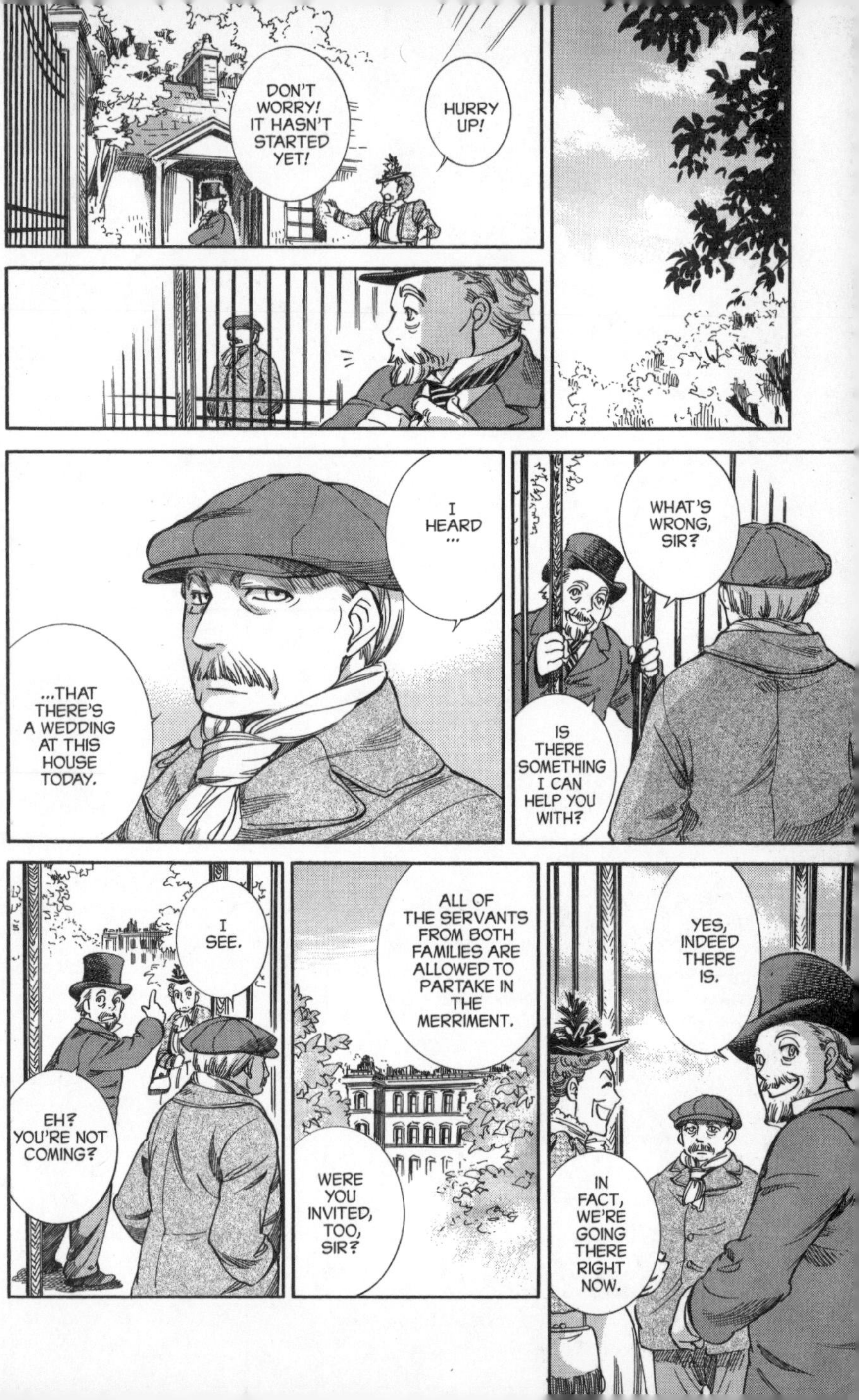
HURRY UP!
DON'T WORRY! IT HASN'T STARTED YET!
WHAT'S WRONG, SIR?
IS THERE SOMETHING I CAN HELP YOU WITH?
I HEARD ...
...THAT THERE'S A WEDDING AT THIS HOUSE TODAY.
YES, INDEED THERE IS.
IN FACT, WE'RE GOING THERE RIGHT NOW.
ALL OF THE SERVANTS FROM BOTH FAMILIES ARE ALLOWED TO PARTAKE IN THE MERRIMENT.
WERE YOU INVITED, TOO, SIR?
I SEE.
EH? YOU'RE NOT COMING?

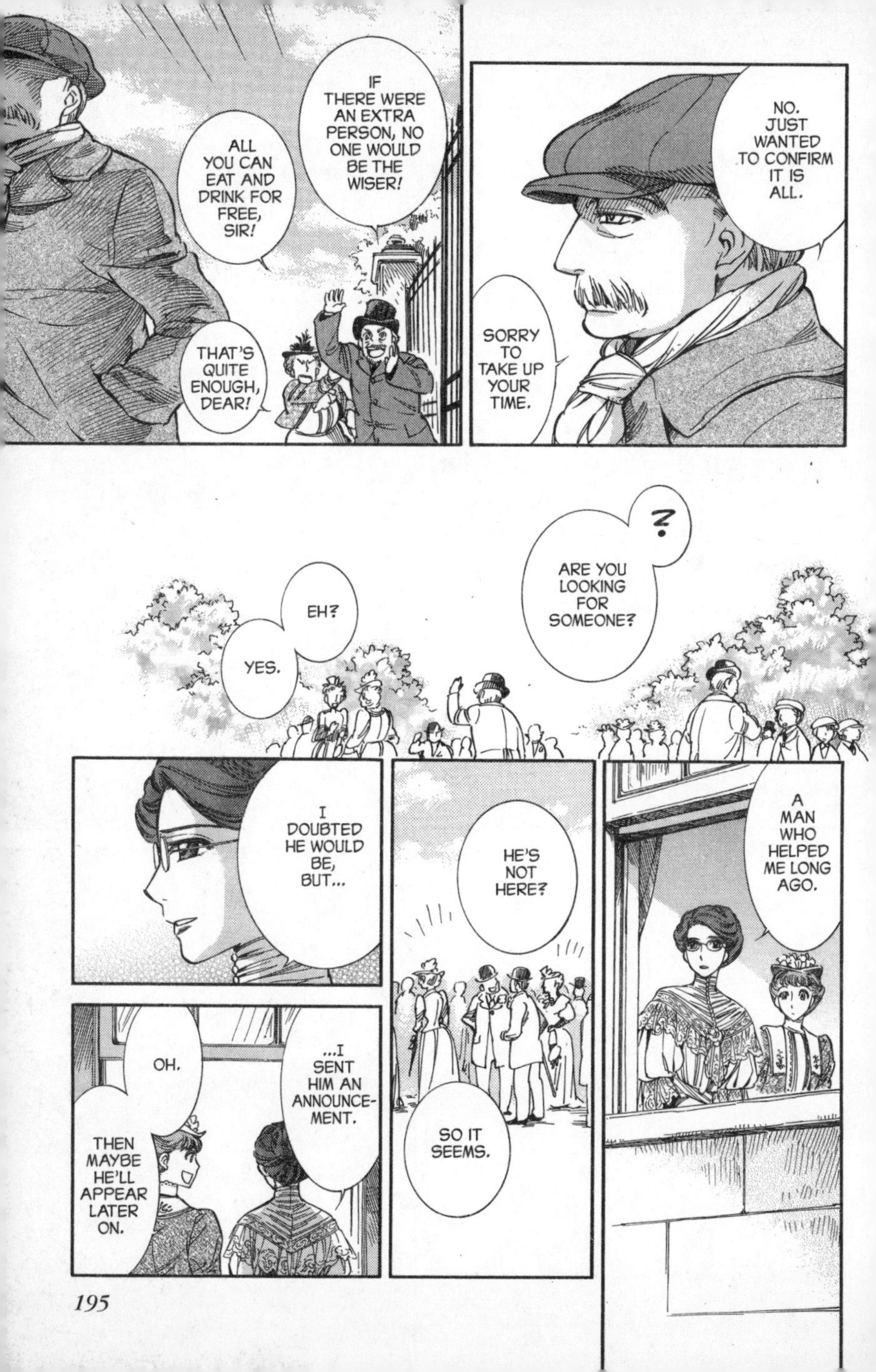
NO. JUST WANTED TO CONFIRM IT IS ALL.
SORRY TO TAKE UP YOUR TIME.
IF THERE WERE AN EXTRA PERSON, NO ONE WOULD BE THE WISER!
ALL YOU CAN EAT AND DRINK FOR FREE, SIR!
THAT'S QUITE ENOUGH, DEAR!
?
ARE YOU LOOKING FOR SOMEONE?
EH?
YES.
A MAN WHO HELPED ME LONG AGO.
HE'S NOT HERE?
SO IT SEEMS.
I DOUBTED HE WOULD BE, BUT...
...I SENT HIM AN ANNOUNCE-MENT.
OH.
THEN MAYBE HE'LL APPEAR LATER ON.

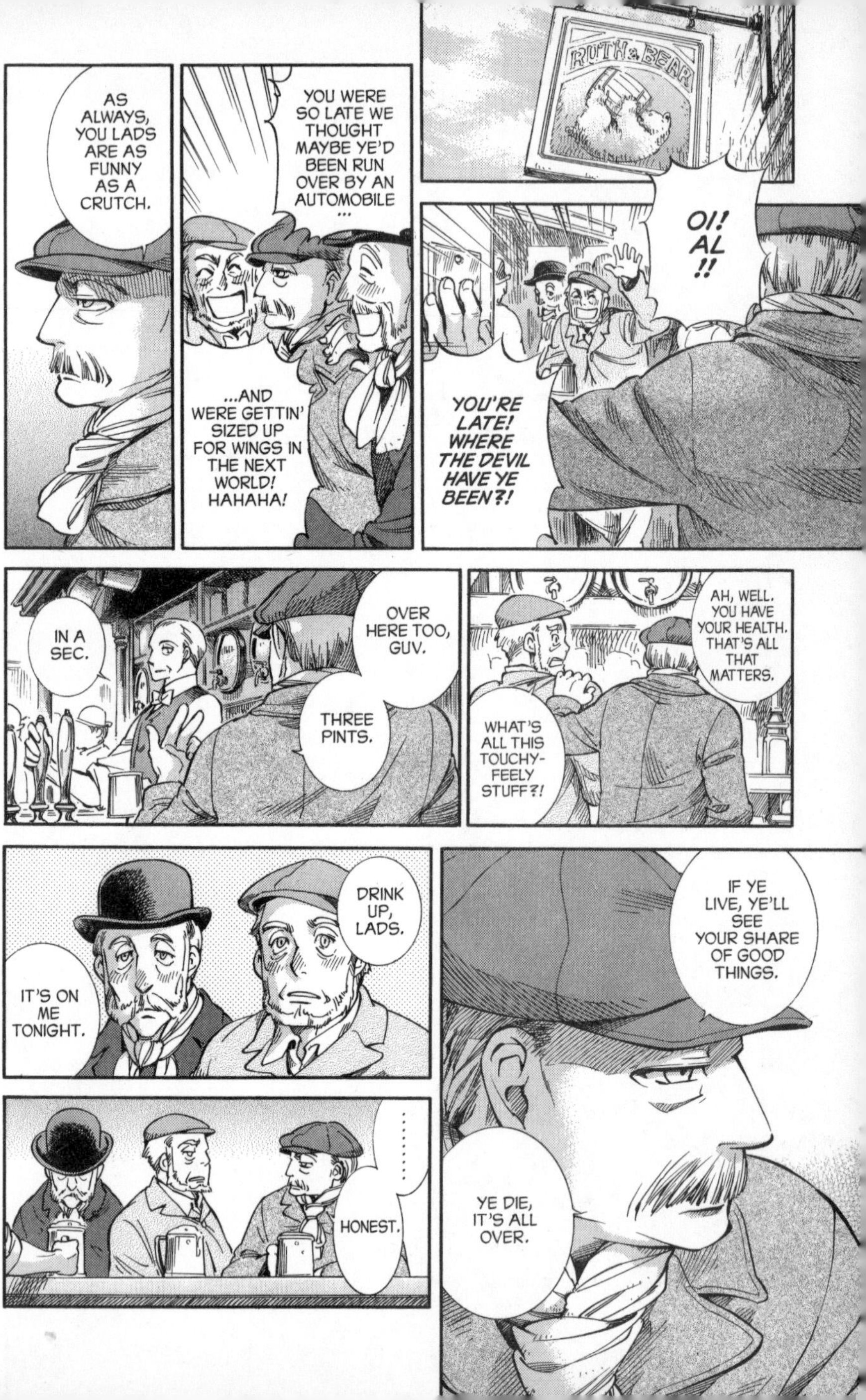
RUTH & BEAR
OI! AL!!
YOU'RE LATE! WHERE THE DEVIL HAVE YE BEEN?!
YOU WERE SO LATE WE THOUGHT MAYBE YE'D BEEN RUN OVER BY AN AUTOMOBILE ...
...AND WERE GETTIN' SIZED UP FOR WINGS IN THE NEXT WORLD! HAHAHA!
AS ALWAYS, YOU LADS ARE AS FUNNY AS A CRUTCH.
AH, WELL. YOU HAVE YOUR HEALTH. THAT'S ALL THAT MATTERS.
WHAT'S ALL THIS TOUCHY-FEELY STUFF?!
OVER HERE TOO, GUV.
THREE PINTS.
IN A SEC.
IF YE LIVE, YE'LL SEE YOUR SHARE OF GOOD THINGS.
YE DIE, IT'S ALL OVER.
DRINK UP, LADS.
IT'S ON ME TONIGHT.
......
HONEST.

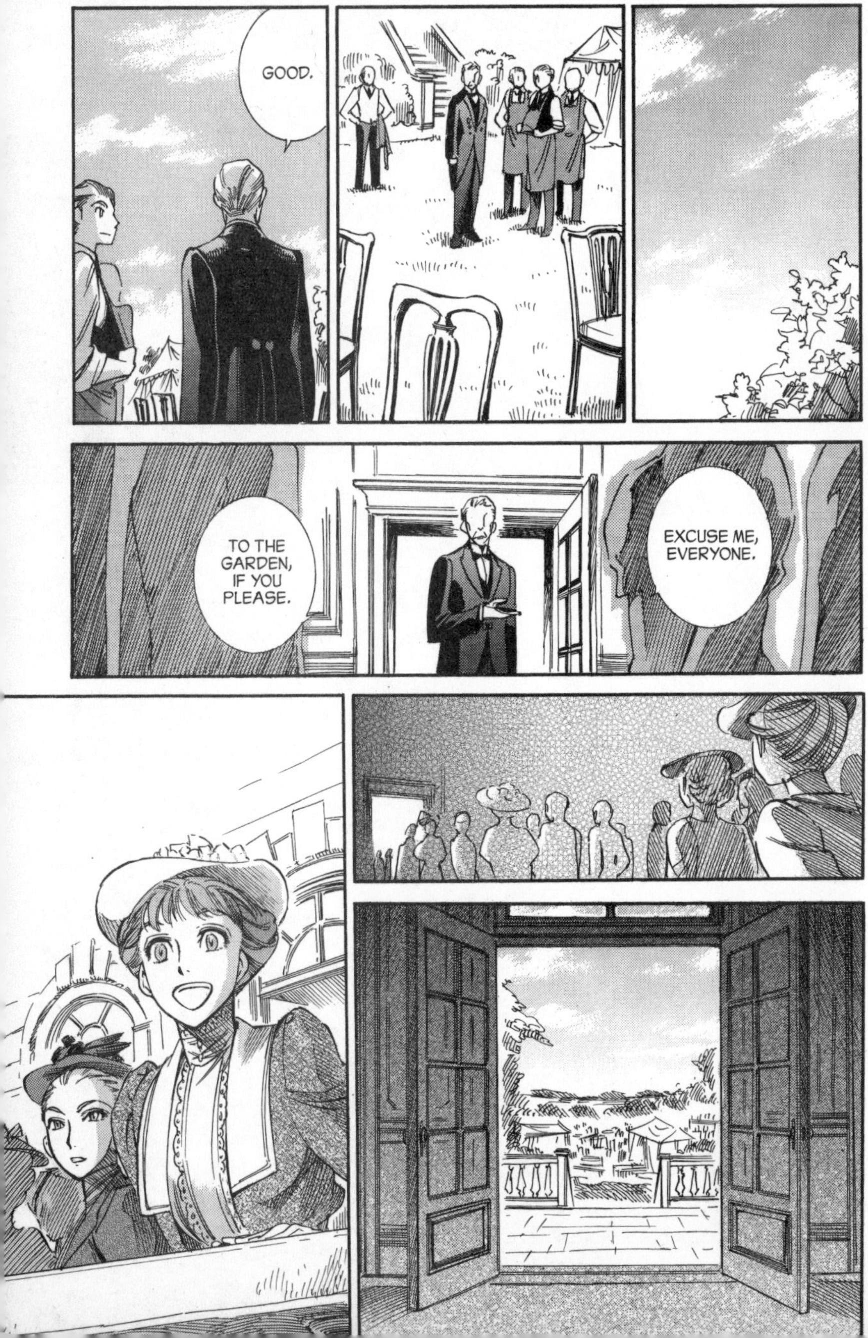
GOOD.
EXCUSE ME, EVERYONE.
TO THE GARDEN, IF YOU PLEASE.

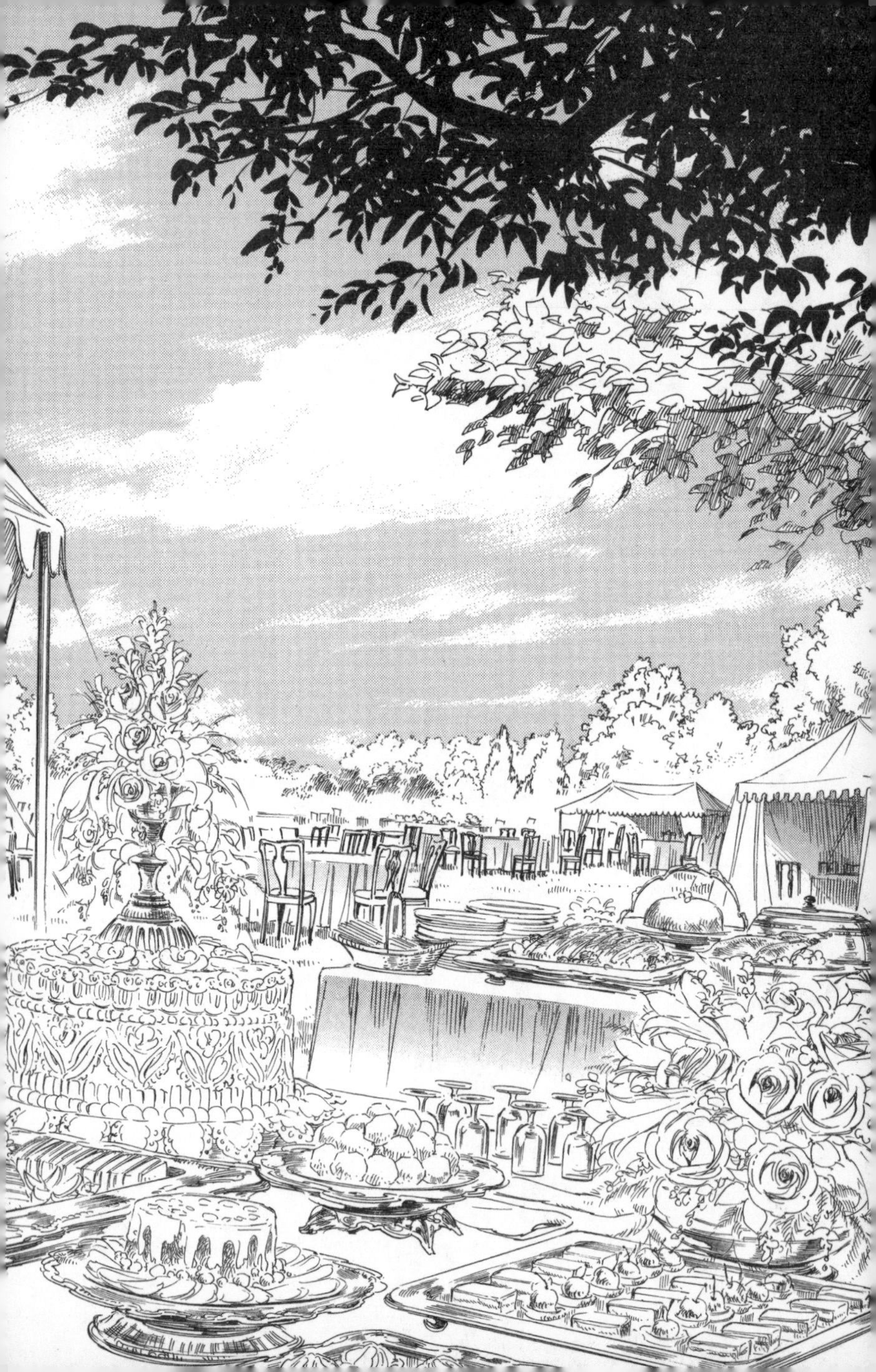

**THE
FINAL
CHAPTER:
A NEW AGE
(part
three)**

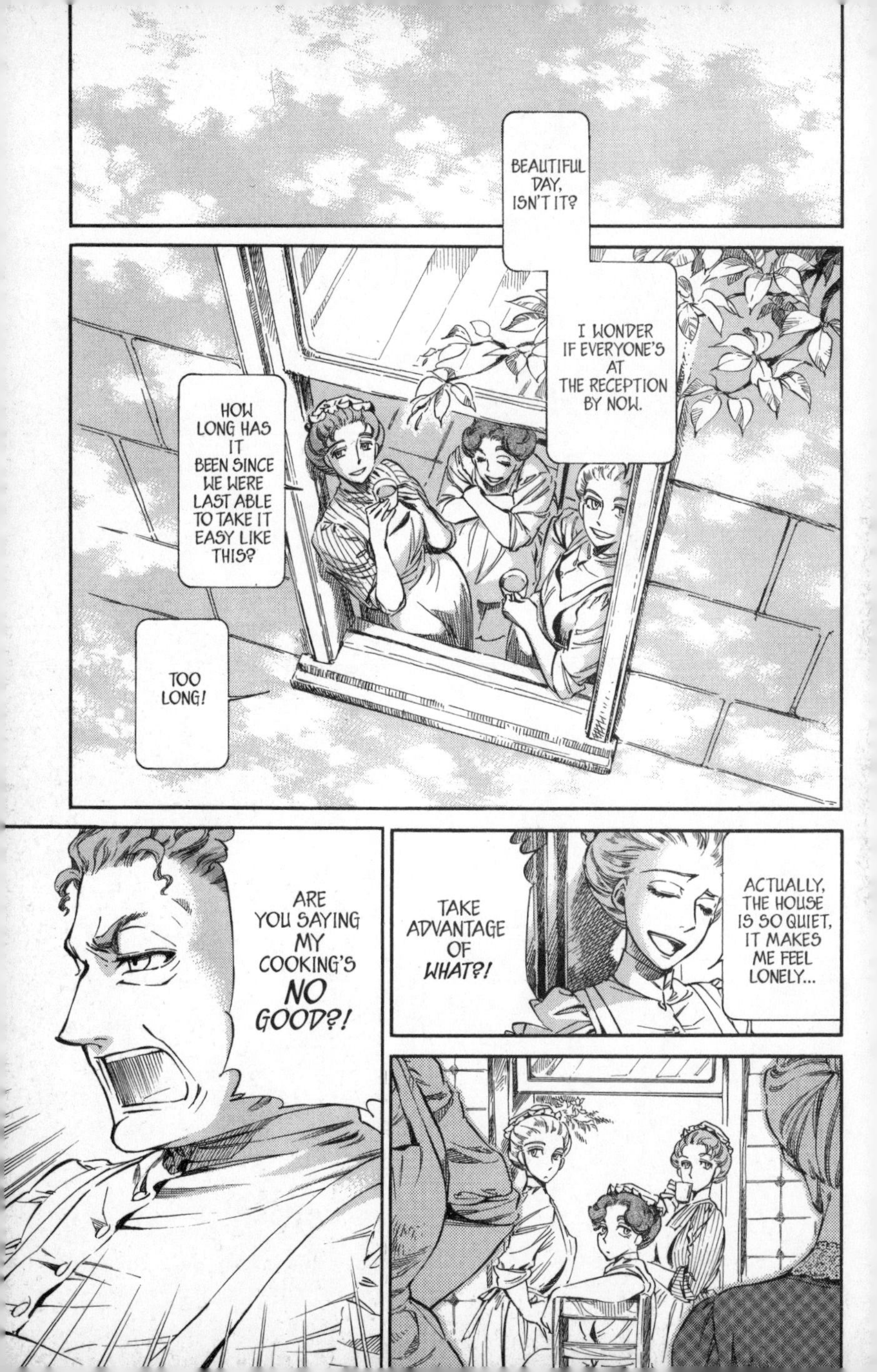
BEAUTIFUL DAY, ISN'T IT?
I WONDER IF EVERYONE'S AT THE RECEPTION BY NOW.
HOW LONG HAS IT BEEN SINCE WE WERE LAST ABLE TO TAKE IT EASY LIKE THIS?
TOO LONG!
ACTUALLY, THE HOUSE IS SO QUIET, IT MAKES ME FEEL LONELY...
TAKE ADVANTAGE OF *WHAT?!*
ARE YOU SAYING MY COOKING'S ***NO GOOD?!***

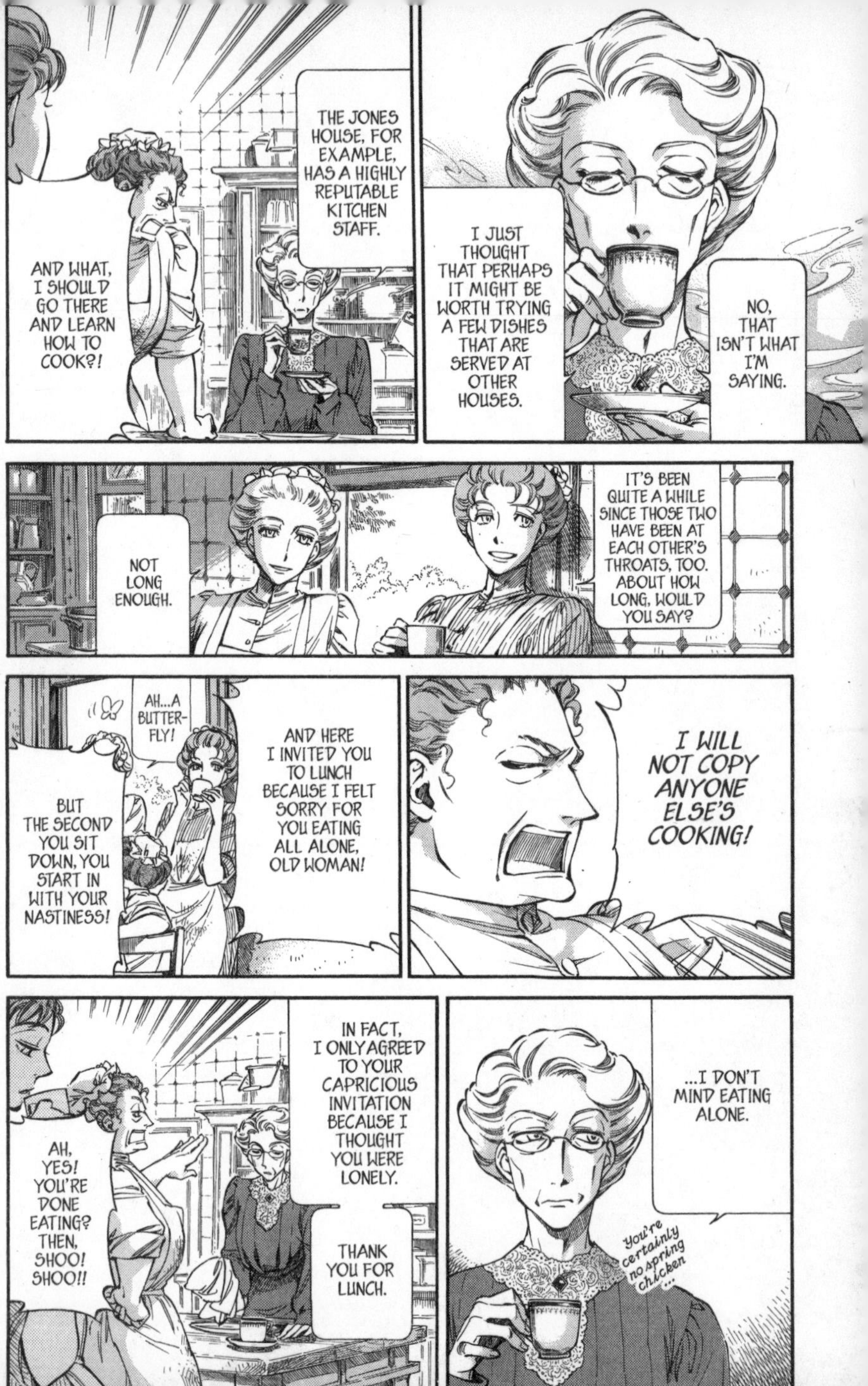
NO, THAT ISN'T WHAT I'M SAYING.
I JUST THOUGHT THAT PERHAPS IT MIGHT BE WORTH TRYING A FEW DISHES THAT ARE SERVED AT OTHER HOUSES.
THE JONES HOUSE, FOR EXAMPLE, HAS A HIGHLY REPUTABLE KITCHEN STAFF.
AND WHAT, I SHOULD GO THERE AND LEARN HOW TO COOK?!
IT'S BEEN QUITE A WHILE SINCE THOSE TWO HAVE BEEN AT EACH OTHER'S THROATS, TOO. ABOUT HOW LONG, WOULD YOU SAY?
NOT LONG ENOUGH.
I WILL NOT COPY ANYONE ELSE'S COOKING!
AND HERE I INVITED YOU TO LUNCH BECAUSE I FELT SORRY FOR YOU EATING ALL ALONE, OLD WOMAN!
AH...A BUTTER-FLY!
BUT THE SECOND YOU SIT DOWN, YOU START IN WITH YOUR NASTINESS!
...I DON'T MIND EATING ALONE.
You're certainly no spring chicken...
IN FACT, I ONLY AGREED TO YOUR CAPRICIOUS INVITATION BECAUSE I THOUGHT YOU WERE LONELY.
THANK YOU FOR LUNCH.
AH, YES! YOU'RE DONE EATING? THEN, SHOO! SHOO!!

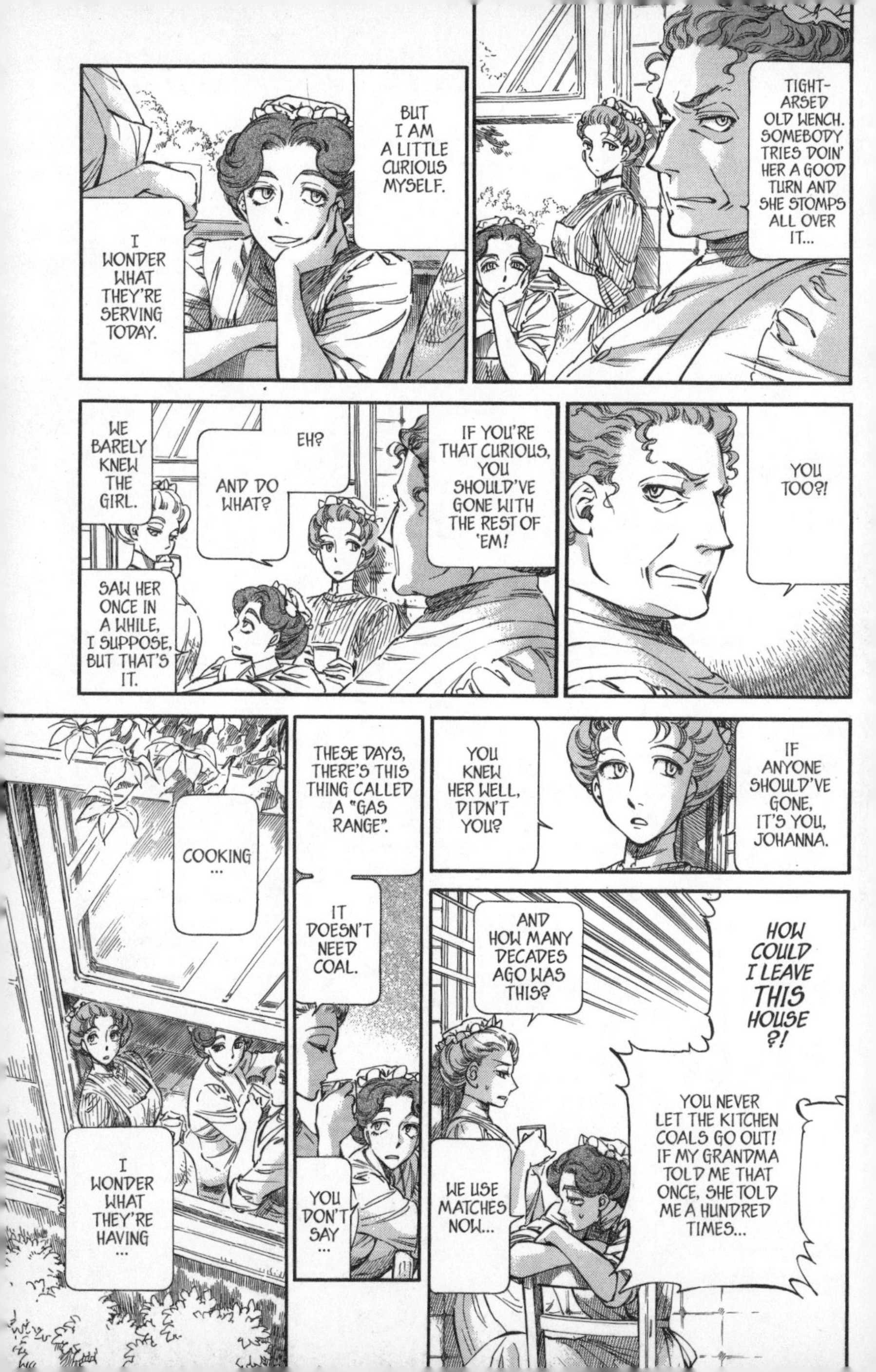
TIGHT-ARSED OLD WENCH. SOMEBODY TRIES DOIN' HER A GOOD TURN AND SHE STOMPS ALL OVER IT...
BUT I AM A LITTLE CURIOUS MYSELF.
I WONDER WHAT THEY'RE SERVING TODAY.
YOU TOO?!
IF YOU'RE THAT CURIOUS, YOU SHOULD'VE GONE WITH THE REST OF 'EM!
EH?
AND DO WHAT?
WE BARELY KNEW THE GIRL.
SAW HER ONCE IN A WHILE, I SUPPOSE, BUT THAT'S IT.
IF ANYONE SHOULD'VE GONE, IT'S YOU, JOHANNA.
YOU KNEW HER WELL, DIDN'T YOU?
HOW COULD I LEAVE THIS HOUSE?!
AND HOW MANY DECADES AGO WAS THIS?
YOU NEVER LET THE KITCHEN COALS GO OUT! IF MY GRANDMA TOLD ME THAT ONCE, SHE TOLD ME A HUNDRED TIMES...
WE USE MATCHES NOW...
THESE DAYS, THERE'S THIS THING CALLED A "GAS RANGE".
IT DOESN'T NEED COAL.
YOU DON'T SAY...
COOKING...
I WONDER WHAT THEY'RE HAVING...

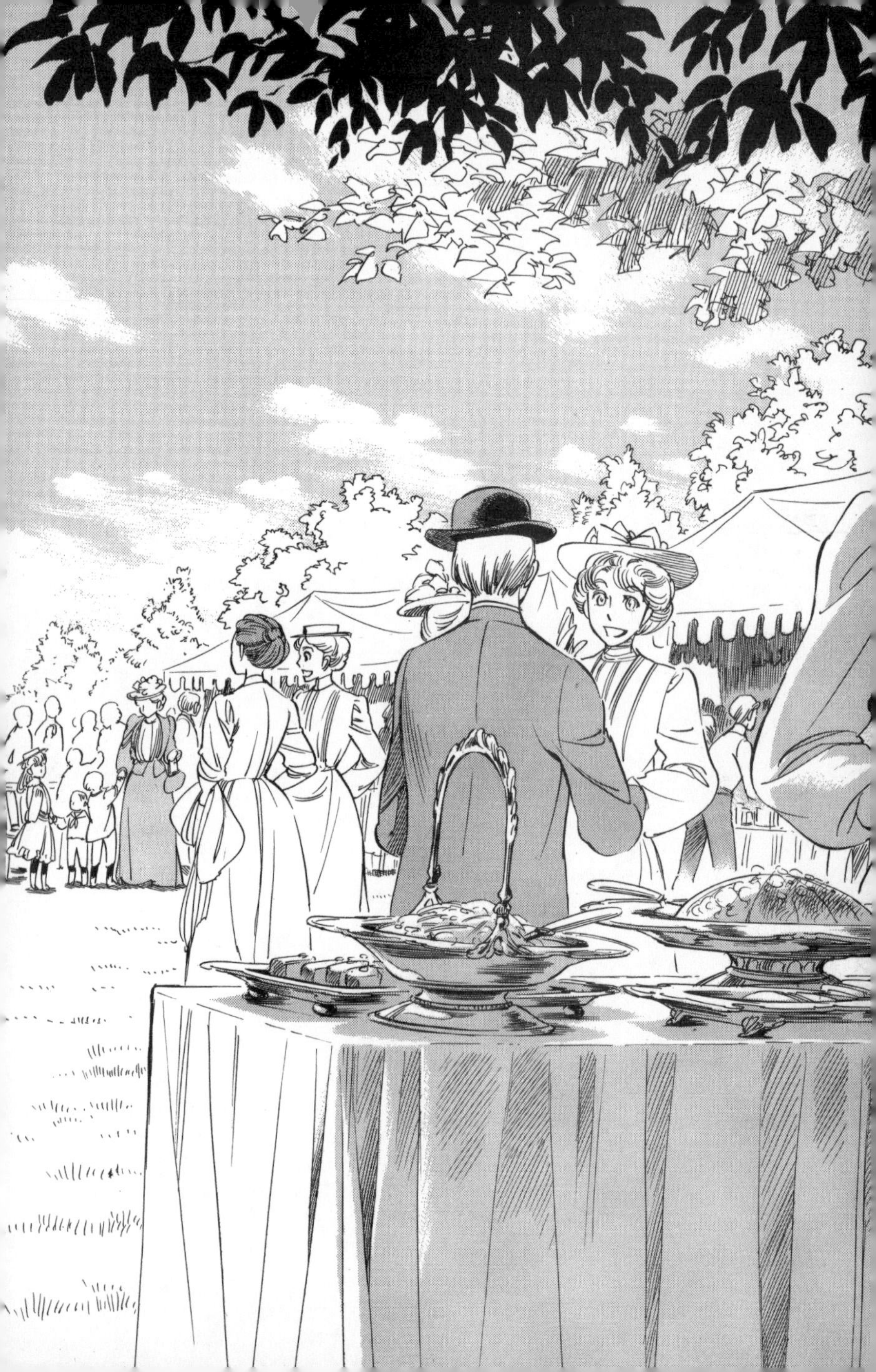

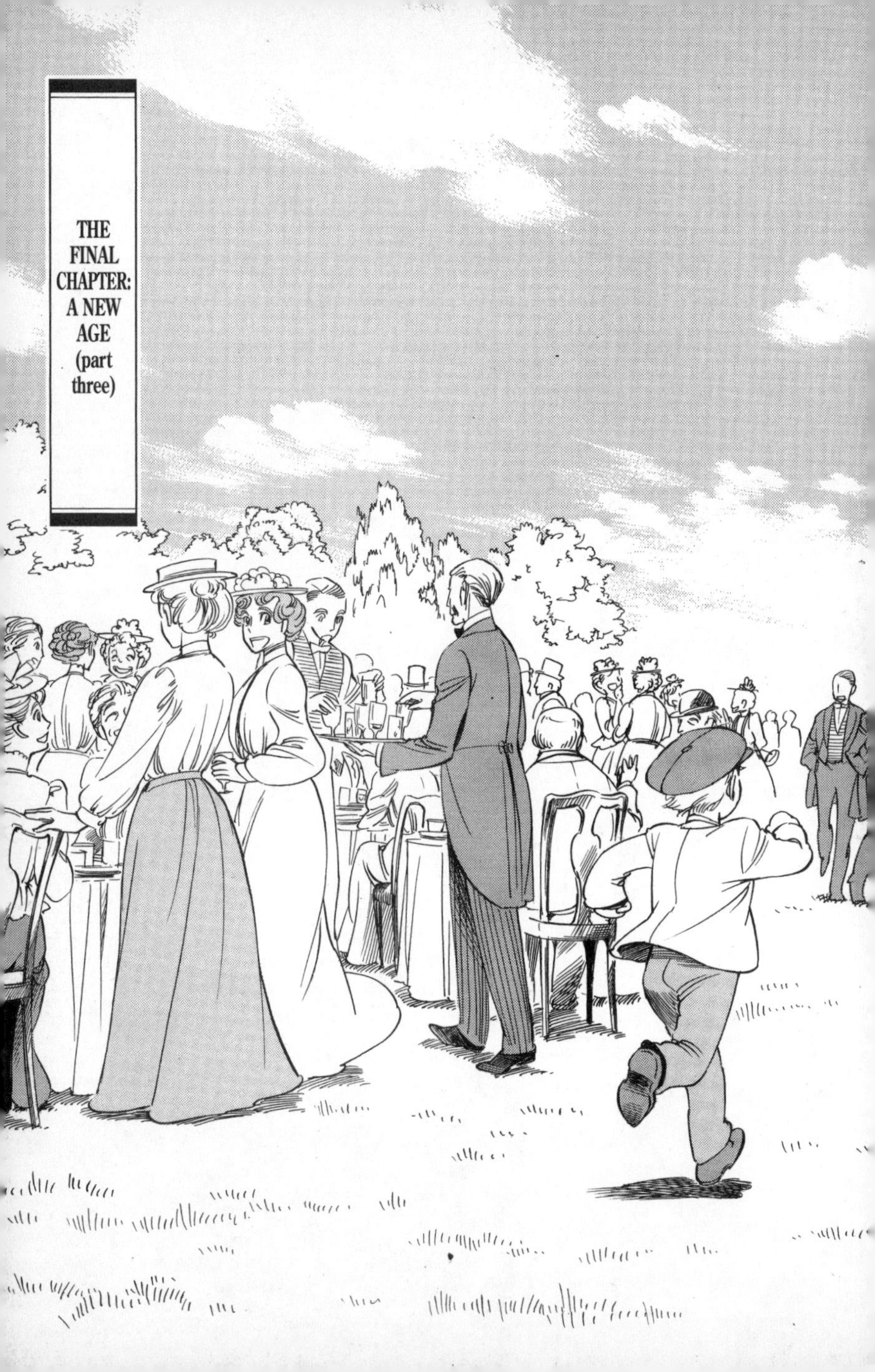
THE FINAL CHAPTER: A NEW AGE (part three)

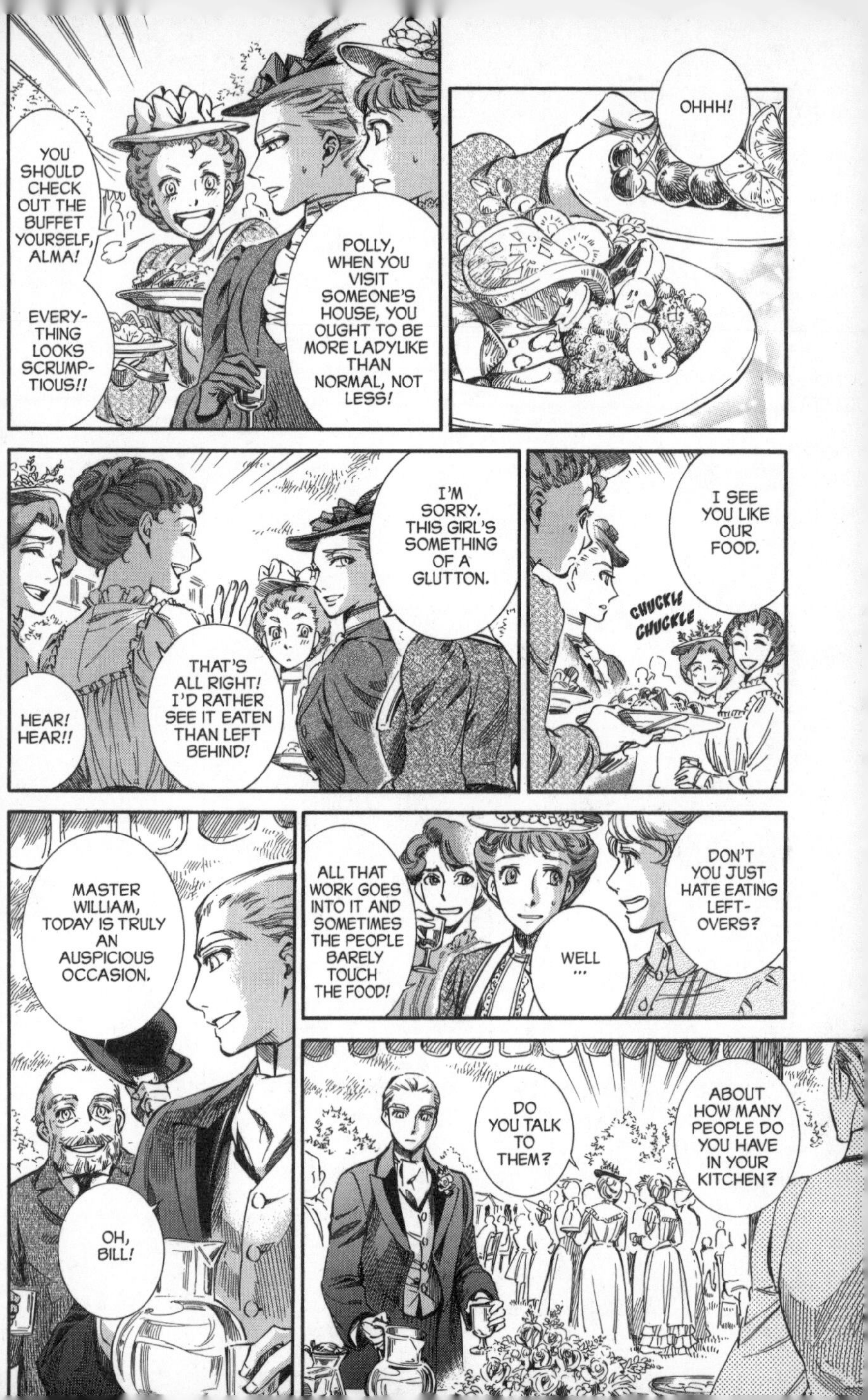
OHHH!
YOU SHOULD CHECK OUT THE BUFFET YOURSELF, ALMA!
EVERY-THING LOOKS SCRUMP-TIOUS!!
POLLY, WHEN YOU VISIT SOMEONE'S HOUSE, YOU OUGHT TO BE MORE LADYLIKE THAN NORMAL, NOT LESS!
I SEE YOU LIKE OUR FOOD.
CHUCKLE CHUCKLE
I'M SORRY. THIS GIRL'S SOMETHING OF A GLUTTON.
THAT'S ALL RIGHT! I'D RATHER SEE IT EATEN THAN LEFT BEHIND!
HEAR! HEAR!!
DON'T YOU JUST HATE EATING LEFT-OVERS?
WELL ...
ALL THAT WORK GOES INTO IT AND SOMETIMES THE PEOPLE BARELY TOUCH THE FOOD!
ABOUT HOW MANY PEOPLE DO YOU HAVE IN YOUR KITCHEN?
DO YOU TALK TO THEM?
MASTER WILLIAM, TODAY IS TRULY AN AUSPICIOUS OCCASION.
OH, BILL!

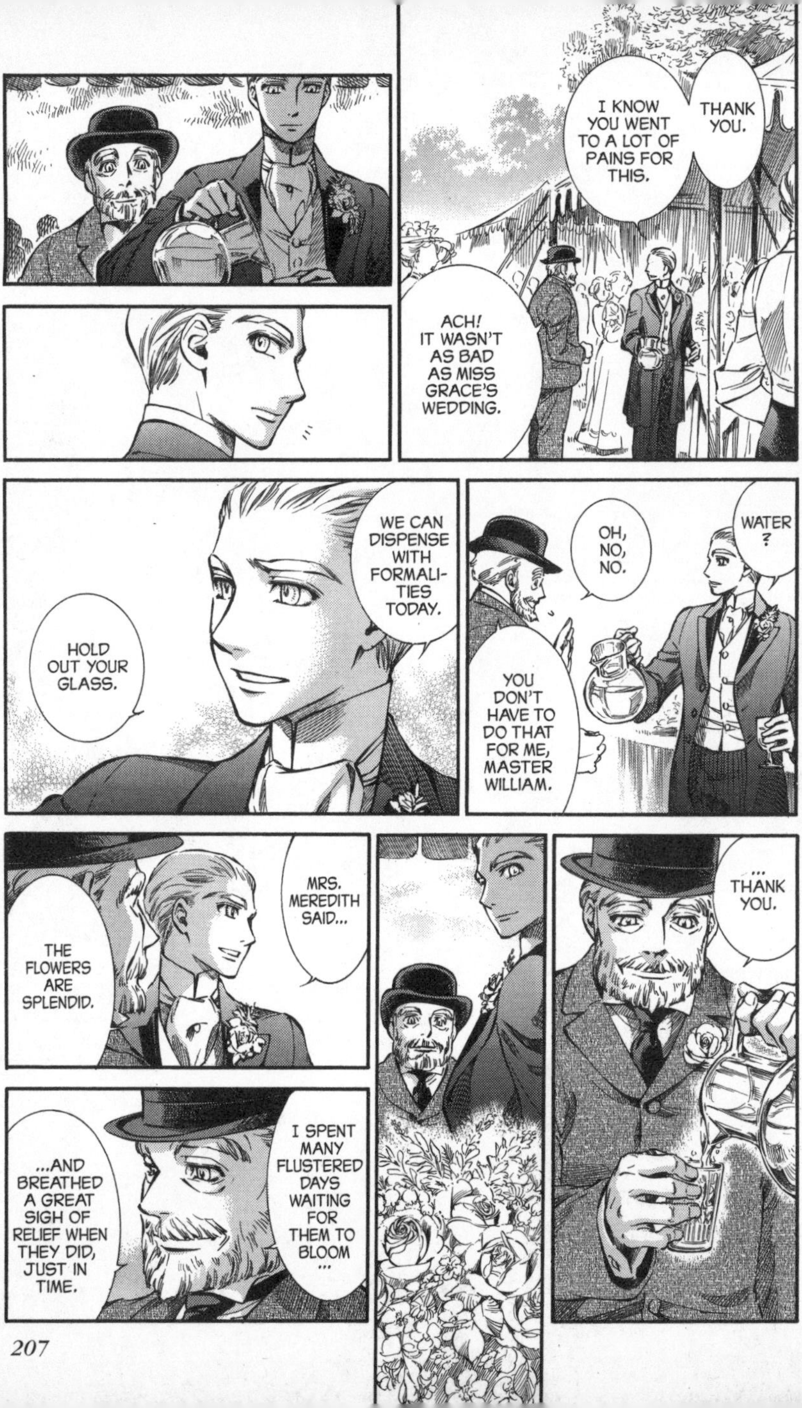
THANK YOU.
I KNOW YOU WENT TO A LOT OF PAINS FOR THIS.
ACH! IT WASN'T AS BAD AS MISS GRACE'S WEDDING.
WATER?
OH, NO, NO.
YOU DON'T HAVE TO DO THAT FOR ME, MASTER WILLIAM.
WE CAN DISPENSE WITH FORMALITIES TODAY.
HOLD OUT YOUR GLASS.
...THANK YOU.
MRS. MEREDITH SAID...
THE FLOWERS ARE SPLENDID.
I SPENT MANY FLUSTERED DAYS WAITING FOR THEM TO BLOOM...
...AND BREATHED A GREAT SIGH OF RELIEF WHEN THEY DID, JUST IN TIME.

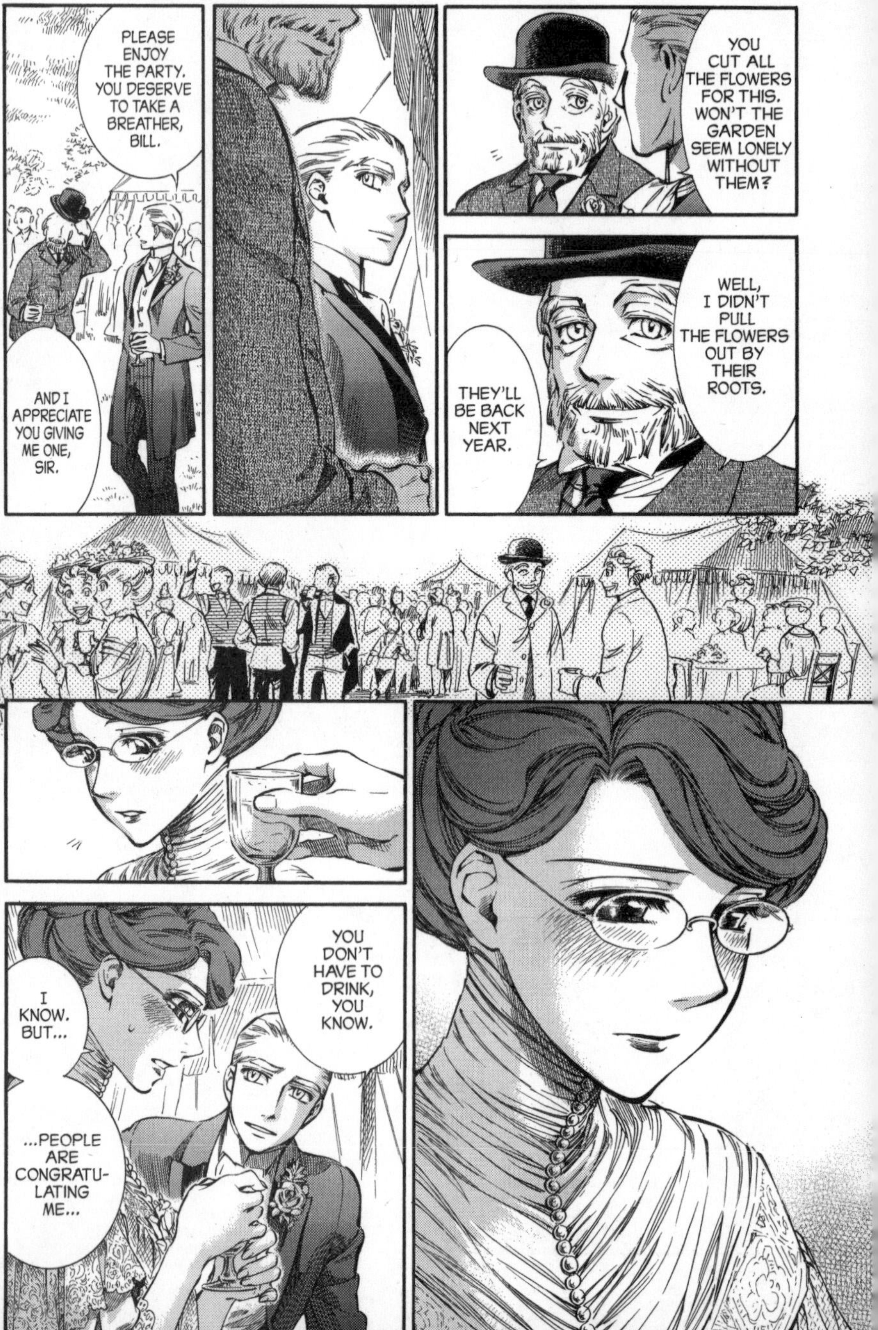
YOU CUT ALL THE FLOWERS FOR THIS. WON'T THE GARDEN SEEM LONELY WITHOUT THEM?
WELL, I DIDN'T PULL THE FLOWERS OUT BY THEIR ROOTS.
THEY'LL BE BACK NEXT YEAR.
PLEASE ENJOY THE PARTY. YOU DESERVE TO TAKE A BREATHER, BILL.
AND I APPRECIATE YOU GIVING ME ONE, SIR.
YOU DON'T HAVE TO DRINK, YOU KNOW.
I KNOW. BUT...
...PEOPLE ARE CONGRATU-LATING ME...

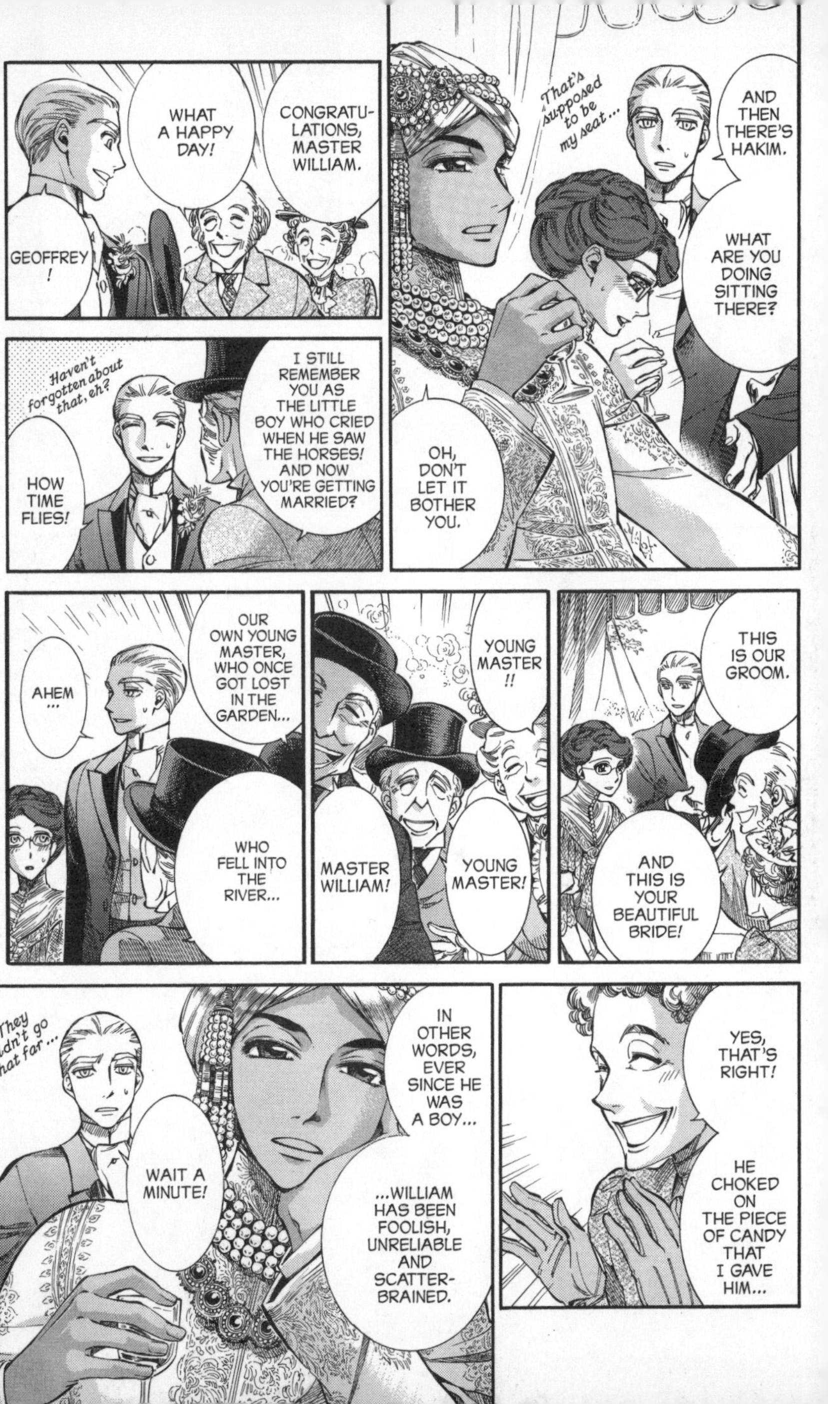
AND THEN THERE'S HAKIM.
WHAT ARE YOU DOING SITTING THERE?
That's supposed to be my seat...
OH, DON'T LET IT BOTHER YOU.
CONGRATULATIONS, MASTER WILLIAM.
WHAT A HAPPY DAY!
GEOFFREY!
I STILL REMEMBER YOU AS THE LITTLE BOY WHO CRIED WHEN HE SAW THE HORSES! AND NOW YOU'RE GETTING MARRIED?
Haven't forgotten about that, eh?
HOW TIME FLIES!
THIS IS OUR GROOM.
AND THIS IS YOUR BEAUTIFUL BRIDE!
YOUNG MASTER!!
YOUNG MASTER!
MASTER WILLIAM!
OUR OWN YOUNG MASTER, WHO ONCE GOT LOST IN THE GARDEN...
AHEM...
WHO FELL INTO THE RIVER...
YES, THAT'S RIGHT!
HE CHOKED ON THE PIECE OF CANDY THAT I GAVE HIM...
IN OTHER WORDS, EVER SINCE HE WAS A BOY...
...WILLIAM HAS BEEN FOOLISH, UNRELIABLE AND SCATTER-BRAINED.
They didn't go that far...
WAIT A MINUTE!

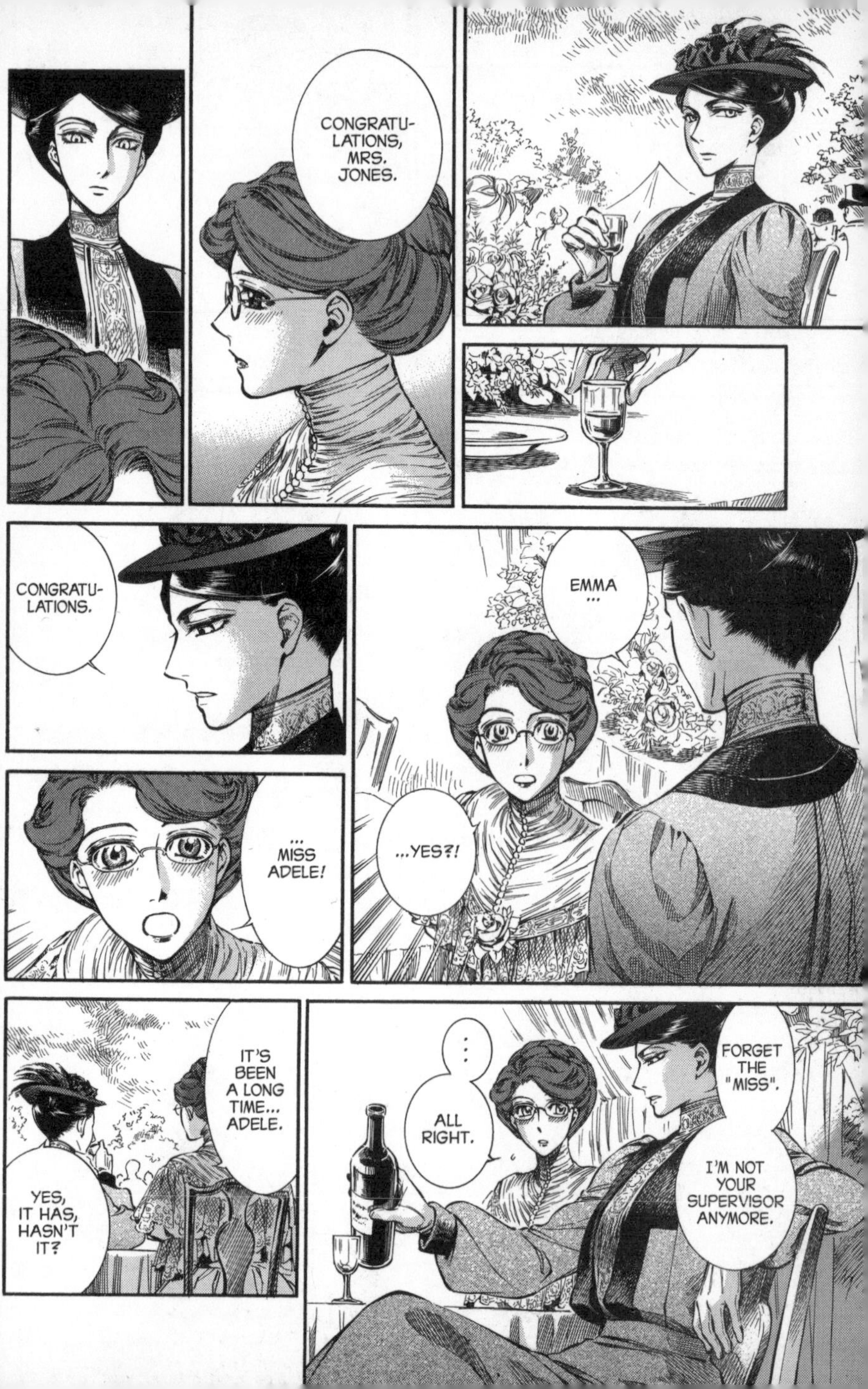
CONGRATU-LATIONS, MRS. JONES.
EMMA ...
...YES?!
CONGRATU-LATIONS.
... MISS ADELE!
FORGET THE "MISS".
I'M NOT YOUR SUPERVISOR ANYMORE.
...
ALL RIGHT.
IT'S BEEN A LONG TIME... ADELE.
YES, IT HAS, HASN'T IT?

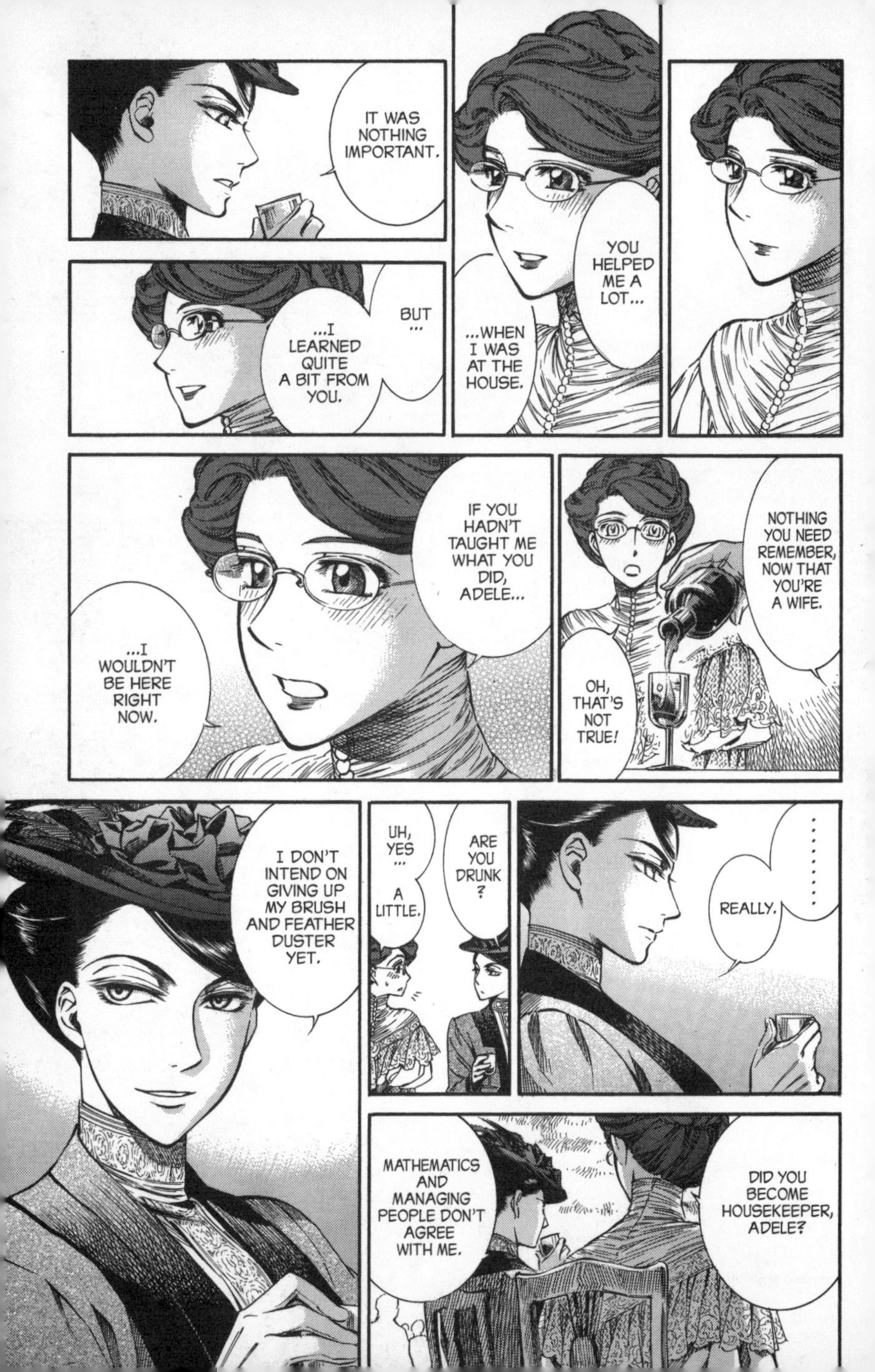
YOU HELPED ME A LOT...
...WHEN I WAS AT THE HOUSE.
IT WAS NOTHING IMPORTANT.
BUT...
...I LEARNED QUITE A BIT FROM YOU.
NOTHING YOU NEED REMEMBER, NOW THAT YOU'RE A WIFE.
OH, THAT'S NOT TRUE!
IF YOU HADN'T TAUGHT ME WHAT YOU DID, ADELE...
...I WOULDN'T BE HERE RIGHT NOW.
....
REALLY.
ARE YOU DRUNK?
UH, YES... A LITTLE.
DID YOU BECOME HOUSEKEEPER, ADELE?
MATHEMATICS AND MANAGING PEOPLE DON'T AGREE WITH ME.
I DON'T INTEND ON GIVING UP MY BRUSH AND FEATHER DUSTER YET.

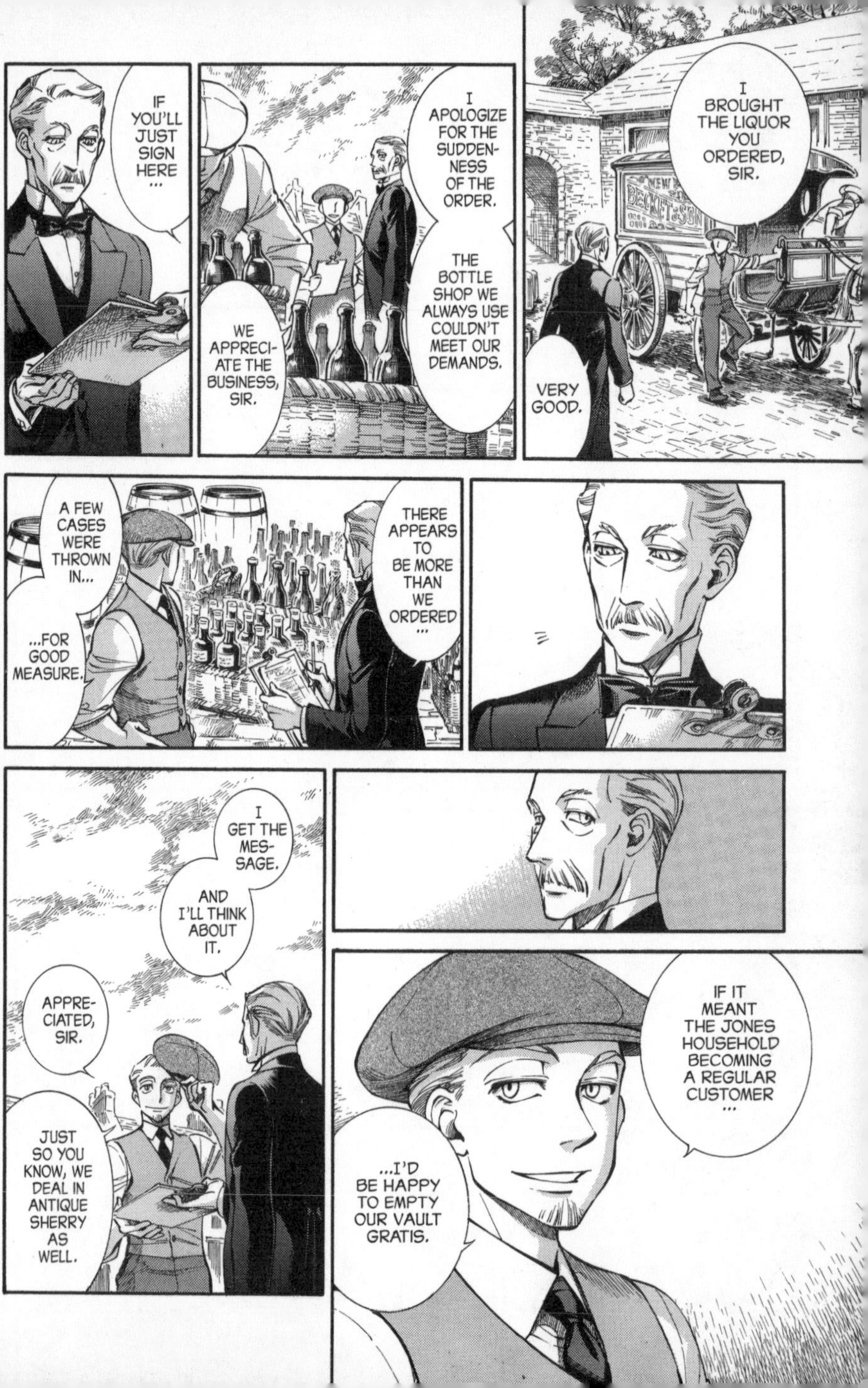
I BROUGHT THE LIQUOR YOU ORDERED, SIR.
BECKET&SON
VERY GOOD.
I APOLOGIZE FOR THE SUDDENNESS OF THE ORDER.
THE BOTTLE SHOP WE ALWAYS USE COULDN'T MEET OUR DEMANDS.
WE APPRECIATE THE BUSINESS, SIR.
IF YOU'LL JUST SIGN HERE...
THERE APPEARS TO BE MORE THAN WE ORDERED...
A FEW CASES WERE THROWN IN...
...FOR GOOD MEASURE.
IF IT MEANT THE JONES HOUSEHOLD BECOMING A REGULAR CUSTOMER...
...I'D BE HAPPY TO EMPTY OUR VAULT GRATIS.
I GET THE MESSAGE.
AND I'LL THINK ABOUT IT.
APPRECIATED, SIR.
JUST SO YOU KNOW, WE DEAL IN ANTIQUE SHERRY AS WELL.

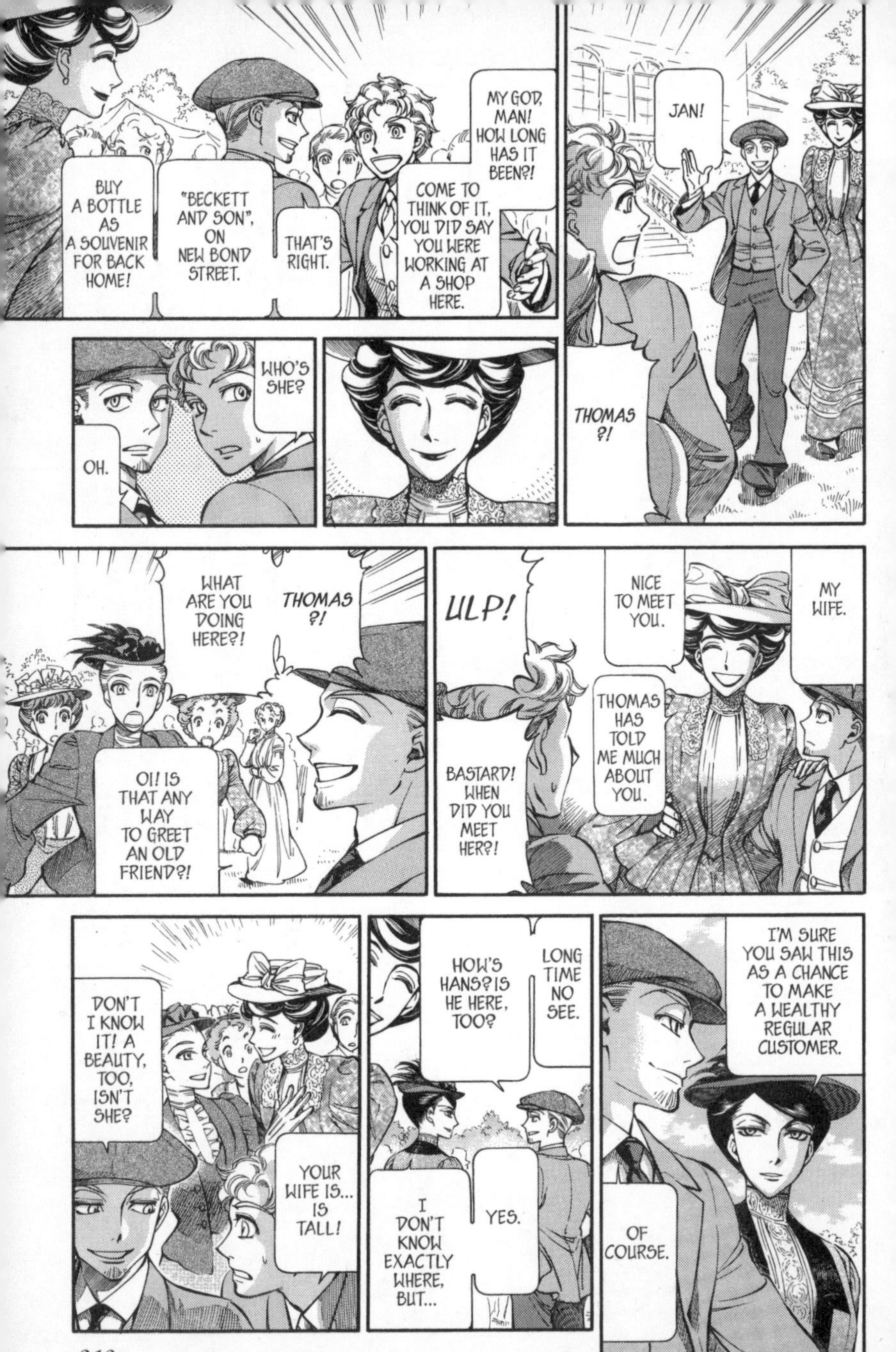
JAN!
THOMAS ?!
MY GOD, MAN! HOW LONG HAS IT BEEN?!
COME TO THINK OF IT, YOU DID SAY YOU WERE WORKING AT A SHOP HERE.
THAT'S RIGHT.
"BECKETT AND SON", ON NEW BOND STREET.
BUY A BOTTLE AS A SOUVENIR FOR BACK HOME!
WHO'S SHE?
OH.
MY WIFE.
NICE TO MEET YOU.
THOMAS HAS TOLD ME MUCH ABOUT YOU.
ULP!
BASTARD! WHEN DID YOU MEET HER?!
THOMAS ?!
WHAT ARE YOU DOING HERE?!
OI! IS THAT ANY WAY TO GREET AN OLD FRIEND?!
I'M SURE YOU SAW THIS AS A CHANCE TO MAKE A WEALTHY REGULAR CUSTOMER.
OF COURSE.
LONG TIME NO SEE.
HOW'S HANS? IS HE HERE, TOO?
YES.
I DON'T KNOW EXACTLY WHERE, BUT...
DON'T I KNOW IT! A BEAUTY, TOO, ISN'T SHE?
YOUR WIFE IS... IS TALL!

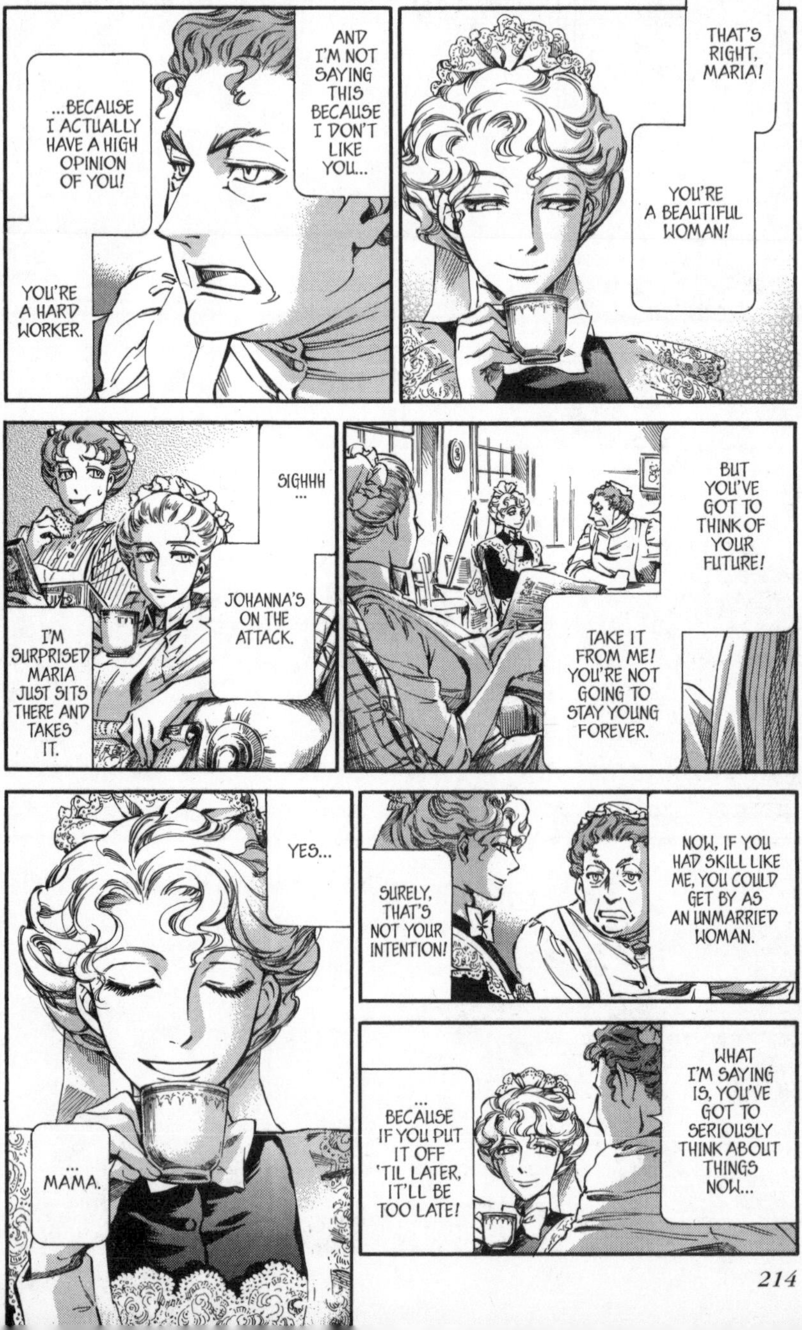
THAT'S RIGHT, MARIA!
YOU'RE A BEAUTIFUL WOMAN!
AND I'M NOT SAYING THIS BECAUSE I DON'T LIKE YOU...
...BECAUSE I ACTUALLY HAVE A HIGH OPINION OF YOU!
YOU'RE A HARD WORKER.
BUT YOU'VE GOT TO THINK OF YOUR FUTURE!
TAKE IT FROM ME! YOU'RE NOT GOING TO STAY YOUNG FOREVER.
SIGHHH...
JOHANNA'S ON THE ATTACK.
I'M SURPRISED MARIA JUST SITS THERE AND TAKES IT.
NOW, IF YOU HAD SKILL LIKE ME, YOU COULD GET BY AS AN UNMARRIED WOMAN.
SURELY, THAT'S NOT YOUR INTENTION!
WHAT I'M SAYING IS, YOU'VE GOT TO SERIOUSLY THINK ABOUT THINGS NOW...
...BECAUSE IF YOU PUT IT OFF 'TIL LATER, IT'LL BE TOO LATE!
YES...
...MAMA.

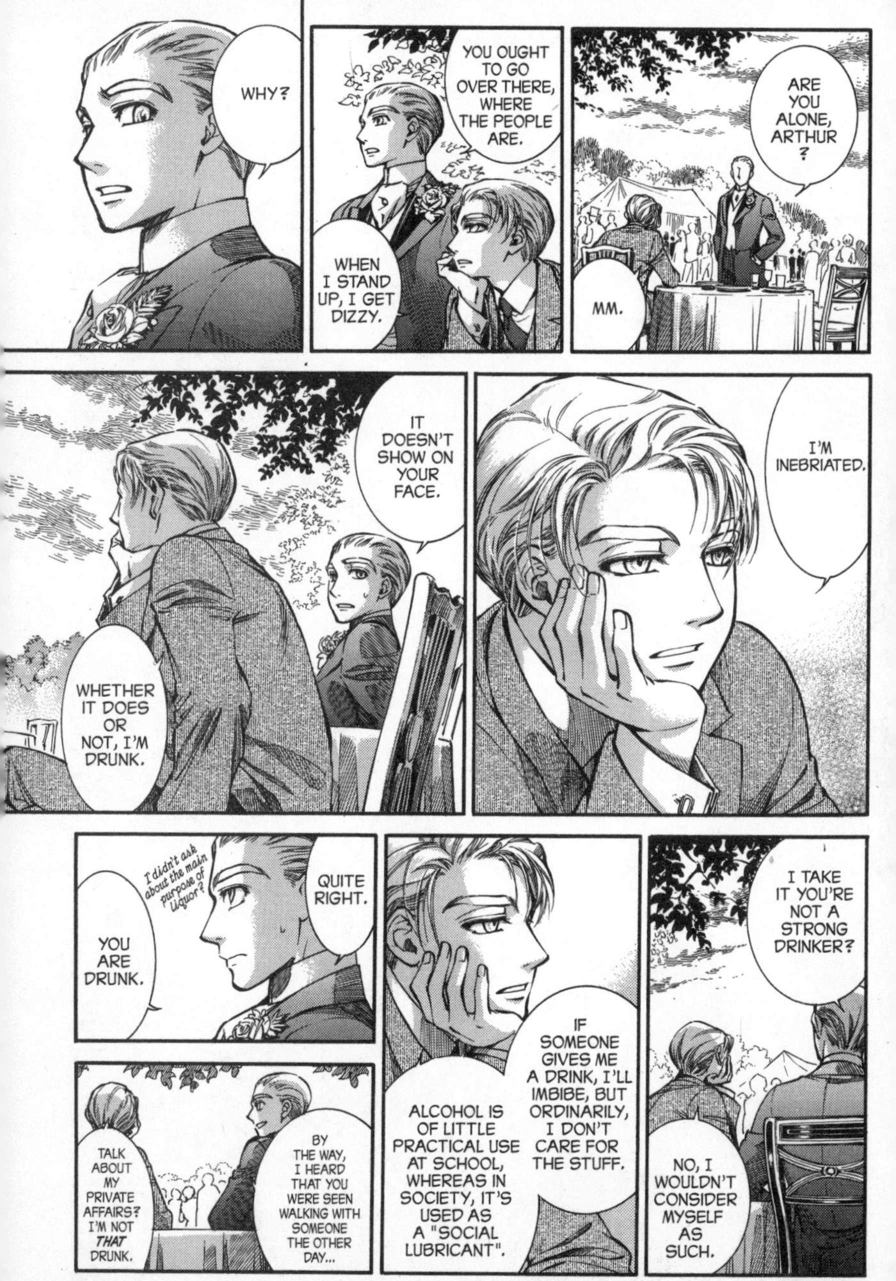
ARE YOU ALONE, ARTHUR?
MM.
YOU OUGHT TO GO OVER THERE, WHERE THE PEOPLE ARE.
WHEN I STAND UP, I GET DIZZY.
WHY?
I'M INEBRIATED.
IT DOESN'T SHOW ON YOUR FACE.
WHETHER IT DOES OR NOT, I'M DRUNK.
I TAKE IT YOU'RE NOT A STRONG DRINKER?
NO, I WOULDN'T CONSIDER MYSELF AS SUCH.
IF SOMEONE GIVES ME A DRINK, I'LL IMBIBE, BUT ORDINARILY, I DON'T CARE FOR THE STUFF.
ALCOHOL IS OF LITTLE PRACTICAL USE AT SCHOOL, WHEREAS IN SOCIETY, IT'S USED AS A "SOCIAL LUBRICANT".
QUITE RIGHT.
I didn't ask about the main purpose of liquor?
YOU ARE DRUNK.
BY THE WAY, I HEARD THAT YOU WERE SEEN WALKING WITH SOMEONE THE OTHER DAY...
TALK ABOUT MY PRIVATE AFFAIRS? I'M NOT *THAT* DRUNK.

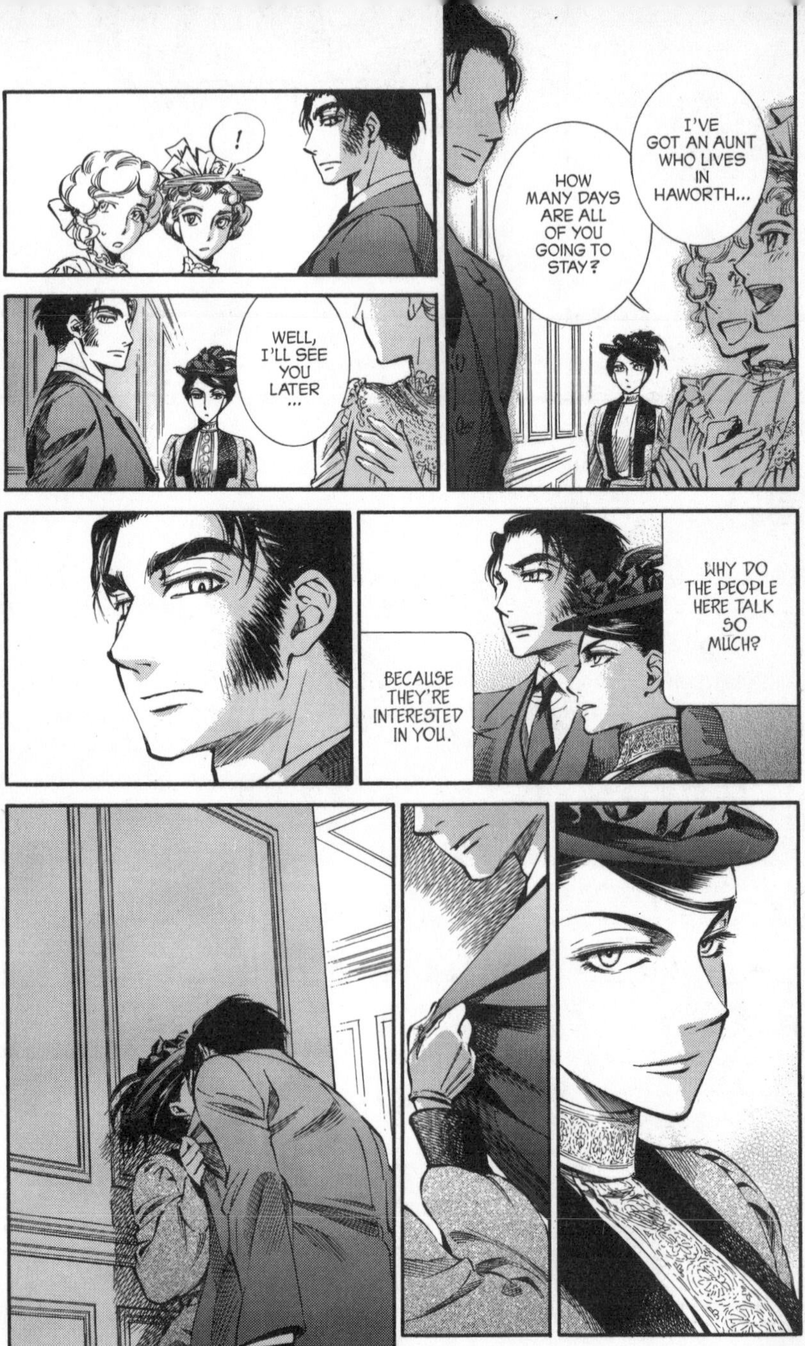
I'VE GOT AN AUNT WHO LIVES IN HAWORTH...
HOW MANY DAYS ARE ALL OF YOU GOING TO STAY?
!
WELL, I'LL SEE YOU LATER ...
WHY DO THE PEOPLE HERE TALK SO MUCH?
BECAUSE THEY'RE INTERESTED IN YOU.

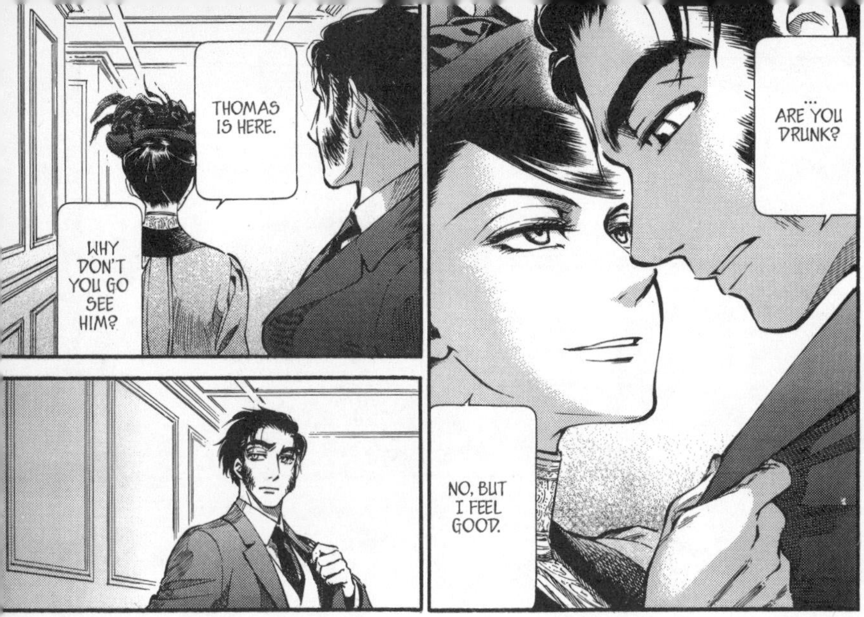
...ARE YOU DRUNK?
NO, BUT I FEEL GOOD.
THOMAS IS HERE.
WHY DON'T YOU GO SEE HIM?

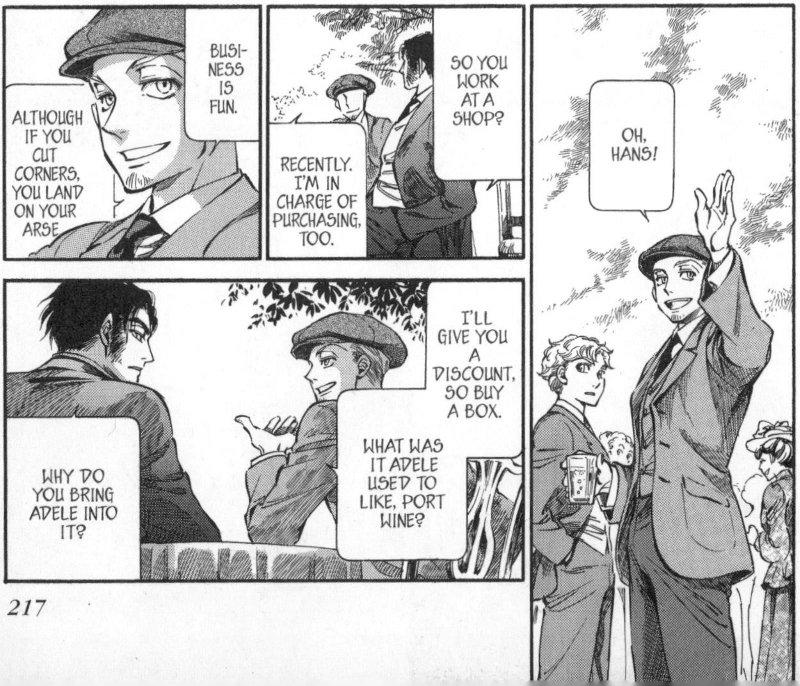
OH, HANS!
SO YOU WORK AT A SHOP?
RECENTLY. I'M IN CHARGE OF PURCHASING, TOO.
BUSINESS IS FUN.
ALTHOUGH IF YOU CUT CORNERS, YOU LAND ON YOUR ARSE.
I'LL GIVE YOU A DISCOUNT, SO BUY A BOX.
WHAT WAS IT ADELE USED TO LIKE, PORT WINE?
WHY DO YOU BRING ADELE INTO IT?

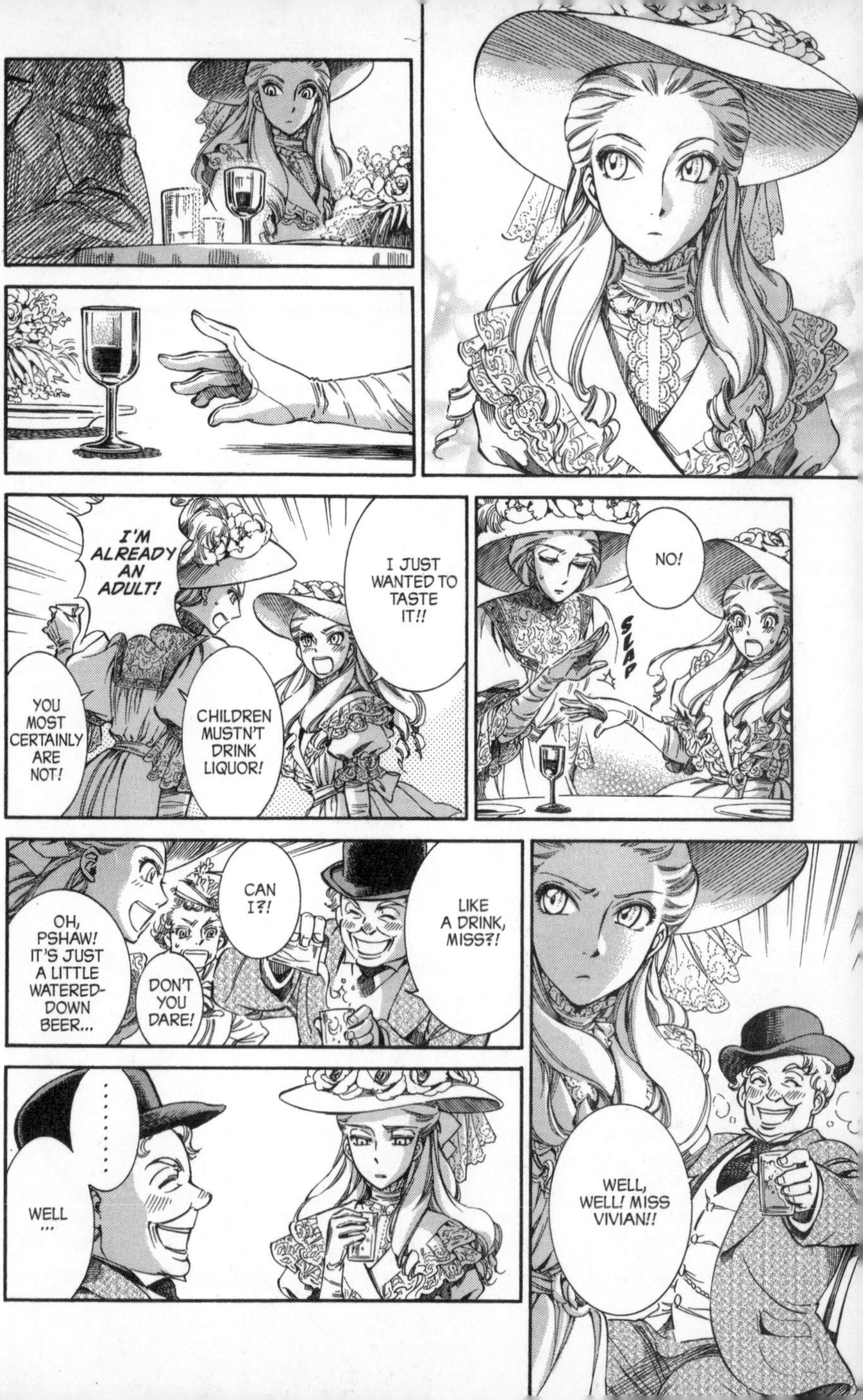

NO!
SLAP
I JUST WANTED TO TASTE IT!!
I'M ALREADY AN ADULT!
CHILDREN MUSTN'T DRINK LIQUOR!
YOU MOST CERTAINLY ARE NOT!
WELL, WELL! MISS VIVIAN!!
LIKE A DRINK, MISS?!
CAN I?!
DON'T YOU DARE!
OH, PSHAW! IT'S JUST A LITTLE WATERED-DOWN BEER...
......
WELL ...

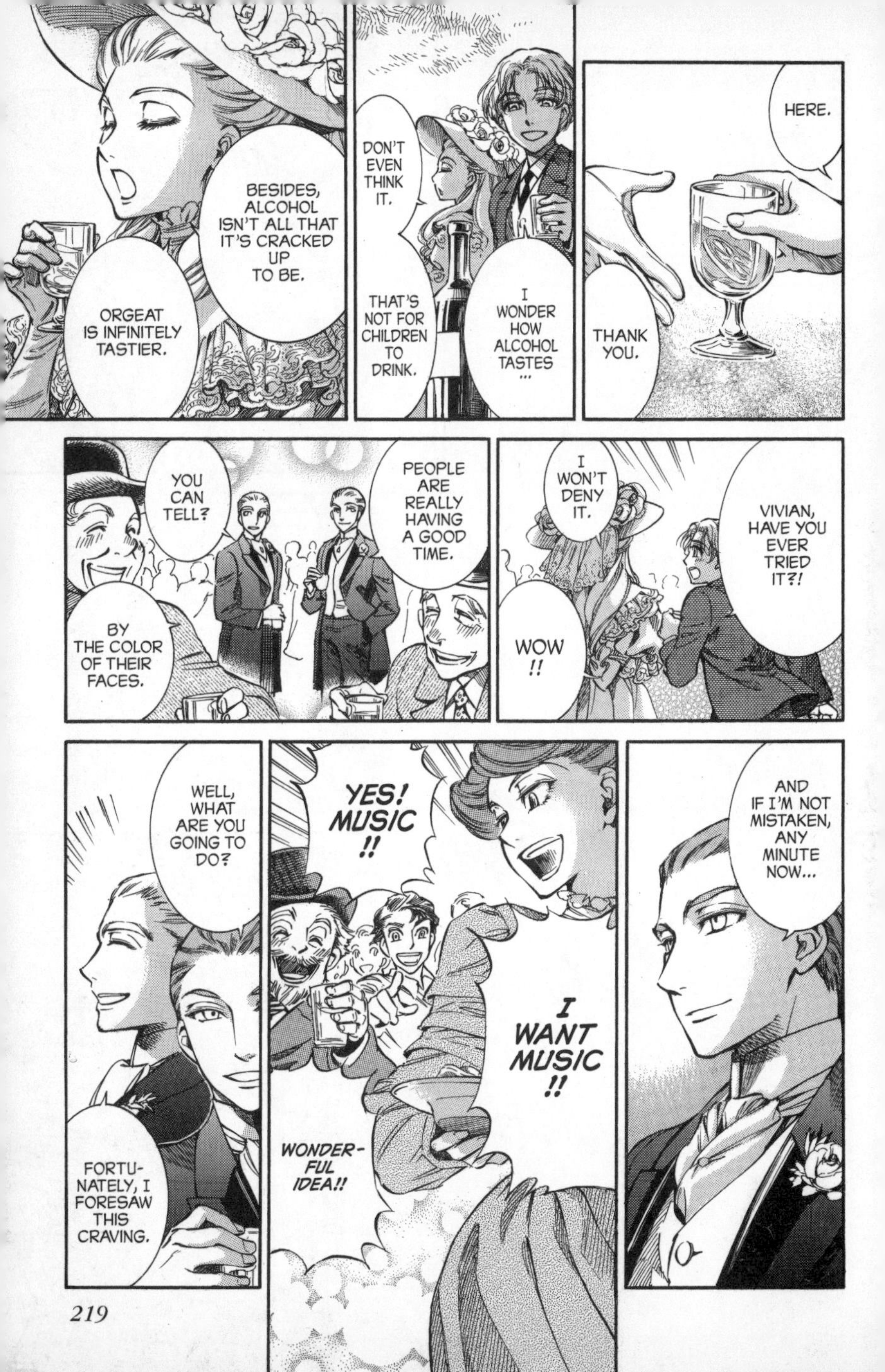

HERE.
THANK YOU.
I WONDER HOW ALCOHOL TASTES...
THAT'S NOT FOR CHILDREN TO DRINK.
DON'T EVEN THINK IT.
BESIDES, ALCOHOL ISN'T ALL THAT IT'S CRACKED UP TO BE.
ORGEAT IS INFINITELY TASTIER.
VIVIAN, HAVE YOU EVER TRIED IT?!
I WON'T DENY IT.
WOW!!
PEOPLE ARE REALLY HAVING A GOOD TIME.
YOU CAN TELL?
BY THE COLOR OF THEIR FACES.
AND IF I'M NOT MISTAKEN, ANY MINUTE NOW...
I WANT MUSIC!!
YES! MUSIC!!
WONDERFUL IDEA!!
WELL, WHAT ARE YOU GOING TO DO?
FORTUNATELY, I FORESAW THIS CRAVING.

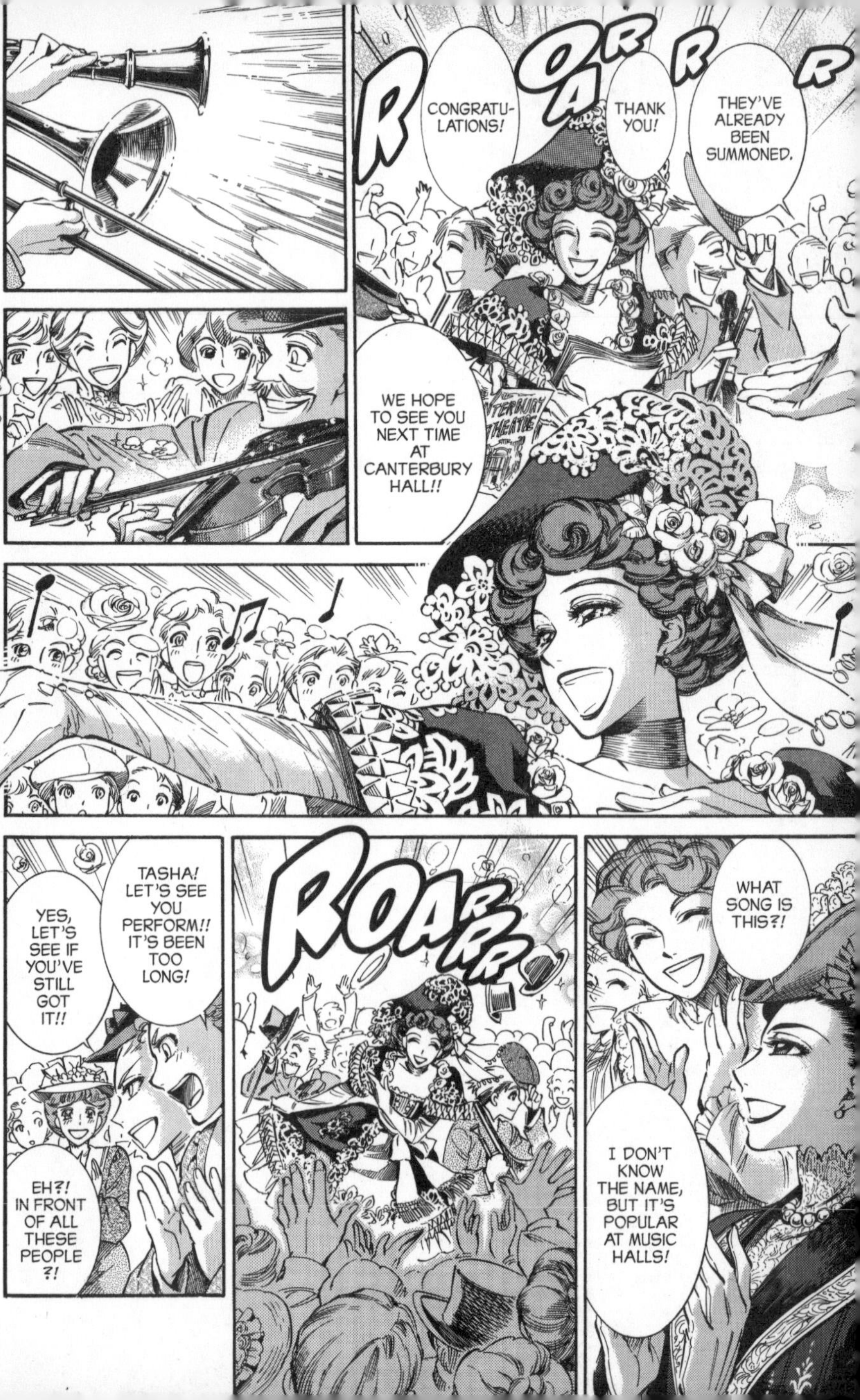
ROARRRR
THEY'VE ALREADY BEEN SUMMONED.
THANK YOU!
CONGRATULATIONS!
WE HOPE TO SEE YOU NEXT TIME AT CANTERBURY HALL!!
WHAT SONG IS THIS?!
I DON'T KNOW THE NAME, BUT IT'S POPULAR AT MUSIC HALLS!
ROARRR
TASHA! LET'S SEE YOU PERFORM!! IT'S BEEN TOO LONG!
YES, LET'S SEE IF YOU'VE STILL GOT IT!!
EH?! IN FRONT OF ALL THESE PEOPLE?!

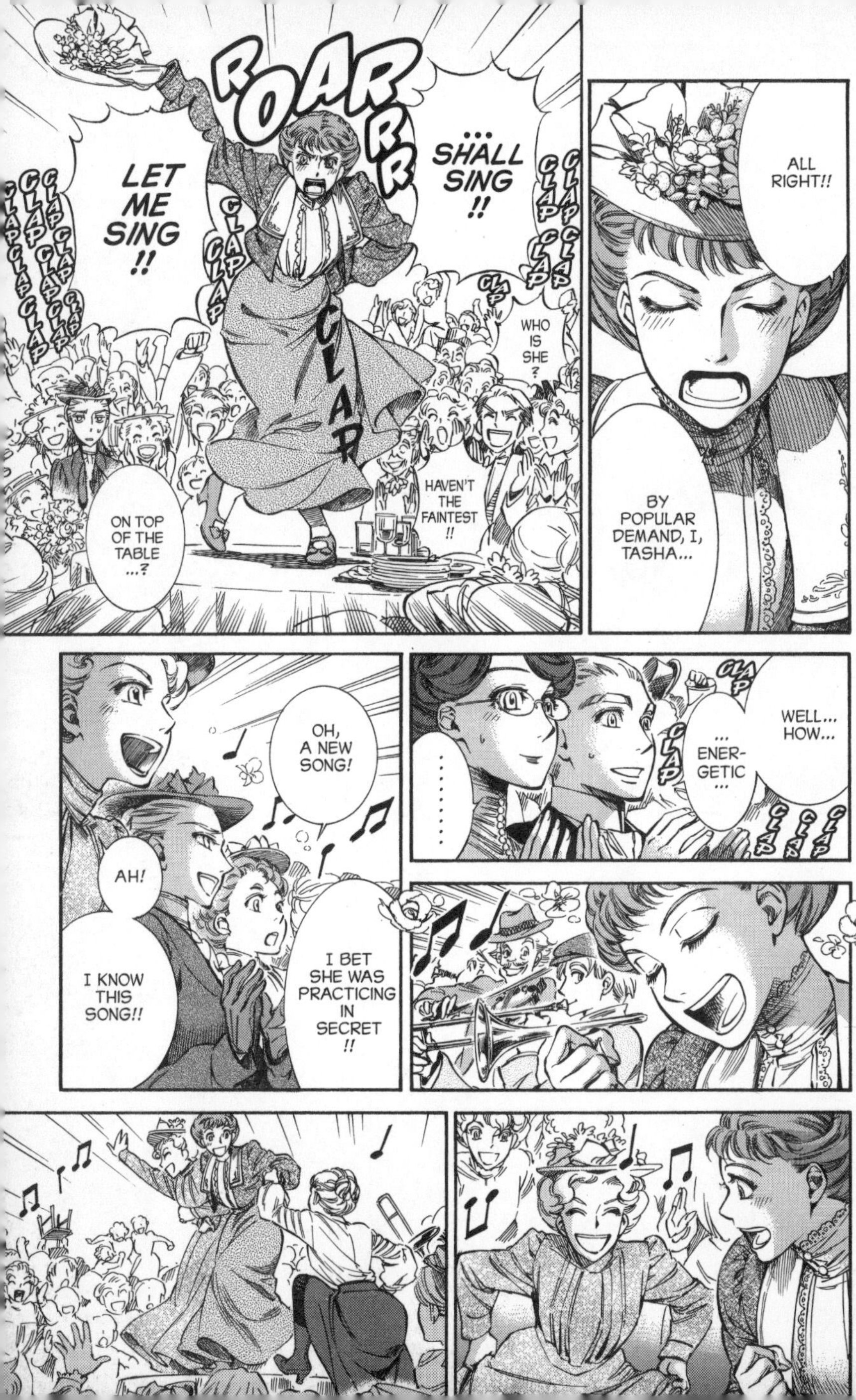
ALL RIGHT!!
BY POPULAR DEMAND, I, TASHA...
...SHALL SING!!
CLAP CLAP CLAP CLAP CLAP
ROARRR
LET ME SING!!
CLAP CLAP CLAP CLAP CLAP CLAP
WHO IS SHE?
CLAP
HAVEN'T THE FAINTEST!!
ON TOP OF THE TABLE...?
CLAP
WELL... HOW...
...ENERGETIC...
CLAP CLAP CLAP
....
OH, A NEW SONG!
I BET SHE WAS PRACTICING IN SECRET!!
AH!
I KNOW THIS SONG!!

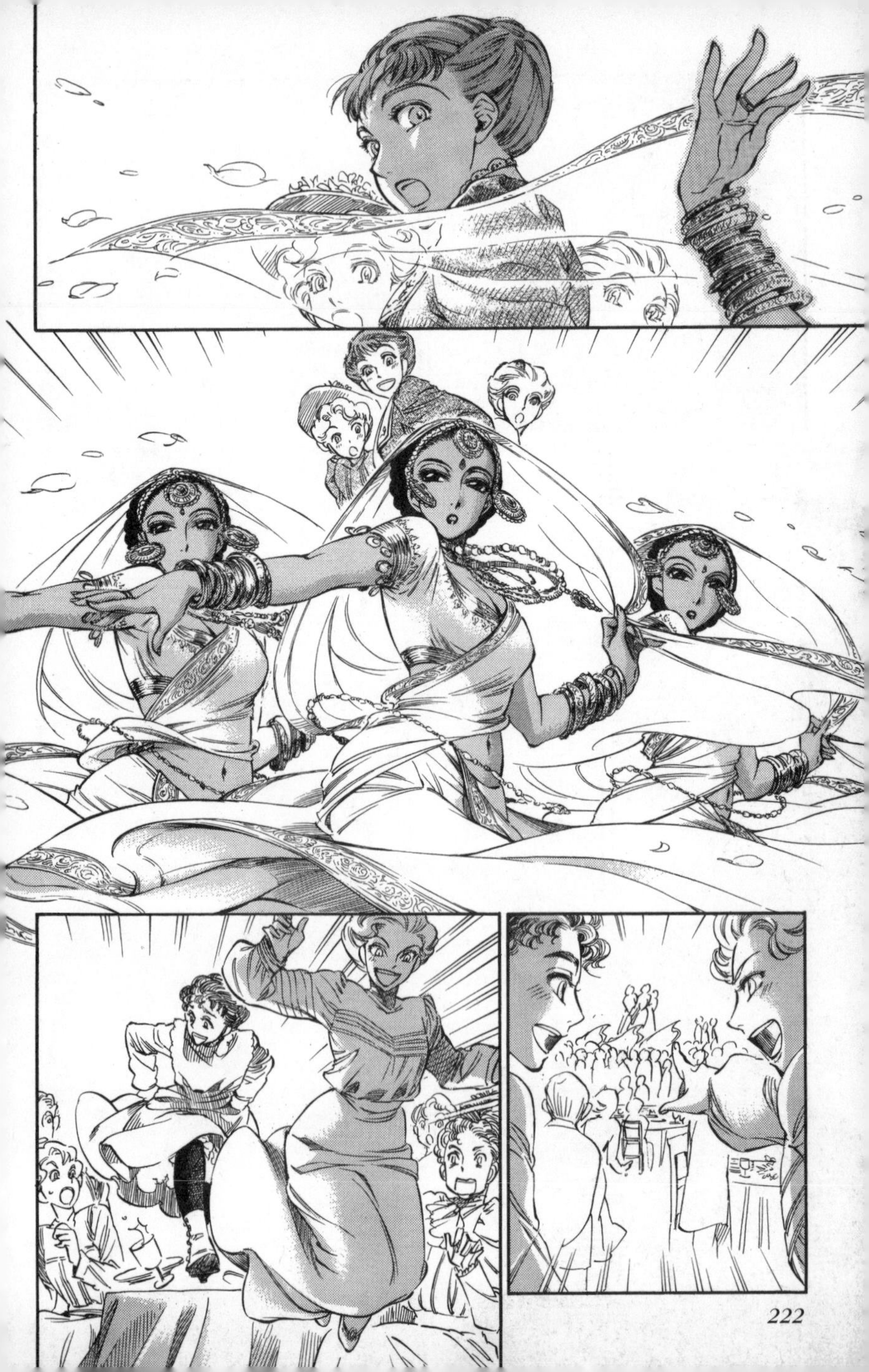

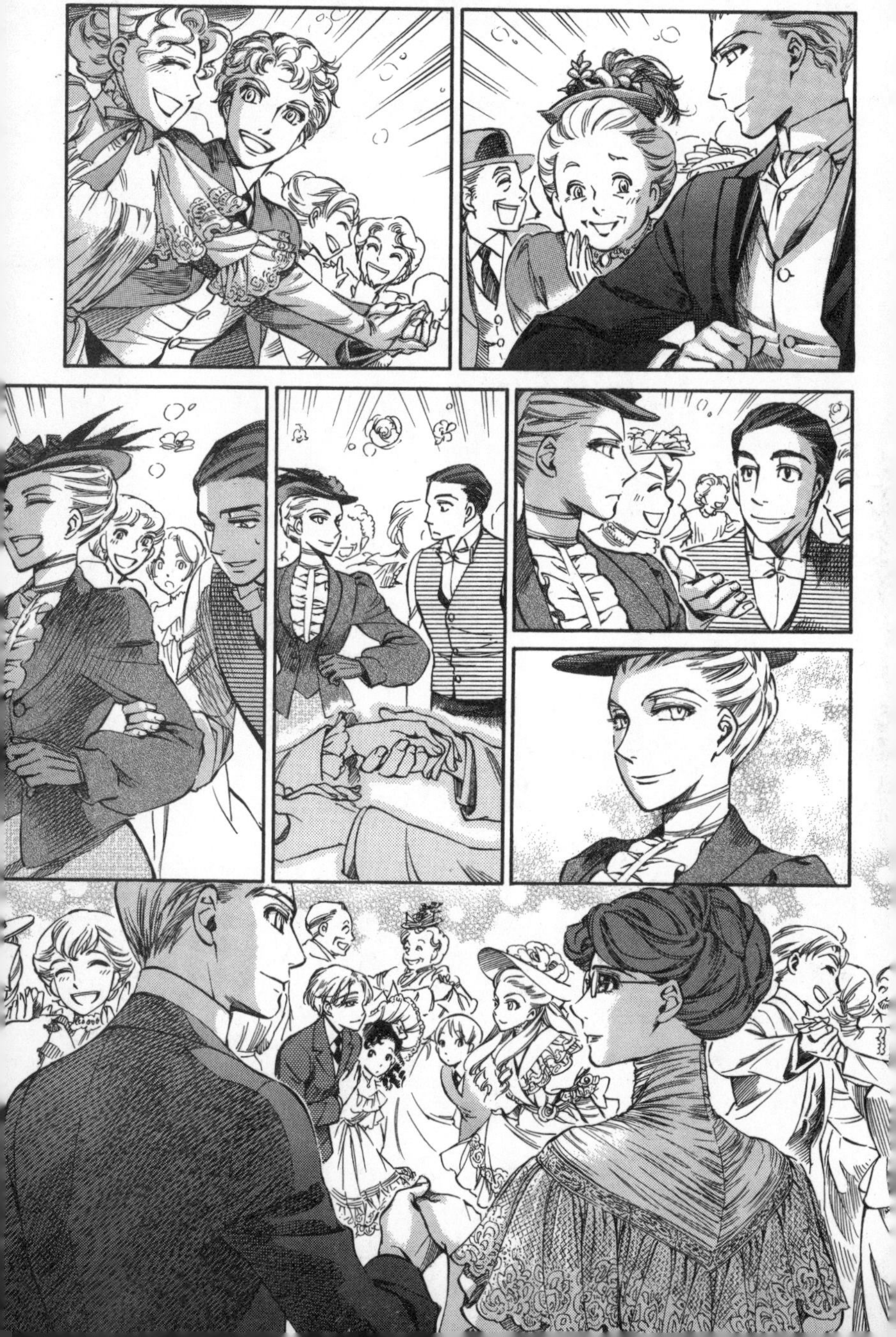

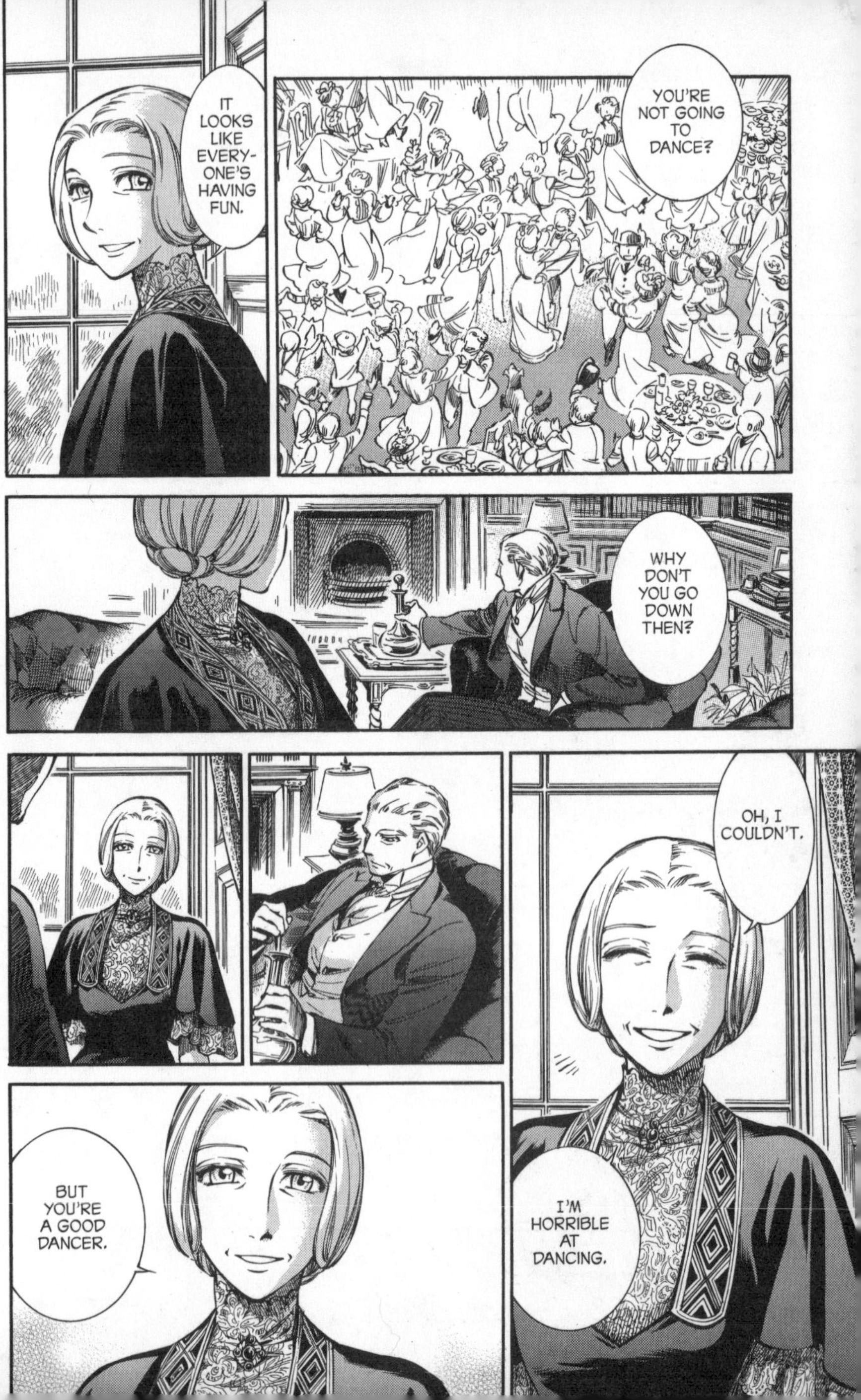
YOU'RE NOT GOING TO DANCE?
IT LOOKS LIKE EVERYONE'S HAVING FUN.
WHY DON'T YOU GO DOWN THEN?
OH, I COULDN'T.
I'M HORRIBLE AT DANCING.
BUT YOU'RE A GOOD DANCER.

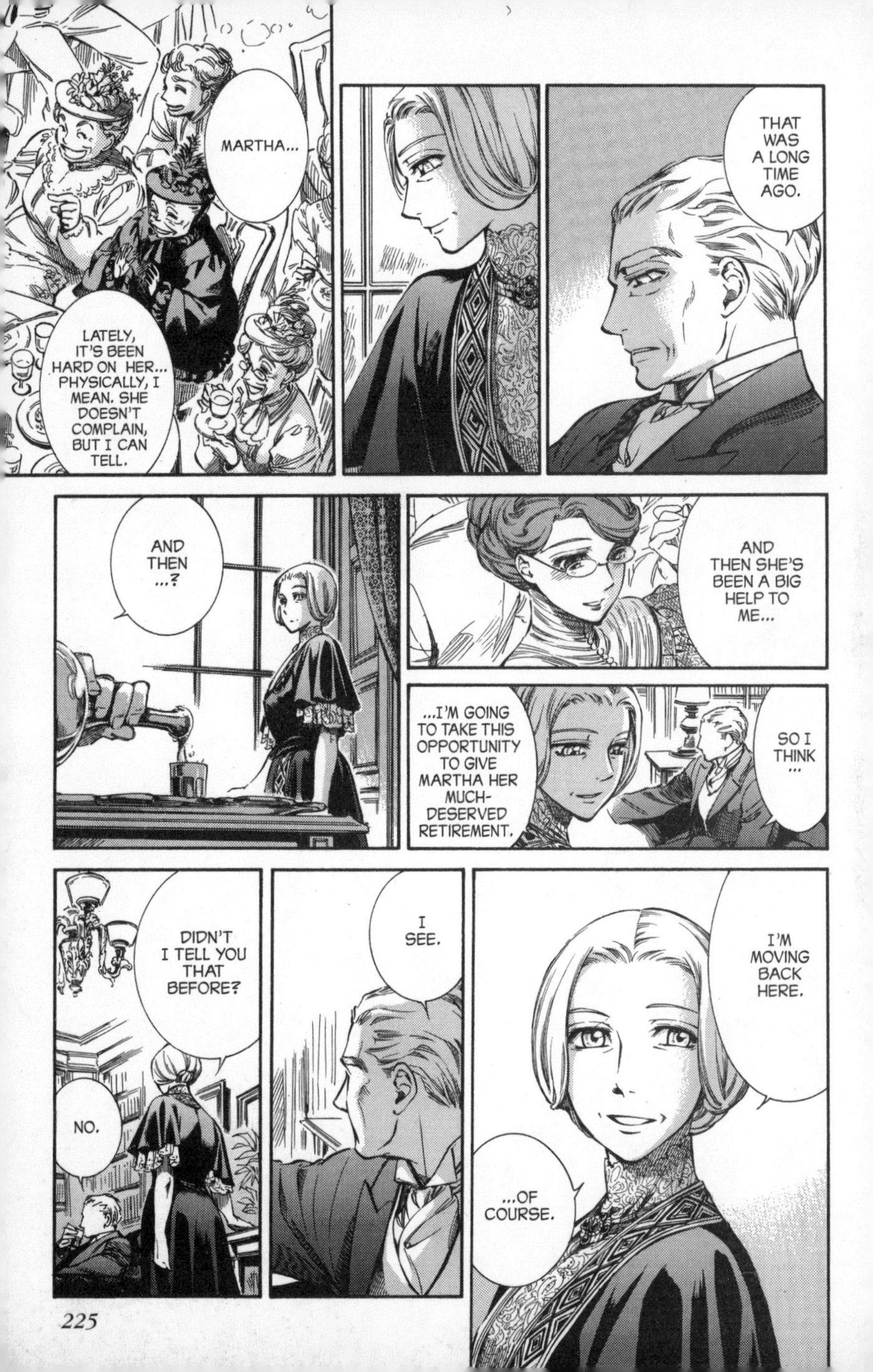
THAT WAS A LONG TIME AGO.
MARTHA...
LATELY, IT'S BEEN HARD ON HER... PHYSICALLY, I MEAN. SHE DOESN'T COMPLAIN, BUT I CAN TELL.
AND THEN SHE'S BEEN A BIG HELP TO ME...
SO I THINK...
...I'M GOING TO TAKE THIS OPPORTUNITY TO GIVE MARTHA HER MUCH-DESERVED RETIREMENT.
AND THEN ...?
I'M MOVING BACK HERE.
...OF COURSE.
I SEE.
DIDN'T I TELL YOU THAT BEFORE?
NO.

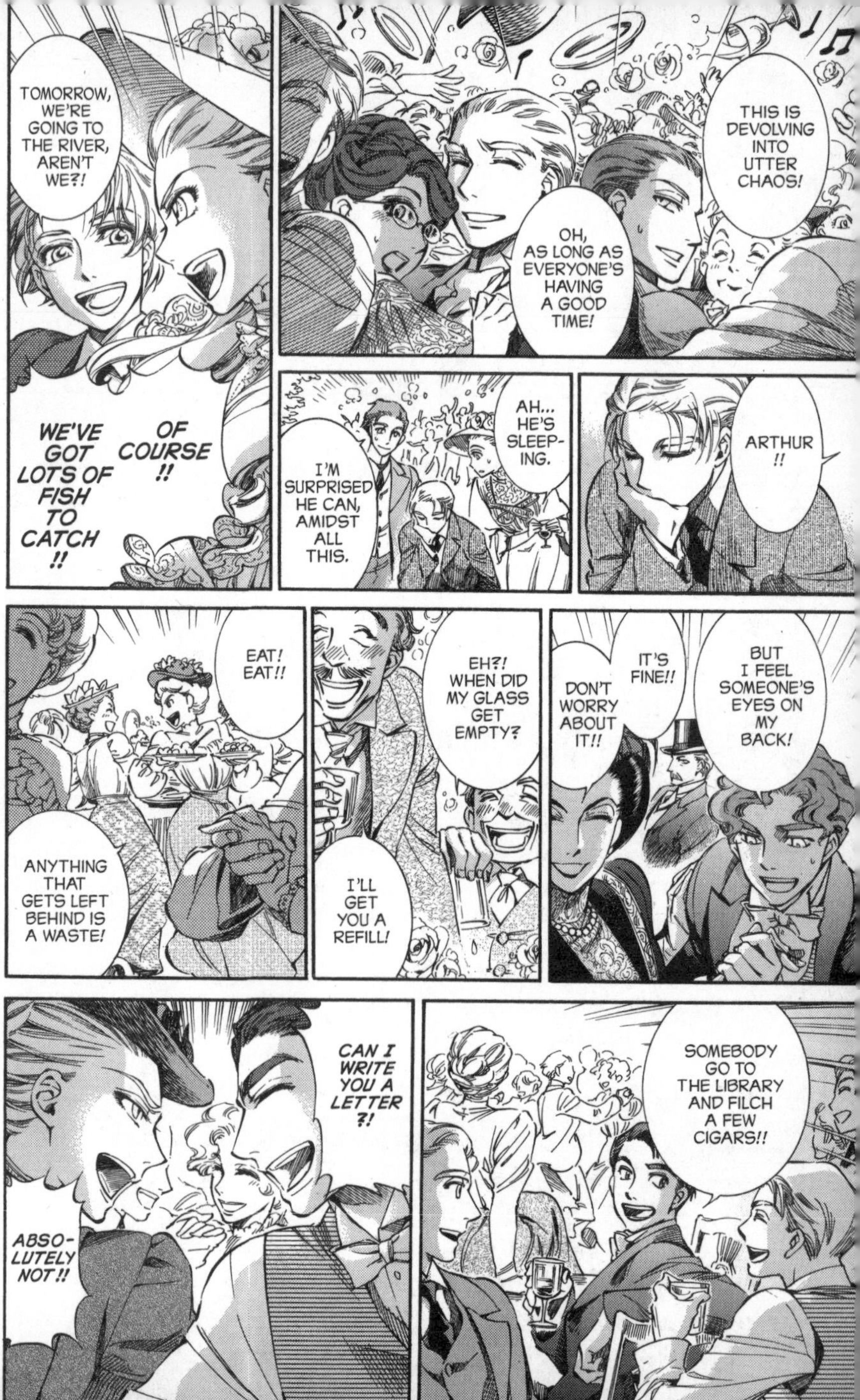
THIS IS DEVOLVING INTO UTTER CHAOS!
OH, AS LONG AS EVERYONE'S HAVING A GOOD TIME!
ARTHUR!!
AH... HE'S SLEEPING.
I'M SURPRISED HE CAN, AMIDST ALL THIS.
TOMORROW, WE'RE GOING TO THE RIVER, AREN'T WE?!
OF COURSE!!
WE'VE GOT LOTS OF FISH TO CATCH!!
BUT I FEEL SOMEONE'S EYES ON MY BACK!
IT'S FINE!!
DON'T WORRY ABOUT IT!!
EH?! WHEN DID MY GLASS GET EMPTY?
I'LL GET YOU A REFILL!
EAT! EAT!!
ANYTHING THAT GETS LEFT BEHIND IS A WASTE!
SOMEBODY GO TO THE LIBRARY AND FILCH A FEW CIGARS!!
CAN I WRITE YOU A LETTER?!
ABSOLUTELY NOT!!

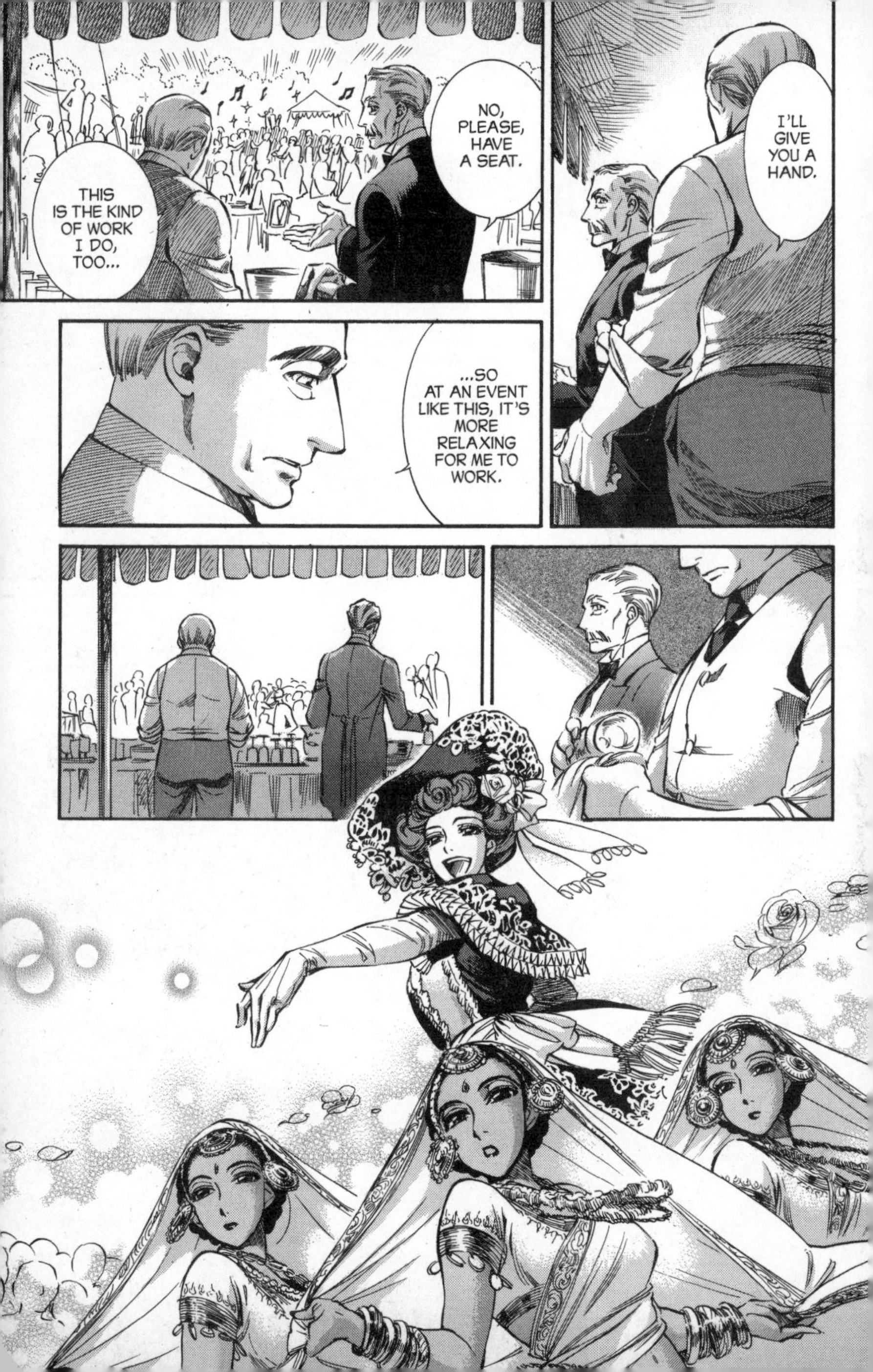
I'LL GIVE YOU A HAND.
NO, PLEASE, HAVE A SEAT.
THIS IS THE KIND OF WORK I DO, TOO...
...SO AT AN EVENT LIKE THIS, IT'S MORE RELAXING FOR ME TO WORK.

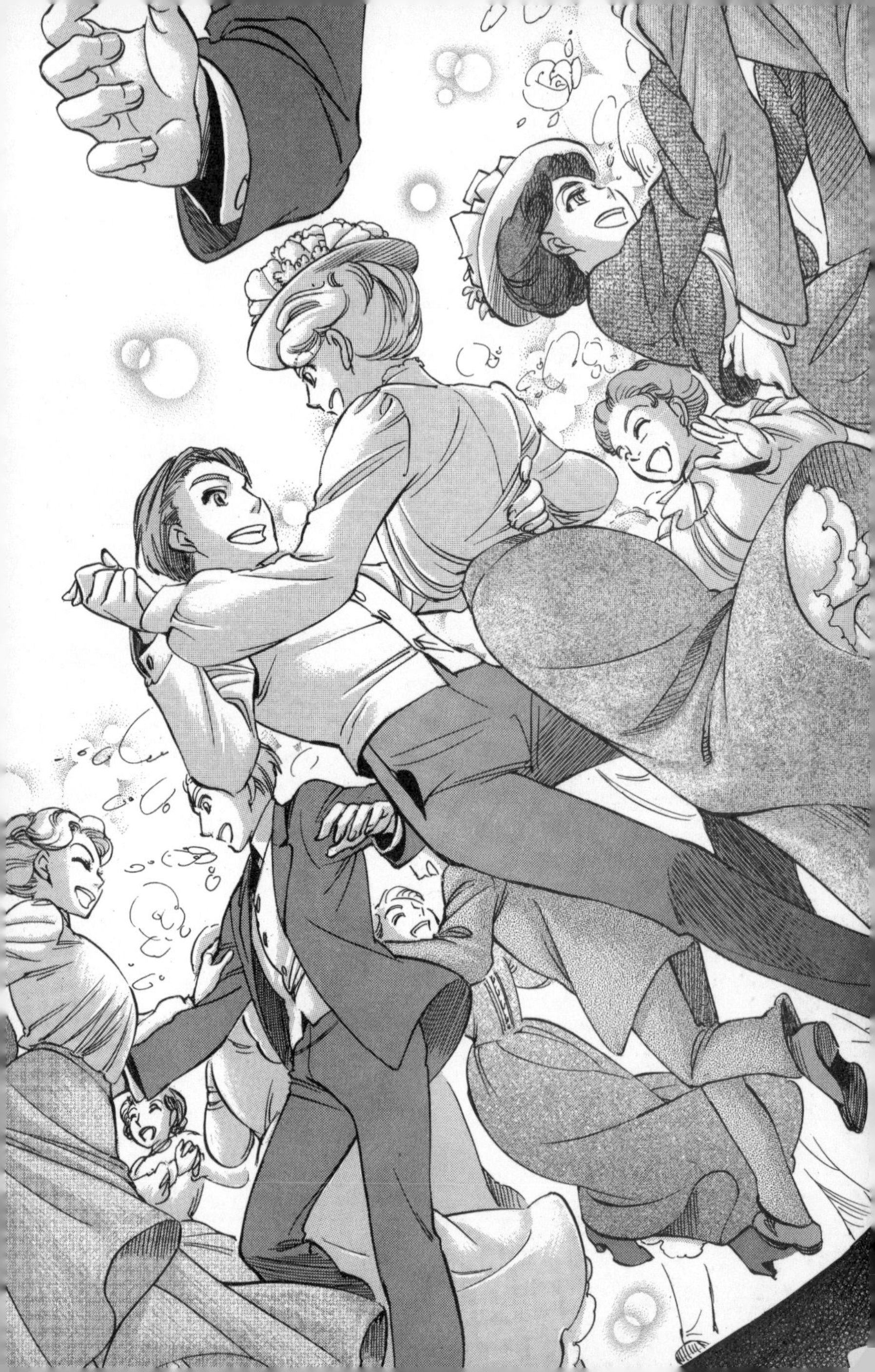

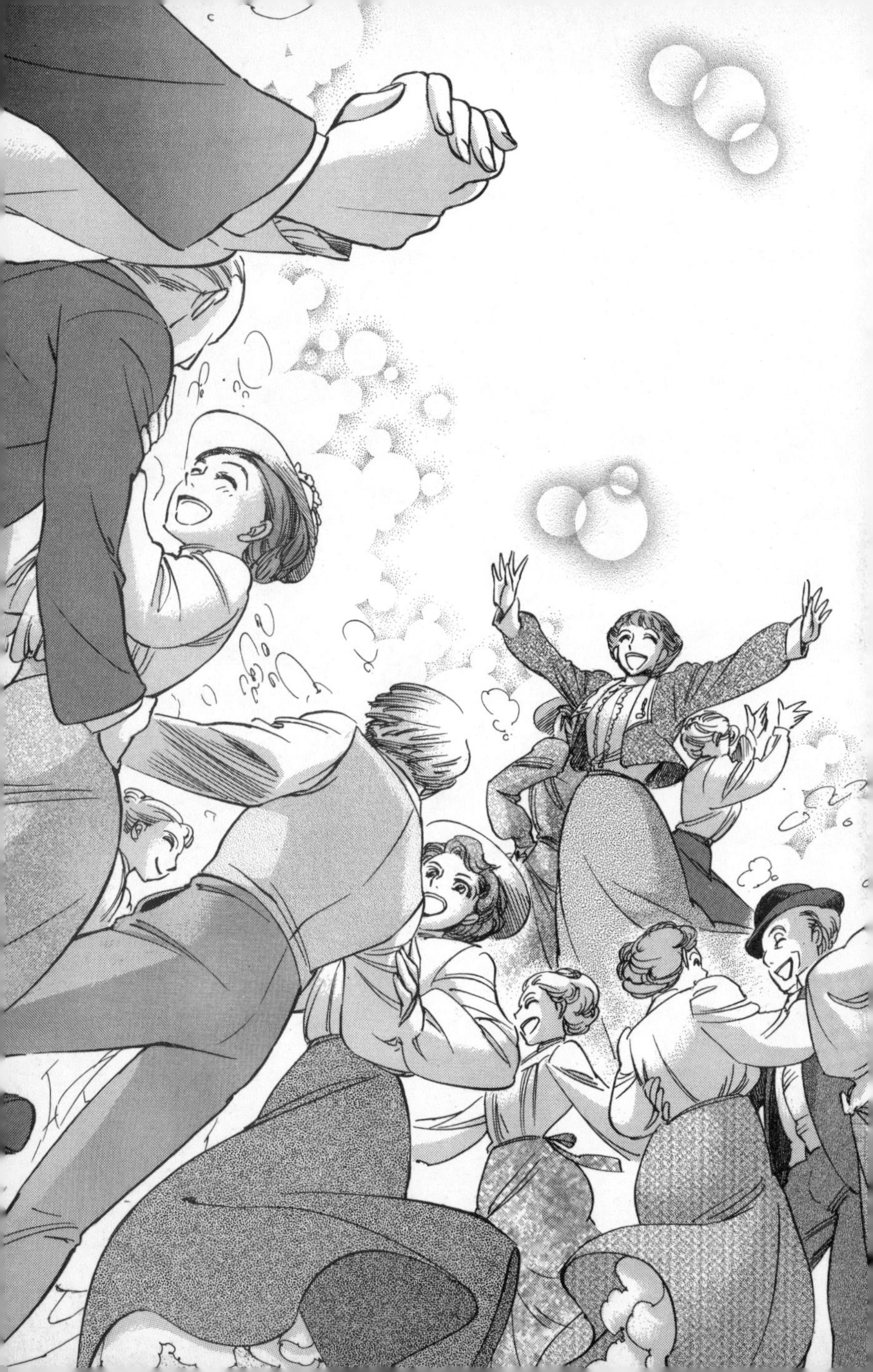

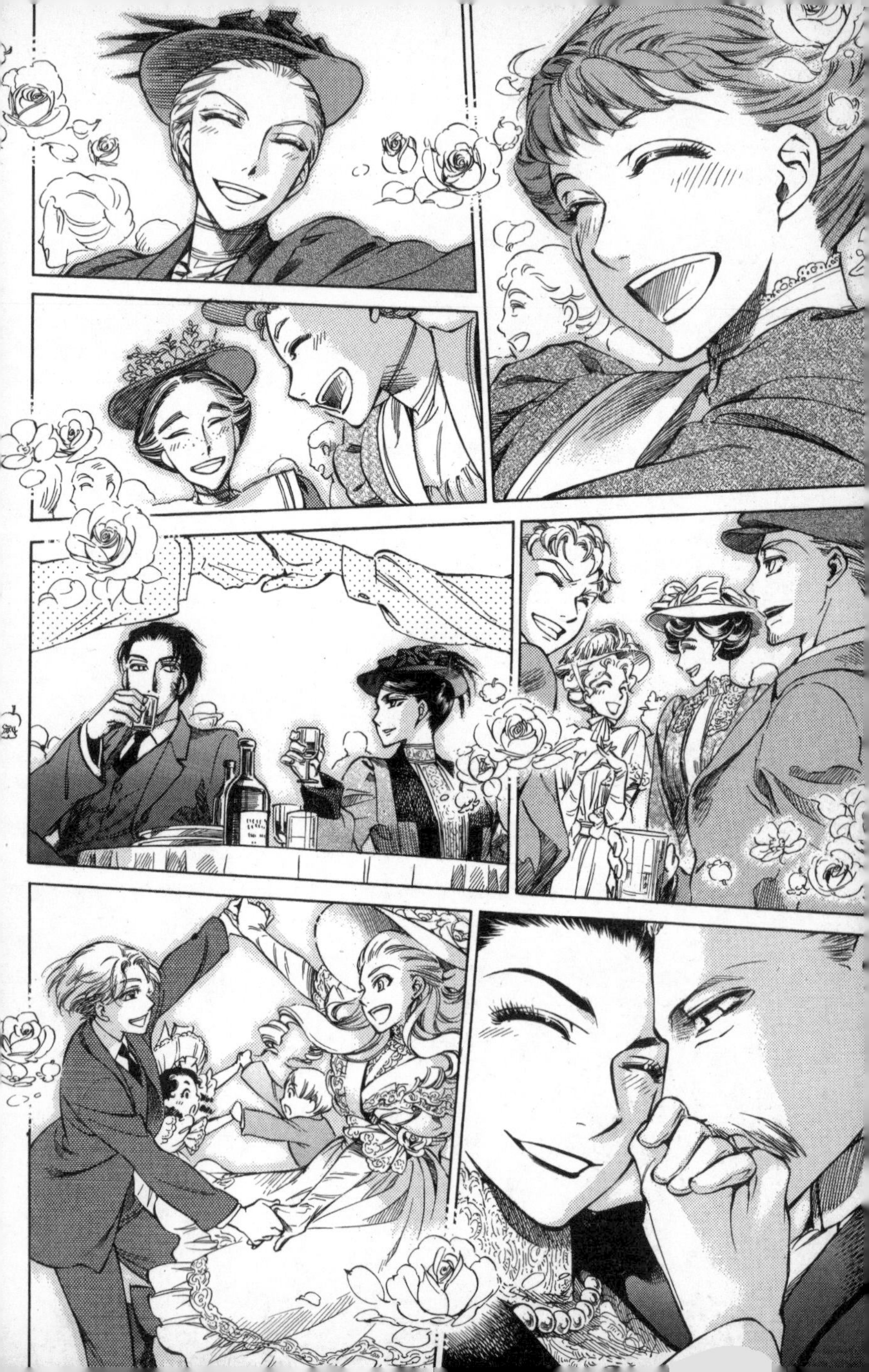

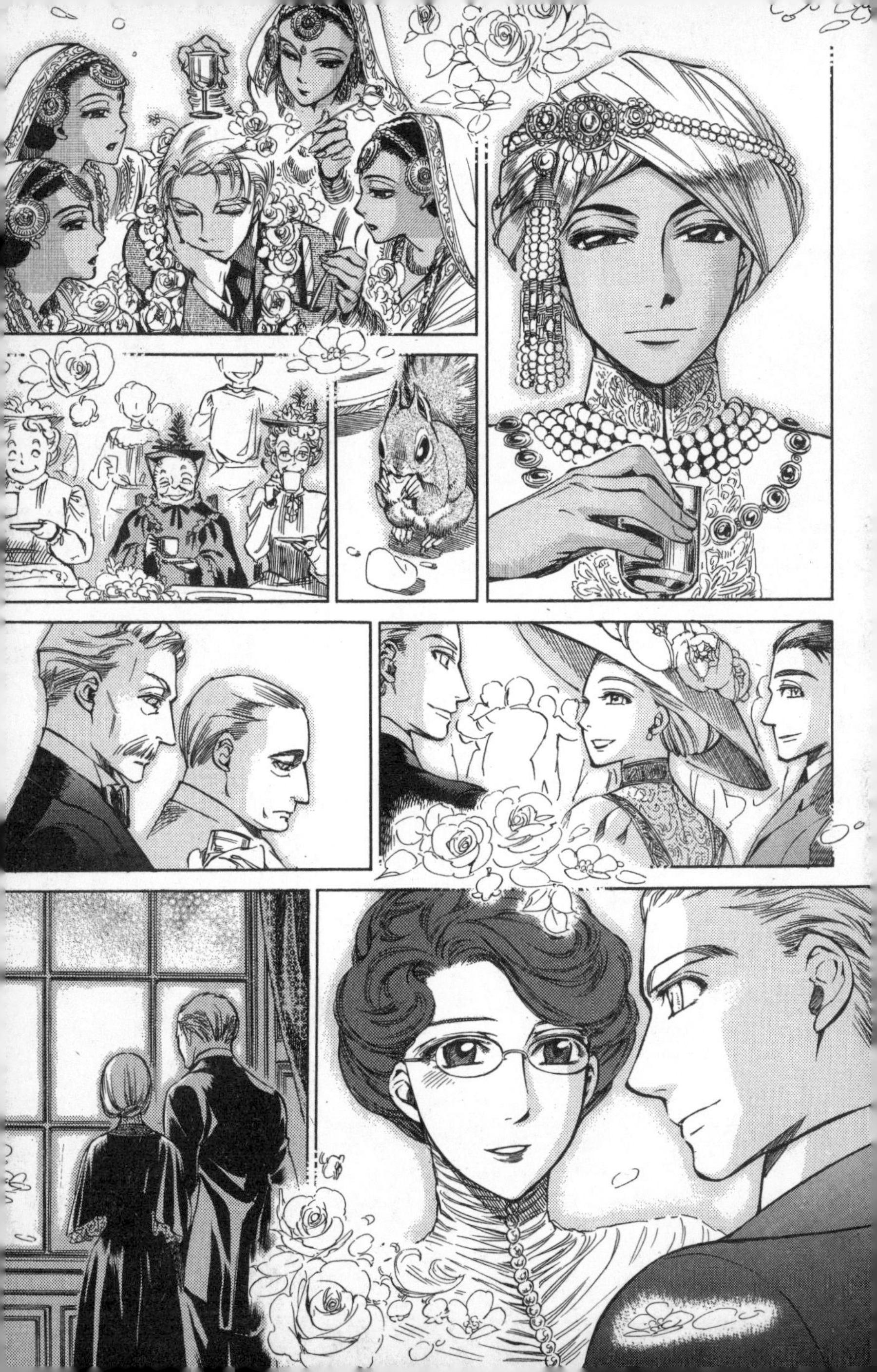

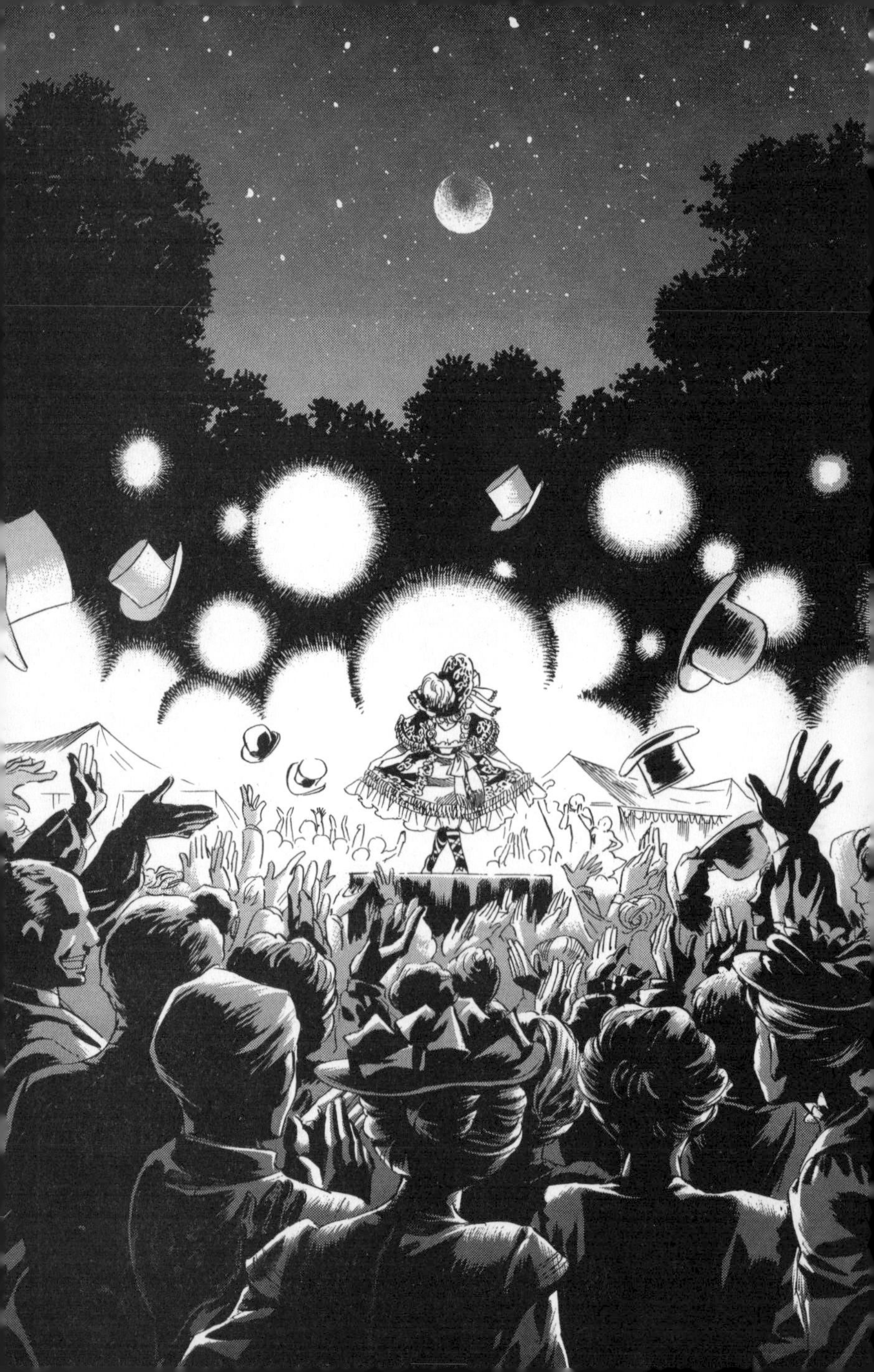

AFTERWORD

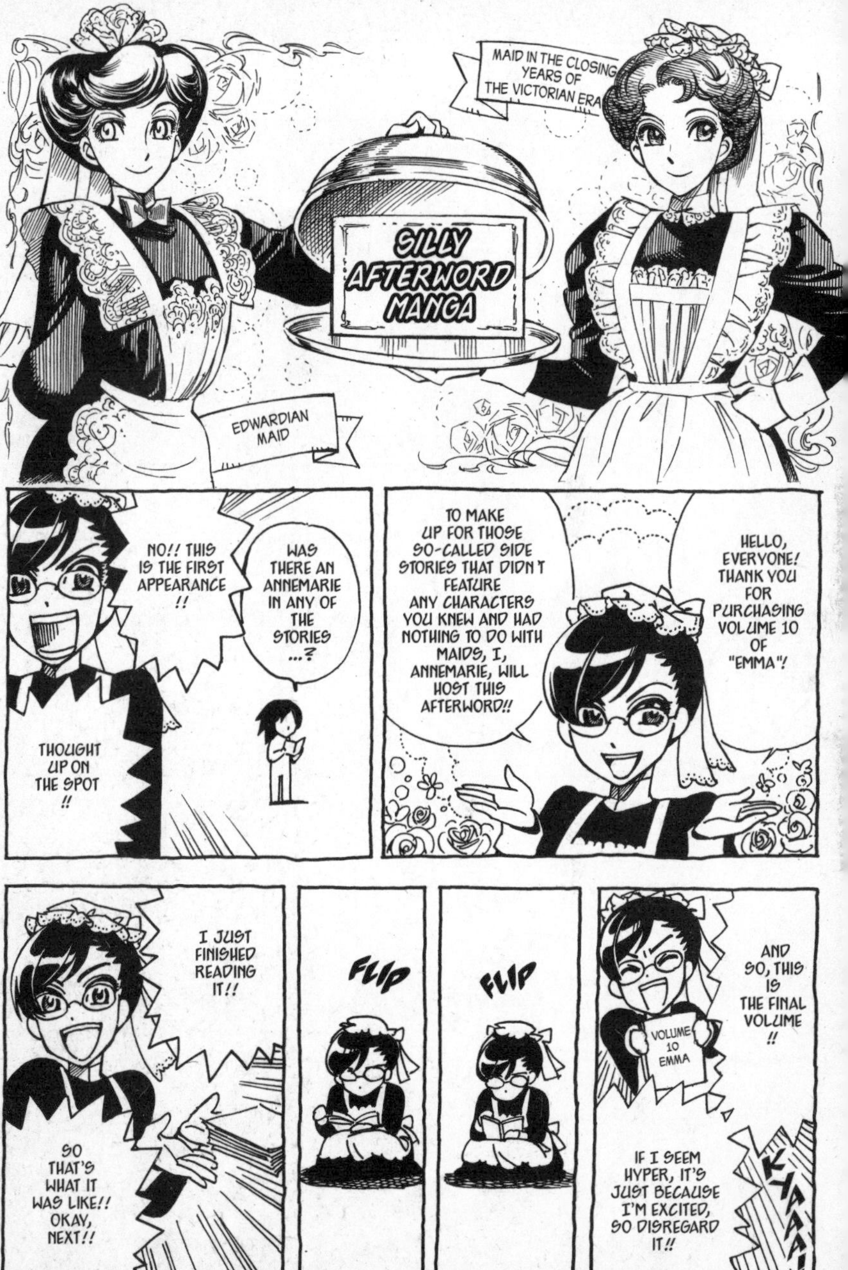
MAID IN THE CLOSING YEARS OF THE VICTORIAN ERA
SILLY AFTERWORD MANGA
EDWARDIAN MAID
HELLO, EVERYONE! THANK YOU FOR PURCHASING VOLUME 10 OF "EMMA"!
TO MAKE UP FOR THOSE SO-CALLED SIDE STORIES THAT DIDN'T FEATURE ANY CHARACTERS YOU KNEW AND HAD NOTHING TO DO WITH MAIDS, I, ANNEMARIE, WILL HOST THIS AFTERWORD!!
WAS THERE AN ANNEMARIE IN ANY OF THE STORIES ...?
NO!! THIS IS THE FIRST APPEARANCE!!
THOUGHT UP ON THE SPOT!!
AND SO, THIS IS THE FINAL VOLUME!!
VOLUME 10 EMMA
KYAAA!
IF I SEEM HYPER, IT'S JUST BECAUSE I'M EXCITED, SO DISREGARD IT!!
FLIP
FLIP
I JUST FINISHED READING IT!!
SO THAT'S WHAT IT WAS LIKE!! OKAY, NEXT!!

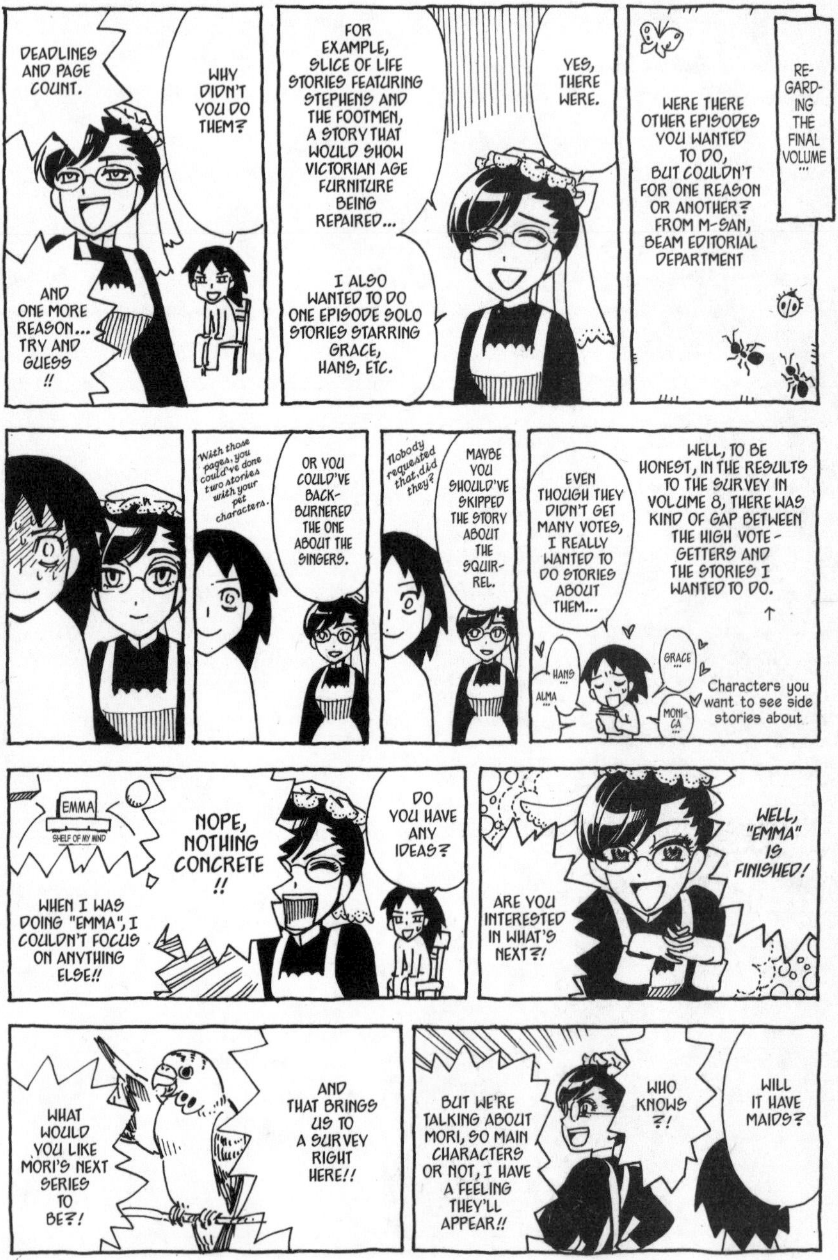
REGARDING THE FINAL VOLUME...
WERE THERE OTHER EPISODES YOU WANTED TO DO, BUT COULDN'T FOR ONE REASON OR ANOTHER?
FROM M-SAN, BEAM EDITORIAL DEPARTMENT
YES, THERE WERE.
FOR EXAMPLE, SLICE OF LIFE STORIES FEATURING STEPHENS AND THE FOOTMEN, A STORY THAT WOULD SHOW VICTORIAN AGE FURNITURE BEING REPAIRED...
I ALSO WANTED TO DO ONE EPISODE SOLO STORIES STARRING GRACE, HANS, ETC.
WHY DIDN'T YOU DO THEM?
DEADLINES AND PAGE COUNT.
AND ONE MORE REASON... TRY AND GUESS!!
WELL, TO BE HONEST, IN THE RESULTS TO THE SURVEY IN VOLUME 8, THERE WAS KIND OF GAP BETWEEN THE HIGH VOTE-GETTERS AND THE STORIES I WANTED TO DO.
EVEN THOUGH THEY DIDN'T GET MANY VOTES, I REALLY WANTED TO DO STORIES ABOUT THEM...
GRACE...
HANS...
ALMA...
MONICA...
Characters you want to see side stories about
MAYBE YOU SHOULD'VE SKIPPED THE STORY ABOUT THE SQUIRREL.
Nobody requested that, did they?
OR YOU COULD'VE BACKBURNERED THE ONE ABOUT THE SINGERS.
With those pages, you could've done two stories with your pet characters.
WELL, "EMMA" IS FINISHED!
ARE YOU INTERESTED IN WHAT'S NEXT?!
DO YOU HAVE ANY IDEAS?
NOPE, NOTHING CONCRETE!!
EMMA
SHELF OF MY MIND
WHEN I WAS DOING "EMMA", I COULDN'T FOCUS ON ANYTHING ELSE!!
WILL IT HAVE MAIDS?
WHO KNOWS?!
BUT WE'RE TALKING ABOUT MORI, SO MAIN CHARACTERS OR NOT, I HAVE A FEELING THEY'LL APPEAR!!
AND THAT BRINGS US TO A SURVEY RIGHT HERE!!
WHAT WOULD YOU LIKE MORI'S NEXT SERIES TO BE?!

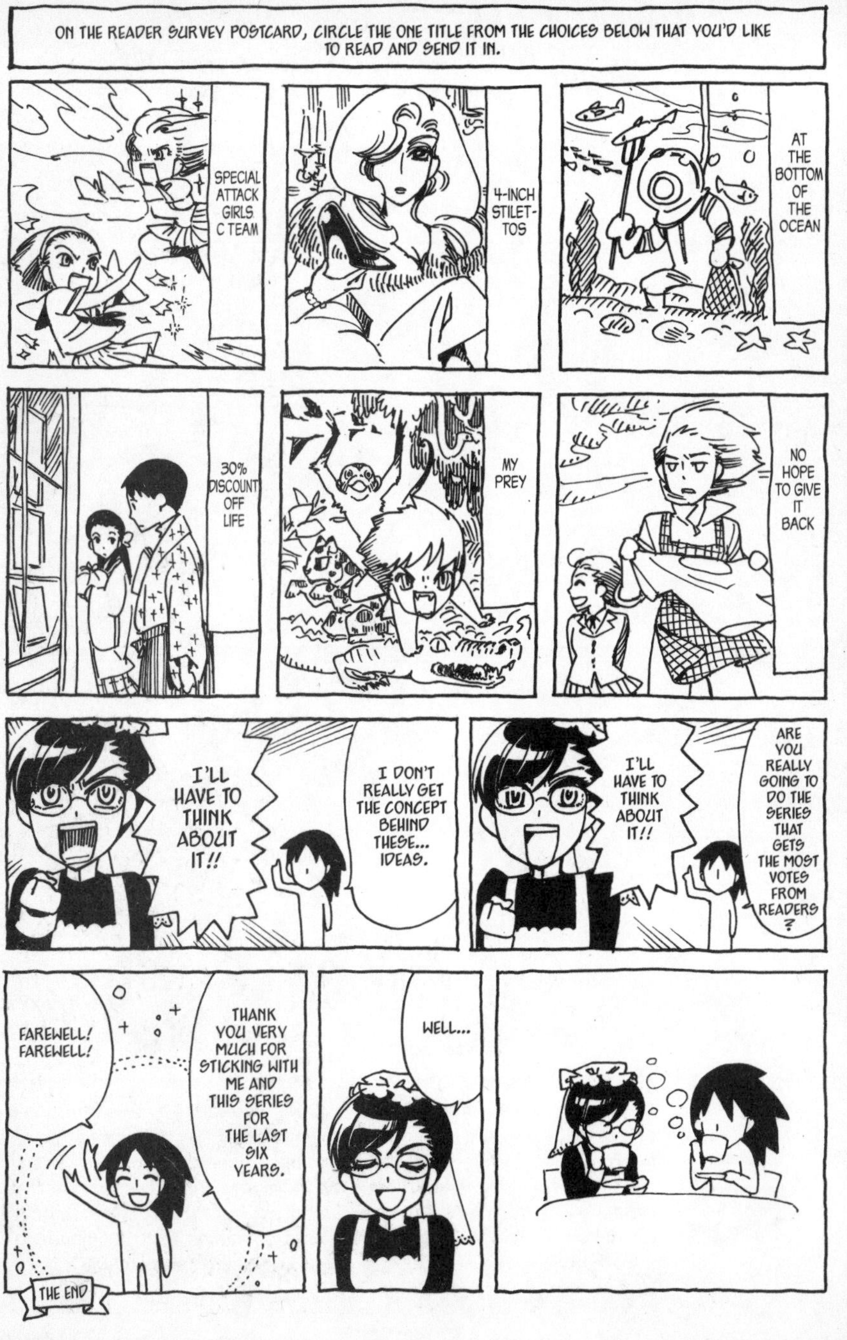
ON THE READER SURVEY POSTCARD, CIRCLE THE ONE TITLE FROM THE CHOICES BELOW THAT YOU'D LIKE TO READ AND SEND IT IN.
AT THE BOTTOM OF THE OCEAN
4-INCH STILET-TOS
SPECIAL ATTACK GIRLS C TEAM
NO HOPE TO GIVE IT BACK
MY PREY
30% DISCOUNT OFF LIFE
ARE YOU REALLY GOING TO DO THE SERIES THAT GETS THE MOST VOTES FROM READERS?
I'LL HAVE TO THINK ABOUT IT!!
I DON'T REALLY GET THE CONCEPT BEHIND THESE... IDEAS.
I'LL HAVE TO THINK ABOUT IT!!
WELL...
THANK YOU VERY MUCH FOR STICKING WITH ME AND THIS SERIES FOR THE LAST SIX YEARS.
FAREWELL! FAREWELL!
THE END

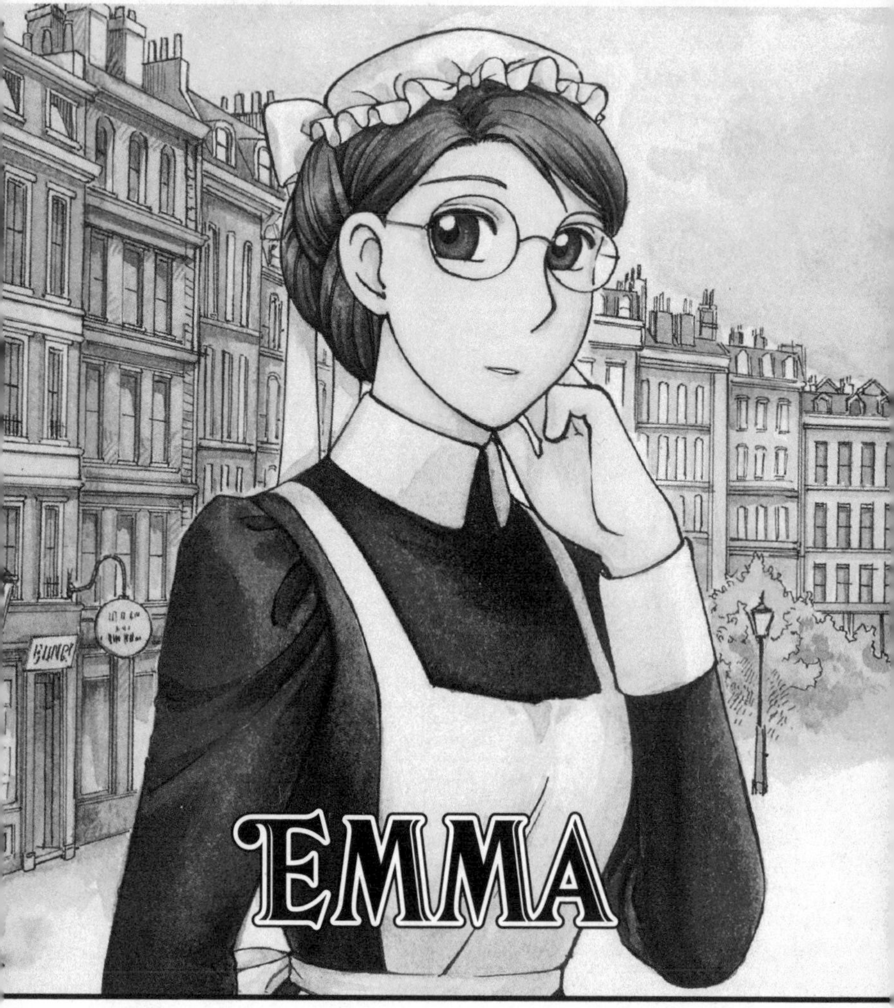
EMMA

EMMA Vol. 10 © 2008 Kaoru Mori. All Rights Reserved.
First published in Japan in 2008 by ENTERBRAIN, INC.

EMMA Volume 10, published by WildStorm Productions, an
imprint of DC Comics, 888 Prospect St. #240, La Jolla, CA
92037. English Translation © 2010. All Rights Reserved.
English translation rights in U.S.A. and Canada arranged by
ENTERBRAIN, INC. through Tuttle-Mori Agency, Inc., Tokyo.
CMX is a trademark of DC Comics. The stories, characters,
and incidents mentioned in this magazine are entirely fic-
tional. Printed on recyclable paper. WildStorm does not
read or accept unsolicited submissions of ideas, stories or
artwork. Printed in Canada.

DC Comics, a Warner Bros. Entertainment Company.

This book is manufactured at a facility holding chain-of-
custody certification. This paper is made with sustainably
managed North American fiber.

Sheldon Drzka – Translation and Adaptation
Janice Chiang – Lettering
Larry Berry – Design
Sarah Farber – Assistant Editor
Jim Chadwick – Editor

ISBN: 978-1-4012-2072-3

SUSTAINABLE FORESTRY INITIATIVE — Certified Fiber Sourcing — www.sfiprogram.org
PWC-SFICOC-260

All the pages in this book were created—and are printed here—in Japanese RIGHT-to-LEFT format. No artwork has been reversed or altered, so you can read the stories the way the creators meant for them to be read.

RIGHT TO LEFT?!

Traditional Japanese manga starts at the upper right-hand corner, and moves right-to-left as it goes down the page. Follow this guide for an easy understanding.

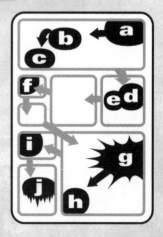